BTEC First

2nd Edition

BUSINESS

Carol Carysforth

Mike Neild

Heinemann Educational Publishers
Halley Court, Jordan Hill, Oxford OX2 8EJ
Part of Harcourt Education
Heinemann is the registered trademark of Harcourt Education Limited

First published 2006

10 09 08 07
10 9 8 7 6 5 4 3

British Library Cataloguing in Publication Data is available from the British Library on request.

10-digit ISBN: 0 435 49907 6
13-digit ISBN: 978 0 435499 07 6

Edited by Sylvia Worth
Editorial management by Alistair Nunn
Designed by Wooden Ark Studio, Leeds
Typeset by Tek-Art, Croydon, Surrey
Printed in China through Phoenix Offset
Original illustrations © Harcourt Education Limited, 2006
Cover design by Peter Stratton
Cover photo: © Corbis
Picture research by Emma Baddeley and Sally Cole

Every effort has been made to contact copyright holders of material reproduced in this book. Any omissions will be rectified in subsequent printings if notice is given to the publishers.

Acknowledgements

The author and publisher would like to thank the following individuals and organisations for permission to reproduce photographs:

Alamy/Pictures colour library – page 1
Rex Features/Phillipe Hayes – page 2
Jeff Morgan/Alamy – pages 6, 13
Rex Features – pages 9, 44, 89, 90a, 298, 357, 368, 369
Rex Features/Alexander Caminada – page 12, 20
Alamy/pictor – page 15
Rex Features/Stephanie Paschal – page 26
Frank Chmura/Alamy – page 28, 235
Bob Johns/expresspictures.co.uk/Alamy – page 29
Rex Features/Alex Segre – pages 30, 377
Corbis/Gideon Mendel – page 45
TopFoto/ImageWorks – page 47
David Pearson/Alamy – page 51
Rex Features/Shilo/Israel Sun – page 58
Corbis/Yang Lui – page 62
Bill Lyons/Alamy – page 76
Alamy/Steven May – page 78
Jeff Greenberg/Alamy – page 79
TopFoto/PA – page 84
Christopher Griffin/Alamy – page 90b
Alan King/Alamy – page 98
Rex Features/Tony O'Brien – page 99
Rex Features/Francis Dean – pages 111, 350
Getty Images/Longview – page 139
Corbis/Helen King – page 142, 148, 153
Harcourt Index – page 152
Corbis/Pinto/Zefa – page 157
Getty Images/Altrendo – page 174
Alamy/Sally & Richard Greenhill – page 179
Getty Images/Jan Koenig – page 181
Doug Steley/Alamy – page 185
TopFoto – pages 186, 293, 333
WoodyStock/Alamy – page 200
ActionPlus/Neil Tingle – page 218
Getty Images/Marc Romanelli – page 224
Getty Images/Lilith Hodge – page 231
Peter Titmuss/Alamy – page 238
Photofusion Picture Library/Alamy – page 241, 268
Education Photos/Alamy – page 254
Rex Features/Image Source – pages 257, 307
Rex Features/Paul Cooper – page 269
Leslie Garland Picture Library/Alamy – page 276
Getty Images/S. Shipman – page 277
Rex Features/Chris Bourchier – page 278
Getty Images – page 283
Rex Features/Sipa Press – page 287
Peter Adams Photography/Alamy – page 290
Getty Images/Wang Leng – page 304
Kim Karpeles/Alamy – page 309
Getty Images/Ghislan & Marie David de Lossy – page 312
Alamy/Robert Clayton – page 318
Alamy/Maria Hesse – page 321
David Pearson/Alamy – page 336
Panos Pictures/David Rose – page 345
Hertfordshire Police/Handout/Reuters/Corbis – page 346
Oote boe/Alamy – page 356
Camera Lucida/Alamy – page 360
David Lyons/Alamy – page 361
Getty Images/Oppenheim Bernhard – page 363
Alamy/Popperfoto – page 382
Mike Goldwater/Alamy – page 388
Image State/Alamy – page 392
Scott Hortrop/Alamy – page 398
Dan Atkin/Alamy – page 400

Contents

About this book

This book has been written especially to help and support you while you are taking the Edexcel BTEC First Certificate or First Diploma in Business. This may be the first time you have taken a business course, or you may have already enjoyed studying business before, perhaps on a GCSE course. In either case, we hope that you will find many of the features of this book interesting and stimulating. Our aim, as authors of this book, is to help you to enjoy your course and understand all the key topics easily.

If you are taking the BTEC First Certificate you will study one core unit (Unit 1) and two specialist units, selected from all the remaining units; whereas on the BTEC First Diploma you will study three core units (Units 1, 2 and 3) and three specialist units. This book contains all the specialist units *except* for Exploring Business Enterprise – which you cannot study if you are taking Unit 9, Starting a Small Business. Talk to your tutor if you are not sure which specialist units you will be studying.

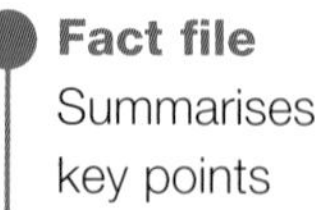

Fact file
Summarises key points

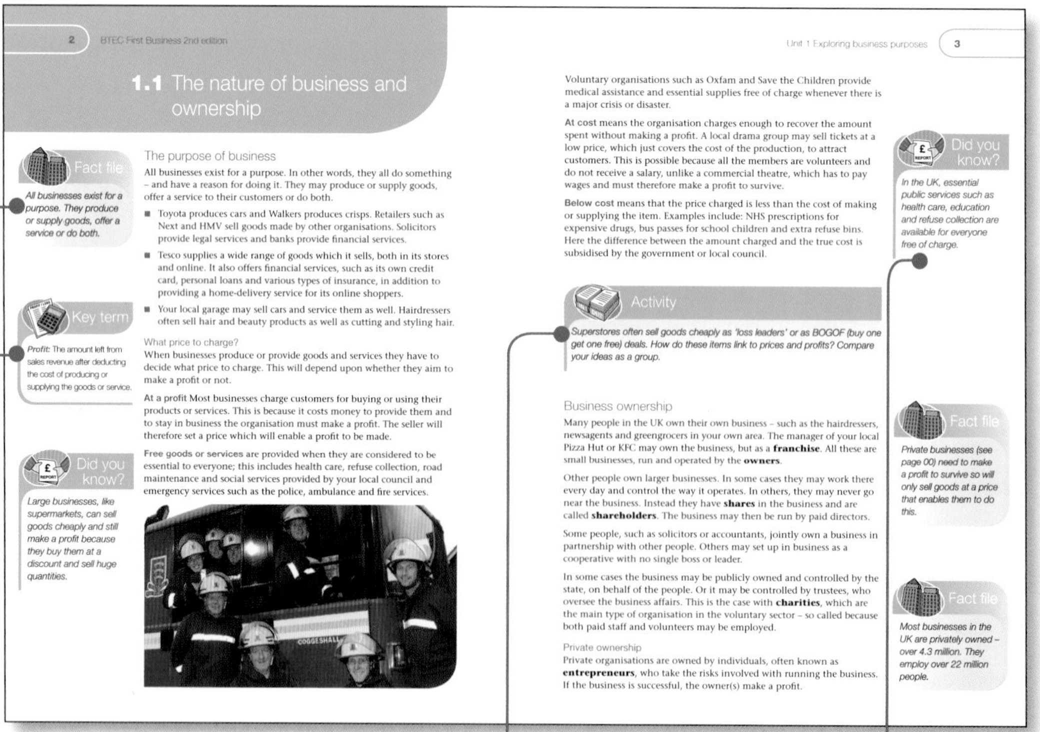

2 BTEC First Business 2nd edition

Unit 1 Exploring business purposes 3

1.1 The nature of business and ownership

Fact file

All businesses exist for a purpose. They produce or supply goods, offer a service or do both.

Key term

Profit: The amount left from sales revenue after deducting the cost of producing or supplying the goods or service.

Did you know?

Large businesses, like supermarkets, can sell goods cheaply and still make a profit because they buy them at a discount and sell huge quantities.

The purpose of business

All businesses exist for a purpose. In other words, they all do something – and have a reason for doing it. They may produce or supply goods, offer a service to their customers or do both.

- Toyota produces cars and Walkers produces crisps. Retailers such as Next and HMV sell goods made by other organisations. Solicitors provide legal services and banks provide financial services.
- Tesco supplies a wide range of goods which it sells, both in its stores and online. It also offers financial services, such as its own credit card, personal loans and various types of insurance, in addition to providing a home-delivery service for its online shoppers.
- Your local garage may sell cars and service them as well. Hairdressers often sell hair and beauty products as well as cutting and styling hair.

What price to charge?

When businesses produce or provide goods and services they have to decide what price to charge. This will depend upon whether they aim to make a profit or not.

At a profit Most businesses charge customers for buying or using their products or services. This is because it costs money to provide them and to stay in business the organisation must make a profit. The seller will therefore set a price which will enable a profit to be made.

Free goods or services are provided when they are considered to be essential to everyone; this includes health care, refuse collection, road maintenance and social services provided by your local council and emergency services such as the police, ambulance and fire services.

Voluntary organisations such as Oxfam and Save the Children provide medical assistance and essential supplies free of charge whenever there is a major crisis or disaster.

At cost means the organisation charges enough to recover the amount spent without making a profit. A local drama group may sell tickets at a low price, which just covers the cost of the production, to attract customers. This is possible because all the members are volunteers and do not receive a salary, unlike a commercial theatre, which has to pay wages and must therefore make a profit to survive.

Below cost means that the price charged is less than the cost of making or supplying the item. Examples include: NHS prescriptions for expensive drugs, bus passes for school children and extra refuse bins. Here the difference between the amount charged and the true cost is subsidised by the government or local council.

Did you know?

In the UK, essential public services such as health care, education and refuse collection are available for everyone free of charge.

Activity

Superstores often sell goods cheaply as 'loss leaders' or as BOGOF (buy one get one free) deals. How do these items link to prices and profits? Compare your ideas as a group.

Business ownership

Many people in the UK own their own business – such as the hairdressers, newsagents and greengrocers in your own area. The manager of your local Pizza Hut or KFC may own the business, but as a **franchise**. All these are small businesses, run and operated by the **owners**.

Other people own larger businesses. In some cases they may work there every day and control the way it operates. In others, they may never go near the business. Instead they have **shares** in the business and are called **shareholders**. The business may then be run by paid directors.

Some people, such as solicitors or accountants, jointly own a business in partnership with other people. Others may set up in business as a cooperative with no single boss or leader.

In some cases the business may be publicly owned and controlled by the state, on behalf of the people. Or it may be controlled by trustees, who oversee the business affairs. This is the case with **charities**, which are the main type of organisation in the voluntary sector – so called because both paid staff and volunteers may be employed.

Private ownership

Private organisations are owned by individuals, often known as **entrepreneurs**, who take the risks involved with running the business. If the business is successful, the owner(s) make a profit.

Fact file

Private businesses (see page 00) need to make a profit to survive so will only sell goods at a price that enables them to do this.

Fact file

Most businesses in the UK are privately owned – over 4.3 million. They employ over 22 million people.

Key term
Provides important definitions

Activity
Enables you to develop your understanding by carrying out tasks and investigations

Did you know?
Introduces topical notes and points of interest

Throughout the text a number of features have been included to help you. We hope you will enjoy using this book, find studying business enjoyable and interesting and be successful on your course. You can find explanations of these features in the diagrams.

How you will be assessed

You will be assessed for each unit you take. Each assessment you take is designed by your tutors to cover specified outcomes which you need to achieve for a pass, merit or distinction grade. The difference between the grades is in the quality of your response. To get a merit grade, you need to show that you can give a higher level of response than for a pass. A distinction grade needs the best response of all. You will see how this works in the assessment practice features in this book which help you to practise to achieve the best grade you can. The assessment practice features demonstrate the level each question is aimed at, and the area of the syllabus that they are testing.

Case study/Assessment practice
Link theory with actual business practice and help work towards you developing the knowledge, the skills and understanding required to gain a pass, merit or distinction grade in your real assessments

Talking point
Give opposite points of view on a topic for you to discuss in class

10 BTEC First Business 2nd edition

Talking point

View 1: If corner shops cease to exist in Britain many people will struggle to buy basic supplies. Something must be done to stop supermarkets taking over.

View 2: Many supermarkets are now opening local stores and also sell goods online. Independent corner shops that charge high prices deserve to go out of business.

With which viewpoint do you agree – and why?

Grading tip

A clear description tells a story for the reader. Make sure you include all the relevant points in a sensible order.

Over to you

1 On Monday you bought a new mobile phone; on Tuesday you renewed your passport; on Wednesday you took your driving test; on Thursday you went to your IT evening class; on Friday you sprained your ankle and had it bandaged in A & E at your local hospital; on Saturday you bought a new T-shirt; on Sunday you went swimming at your local sports centre.

As a group decide which goods or services were provided at a profit, free, at cost or below cost. Then suggest two other goods or services for each category.

2 Identify the ownership of each of the following business organisations. Then suggest how the type of ownership affects the price charged for the goods or services each one offers.
a) *Amazon (www.amazon.co.uk)*
b) *The ambulance service (eg www.londonambulance.nhs.uk/)*
c) *Citizens Advice Bureau (www.citizensadvice.org.uk/)*

3 **a)** *Copy out the table below then, as a group, suggest the names of businesses in your area, or the names of businesses which you know from advertising or researching on the Internet to complete it. Ideally try to suggest two or three businesses for each category.*

THE SIZE AND SCALE OF DIFFERENT BUSINESSES	
Size	**Name of business**
Small business (Under 10 employees) Small business (10 to 50 employees) Medium sized business (50 to 250 employees) Large sized business (250+ employees)	
Scale	
Local area only Regional area covered National business European business Global business/multinational	

b) *For each business you have identified, suggest reasons why it is the size and scale it is. Compare your ideas with other members of your group.*
c) *Write a clear and accurate description of the purpose, ownership, size and scale of any* ***one*** *business of your choice in this list.*

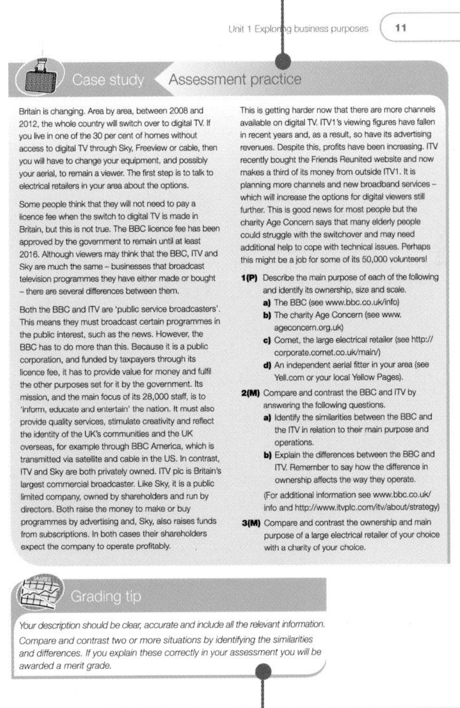

Unit 1 Exploring business purposes 11

Case study Assessment practice

Britain is changing. Area by area, between 2008 and 2012, the whole country will switch over to digital TV. If you live in one of the 30 per cent of homes without access to digital TV through Sky, Freeview or cable, then you will have to change your equipment, and possibly your aerial, to remain a viewer. The first step is to talk to electrical retailers in your area about the options.

Some people think that they will not need to pay a licence fee when the switch to digital TV is made in Britain, but this is not true. The BBC licence fee has been approved by the government to remain until at least 2016. Although viewers may think that the BBC, ITV and Sky are much the same – businesses that broadcast television programmes they have either made or bought – there are several differences between them.

Both the BBC and ITV are 'public service broadcasters'. This means they must broadcast certain programmes in the public interest, such as the news. However, the BBC has to do more than this. Because it is a public corporation, and funded by taxpayers through its licence fee, it has to provide value for money and fulfil the other purposes set for it by the government. Its mission, and the main focus of its 28,000 staff, is to 'inform, educate and entertain' the nation. It must also provide quality services, stimulate creativity and reflect the identity of the UK's communities and the UK overseas, for example through BBC America, which is transmitted via satellite and cable in the US. In contrast, ITV and Sky are both privately owned. ITV plc is Britain's largest commercial broadcaster. Like Sky, it is a public limited company, owned by shareholders and run by directors. Both raise the money to make or buy programmes by advertising and, Sky, also raises funds from subscriptions. In both cases their shareholders expect the company to operate profitably.

This is getting harder now that there are more channels available on digital TV. ITV1's viewing figures have fallen in recent years and, as a result, so have its advertising revenues. Despite this, profits have been increasing. ITV recently bought the Friends Reunited website and now makes a third of its money from outside ITV1. It is planning more channels and new broadband services – which will increase the options for digital viewers still further. This is good news for most people but the charity Age Concern says that many elderly people could struggle with the switchover and may need additional help to cope with technical issues. Perhaps this might be a job for some of its 50,000 volunteers!

1(P) Describe the main purpose of each of the following and identify its ownership, size and scale.
a) The BBC (see www.bbc.co.uk/info)
b) The charity Age Concern (see www.ageconcern.org.uk)
c) Comet, the large electrical retailer (see http://corporate.comet.co.uk/main/)
d) An independent aerial fitter in your area (see Yell.com or your local Yellow Pages).

2(M) Compare and contrast the BBC and ITV by answering the following questions.
a) Identify the similarities between the BBC and the ITV in relation to their main purpose and operations.
b) Explain the differences between the BBC and ITV. Remember to say how the difference in ownership affects the way they operate.

(For additional information see www.bbc.co.uk/info and http://www.itvplc.com/itv/about/strategy)

3(M) Compare and contrast the ownership and main purpose of a large electrical retailer of your choice with a charity of your choice.

Grading tip

Your description should be clear, accurate and include all the relevant information.

Compare and contrast two or more situations by identifying the similarities and differences. If you explain these correctly in your assessment you will be awarded a merit grade.

Over to you
Reinforce each section by questions or problems to complete on your own or in a group

Grading tip
Explains the outcomes required to get higher grades

Author's acknowledgements

The authors would like to record their gratitude to all those who have helped with the creation of this book by providing expert guidance in a number of areas.

Special thanks are due to the following people who helped us to create realistic and appropriate case studies: Catherine Carysforth, LLB, whose experience proved invaluable for the legal practice case study; Alastair Lee, for divulging the joys and traumas he experienced when he started his own business Posing Productions; Paul Carysforth for sharing with us his e-business expertise; David Robinson and his PA, Julie McCabe for helping us with the case study on customer relations at Richer Sounds; Rachel Bretherton for talking about her job role as a school administrator; Carolyn Briggs-Conway who took us through the intricacies of selling in the hair and beauty industry. Thanks are also due to Jerry Brees and Matt Neild for providing prompt and useful help when it was needed!

No book of ours would ever reach the shelves without the combined efforts of Mary James, our publishing manager, and her team at Harcourt. We are especially grateful to Jilly Hunt, our publisher on this project, who continually amazes and impresses us by her seemingly endless patience and unflappability; Alistair Nunn, who coordinated the editorial work magnificently; Sylvia Worth, Helen Kemp and Liz Evans, editors, for helping us to fit our quart into a pint pot so beautifully!

Carol Carysforth and Mike Neild
August 2006

Dedications

To Jilly and Darren – with every wish for a long and happy married life.

To all our family – past, present, future and currently expected! With love.

1 Exploring business purposes

We are all surrounded by many different types of businesses – from small local firms to large international enterprises. Some produce or sell goods, others provide a service. Each has aims which vary depending upon the business, its size and how it is owned. This unit introduces you to the range of businesses that exist and helps you to understand how they operate.

What you need to learn

- The nature of businesses and how they differ in terms of their ownership, size and scale
- How business activities in Britain are classified
- The purpose of setting aims and objectives in business
- The main functional areas within business organisations

1.1 The nature of business and ownership

Fact file

All businesses exist for a purpose. They produce or supply goods, offer a service or do both.

Key term

Profit: The amount left from sales revenue after deducting the cost of producing or supplying the goods or service.

Did you know?

Large businesses, like supermarkets, can sell goods cheaply and still make a profit because they buy them at a discount and sell huge quantities.

The purpose of business

All businesses exist for a purpose. In other words, they all do something – and have a reason for doing it. They may produce or supply goods, offer a service to their customers or do both.

- Toyota produces cars and Walkers produces crisps. Retailers such as Next and HMV sell goods made by other organisations. Solicitors provide legal services and banks provide financial services.
- Tesco supplies a wide range of goods which it sells, both in its stores and online. It also offers financial services, such as its own credit card, personal loans and various types of insurance, in addition to providing a home-delivery service for its online shoppers.
- Your local garage may sell cars and service them as well. Hairdressers often sell hair and beauty products as well as cutting and styling hair.

What price to charge?

When businesses produce or provide goods and services they have to decide what price to charge. This will depend upon whether they aim to make a profit or not.

At a profit Most businesses charge customers for buying or using their products or services. This is because it costs money to provide them and to stay in business the organisation must make a profit. The seller will therefore set a price which will enable a profit to be made.

Free goods or services are provided when they are considered to be essential to everyone; this includes health care, refuse collection, road maintenance and social services provided by your local council and emergency services such as the police, ambulance and fire services.

Voluntary organisations such as Oxfam and Save the Children provide medical assistance and essential supplies free of charge whenever there is a major crisis or disaster.

At cost means the organisation charges enough to recover the amount spent without making a profit. A local drama group may sell tickets at a low price, which just covers the cost of the production, to attract customers. This is possible because all the members are volunteers and do not receive a salary, unlike a commercial theatre, which has to pay wages and must therefore make a profit to survive.

Below cost means that the price charged is less than the cost of making or supplying the item. Examples include: NHS prescriptions for expensive drugs, bus passes for school children and extra refuse bins. Here the difference between the amount charged and the true cost is subsidised by the government or local council.

Did you know?

In the UK, essential public services such as health care, education and refuse collection are available for everyone free of charge.

Activity

Superstores often sell goods cheaply as 'loss leaders' or as BOGOF (buy one get one free) deals. How do these items link to prices and profits? Compare your ideas as a group.

Business ownership

Many people in the UK own their own business – such as the hairdressers, newsagents and greengrocers in your own area. The manager of your local Pizza Hut or KFC may own the business, but run this as a **franchise**. All these are small businesses, run and operated by the **owners**.

Other people own larger businesses. In some cases they may work there every day and control the way it operates. In others, they may never go near the business. Instead they have **shares** in the business and are called **shareholders**. The business may then be run by paid directors.

Some people, such as solicitors or accountants, jointly own a business in partnership with other people. Others may set up in business as a cooperative with no single boss or leader.

In some cases the business may be publicly owned and controlled by the state, on behalf of the people. Or it may be controlled by trustees, who oversee the business affairs. This is the case with **charities**, which are the main type of organisation in the voluntary sector – so called because both paid staff and volunteers may be employed.

Fact file

Private businesses (see page 4) need to make a profit to survive so will only sell goods at a price that enables them to do this.

Fact file

Most businesses in the UK are privately owned – over 4.3 million. They employ over 22 million people.

Private ownership

Private organisations are owned by individuals, often known as **entrepreneurs**, who take the risks involved with running the business. If the business is successful, the owner(s) make a profit.

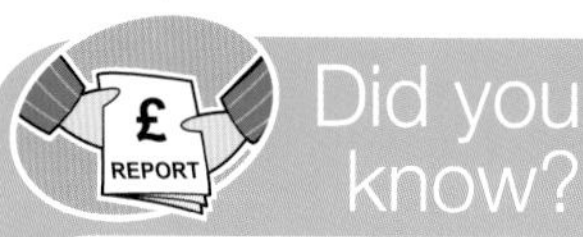

Did you know?

The John Lewis Partnership is a special type of partnership. All 64,000 staff are partners and receive a share of the profits as a bonus each year. In 2006 the bonus amounted to almost eight weeks' pay for each employee. Find out more at www.johnlewispartnership.co.uk.

Activity

Look in your local **Phone book** *or* **Yellow Pages** *and find examples of sole traders, partnerships, Limited companies (Ltd) and public limited companies (plcs) in your area. Compare your list with those made by other people in your group.*

Fact file

Profit is the owners' reward for taking risks and for running the business. The owners can keep all the profit after paying the business expenses and any tax due.

There are four main types of privately owned organisation.

- **A sole trader** is the name for the smallest type of business. It is owned by one person, even though there may be several employees. A sole trader is personally responsible for every aspect of the business, from keeping the premises clean to doing the accounts and paying the tax due on the profits. Examples include plumbers, decorators, hairdressers and some local retailers. The sole trader can keep all the profit each year, after paying tax.

- **A partnership** is owned and run by two or more people. The partners are then jointly responsible for running the business. Most partnerships are small, such as local accountants, solicitors, doctors and vets. However, a few larger organisations are run on the basis that the employees become partners when they join the company.

- **A private limited company** is easily identified because its name always ends with the abbreviation 'Ltd'. The owners each own a share of the business and are therefore known as shareholders. If the company is successful the shareholders will receive a financial reward in the form of dividends. Many private companies are family businesses in which the owners have two roles. As well as being shareholders they are also directors and run the company.

- **A public limited company** is the largest type of business. These companies end their name with the letters 'plc.' The shares are usually traded on the Stock Exchange and can be owned by members of the public and institutional investors, such as large banks or insurance companies. The directors are paid a salary to run the company and may, or may not, own shares. Selling shares to the public means that this type of company can raise large amounts of money to expand or develop the enterprise. Two variations on these types of businesses are given below.

- **Franchises** In this situation a business is started using the name of a well known organisation. The owner of the small business (the franchisee) pays the larger company (the franchisor) a share of the profit and a fee to use the name. In return, he or she is given help and support to run the business. Examples of franchise businesses include Prontoprint, Kentucky Fried Chicken, Body Shop and Benetton.

- **Workers' cooperatives**, where the business is jointly owned and run by the workers. All the profits are shared and the owners make joint decisions about how the business should be run. Workers' cooperatives in Britain are normally quite small, unlike the CRS – the Cooperative Retail Society – which is owned by its customers and operates all over the country.

You can find out more about different types of private organisations in Unit 9, pages 374 and 375.

Public ownership

Some enterprises in the UK are owned or controlled by the state such as government departments and organisations funded by the government. They include the following.

Government departments deal with different matters at national level. These include education, the NHS, social security benefits, defence, the police and prison service, environmental issues and concerns, major road building programmes and the collection of taxes.

Local authorities provide services for the local community. These vary, depending upon the area, so that the services in a rural community are different from those offered in a city. The range of services offered is shown in the diagram below.

An ***entrepreneur*** is a person who risks his or her own money to build up a successful business.

Private ownership relates to businesses owned by individuals who aim to make a profit.

■ *Some of the services provided by local councils*

Health trusts receive money from the government to deliver health care without making a profit.

Public corporations are government-owned businesses, such as the BBC and the Royal Mail service. These businesses are expected to operate profitably, just like private organisations.

Public ownership relates to businesses owned by the state.

Charities and voluntary organisations

Voluntary organisations, including charities, are so called because many staff, such as many of those you see in charity shops in your town, may work there without being paid. They are also called 'not-for-profit' organisations because they focus on using their income to provide a service to those in need. They aim to make a **surplus** every year, after necessary expenses, which is used to support and promote their own particular cause.

Did you know?

About six million people work in the public sector. They include health workers, teachers, the Civil Service and staff in your town hall.

Some charities receive government subsidies and tax relief but must abide by a number of regulations, overseen by the Charity Commission. Trustees are appointed to ensure that the money raised is managed carefully and that accurate records are kept. Being a trustee is a voluntary, unpaid position.

Today large charities are run on a professional and business-like basis. They are divided into departments and employ professional fund-raisers and administrators. They spend money on advertising and promoting the charity.

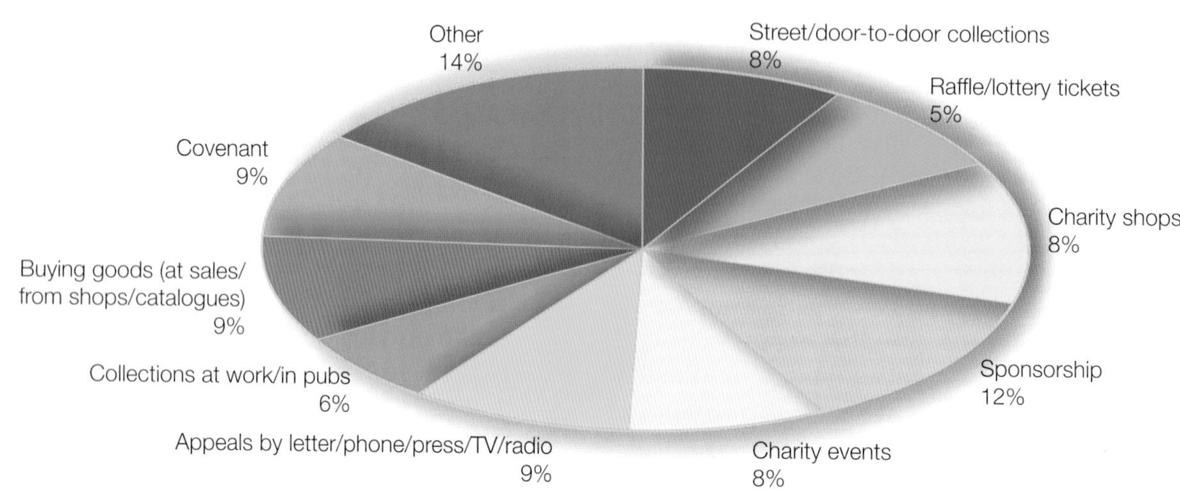

■ *How charities raise their money (adapted from CA/NCVO research report, August 2003)*

Activity

Choose a large charity which interests you. Use Google to go to its website and find out about its work, including how it raises its money and how much was raised and spent last year.

Did you know?

There are over 160,000 charities and over 200,000 community groups in the UK. They employ 1.5 million professional staff and 6 million volunteers. In 2004 the income of the top ten charities was over £1.6 billion. Find out more at www.charity-commission.gov.uk.

The size of businesses

The **size** of an organisation is easy to understand. Some businesses are very small and may only consist of one person, or a few staff – such as a taxi driver or your local newsagent. Others, such as Boots, Marks and Spencer and manufacturers Heinz and Toyota, are very large and may employ thousands of people. Large businesses enjoy several benefits because of their size, known as **economies of scale**. Tesco and Asda can buy stocks more cheaply than your local grocer because suppliers are eager for large supermarkets to stock their goods, so will sell them at larger discounts. They can also afford to advertise on national television, so that everyone knows their name.

You can assess the size of a business if you know about any of the factors outlined below.

The number of employees This is the easiest way to assess a business but if many employees are part-time, this may not be a reliable guide.

Number of employees and size of organisation			
Micro	Small	Medium	Large
1 – 5	6 – 99	100 – 249	250+

■ *Size of an organisation, assessed by the number of employees*

Key terms

Voluntary organisations are not-for-profit organisations that provide a service, such as charities, and are run by professional staff and volunteers.

A ***surplus*** in the voluntary sector is the amount remaining from donations and fund-raising activities after essential expenses have been paid.

The sales turnover This is the value of goods sold or the income from services. A small business may sell about £1 million of goods each year whilst a medium-sized business would aim for sales of £10 million or more.

The scale of its operations Usually, there is a link between size and scale but be careful! Today, the Internet enables many small businesses to operate nationally or internationally through their websites.

Did you know?

In 2005 Google employed fewer than 5,000 staff but it operates on a global basis.

The scale of a business

The **scale** relates to the area over which the business operates. Some firms supply only a small area, such as your local convenience store. Others trade on much wider basis, perhaps across a region, all over the country, throughout Europe or even globally.

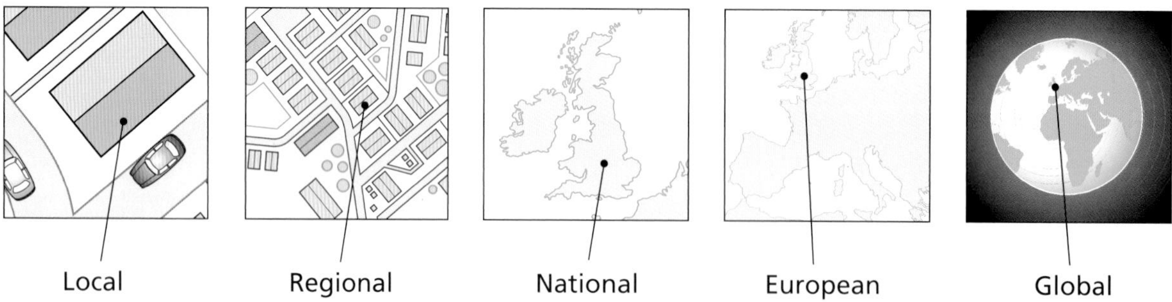

■ *The different scale of business operations*

Key terms

Sales turnover is the amount of money the business obtains by selling its goods or services.

Economies of scale are the financial benefits of operating on a large scale, such as buying goods more cheaply and national advertising.

Did you know?

Some large private limited (Ltd) companies operate on an international scale. United Biscuits has sites all over Europe and Virgin Atlantic operates on a global basis.

Fact file

There are risks and costs involved with increasing the size and scale of a business that entrepreneurs must take into account.

The factors which influence the scale of business operations are shown below. These will all affect any decisions to expand operations over a wider area.

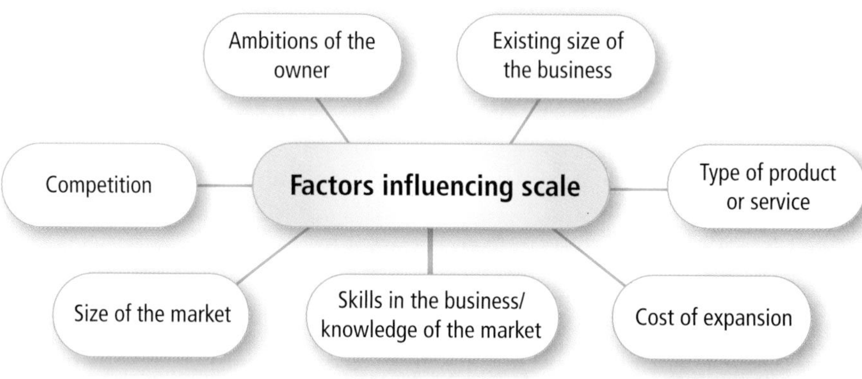

■ *Factors influencing scale*

Existing size of the business Small businesses are less likely to have the money, staff or expertise to operate on a large scale. Therefore a 'one-man business' – such as your local DJ – can only work in a small area. A small business which tries to expand too quickly may let down customers because it cannot meet its commitments.

Type of goods and services Some services are specific to a region or country. Most solicitors and accountants concentrate on UK laws and regulations and only the largest firms employ international specialists. Services required worldwide, such as those provided by banks, cinemas and hotels, enable many of these businesses to operate on an international basis.

Products with global appeal, such as computers, clothes, cars, chocolate and cameras, can be sold in many countries.

Highly perishable goods, like bread or cakes, are costly to transport a long distance – so most bakeries operate on a local or regional basis. Heavy goods, like stone or concrete, are also expensive to transport over long distances.

Skills in the business and knowledge of the market It is not wise to expand – especially abroad – without researching the foreign market first. There may be many regulations and laws to consider as well as ethnic and cultural differences to take into account.

Cost of expansion Increasing the scale of a business costs money – from opening branch offices to adapting a product for a foreign market and advertising to attract new customers. Small businesses often have problems raising money and unsuccessful expansion can threaten the whole business.

Size of market It is only sensible to expand if there are enough potential customers. This is why you do not find large stores in remote areas – there simply are not enough customers nearby to make it worthwhile.

Competition The number of competitors will feature heavily in a firm's decision to expand – even to a nearby town.

Ambitions of the owner Some entrepreneurs are very ambitious and want their business to grow as large as possible. Richard Branson (Virgin) and Stelios Haji-Ioannou (easyJet) are two examples. Others may be happier with a quiet life, providing their business is making enough profit to meet their needs.

Activity

Identify one business in your own area that you know well and clearly describe its size and scale. Suggest two reasons why it operates on the scale it does.

Did you know?

Tesco spent three years researching the market in China and sent Tesco staff to live with a Chinese family to see how they shopped and spent their leisure time.

Did you know?

Two thousand independent corner shops are closing every year because they cannot compete with supermarkets. An all-party group of MPs has concluded there will be none left by 2015.

Key terms

Scale means the size of the area over which the business operates.

Multinationals are businesses which produce goods in many countries and sell to a worldwide market.

SMEs are small or medium-sized enterprises. Most businesses in Britain are in this category.

Talking point

View 1: If corner shops cease to exist in Britain many people will struggle to buy basic supplies. Something must be done to stop supermarkets taking over.

View 2: Many supermarkets are now opening local stores and also sell goods online. Independent corner shops that charge high prices deserve to go out of business.

With which viewpoint do you agree – and why?

Grading tip

A clear description tells a story for the reader. Make sure you include all the relevant points in a sensible order.

Over to you

1 *On Monday you bought a new mobile phone; on Tuesday you renewed your passport; on Wednesday you took your driving test; on Thursday you went to your IT evening class; on Friday you sprained your ankle and had it bandaged in A & E at your local hospital; on Saturday you bought a new T-shirt; on Sunday you went swimming at your local sports centre.*

As a group decide which goods or services were provided at a profit, free, at cost or below cost. Then suggest two other goods or services for each category.

2 *Identify the ownership of each of the following business organisations. Then suggest how the type of ownership affects the price charged for the goods or services each one offers.*

a) *Amazon (www.amazon.co.uk)*
b) *The ambulance service (eg www.londonambulance.nhs.uk/)*
c) *Citizens Advice Bureau (www.citizensadvice.org.uk/)*

3 a) *Copy out the table below then, as a group, suggest the names of businesses in your area, or the names of businesses which you know from advertising or researching on the Internet to complete it. Ideally try to suggest two or three businesses for each category.*

THE SIZE AND SCALE OF DIFFERENT BUSINESSES	
Size	**Name of business**
Micro business (Under 6 employees) Small business (6 to 99 employees) Medium-sized business (100 to 249 employees) Large-sized business (250+ employees)	
Scale	
Local area only Regional area covered National business European business Global business/multinational	

b) *For each business you have identified, suggest reasons why it is the size and scale it is. Compare your ideas with other members of your group.*

c) *Write a clear and accurate description of the purpose, ownership, size and scale of any* ***one*** *business of your choice in this list.*

Case study — Assessment practice

Britain is changing. Area by area, between 2008 and 2012, the whole country will switch over to digital TV. If you live in one of the 30 per cent of homes without access to digital TV through Sky, Freeview or cable, then you will have to change your equipment, and possibly your aerial, to remain a viewer. The first step is to talk to electrical retailers in your area about the options.

Some people think that they will not need to pay a licence fee when the switch to digital TV is made in Britain, but this is not true. The BBC licence fee has been approved by the government to remain until at least 2016. Although viewers may think that the BBC, ITV and Sky are much the same – businesses that broadcast television programmes they have either made or bought – there are several differences between them.

Both the BBC and ITV are 'public service broadcasters'. This means they must broadcast certain programmes in the public interest, such as the news. However, the BBC has to do more than this. Because it is a public corporation, and funded by taxpayers through its licence fee, it has to provide value for money and fulfil the other purposes set for it by the government. Its mission, and the main focus of its 28,000 staff, is to 'inform, educate and entertain' the nation. It must also provide quality services, stimulate creativity and reflect the identity of the UK's communities and the UK overseas, for example through BBC America, which is transmitted via satellite and cable in the US. In contrast, ITV and Sky are both privately owned. ITV plc is Britain's largest commercial broadcaster. Like Sky, it is a public limited company, owned by shareholders and run by directors. Both raise the money to make or buy programmes by advertising and, Sky, also raises funds from subscriptions. In both cases their shareholders expect the company to operate profitably.

This is getting harder now that there are more channels available on digital TV. ITV1's viewing figures have fallen in recent years and, as a result, so have its advertising revenues. Despite this, profits have been increasing. ITV recently bought the Friends Reunited website and now makes a third of its money from outside ITV1. It is planning more channels and new broadband services – which will increase the options for digital viewers still further. This is good news for most people but the charity Age Concern says that many elderly people could struggle with the switchover and may need additional help to cope with technical issues. Perhaps this might be a job for some of its 50,000 volunteers!

1(P) Describe the main purpose of each of the following and identify its ownership, size and scale.
- **a)** The BBC (see www.bbc.co.uk/info)
- **b)** The charity Age Concern (see www.ageconcern.org.uk)
- **c)** Comet, the large electrical retailer (see http://corporate.comet.co.uk/main/)
- **d)** An independent aerial fitter in your area (see Yell.com or your local Yellow Pages). ***(P1)***

2(M) Compare and contrast the BBC and ITV by answering the following questions.
- **a)** Identify the similarities between the BBC and the ITV in relation to their main purpose and operations.
- **b)** Explain the differences between the BBC and ITV. Remember to say how the difference in ownership affects the way they operate. ***(M2 part)***

(For additional information see www.bbc.co.uk/info and http://www.itvplc.com/itv/about/strategy)

3(M) Compare and contrast the ownership and main purpose of a large electrical retailer of your choice with a charity of your choice. ***(M2 part)***

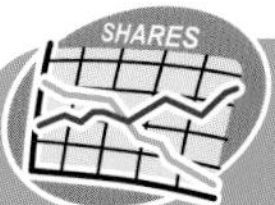

Grading tip

Your description should be clear, accurate and include all the relevant information.

Compare and contrast two or more situations by identifying the similarities and differences. If you explain these correctly in your assessment you will be awarded a merit grade.

1.2 The classification of business activities

Activity

Learn more about British businesses at www.britishcompanies.co.uk. Click on the type of goods that interest you to read about growers, manufacturers, wholesalers and retailers. Click on the bold names in the lists to go to the company website.

All businesses are classified into industrial sectors based on what they do.

- **The primary sector** comprises all businesses involved in producing raw goods, such as farming and mining.
- **The secondary sector** is made up of businesses that manufacture or construct goods, such as Dairy Crest or Barratts, the house builders.
- **The tertiary sector** includes all the businesses that provide a service to businesses and/or individuals, such as retailers and banks.

The names of the sectors show that they are linked as a sequence – often referred to as the **chain of production**. Primary is the first stage, secondary is the second and tertiary is the third. You can see how this works on the illustration below.

Key term

Industrial sectors are the primary, secondary and tertiary sectors which together cover all the business activities in the UK.

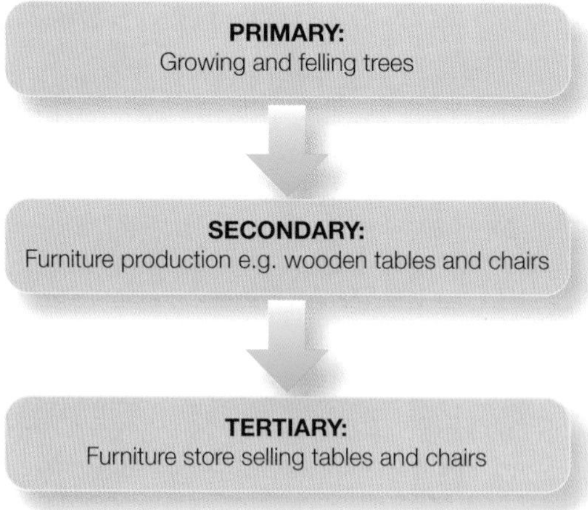

■ *The chain of production*

Did you know?

Fishing fleets have declined because of the introduction of fishing quotas to protect fish stocks but the number of fish farms has increased.

The primary sector

The primary sector includes all those businesses which produce or obtain raw materials or natural products from the land or the sea. There are four main categories in this sector.

Agriculture, hunting and forestry

This category covers the production of crops, such as vegetables and cereals, and animal farming as well as landscape gardening and horticultural businesses.

Forestry and logging

This category includes all businesses involved with planting, conserving and felling timber as well as Christmas tree growers such as Festive Forestry at www.festiveforestry.co.uk. Although the overall woodland area and the amount of softwood grown in Britain has increased in the past ten years, Britain does not grow enough to meet its needs and imports wood from abroad.

Fishing

This group includes fishing fleets as well as fish farms, such as trout hatcheries, salmon farms and freshwater mussel growers.

Mining and quarrying

This group includes coal mines, oil and natural gas extraction, quarrying of all types of stone, slate, gravel, sand and clay and salt production.

Activity

Find out about the primary sector online. The Defra website at www.defra.gov.uk covers fishing and farming; forestry may be found at www.forestry.gov.uk and coal mining at www.rjb.co.uk. Go to www.tarmac.co.uk and www.lafarge-cement-uk.co.uk to find out about quarrying and www.saltinfo.com and www.british-salt.co.uk to investigate salt production.

The secondary sector

The secondary sector includes all those businesses which manufacture, process or assemble products. This sector also covers energy production and the construction industry.

Manufacturing

This includes all businesses which make or produce goods in the UK, regardless of their size or what they make. The Office for National Statistics divides manufacturing companies into different product groups. This is helpful because it enables you to see which types of manufacturers are thriving and which are not (see page 14).

Fact file

The primary sector involves growing, extracting or converting natural resources into raw materials.

Product groups

Food products, beverages and tobacco, e.g. meat and poultry, fish freezing, fruit and vegetable processing, dairy products and ice cream, breakfast cereals, pet food, bread, sweets, chocolate, wines, mineral water, soft drinks, beer and tobacco.

Textiles and textile products, e.g. cotton and woollen goods, soft furnishings, carpets, knitted and leather clothes.

Leather and leather goods, e.g. handbags, luggage and footwear.

Wood and wood products (excluding furniture), e.g. sawmilling, wood containers, plywood and veneers.

Pulp, paper products, publishing and printing, e.g. paper, cartons and boxes, wallpaper, book and newspaper publishing, reproducing sound or video recordings or computer media.

Coke, refined petroleum products and nuclear fuel processing

Chemicals, chemical products and man-made fibres, e.g. chemicals, industrial gases, dyes, plastic, synthetic rubber, paint, printing ink, pharmaceuticals, soap, detergents, perfume, glue, man-made fibres, manufacturing unrecorded media (e.g. blank CDs).

Rubber and plastic products, e.g. rubber tyres, plastic tubes and packaging, plastic floor coverings.

Non-metallic mineral products, e.g. glass, ceramic goods (such as sinks, baths and tiles), bricks and cement manufacture, finishing of ornamental and building stone.

Basic metals and fabricated metal products, e.g. iron, steel, aluminium, lead, zinc, tin and copper goods, central heating radiators and boilers, cutlery, tools, locks, wire, screws.

Other machinery and equipment*, e.g. pumps, compressors, furnaces, ventilation equipment, agricultural machinery, power tools, earth-moving machinery, domestic appliances.

Electrical and optical equipment*, e.g. office machinery, computers, electric motors, batteries, electric lamps, televisions and radios, medical and surgical equipment, cameras, watches and clocks.

Transport equipment, e.g. motor vehicles, trailers, caravans, motor vehicle parts and accessories, ships, boats, trains, aircraft and spacecrafts, motorcycles and bicycles.

Other manufacturing not listed above, e.g. furniture, mattresses, jewellery, musical instruments, sports goods, games and toys, brooms and brushes; recycling of scrap metal.

* Engineering industries.

■ *Manufacturing in the UK*

Engineering

Engineers are employed in manufacturing industries, mainly in relation to the design and functioning of machinery and equipment. Light engineering companies make small items where precision is important, such as scientific equipment. Heavy engineering companies make goods comprising large sections of metals, such as ships or cranes.

Activity

Identify the type of manufacturing businesses that exist in your area today by looking in your local ***Yellow Pages****. Compare your findings as a group.*

Energy production

In addition to products, we all need electricity, gas and water. This group of organisations includes those that produce and distribute gas and electricity, such as Powergen and London Energy, and those which collect and distribute water. This includes regional water companies, such as Anglian Water Services and water collection and bottling companies. In the future Britain is looking at obtaining more energy from alternative sources, such as wind farming and tidal energy. These businesses, too, will be classified in this group.

Fact file

The secondary sector manufactures goods. It converts raw materials into products for sale to businesses and private individuals.

Construction

This group includes house builders and civil engineering companies. Between them they construct all types of buildings as well as motorways, bridges, roads and railways. Also included are electricians who work on building sites and plumbers, plasterers, joiners, painters and glaziers.

The tertiary sector

This sector includes every type of business that offers a service.

- **Private services** are purchased by businesses and individuals. They are offered by privately owned businesses including retailers, accountants, banks, communications companies, consultants, private clinics and hospitals, publishers, transport and distribution firms, travel agencies and many others.
- **Public services** are provided locally and nationally by the government and local authorities, for example education, emergency services, housing, law and order, defence and military activity, social services, local planning, recreational facilities and so on.

Four out of every five people in the UK today work in the tertiary sector.

- **Voluntary and not-for-profit services** are provided by charitable and voluntary organisations in areas such as social care, community health care, global development, environmental and wildlife protection.

The Office for National Statistics groups services slightly differently, because different types of business may offer the same service. Education, for example, is provided both by state schools and by private (independent) schools. Health care is similar, and voluntary organisations such as MIND or Help the Aged may also be involved. The official categories are shown in the table below.

Main groupings
Wholesale and retail trade, e.g. all wholesalers and retailers, including market stalls and dispensing chemists, plus repair/maintenance businesses such as garages, watch repairers, cobblers.
Hotels and restaurants including camping sites, youth hotels, holiday centres, take-away food shops and stands, pubs and bars.
Transport, storage and communication, e.g. taxis, furniture removals, freight transport by road, rail, sea, canals and air, all passenger transport, pipelines, cargo handling and storage, travel agencies and tour operators, post and courier services, telecommunications.
Financial services, e.g. banks, building societies, finance houses, insurance companies and pension funds.
Real estate, renting and business activities, e.g. estate agents, car hire firms, all rental firms, computer consultants, software developers, office equipment repairers, solicitors, accountants, market research companies, quantity surveyors, architects, advertising agencies, recruitment companies, security firms, industrial cleaners, photographers, secretarial agencies, call centres, debt collectors, exhibition organisers.
Public Administration and Defence, e.g. government agencies which oversee health care, education and other services, defence activities, the justice system, the police and fire service.
Education, e.g. all schools, colleges and universities, driving schools, private training firms.
Health and Social work, e.g. hospitals and nursing homes, doctors, dentists, vets, social workers.
Other community, social and personal service activities, e.g. sewage and refuse disposal, professional organisations and trade unions, religious and political organisations, film and video production and distribution, radio and television, theatres, fair and amusement parks, news agencies, libraries, museums, sports centres, dry cleaners, funeral directors, hairdressers, beauty therapists, gyms and fitness centres, nature reserves.

■ *The tertiary sector*

Distribution is the moving of goods around the country to where they are required. Large distribution centres near motorways store goods before they are transported to local shops and stores.

Wholesalers buy large quantities of items and sell these in smaller quantities to retailers.

The tertiary sector provides services to businesses and individuals.

The growth and decline of sectors

Classifying businesses means that it is easier to identify trends in different sectors and industries and compare these. Businesses may change what they do, for various reasons:

- businesses are attracted towards profitable activities and away from unprofitable ones. This is why some farmers now run holiday homes
- cheap foreign imports can force the closure of some British companies, such as shoe and textile manufacturers
- technological developments change the demand for goods and services – such as computer maintenance services and Internet service providers
- fashion, trends and lifestyles affect the type of goods and services we want to buy.

This has two effects:

- whole sectors can grow or decline
- within different sectors, certain types of businesses may flourish whilst others may not.

Activity

As a group, name ten businesses that have opened in your area since you were born. Then identify ten that have closed since your parents were young by asking older relatives, visiting a library or researching online. Suggest reasons for these changes and say which sectors have been affected.

Whole sector changes

Once, most people in Britain worked on the land. Then the UK led the world in manufacturing. Today, we import most of our manufactured goods from abroad and more people are employed in the tertiary sector. We know this because we can measure changes by looking at different types of figures.

Employment by sector An increase in the number of jobs usually means that a sector is growing. If you look at the chart of employment by sector below, you will see that in recent years employment has:

- fallen in the primary and secondary sector
- increased in the tertiary sector.

Fact file

The primary and secondary sectors are declining in the UK whilst the tertiary sector is growing.

Year	Primary (%)	Secondary (%)	Tertiary (%)
1993	2.2	24.0	73.8
1998	2.0	23.0	75.0
2000	1.7	21.8	76.5
2003	1.4	19.9	78.7
2005	1.4	17.0	81.6

■ *Share of UK employment by sector*

Sometimes, however, employment may appear to increase more than it really does because many employees are part-time workers. In retailing and catering, for example, there are more part-time workers than there are in manufacturing.

Did you know?

*Output per person is known as **productivity**. As this increases, the cost of producing each item is less, therefore goods can be sold more cheaply.*

Key terms

Consumer demand is the degree to which consumers want to buy certain products or services.

Employment is the number of people employed in a sector or industry.

Share of employment is the percentage of working people involved in a sector of industry.

Output is the amount of goods produced and their value.

Activity

Banks now employ fewer staff but their output (i.e. the number of transactions processed) has increased. Suggest reasons for this.

Sector output All businesses produce output. A fisherman's output is the number of fish caught, a manufacturer's is the number of goods made and a retailer's is the number sold, and so on. It is possible for the output of a sector to be growing but for the sector to be declining in relation to other sectors. This is the case with manufacturing in the UK. Output has steadily increased because of modern technology and greater efficiency – so more goods are now made by fewer people. However, manufacturing's share of output in relation to the other sectors has fallen considerably as you can see by the table below.

Year	Primary (%)	Secondary (%)	Tertiary (%)
1993	4.1	28.9	67.0
1998	4.0	28.7	67.3
2000	3.5	26.5	70
2003	3.1	22.5	74.4
2005	3	22	75

■ *Approximate share of UK output by sector*

Activity

Compare the employment and output tables above and identify where any differences occur.

Specific changes

Several specific changes have taken place in different sectors. Some areas have grown (✔) and some have declined (✘) as you can see in the table below.

Sector	Change
Primary	✔ Organic food producers, wind farms, fish farms, oil and natural gas extraction ✘ Fishing fleets, coal mining, quarrying
Secondary	✔ Food and drink, drugs and pharmaceuticals, weapons and ammunitions, energy (electricity gas and water), construction, electrical and optical equipment, paper and publishing ✘ Heavy engineering (e.g. ship building); textiles, leather and clothing, fur products, knitwear, wood products, iron and steel, machinery and equipment
Tertiary	✔ Computer services, other business services, wholesale and retail, financial services, real estate (e.g. estate agencies), travel and recreation, security services, education, health and social work, hotels and restaurants ✘ Public administration (e.g. the Civil Service), defence, secretarial services

■ *Specific changes in sectors*

Some changes affect output or employment over a long period, such as falling demand for British textiles because of cheaper foreign imports. However, specific events and fashions can have a short-term impact, such as the modern trend for wooden flooring, which has affected the carpet industry.

Did you know?

By 2003, business and financial services contributed more than twice as much to the UK economy than all of the manufacturing industries put together.

Activity

Investigate sectors at www.prospects.ac.uk. In groups, select 'explore job sectors' and click on a sector to find out what has happened to that industry in the past, what is happening now and what is predicted for the future. Then compare your notes with other groups.

Over to you

1 a) *Identify the industrial sector in which each of the following people works:*

plumber	*oil driller*	*teacher*
journalist	*engineer*	*lorry driver*
vet	*dog breeder*	*website designer*
actor	*sales assistant*	*paramedic*

b) *Work in pairs. Write down six occupations that are as unusual as possible. Exchange your list with your partner so that you each identify the sector relating to the jobs on the other person's list.*

2 a) *Working in small groups, suggest reasons for the growth or decline of five of the industries shown in the table on page 18. Share your ideas with other groups who have discussed other industries.*

b) *Identify how each of the following events may affect different industries and sectors and explain whether each is likely to signify a long-term trend or a short-term change:*

- ***i)*** *London winning the Olympic bid for 2012*
- ***ii)*** *worries about bird flu*
- ***iii)*** *the popularity of music downloads and MP3 players*
- ***iv)*** *more working mothers.*

Talking point

View 1: It doesn't matter if manufacturing disappears in Britain because we can import any goods we want from abroad.

View 2: Manufacturing provides jobs and helps Britain to earn money from abroad. The government should give grants and loans to encourage new hi-tech businesses.

With which viewpoint do you agree – and why?

Case study Assessment practice

In the 1920s the British coal industry employed 1.2 million men, but output was low at 200 tonnes per man per year. Today, UK Coal, the largest UK producer, employs just over 5,000 people and produces about 15 million tonnes a year. Average output in the industry is now far higher at 4,000 tonnes per person per year.

Despite this the demand for coal in Britain has fallen dramatically since 1950 from over 200 million tonnes a year to around 60 million. The main users today are coal-fired power stations and, to meet their needs, about 40 million tonnes of coal is now imported every year.

1(P) **a)** Describe what is meant by the primary, secondary and tertiary classification of business activities.

b) In which classification would you place the coal industry?

c) Suggest two or three local and national examples for each sector. ***(P2)***

2(M) Explain changes in the coal industry by answering the following questions.

a) Has employment in the industry increased or decreased since 1920?

b) How has demand for coal changed since 1950? Suggest two reasons for this.

c) Has productivity increased or decreased in the coal industry since 1920? Explain how you know.

d) Suggest one reason why this change has occurred.

e) How do you think this affects the price of coal – and why? ***(M2 part)***

3(M) **a)** Identify six other areas of primary, secondary and tertiary business activities that have grown or declined in recent years.

b) Explain the reasons for these changes. ***(M2 part)***

Grading tip

'Explaining' means that you must give a reason rather than just a description. You need to say 'how' or 'why' something has happened.

1.3 Aims and objectives in different sectors

The aims of businesses

All businesses have aims they want to achieve. These are the long-term visions or goals of a business.

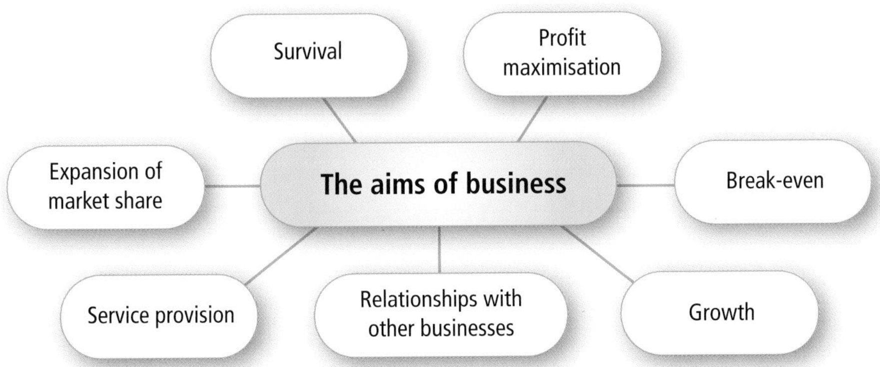

■ *The aims of business*

- Privately owned businesses aim to make a profit, as you saw on page 3 and most will want to increase this each year. Some will aim for **profit maximisation**, which means making as much profit as possible.
- If trading is difficult, for some reason, then making good profits may be unrealistic. In this situation, the business may aim just to **survive**, until times improve.
- One method of surviving is to aim to **break-even** over a certain period. This means making enough money to cover the total costs involved in producing and selling the goods or services and running the business. There is no profit, but there is no money lost, either. You will learn more about break-even in Unit 3.
- The business may aim for **growth**, so that it sells more goods or services. This may mean expanding by opening other branches or buying out a competitor.
- Another aim may be **service provision**. This may mean offering a new service or improving current services to attract more customers, such as businesses which extend their websites to allow customers to order and pay for goods online and track deliveries.
- Many businesses have a constant aim of expanding their **market share**. This normally means taking business away from their competitors.
- Some business aim to improve or **develop their relationships with other businesses**. This may involve joint initiatives to offer goods or services to more people.

Although a business may have more than one aim, it is sensible not to have too many. Most focus on two or three which are appropriate to the main purpose of the business.

Activity

Find out the main aims of your school or college and the type of relationships it has with other businesses.

Fact file

Aims are set to provide a focus for the organisation. The aims and objectives will always link to the main purpose of the organisation.

Key terms

Profit maximisation involves making as much profit as possible.

Break-even is covering the costs of running the business without making a profit.

Market share is the share of the consumer market for that product or service held by a supplier.

Key terms

Aims are the longer-term visions or goals of a business.

Objectives are specific, measurable targets to help achieve an aim.

Fact file

*Objectives are **targets** to be attained. These are communicated to staff and departments who then know which targets they must achieve for the business to realise its aims.*

Activity

Decide on one personal aim you have this year. Then write two SMART objectives to help you achieve this. Compare your ideas with others in your group.

Business objectives

Objectives are more specific than aims. They are **targets** which are set to help to achieve the overall aims of the business. You may have several personal aims you want to achieve – to get fitter, save for a holiday next year, achieve your BTEC First Diploma but you are unlikely to achieve your aim unless you set objectives. This is because aims often seem overwhelming. They are easier to achieve if they are broken down into smaller steps – such as doing 20 minutes exercise every day to get fit, or regularly saving £10 a week to go on holiday.

SMART objectives

A problem with some objectives is that they are not very clear or specific. You may decide to join a gym but then only go when you feel like it; you may decide to save for a holiday without setting a specific amount. In both cases you may fail to fulfil your aims. This type of problem can be overcome by setting SMART objectives which are:

Specific There is a clear definition, often including a number, for example saving £20 a week.

Measurable This means achievement can be checked. Banking your savings means your bank statement will record and measure your achievement.

Achievable This means you can attain your target if you stretch yourself a little – so saving £20 a week may be achievable without having to make too many sacrifices.

Realistic This means the target is sensible so that you stand a chance of achieving it. You could not save £20 a week if you did not have a job that paid at least that amount.

Time-related Every objective should have a date for achievement or review. Therefore, you could set a time limit to review your progress after three months.

It should be fairly obvious from this list that it is very difficult to wriggle out of an objective that is SMART. You either achieve it or you don't!

Aims and objectives in different sectors

Aims and objectives are designed to help an organisation to achieve its key purpose and provide a focus for staff. They vary between organisations in different sectors because these businesses have different purposes.

- **Private sector businesses** provide goods and/or services and must make a profit to survive. They can only break-even (or make a loss) for a very short time or the business would have to close.
- **Public sector businesses** are owned by the state and provide many essential services free of charge and others at or below cost price.
- **Voluntary sector organisations** raise money which is used to support a particular cause. They do not aim to make a profit but to generate a surplus, after the costs of the business have been deducted.

The table below shows how these purposes affect the aims that are set.

Did you know?

Because public sector businesses receive public money raised through taxes their ability to achieve targets is often highlighted in performance tables, such as school and hospital league tables.

	Private sector	Public sector	Voluntary sector
Business examples	Manufacturers, retailers, banks, builders, solicitors	Government departments, local councils, NHS hospitals, state schools	Community groups and charities such as Oxfam and Cancer Research UK
Purpose	To provide goods and/or services To make a profit	To provide a quality service to the community	To provide a free service for the needy To promote a particular cause
Examples of aims	Maximise profits by increasing sales and keeping costs low Increase market share Expand or develop the business	Improve service provision Operate within budget (i.e. break-even)	Increase surplus. Increase services offered
Examples of objectives	Increase sales Increase number of customers Reduce costs	Meet customer targets (e.g. patient waiting times) Keep costs low	Increase revenue from donations Reduce costs

■ *How purposes of organisations in different sectors affect their aims*

Fact file

A mission or vision statement explains the main purpose of the business and the activities it is doing to achieve this. Many include the organisation's aims and objectives.

Many large organisations have a **mission statement**, especially those in the public and voluntary sectors. Some businesses call this their vision statement and others have both a mission statement and a vision statement.

Because mission statements reflect the main purpose of the business you will again see a difference depending upon the sector. They will also often include the aims and/or objectives of the business.

- Privately owned businesses mention **customers, employees**, the **cost** of their products or **value** for money.
- Publicly owned organisations often mention the **service** they provide and the **work they do** as well as including statements on quality, efficiency and customer service.
- Voluntary organisations focus on the **services** they provide, the **causes** they support or their **aims** in helping the needy.

Did you know?

You will rarely see the word 'profit' included in any mission statement but that does not mean it is not a key aim of all private businesses!

Activity

Obtain the mission statement of your school or college. As a group, decide how this relates to the sector it is in, its ownership and its main purpose. Then ask your tutor to explain the current aims and objectives and discuss how these link to the sector and the purpose of the organisation.

Did you know?

*The website suffix will often tell you the ownership of a business. **.co.uk** and **.com** is the private sector; **.gov** is the public sector, **.org** is the usually the voluntary sector.*

Over to you

1. *Working in small groups, suggest two appropriate aims for each of the following organisations and one suitable objective to link to each one. Then compare your ideas with other groups.*
   a) *GP*
   b) *hotel*
   c) *children's charity*
   d) *retail store*
   e) *police force*
2. **a)** *Read the following mission statements and identify the ownership of each organisation.*
   b) *Suggest one appropriate aim that each business may have.*
   c) *Explain why aims and objectives are set by businesses.*

continued ▶

Over to you *continued*

A Apple is committed to bringing the best personal computing experience to students, educators, creative professionals and consumers around the world through its innovative hardware, software and Internet offerings.

B Sport England is working with others to create opportunities for people to get involved in sport, to stay in sport and to excel and succeed in sport at every level.

C Google's mission is to organise the world's information and make it universally accessible and useful.

D The NSPCC's mission is to end cruelty to children. Their vision is a society in which all children are loved, valued and able to fulfil their potential – in other words, a society that will not tolerate child abuse, whether sexual, physical, emotional, or neglect.

E The mission of Cheltenham Animal Shelter is to return to health the sick, find homes for the lost and give dignity to the aged.

F The mission of the DVLA is to contribute to safer, cleaner motoring, maintaining accurate driver and vehicle licensing and registration records and providing other integrated services. Its vision is to be the trusted partner – right at the heart of road safety.

3 *Working in small groups, and in agreement with your tutor, investigate the aims and objectives of differently owned organisations online. Some suggested businesses are given below but you may prefer to choose others you know well in your own area.*

- *A public sector organisation, for example, your local council, local police authority, the Foreign and Commonwealth, Office of Fair Trading, Sport England or university of your choice.*
- *A large charity of your choice, for example, Oxfam, NSPCC, or Cancer Research UK.*
- *A privately owned organisation, for example, BT, Boots, Marks and Spencer, Unilever, HBOS, or Carphone Warehouse.*

a) *Describe the aims and objectives of the organisation you have investigated.*

b) *Explain how you think the aims and objectives relate to the type of ownership for your chosen business.*

Talking point

View 1: Targets are a good thing because they focus people's attention on working harder at the things that matter.

View 2: Targets cause problems. If they are too hard people lose interest. They also get fed up if the targets get harder every year.

With which viewpoint do you agree – and why?

Did you know?

You will find out more about a business online if you click on the 'About Us' or 'Corporate Information' sections of the website.

Case study Assessment practice

Subway is a sandwich chain that is expanding rapidly. It is a franchise, so needs to attract potential owners, who are willing to invest their savings or borrow money to run their own outlet. They need about £6,000 to open a branch but this may vary, depending upon the location and size of the shop.

The website states that Subway's mission is 'to provide the tools and knowledge to allow entrepreneurs to successfully compete in the Quick Service Restaurant industry worldwide, by consistently offering value to consumers through providing great tasting food that is good for them and made the way they like it'. One main aim is to expand its operations – it wants to increase its UK and Irish stores to 2010 by the same year – from 615 stores in 2005. You can find out more at www.subway.co.uk – particularly the 'About Us' and 'FAQs' pages.

1(P) **a)** What is a franchise? (If you have forgotten, look back to page 4).

b) What is an entrepreneur?

c) Why are new entrepreneurs essential for Subway to meet its aim of expansion? ***(P1 part P3 part)***

2(P) Describe why Subway sets aims and objectives for its business. Refer to examples on its website to illustrate your answer. ***(P3)***

3(M) Jack is interested in opening a sandwich shop because he has always wanted to own his own business. At the moment he works in the finance department at a local NHS hospital.

Compare and contrast the ownership and the type of aims and objectives he would set for his own business with those of a major NHS hospital. ***(M1 part)***

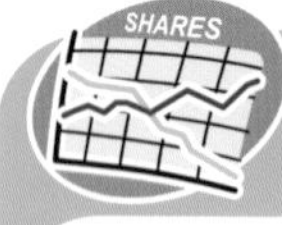

Grading tip

When you compare and contrast, make sure you identify both similarities and differences. In this question, remember that the aims and objectives will be affected by the ownership of each business, as well as by its main purpose.

1.4 The main functional areas within business organisations

Even in the smallest business a number of key tasks, or functions, must be done regularly. Stock must be bought, bills must be paid, customers must be served and customer enquiries must be answered. In a small firm all these jobs may be done by one or two people. In a large organisation, people specialise in different tasks. Tesco and Sainsbury's, for example, have buyers to purchase the stock, accounts staff to pay the bills, checkout staff to serve customers and customer service staff to answer queries.

Fact file

All businesses have key functions to carry out, such as dealing with customers and paying bills.

Functional areas in business

In a large organisation, it is usually easier to identify separate functional areas because people work together in departments. Each department carries out the tasks that relate to its particular area. The main ones you are likely to meet in business are shown below.

Activity

Suggest the key functions that are carried out in your school or college and see if your tutor agrees.

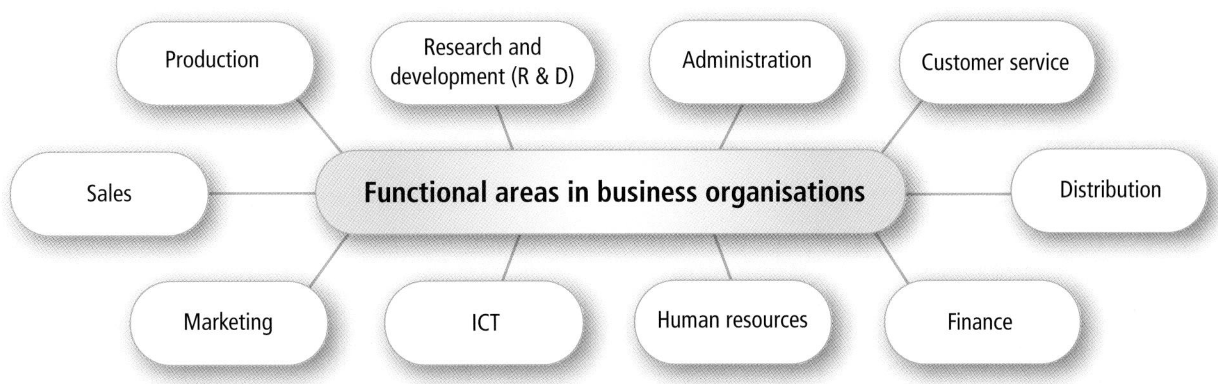

■ *Main functional areas in business*

The purposes of functional areas

The main purpose of functional areas is to ensure that all important business activities are carried out efficiently. This is essential if the business is to achieve its aims and objectives. In addition, specific areas will be responsibility for supporting specific types of aims and objectives, for example:

- sales and marketing will be involved in achieving targets linked to developing new markets or increasing sales
- human resources will be involved in arranging staff training activities and supporting the continuous professional development of all staff

Key term

Functional area relates to a person, area or department responsible for a particular business function, for example, finance, sales or customer service.

Fact file

Functional areas vary between organisations, depending upon the type of work carried out. For example, retailers do not need a production function.

Did you know?

CPD (Continuous professional development) means taking responsibility for your own future development at work by identifying opportunities that will enable you to improve and progress your knowledge and skills.

Did you know?

Administrative salaries can range from £10,000 per annum to over £30,000 per annum. Many recruitment agencies publish salary surveys and reports, such as www.secsinthecity.co.uk and www.kellyservices.co.uk.

- finance will be expected to monitor and support aims and objectives linked to keeping costs low to improve profitability
- production will be set targets relating to quality or meeting planned production schedules.

The administration function

Administration is a support function required by all businesses – and this does not mean just doing keyboarding or filing. Senior administrators carry out a wide range of tasks, from monitoring budgets to interviewing new staff for their departments.

Routine administrative tasks include opening the mail, preparing and filing documents, sending emails and faxes. Others require more creativity and flexibility, such as arranging travel or important events, from staff meetings to visits by foreign customers. Most administrators also deal with external customers who judge the business on the way their enquiry is handled. Poor or sloppy administration can be disastrous for a company's image and reputation. A lost order, badly typed letter, important message that is not passed on or wrong date scheduled for a meeting can cause problems and may lose customers. Efficient administration means that everything runs smoothly and managers can concentrate on the task of running the business.

In a small organisation, an administrator is often a 'jack-of-all-trades' who can turn a hand to anything – from checking and paying invoices to keeping the firm's website up to date. In a larger firm administration may be carried out in every department, rather than just one. A sales administrator may make overseas travel arrangements whereas an administrator in human resources would arrange job interviews.

A summary of the range of tasks administrators carry out is given below. You will learn more about administration if you study option unit 6.

Administration functions

- Collecting, distributing and dispatching the mail
- Storing and retrieving paper and electronic records
- Organising meetings and preparing meeting documents
- Responding promptly to enquiries
- Preparing documents using word processing, spreadsheet and presentation packages, such as PowerPoint
- Researching information
- Sending and receiving messages by telephone, fax and email
- Making arrangements for visitors
- Making travel arrangements
- Purchasing supplies of office stationery and equipment
- Making arrangements for events, such as interviews or sales conferences

Activity

Talk to one of the administrators in your school or college about the work carried out in their office – but remember it is not polite to ask anyone how much they earn!

The customer service function

All businesses must look after customers or clients who have an enquiry, concern or complaint. Today, customer expectations are high. When people contact a business they expect a prompt, polite and knowledgeable response. Unless they get a high level of service they are likely to take their business elsewhere in the future.

For this reason, many businesses have customer service staff – or a customer service department – where trained staff handle enquiries and complaints positively and professionally. This does not mean that other staff can ignore customers and their needs. It simply means that one group specialises in assisting customers.

Organisations that manufacture and sell complex industrial products usually employ technical specialists or engineers in customer service to give detailed advice and information. An example is BAE Systems, which sells aeroplanes such as the Eurofighter and Hawk jets. Answering queries

Technicians, engineers and consultants often undertake customer service functions in industry when specialist knowledge is required.

related to these products obviously needs specialist knowledge. Similarly, computer suppliers like Dell or PC World, and Internet service providers like BT have trained IT specialists to handle customer problems – whether from other businesses or from individuals.

Customer service staff also deal with complaints and problems. Most businesses have a special procedure for dealing with customer complaints, to ensure these are dealt with quickly and consistently. In some cases, action is needed to make sure the problem does not occur again. Customer service staff must also be aware of the legal rights of customers – and this means having a knowledge of consumer law. You will learn more about Customer Relations in Unit 2.

Activity

As a group, compare your best and worst customer service moments as customers. What lessons can you learn from these?

Customer service functions

- Answering customer enquiries about products and services
- Providing specialist information and advice to meet customer needs
- Solving customer problems
- Providing after-sales service, including replacing damaged goods, arranging for repairs or for spare parts to be obtained and fitted
- Dealing with customer complaints according to company procedures
- Analysing records of customer complaints to resolve problem areas
- Using customer feedback to improve customer service and satisfaction

Did you know?

*The term **supply chain** is sometimes used to describe each stage of the process from the finished goods leaving a factory to their arrival in a store.*

The distribution function

Distribution means ensuring that goods are delivered to the right place on time and in the right condition. Some companies, such as Amazon and Debenhams, deliver direct to the customer, particularly when goods are bought online. Other businesses, including B & Q and Sainsbury's, hold stocks in giant regional warehouses, for delivery to stores around the area. Superstores may use special vehicles, which can also carry chilled or frozen items. Other businesses have to move more difficult loads or hazardous substances, such as large engineering parts, cars or chemicals.

Distribution involves more than just arranging for goods to be collected. For it to be cost-effective, costs must be kept as low as possible. This means, for example:

- planning vehicle routes to avoid back-tracking. This keeps fuel costs down and saves time
- ensuring that vehicles do not return empty. This is only possible if goods are both delivered and collected. Vehicles that only deliver goods normally operate on a regional or local basis to minimise 'empty journey' time.

Working out the routes for many vehicles, with different loads – some urgent and some not – can be very complicated. Computer programs are used by staff skilled in **logistics** to work out the best routes.

Many organisations **outsource** both storage and distribution to external contractors. This means paying a specialist firm to do the work. This is often cheaper than employing experts in the business.

Key terms

Outsourcing involves hiring a specialist firm to do specific work, such as distribution companies, security firms and payroll agencies.

Logistics is planning and controlling the movement of goods.

Distribution functions

- Ensuring all goods are appropriately stored before dispatch
- Ensuring goods for dispatch are securely packed and correctly labelled
- Checking vehicle loads are safe and secure
- Ensuring goods are despatched at the right time
- Checking that all deliveries match orders precisely and notifying sales if there is a discrepancy
- Completing the delivery documents
- Planning and scheduling vehicle routes
- Notifying sales staff of delivery schedules so that customers can be informed
- Dealing with distribution problems, e.g. through bad weather or vehicle breakdown

Did you know?

Eddie Stobart is a distribution firm with its own fan club! Find out more at www.eddiestobart.co.uk.

The finance function

Most entrepreneurs consider this is the most important function in the business. This is because all businesses need a regular stream of income to pay the bills. Finance staff record all the money earned and spent so that the senior managers always know how much profit (or loss) is being made by each product or each part of the business and how much money is currently held by the business. This enables critical decisions to be made rapidly and accurately because they are based on accurate information. In some cases, this can mean the difference between the success or failure of the business as a whole, as you will see in Unit 3.

Activity

Find out more about logistics and distribution at www.exel.com/exel/home. Click on 'About Us' then 'Solutions' and 'Industries' to find out how distribution solutions vary for different sectors.

Fact file

An efficient finance function is crucial for businesses to achieve aims and objectives linked to improving profits and lowering costs.

Key terms

Reserves are profits kept back for later reinvestment in the business.

Interest rates show the cost of borrowing money.

Did you know?

Computerised tills automatically record data on the computer system so that transactions can be analysed by product, customer, staff and store. Many systems also automatically update stock levels.

In many large businesses, different types of financial experts are employed:

- **management accountants** monitor departmental budgets and current income from sales, prepare cash flow forecasts and specialise in analysing day-to-day financial information and keeping senior managers informed
- **financial accountants** are concerned with the preparation of the statutory accounts. All companies must provide a Balance Sheet and Profit and Loss Account each year, and most produce a cash flow statement as well. You will learn about cash flow in Unit 3
- **credit controllers** monitor overdue payments and take action to recover bad debts. You will find out more about credit control in Unit 3.

Finance staff support the accountants by keeping financial records, chasing up late payments and paying for items purchased. Today, virtually all businesses use computer accounting packages to record financial transactions and prepare their accounts as well as spreadsheets to analyse financial data. Some finance departments prepare the payroll and pay staff salaries, but others outsource this to a specialist bureau.

Finally, businesses will often need money to fulfil specific aims and objectives linked to growth, expansion or simply updating their equipment or machinery. These items may be bought from money held back (reserved) from past profits, but usually additional money will be needed. If the business needs to borrow money it will want the cheapest interest rates possible and also want good repayment terms. Deciding where to obtain these funds is a specialist job and normally the task of the senior financial manager.

Finance functions

- Producing invoices, checking payments are received and chasing up overdue payments
- Recording money received
- Checking and paying invoices received
- Preparing the payroll and paying staff salaries
- Monitoring departmental budgets to check managers are not overspending
- Issuing regular budget reports to all departmental managers
- Producing cash flow forecasts and regular financial reports for senior managers
- Advising senior managers on sources of finance for capital expenditure
- Producing the statutory accounts each year

Activity

Discuss the way in which money is handled and transactions are recorded in any businesses where members of your group have jobs.

The human resources (HR) function

The human resources of a business are its employees. Wise organisations look after their staff on the basis that if they are well trained and committed to the aims of the business, the organisation is more likely to be successful.

HR is responsible for recruiting new employees and ensuring that each vacancy is filled by the best person for the job. This is important because the recruitment process is expensive and time-consuming. Hiring the wrong person can be costly and cause problems both for the individual and the firm.

Normally, new employees attend an **induction programme** which tells them about the business, their rights and responsibilities as employees, the company rules and the requirements of their new job. Arranging appropriate training and assisting with the continuous professional development of staff is another aspect of HR (see page 28). Training may be carried out in-house or staff may attend external courses.

HR aims to ensure that the business retains good, experienced staff. Analysing staff turnover figures will show the rate at which people leave the organisation. If these are high, it is important to identify and remedy any problem areas. Whilst people may leave for justifiable reasons, such as moving to another area or for promotion elsewhere, dissatisfaction with the job or the company should be investigated. Some organisations hold exit interviews to find out staff views on the business when they leave.

Did you know?

Human resources used to be called ***personnel*** *and you may still see this term used in some companies.*

Employees normally have basic expectations of their employer. They expect to be treated and paid fairly, to have appropriate working conditions, to have training opportunities which will improve their promotion prospects, and support if they are ill or have serious personal problems. They also want a varied and interesting job and praise when they have worked particularly hard or well. These factors help **motivation**, which means staff are keen to work hard – and this benefits everyone. HR can help this process by monitoring working conditions, having staff welfare policies and ensuring that company pay rates are fair and competitive.

Many organisations have **staff associations**, which monitor the views and conditions of staff and make these known. In other businesses **trade unions** may represent the workers, especially on pay and conditions. Senior HR staff liaise with these organisations, keep them informed of changes and developments and are also involved in any negotiations with senior management.

Today, all employees and employers have legal rights and responsibilities in relation to health and safety, data protection (which restricts the type of information which can be held on employees and customers and how it is used) and employment. HR staff must ensure that the business complies with current laws and stays up to date with legal changes and developments. You will find out more about this if you study option unit 5.

Human resources functions

- Advertising job vacancies
- Notifying staff of promotion opportunities
- Receiving and recording all job applications, arranging interviews and notifying candidates of the result
- Sending a contract of employment and other essential information to new staff
- Arranging staff training and encouraging continuous professional development
- Monitoring the working conditions of staff
- Checking health and safety and keeping accident records
- Recording sick leave and reasons for absence
- Carrying out company welfare policies, e.g. long-service awards and company loans
- Advising managers on the legal rights and responsibilities of the company and its employees
- Keeping records of grievances and disciplinary actions and their outcome
- Monitoring the terms and conditions of employment, including wage rates
- Maintaining staff records
- Liaising with staff associations or trade unions which represent the workforce

Activity

What would motivate you to do a good job? List the top five factors that would encourage you to work hard, then compare your list with other people in your group.

The ICT function

Today, even the smallest businesses need someone who understands ICT and what to do if something goes wrong. This is vital, because the number of crucial business tasks now carried out on computer and the importance of the data stored in the system mean that any system failure can be catastrophic.

Most organisations have a computer network where staff computers are linked through servers. Maintaining the servers, installing new (communal) software and additional hardware, such as printers and scanners, is all part of the ICT function. ICT staff may also be involved in the purchase or issue of computer supplies, such as cabling and network cards and consumables such as printer cartridges – to ensure that they are compatible with the system.

ICT specialists will be expected to update senior managers on technological developments which would benefit the company. In addition, current equipment will need replacing and software upgrading at regular intervals.

Above all, ICT is responsible for system security. Making sure that only authorised users have access to the system, protecting the system against viruses and hackers and ensuring there is a full back-up system to restore critical data in an emergency is vitally important.

Finally, ICT specialists will help and assist other users – from repairing problems and glitches to advising on the use of new software or updating the company Intranet. The business website is likely to be technically maintained by the ICT staff, but the content will normally be devised by marketing staff – as you will see below. You will learn more about this if you study option unit 8.

ICT functions

- Recommending new/updated systems and software to keep abreast of technological developments and the needs of the business
- Buying and installing new hardware and software and providing information or training as appropriate
- Assisting users who have computer problems
- Repairing the computer system when required
- Advising on/obtaining/issuing computer supplies and consumables
- Connecting new or additional equipment to the system
- Installing a security system which limits access to authorised users and protects against hackers and viruses
- Technically maintaining the company website
- Monitoring staff computer use for compliance with the company IT policy
- Operating a back-up system for critical data so this can be recovered quickly in an emergency

Key terms

A ***server*** is a computer which allows access to files and programs stored as shared resources on a computer network.

A ***network*** is a system of linked computers which can communicate and share information.

An ***Intranet*** is a private area on the network on which the information stored can be accessed only by authorised users.

Activity

Find out the IT policy at your school or college and the security measures that are in force to safeguard the system.

Fact file

Marketing was famously described as 'looking at the business through the customer's eyes'.

The marketing function

Marketing is all about identifying and meeting customer needs. Many businesses consider this so important that they are said to be marketing-led. In this case, everyone in the organisation is trained to put the customer first – from the production worker, who has to produce high-quality goods, to the accounts clerk, who must respond to a customer enquiry promptly and accurately.

Another way to understand marketing is through the **marketing mix** which consists of four Ps.

- **Product** – Who are our customers? What do they want to buy? Are their needs changing? Which products are we offering and how many are we selling? What new products are we planning? In which areas are sales growing – and how can we sustain this? For which products are sales static – and how can we renew interest? Which sales are falling and what, if anything, can we do?
- **Price** – How much should we charge? Should we reduce the price at the start to attract more customers – or charge as much as we can when we can? Can we charge different prices to different types of customers? What discounts can we give? What services or products should we give away or sell very cheaply – and what benefits would this bring?
- **Promotion** – How can we tell people about our products? Should we have specialist sales staff? Where should we advertise to attract the attention of our key customers? How else can we promote the product – should we give free samples or run a competition? Where and how can we obtain free publicity? Should we send direct mail shots and, if so, what information should we include?
- **Place** – How can we distribute our product(s)? Should we sell direct to the customer or through retailers? Do we need specialist wholesalers or overseas agents to sell for us? What can we sell over the telephone? How can the Internet help us to sell more?

Did you know?

E-marketing *relates to electronic and online promotions, such as email newsletters, website competitions and advertising on search engines like Google, often on a pay-per-click basis.*

All these questions are considered by marketing staff. They start by carrying out market research to identify customer needs. Products are then developed (or adapted) or services offered to meet these needs. If this is done well, it gives the company an edge over its competitors. This happened when Apple introduced the iPod.

It is no use developing new products or services if no one knows about them. Marketing is therefore responsible for the promotional activities which tell the customer what is available, such as by advertising, sales promotions and publicity campaigns.

Key term

A ***publicity campaign*** is a linked combination of marketing activities, often used for a new product launch.

The company website is a major way of communicating with prospective and actual customers and the style and content is usually the responsibility of marketing staff who ensure it is kept up to date. They may also send regular newsletters to registered users of their site by email. Monitoring the popularity of the website and obtaining information on the customers who use it may be undertaken by the company or outsourced to a specialist agency.

Marketing functions

- Carrying out market research to obtain feedback on potential and existing products and/or services
- Analysing market research responses and advising senior managers of the results and implications
- Promoting products and services through a variety of advertising and promotional methods, e.g. press, TV, online, direct mail, sponsorship and trade shows or exhibitions
- Obtaining and updating a profile of existing customers to target advertising and promotions appropriately
- Producing and distributing publicity materials, such as catalogues or brochures
- Designing, updating and promoting the company website

Find out what promotional activities are undertaken by your school or college and why these have been chosen.

The sales function

Sales is a crucial function for all businesses. It is pointless having superb products or services if no one buys them. For that reason, most businesses have sales targets as part of their aims and objectives. Meeting these is the responsibility of the sales staff or sales team.

The job of the sales staff varies, depending upon the industry. Shops that sell basic products, such as chocolates or magazines, do not need to do much selling. Most customers call in to buy something, choose the goods they want, pay and leave.

Customers expect more help and advice if they want to buy a complex or expensive item, such as a television or car. Stores which sell these types of products therefore need trained sales staff who are friendly, knowledgeable and can describe and/or demonstrate their products and link these to the customer's specific needs.

Organisations train sales staff to spot when an extra sale may be made to a customer. This is why you are offered shoe cleaner when you buy shoes and paper when you buy a computer printer!

Business buyers also expect a high-quality service and in-depth advice and information. They may want to buy highly complex and expensive industrial equipment and need to negotiate special finance arrangements – particularly if they are overseas buyers. Business buyers will also expect discounts for bulk purchases. Sales representatives often travel to meet potential customers, as well as routinely visiting existing customers to ensure their needs are being met.

Employing a skilled sales force is expensive, especially if they are paid bonuses or commission. However, there are many benefits as an effective sales person can convert many enquiries into firm sales and build strong links with customers to encourage repeat business.

There are strong links between marketing and sales – and in many businesses this may be a 'joint' department. Sales can pass on important customer feedback to help marketing colleagues, as you will see on page 42.

All sales staff should know there are a number of laws that protect customers and understand which type of sales activities are legal and which are not. You will find out more about selling if you study option unit 7.

Talking point

View 1: The best way to sell goods is to display stock effectively and then leave customers alone to look around in peace.

View 2: The best way to sell goods is to employ sales staff who will chat to customers about their needs and requirements.

With which viewpoint do you agree – and why?

Sales functions

- Organising sales promotions
- Responding to customer enquiries
- Selling the product or service to customers, either over the telephone or face to face
- Preparing quotations or estimates for customers
- Negotiating discounts or financial terms for business customers
- Providing technical advice
- Keeping customer records up to date

The production function

Production refers to the manufacture or assembly of goods. Production staff must ensure that goods are produced on time and are of the right quality. Quality requirements can vary considerably. Whilst an error of 0.5 mm would not matter much for a chair or table, for an iPod or DVD player it would be critical.

Checking quality does not mean just examining goods after they have been produced. Today quality is 'built-in' at every stage of the process, starting with the raw materials. Many buyers set down a detailed specification for the goods they order, such as Marks and Spencer which sets down precise standards for all its producers. For clothing, this includes the type and weight of material and the thread and fastenings too.

Did you know?

Today many businesses buy goods online. This speeds up the buying process and means there is less need to keep large stocks on the premises.

Buying raw materials is done by specialist purchasing staff, who take out contracts with regular suppliers and make sure that the terms of the contract are met in relation to delivery, cost, quantity and quality. They also ensure that all items are checked on delivery and refer any problems back to the supplier. The materials must be purchased at a competitive price. This is not necessarily the cheapest price, but takes account of other factors, such as the reliability of the supplier, the quality required and the delivery date.

Raw materials will be stored near to the production area in a separate area. If a manufacturer uses a large number of parts – such as a car producer – storage can be very expensive, in terms of the space required and the manpower to oversee the stock. For this reason, many manufacturers today operate a **just-in-time** (JIT) system. This involves having an agreement with specific suppliers to provide small quantities, quickly, when they are needed. This benefits both parties. The suppliers know that they have a regular buyer. The manufacturer no longer needs to store large quantities of goods or worry about having sufficient stocks on the premises all the time.

Today, many production processes are automated. This means that machines or robots do all the routine or dangerous jobs. At a bottling plant, for example, the cleaning, filling and labelling of the bottles is all done as a continuous process by machines. Operators check that the production 'line' is functioning correctly by checking consoles and computer screens, as well as by watching the work as it progresses. Some industries use Computer Integrated Manufacturing, where the control of the process is done by computer.

Purchasing is often a separate function. It is only linked to production in a manufacturing organisation.

When a process cannot be automated, teams of operators may work together and take responsibility for a sequence of operations. This makes the job more interesting and makes it easier to ensure high quality. This system is also more flexible because changes can easily be introduced at any stage by giving instructions to specific teams. It is therefore used by many car manufacturers who often want to vary certain models.

In 2005 Toyota's sales targets were set with the aim of making it the biggest car producer in the world.

The production function also includes all the following aspects of production:

- **production planning** involves deciding what will be made, when, and which machines and operators will be used. A realistic timescale must be predicted, bearing in mind other jobs that are in progress.
- **production control** means constantly checking progress to make sure that production plans are met – and taking remedial action if problems occur. This could be because of machinery breakdown, substandard raw materials or labour shortages.
- **machine utilisation control** is concerned with minimising problems by keeping all the equipment and machinery in good working order. This involves checking to ensure none is overloaded or overused, without being routinely checked and maintained. This is important because if a machine malfunctions it may produce damaged goods. If it breaks down altogether then production of that product will cease. Because this aspect is so important, many organisations have a maintenance plan, which shows the dates on which machines will be out of operation for inspection and servicing. These dates are then taken into consideration when production plans are made.
- **staff utilisation control** concentrates on making sure all the staff are working effectively and efficiently and concentrating their efforts on key production areas and targets. This is very important in industries which are labour-intensive and use more people than machines, such as assembling circuit boards or sewing jeans.
- **final quality checks** make certain that the product is of the correct standard. This can be done in several ways. Each item may be examined by hand – or passed through a machine which checks that the size and tolerance is correct. Alternatively, items may be selected for inspection on a random sampling basis. This would be the case if a large number of identical items is being produced, such as cups or biros.

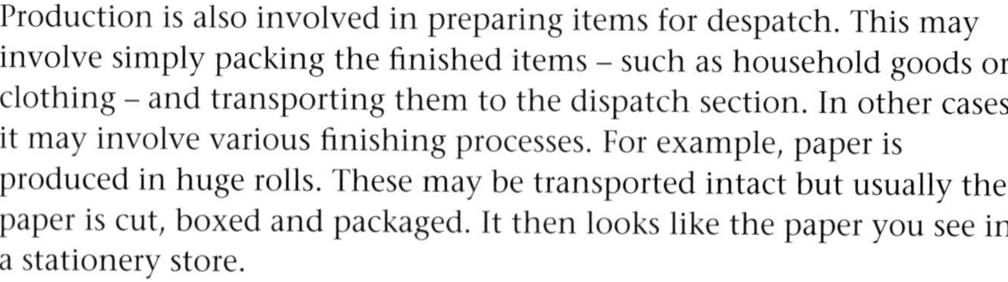

Production is also involved in preparing items for despatch. This may involve simply packing the finished items – such as household goods or clothing – and transporting them to the dispatch section. In other cases, it may involve various finishing processes. For example, paper is produced in huge rolls. These may be transported intact but usually the paper is cut, boxed and packaged. It then looks like the paper you see in a stationery store.

Activity

Investigate production processes online. At the Toyota site www.toyotauk.com/main/index.jsp click on 'How we Manufacture' to find out more. You will need Adobe Acrobat on your system to download the pdf files. Talk to your tutor if you do not know what this means.

Production functions

- Ordering (often buying) stocks of raw materials from approved suppliers
- Storing and checking the stocks of raw materials
- Planning production schedules to maximise machine capacity and staff levels
- Producing or assembling the finished product
- Checking the quality of the product throughout the production process
- Checking production is on schedule and resolving delays or problems
- Packing and storing the final products before distribution
- Scheduling routine machinery inspections and maintenance
- Carrying out repairs to machinery and equipment as required

The research and development (R & D) function

This function is concerned with new product developments as well as improvements to existing products or product lines. In many industries, it also involves product design as well.

Did you know?

Many organisations are secretive about R & D because of the costs involved in new product developments. Staff who work on new projects are sworn to secrecy, to ensure competitors do not find out about them.

Improvements to existing products are often ongoing as a result of market research or customer feedback. You can see these improvements around you all the time – such as ring-pull cans, microwavable containers for ready meals, transparent jug kettles and memory sticks for computers.

New products may be developed because of scientific or technological scientific advances, such as mobile phones, new drugs, WiFi and satellite navigation systems. Or they may occur because someone has a good idea – such as Google or the Apple iPod.

The word 'research' may conjure up ideas of scientists peering into microscopes but this is not always appropriate because research can be divided into two types. **Pure research** aims to help us to learn and understand more about anything – from outer space to DNA. It is mainly carried out by universities and scientific establishments. **Applied research** is focused investigation into how new discoveries can be used to improve products – such as non-stick pans, which were developed from space research. This is the type of research done in business organisations.

R & D staff aim to work with designers to develop a usable product that can be manufactured at a reasonable cost, sold at a competitive price and is safe to use. The activities undertaken, however, can vary considerably, depending upon the industry. Trying to discover new, safe drugs is very different to improving car performance. For that reason, R & D attracts staff who are very experienced in their own industry and also in their own field – from software developers to food technologists.

Many organisations aim to continually improve *both* product design and performance. **Industrial design** relates to the appearance of a product – from a computer to a car, or even the packaging of a standard product – from perfume to soap. Designers want their product to stand out from its competitors and to look attractive, such as the iMac. Today, most products are designed using Computer Aided Design (CAD) packages, which enable a designer to sketch a basic shape and then vary the dimensions, angles and sizes of certain parts. The product can even undergo stress testing by computer. **Engineering design** relates to product performance; for example, for a computer, this means more memory and greater operating speed.

Technological advances through R & D not only affect our lives but also the ways in which businesses operate. New developments in computer software and hardware have changed the way all departments create, store and share data and communicate with their customers; and new types of machinery and equipment have revolutionised many production processes.

R & D functions

Note that the exact activities will depend upon the industry.

- In the pharmaceutical industry, scientists research and develop new medicines and drugs
- In the food industry, technologists work with chefs to prepare new products such as ready meals, sauces or flavourings
- Electronic and IT companies concentrate on new technology products and software, such as HD televisions, the X-box 360 and Sony PS3
- In the aerospace and car industries, engineers focus on improving performance and safety whilst reducing emissions or noise. Designers concentrate on the shape and look, both internally and externally

Activity

Discuss with your tutor how the different functional areas of your school or college help to achieve its aims and objectives.

Relationships between different functional areas

No functional area in a business organisation can work in isolation. In a small firm, links and interactions between people responsible for different functions are usually informal and continuous. Sales people know which customers still owe money and must not be sold any more goods on credit until a bill has been paid; the manager knows which members of staff are keen and hardworking, without being told, and a customer query can quickly be solved by asking everyone in the office for advice.

The situation is different in a larger organisation because people may work in separate areas or departments and rarely meet each other. However, all areas still need information and support from each other for the organisation to operate effectively. Constant communication and cooperation is essential for the business to achieve its aims and objectives. This often means that joint decisions have to be made between departmental managers, or their staff, to take account of everyone's needs.

Some of the reasons why departmental links are essential are shown in the table below, which identifies some of the key issues over which functional areas need to communicate.

Functional areas support business aims and objectives by achieving targets appropriate to their own area of work.

Functional area	Links
Sales and Production	Sales must know production schedules and agree delivery dates of orders with Production so customers are not promised dates which cannot be met. Production must tell Sales about production problems which will affect customers.
Sales and Finance	Finance must know about customer enquiries to check their credit rating before sales are made. Finance will be involved when discounts are agreed or when there are problems with customer payments.
Distribution and Finance	Finance must know when goods have been despatched so that invoices can be sent out.
Distribution and Sales	Sales must be able to inform customers when deliveries are due and be aware of any problems.
Sales and Marketing	Must liaise over sales promotions and adverts so that sales staff can expect/handle enquiries.
Finance and all other departments	Finance monitors departmental spending and the achievement of financial targets.
Human Resources and Finance	Will liaise over salary increases and bonuses.
Customer Service, Sales and Marketing	Customer Service must pass on customer feedback that could affect future product developments or future sales.
R & D and Production	Liaise over new product developments and methods of production.
Human Resources and other functional areas	HR handles job vacancies, promotion opportunities, training courses and CPD for all areas/staff.

■ *Links between functional areas*

Over to you

1 *Investigate a famous business online at www.cadburyschweppes.com/EN/AboutUs/. Do not worry if you don't understand everything on the site, simply try to get an overview of how a well-known organisation operates. Then combine your findings as a group to answer the following questions.*

a) *Describe the size and scale of the business.*
b) *What is its core purpose as stated in the mission statement?*
c) *What are the main goals of the business?*
d) *Explain how the business priorities link to the goals.*
e) *What are the main functional areas and what do you think is the main purpose of each one?*
f) *As a group, suggest how the functional areas may interact to achieve the goals of the business.*

2 *Simonstone Safety Products makes airbags for cars. It aims to expand its operations over the next two years. It has the following departments: Marketing, Distribution, Sales, Production, R & D, HR, Customer Service, ICT and Finance.*

a) *For each target listed below, identify the functional area which would be mainly responsible for its achievement:*
  i) *increase output by 15 per cent*
  ii) *reduce outstanding debt levels*
  iii) *employ 20 new production operatives*
  iv) *develop 'intelligent' airbags which adjust for individual occupants*
  v) *redesign the company website to be more appealing with extra features*
  vi) *increase sales by 20 per cent.*

b) *Identify three issues over which different functional areas would need to liaise, and explain which departments would be involved.*

c) *Suggest the likely effect on the achievement of the targets if each of the following situations occurred:*
  i) *sales and customer service cannot agree on who should respond to customer enquiries by email*
  ii) *customer feedback is analysed each month by a team from marketing, sales, production, customer service and R & D and an action plan drawn up*
  iii *machine breakdowns cause a serious backlog in production – but staff keep the problem to themselves*
  iv) *the sales manager frequently goes abroad on business and no one in the department seems to know his travel plans.*

Case study Assessment practice

In the 1920s Britain started snacking on crisps – and has not stopped since. But not all crisp companies have been equally successful. Recently, Golden Wonder, which once had the largest crisp factory in the world in Corby, has had serious problems. Struggling to compete against Walkers, which dominates Britain's crisp market, it lost money in 2004 and 2005. It was only rescued from total collapse at the last minute when it was bought by Northern Ireland crisp firm Tayto in February 2006, saving over 500 jobs.

Walkers claims that 11 million people eat its crisps every day. The combination of Gary Lineker's endorsement and the continual expansion of flavours has proved a huge hit.

Another reason for its success is its ability to meet new challenges. In 2006, in response to publicity about unhealthy snack foods, Walkers changed its production method and reduced the amount of saturated fat and salt in its crisps. It also opened a new plant in Skelmersdale and now has operations at ten locations in the UK.

1(P) Find out more about Walkers at its website www.walkers.co.uk and describe its production and quality processes. ***(P4 part)***

2(P) Identify two appropriate aims and objectives for Walkers crisps and suggest why these were set. ***(P3)***

3(P) Walkers is owned by PepsiCo which owns other brands, such as Quakers and Tropicana. PepsiCo describes its functions as business areas. Access these at www.pepsicocareers.co.uk/careers.php and read the profiles of people who work in each area. Then identify the business areas that would be responsible for the achievement of the aims and objectives you suggested in 2 above. ***(P4 part)***

4(M) As a group, decide how these areas will need to interact on a regular basis and then explain this in your own words. ***(M3 part)***

5(D) Walkers has been more successful at meeting its aims and objectives than Golden Wonder so far. As a group, evaluate the ways in which the functional areas may have contributed to each organisation's success or failure by answering the following questions.

- **a)** Suggest the ways in which the functional areas must have operated at Walkers for it to be successful.
- **b)** Suggest problems that could have occurred between functional areas at Golden Wonder that may have contributed to its problems.
- **c)** Suggest how being owned by Tayto might make a difference.
  (You can find out more about Golden Wonder and Tayto at their websites www.goldenwonder.com and www.tayto.com.) ***(D1)***

Then write a summary of the discussion in your own words.

Grading tip

A detailed explanation should include reasons or examples to support the statements you are making.

Evaluating something means reviewing the information and forming a conclusion based on your evidence. You should always include the evidence that supports your views in your answer.

2 Developing customer relations

All businesses deal with customers and must meet their needs consistently to be successful. In this unit you will learn how to provide professional customer care and see how businesses evaluate their customer service to identify where improvements can be made.

What you need to learn

- How customer service is provided in business
- How to apply appropriate presentation and interpersonal skills in customer service situations
- How consistent customer service contributes to customer satisfaction
- How to monitor and evaluate customer service

2.1 Understand how customer service is provided in business

Did you know?

Many people work in teams to deliver customer service, in other cases two departments may link together to provide a more effective service. Find out more at the ICS website at www.instituteofcustomerservice.com.

Did you know?

Social Service departments call their reception staff 'customer care officers' because they are dealing all day with the department's customers or clients.

Customer needs and expectations

All businesses aim to provide good customer service but some are more successful than others. Those that are well known for providing excellent customer care are often those with the following characteristics:

- they understand what customer service really means
- they understand their customers and aim to fulfil their needs in every respect
- all the staff in the organisation, at every level, are committed to achieving this aim.

Definition of customer service

The first step in delivering excellent customer service is to understand what this means – and there are many definitions. A simple one is given below:

> *Customer service is the ability of an organisation to recognise and consistently meet its customers' needs.*

The Institute of Customer Service (ICS) has a longer definition which recognises the role played by everyone in an organisation in delivering customer service:

> *Customer service is the sum total of what an organisation does to meet customer expectations and produce customer satisfaction. Customer service generally involves service teamwork and service partnerships. Although somebody may take a leading part in delivering customer service it normally involves actions by a number of people in a team or in several different organisations. (Source: ICS website)*

Identifying customer needs

If effective customer service involves satisfying customer needs, the next step is to know how to identify these. All customers contact an organisation because they need something. The diagram below shows the most common reasons.

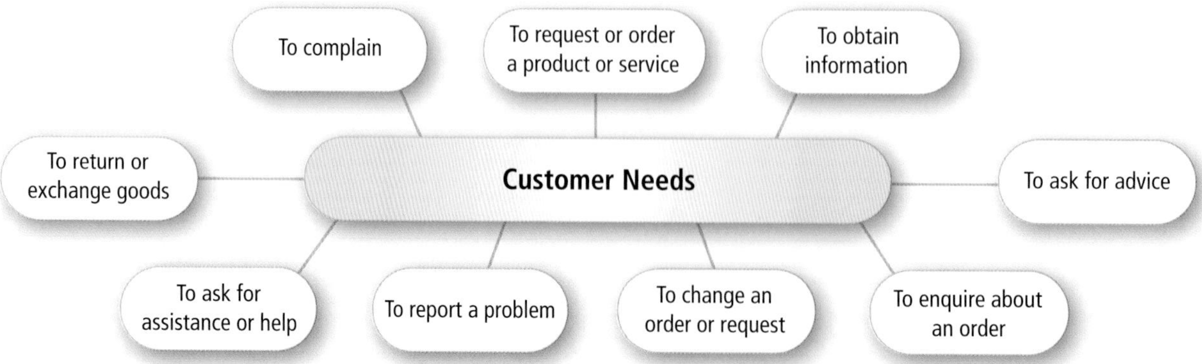

■ *The range of customer needs related to obtaining goods and services*

Did you know?

Customers have preferences as well as needs. You may buy a present online but prefer to have it gift wrapped and delivered direct to the recipient. Excellent customer service involves identifying and fulfilling both the needs and preferences of customers.

Many businesses have specific methods for quickly identifying customer needs. Restaurants display a menu at the door so that passers-by can see what is on offer and whether it will meet their needs. Many suppliers issue brochures or catalogues and employ staff with detailed product knowledge to answer queries. Supermarkets and department stores rely on large signs and distinctive product displays so that customers can find items easily. Floor staff can answer basic queries and customer service staff are employed to deal with more complicated issues.

Organisations that provide expensive products or complex services, such as a car dealership or a bank, train specialist staff how to ask appropriate questions to establish a customer's needs. Learning how to establish and confirm a customer's needs quickly and accurately is important and is far more likely to result in a satisfied customer.

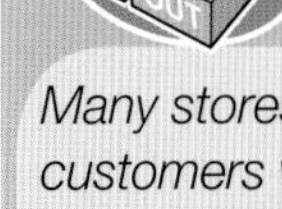

Activity

Many stores have customers who often need to buy something quickly. As a group suggest ways in which different businesses can specifically meet the needs of people in a hurry.

Customer expectations

When customers contact an organisation they expect certain fairly obvious things to happen– such as being treated honestly and politely. However, the expectations of customers often differ.

■ *Factors that influence customer expectations*

Customer service means providing a service that consistently meets or exceeds customer needs.

Customer needs are the main requirements of a customer.

Customer expectations are what a customer expects to happen, usually based on previous experience.

Fact file

Customers make contact with an organisation when they want something, but their needs and expectations vary depending upon many factors.

Activity

Customer expectations increase as prices rise. In groups, identify how your expectations would change for four items of your choice, between the cheapest option and the dearest. To start, think about spending a night in a hostel against a luxury hotel!

Did you know?

Accuracy and reliability are vital if the consequences of an error could cause serious problems. A mistake with an airline booking is never good news but is worse if the traveller is going to an important business meeting, rather than on holiday.

Accuracy and reliability

Accuracy and reliability are important for two reasons. Each is:

- a basic customer need and expectation
- normally a legal requirement.

Therefore, if you provide inaccurate information or fail to do what you have promised you will not only disappoint or anger the customer but may even find yourself legally liable (see Unit 7, page 284).

Reasonable customers will usually forgive minor errors that can be quickly corrected, especially if they receive an apology. They will be less forgiving if they are sent the wrong goods or if a mistake or inefficiency will cause them considerable inconvenience.

Similarly, if their goods are delivered one day late this is different from a week late – and everyone knows horror stories about people staying off work for service engineers who do not turn up.

Providing information and advice

Many customers need information or advice before they can choose the best product or service to meet their needs. However, there is a difference between the two.

Fact file

Alll customers expect to receive accurate information and reliable services. Advice is more personal than information and may need to be given in confidence.

Information you provide must be accurate and complete. This means that you must know what you are talking about. You may be asked to provide information on specific products or services, or be asked a question about your organisation. You are only likely to be able to answer every enquiry you may receive when you have worked in an organisation for some time. However, from the start you can arm yourself with some basic facts, such as

- the correct address, phone number and website address of the organisation and its opening hours
- the people to whom you can refer specific types of queries or problems
- the range of products or services your employer supplies (and those it doesn't)
- the literature and printed information you can give or send to callers
- organisational rules for dealing with problems
- who to ask for help if you can't answer a query.

Advice is usually more personal and specific than information. It normally involves knowing more about the customer's needs and preferences. For example, if you work in a computer shop you may provide information on a range of printers. You can only give advice on which one would be best if you know why and how often your customer wants to use it and how much he or she is prepared to spend.

Activity

At your own college or school, find out which members of staff can give general information about courses to prospective students, who can provide advice and the type of advice that is given in private. Then decide the reasons for any differences.

Providing assistance and help

Sam works for a computer store. On Monday morning he helped a customer to find the software she wanted. Later that day she phoned him to say she had a problem installing it and asked him to help her again. Quite obviously there is a considerable difference between these two requests.

Businesses are aware of the type of assistance and help they are usually asked to provide and this is – or should be – reflected in the services they offer. Some examples are given in the table below.

	For common queries	For specific or technical queries
Online	Website, especially FAQs pages	'Contact us' option to send email
Telephone	Call centre	Specialist advisory staff
Face to face	Receptionist, all other staff	Sales or technical staff Customer service staff
Printed material	Advertisements, leaflets and point-of-sale materials	Brochures and technical literature

■ *Methods of offering assistance and help*

Did you know?

In one DIY store, staff were walking around with T-shirts emblazoned with 'Ask me how to get 10% discount' but when stopped several hadn't a clue how to answer!

It is important to be aware of new promotions and advertisements that customers may have read and then enquire about, so that you can respond appropriately, without looking silly.

Activity

Some organisations are in the business of providing assistance and help to their customers all the time – such as the AA, RAC and Green Flag. As a group, suggest the skills and attributes needed by the people who work for them.

Fact file

All staff have a responsibility to assist customers, some of whom may have special or individual needs that must be taken into consideration.

Dealing with special needs

All customers like to think they are special – but some have specific special needs. These may include the following:

- **an unusual request or enquiry** such as wanting a leaflet in a different language or asking if a product can be adapted in some way

Did you know?

***Positive thinking** means regarding unusual requests as a challenge, not an inconvenience!*

- **special circumstances** such as having to return to work quickly or only being in the area a short time – so their request is more urgent
- **personal characteristics** that affect their needs. Elderly people may need more time to make a decision, young children may need special facilities, visitors may be vegetarian or their culture may affect what they can eat and drink (see page 54)
- **mobility problems or a physical impairment** that affects their needs (see page 55).

Today, most organisations take pride in their ability to meet the special needs of all their customers and this needs the cooperation of their staff. The first step is for the business to identify the possible special needs of its customers and then try to meet these. This is why superstores have parent parking spaces, a range of different trolleys (including powered wheelchairs in some stores), baby changing rooms and cafés. The second step is to train staff to respond positively to unusual requests.

Activity

Working in groups, suggest how the following businesses aim to meet the special needs of their customers and compare your ideas: an airport, a large city centre museum, a top tourist attraction, a large hotel, a college or school.

Dealing with problems

Customers have a problem if their needs and expectations have not been met or if something has happened to change their requirements. Some problems are relatively minor and you will be expected to deal with them yourself or, at the very least, to use your own initiative in finding out what to do, and doing it. Serious problems should be referred immediately to your supervisor. Always remember:

- never overstep your own job role by taking action or making promises that are not in your power to keep. If you suspect a customer's problem is beyond you, ask for advice (see page 64)
- never give the customer the impression that their problem is unimportant or unsolvable, no matter what it is. Write down the details, decide how you can best help and reassure the customer that you will do all you can to help. Then do so.

You will learn more about dealing with specific types of problems on page 75.

Key terms

Information relates to details of a product or service.

Advice is the guidance on the product or service that would best meet the customer's needs.

Customer service targets are specific targets staff must achieve when they are dealing with customers.

Organisational targets

Many organisations set targets – sometimes known as **performance indicators** (PIs) – for customer service. This sets goals for staff to achieve. In the public sector, many organisations have specific customer service standards that they must achieve.

If you have studied Unit 1 then you already know that targets should be specific and measurable – and this also applies to customer service targets.

Achievement is usually measured by analysing information (such as the speed at which requests were acknowledged) or by obtaining customer feedback (see pages 79 and 80).

Examples of targets may include:

- responding to all written enquiries within six working days
- seeing 95 per cent of customers who ring for an appointment within two days
- answering the telephone within 20 seconds.

Activity

Find out the customer service targets – or their equivalent – in place in your school or college and how their achievement is measured.

Health, safety and security

No one ever expects to be in danger at work or when they visit a business. If an accident happened through negligence on the part of the organisation then, under the Health and Safety at Work Act (see page 206), the business would be liable. For this reason, organisations provide health and safety training for staff, have emergency evacuation procedures and carry out risk assessments to minimise the likelihood of an accident occurring. If a risk cannot be eliminated a safety sign will warn everyone of the hazard – such as a wet floor or people working overhead.

Visitors to an organisation need to know what to do in an emergency. If you stay in a hotel you will find evacuation instructions on the back of the room door; if you attend a course then you should be told during the first session what to do if the alarm sounds; people visiting a business organisation are likely to find the instructions on the reverse of their visitor pass.

The type of security measures required will depend upon the nature of the business. An airline has different types of responsibilities to a bank or a supermarket. Most businesses take steps to protect staff and customers against obvious risks, from putting good lighting and CCTV cameras on car parks used at night to having precautions in place for staff who handle cash. Businesses that receive online payments must have a secure area on their website to deter fraudsters (see Unit 3, page 136) and all businesses must protect the data they hold on staff and customers. Any bad publicity as a result of personal details being divulged or from identity theft through lack of IT security would probably lose them business.

Did you know?

You have a legal responsibility to cooperate with your employer on all health and safety matters.

Fact file

Providing safe premises and minimising risks are legal requirements for all organisations under the Health and Safety at Work Act. Protecting personal details held on customers and staff is a legal requirement under the Data Protection Act.

Did you know?

'Front office' staff – such as receptionists and sales staff – deal directly with external customers. Although 'Back office' staff – such as IT specialists or production workers – rarely deal with external customers, their work and support is essential to those who do.

Activity

Find out how visitors to your college or school are informed of emergency evacuation procedures. Then check out the security measures that are in force, both to protect the IT systems and the physical safety of staff and students.

Internal and external customers

A customer is anyone who has the right to ask you or expect you to provide a service as part of your job role. For most people this means that they have two types of customers at work – internal and external.

Internal customers

Did you know?

At the Barbican in London 'backroom' staff deal with external customers at evenings or weekends to ensure they understand about front-line customer service.

■ *Examples of internal customers*

Your internal customers are all the colleagues who need your assistance to fulfil their obligations to their own customers. A request from your boss to help someone out, or from the cleaner to move your bag, are 'customer requests', because neither of them can do their own job properly if you do not cooperate. If, for any reason, you cannot respond positively to a request from an internal customer then you should refer it to someone else. The only time you should refuse a request is if, by meeting it, you would have to do something that is not allowed or is outside your job role (see page 73).

In many organisations, teams helping to deliver customer service are unseen and often forgotten by customers. They include baggage handlers in an airport, chefs in a restaurant, chambermaids in a hotel and mechanics in a garage. If something goes wrong – a suitcase is damaged, food is cold, the room has no towels or a car is not ready as promised, the customer will complain to someone on the 'front desk' – who is then dependent upon the cooperation of one of the service team to put matters right.

Activity

You have just bought tickets to see your favourite band play at a concert. As a group, suggest at least five types of people whose 'behind the scenes' roles are essential for the performance to take place.

External customers

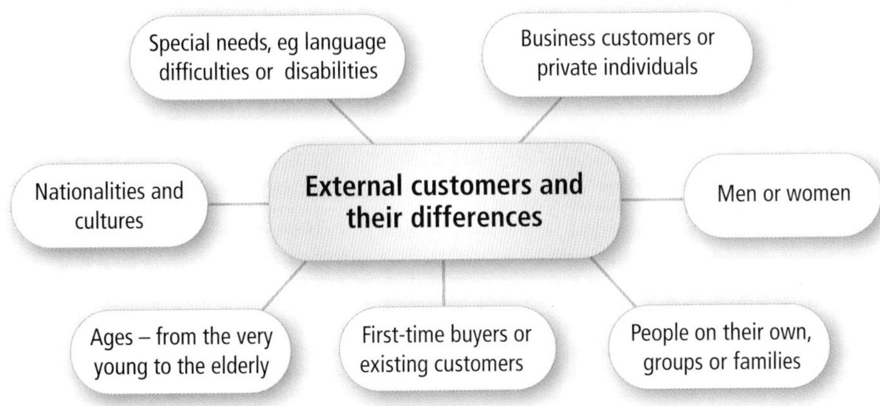

■ *External customers and their differences*

With your tutor's help, identify the roles of people in your college or school who contribute to your overall experience as a student but whom you rarely see.

External customers contact or visit an organisation because it can provide something they need. Some businesses have a wide variety of customers because most people need or use their goods or services, such as a supermarket, airport or hospital. Others provide products or services which are of interest only to certain types of people. A nursery concentrates on children, whereas a care home focuses on the needs of the elderly. Some companies also supply to specific groups: Saga only provides its travel, insurance and other services to people over the age of 50 whereas Club 18-30 targets a different group. In this situation it is easier to focus on the needs of the customer because they are more defined.

Business customers versus private individuals Some organisations only deal with other businesses, such as manufacturers of industrial equipment. Their customers will have precise needs, linked to a specific buying procedure. They will expect prompt and professional responses to their requests, no matter how complex. They are also likely to want special financial deals, discounts for bulk purchases and 'after-sales' service, such as maintenance or spare parts. Other businesses only deal with private individuals, such as hairdressers and hospitals. Many organisations have both business and private customers, but the staff who deal with them may work in separate departments and be specially trained to meet their different needs.

New versus existing customers Most organisations need to attract new customers to stay in business and will use marketing and promotional methods to do this. However, such activities should not be carried out at the expense of losing existing customers. Customer loyalty is to be treasured, which is why many organisations give rewards or discounts to long-term customers. Regular customers may expect staff to know their name, purchasing history and usual preferences – particularly if they are business customers.

Telecoms providers are one type of business that offers different services to both business and private customers. Check out how these differ on the BT site at www.bt.com/index.jsp. Then suggest two other types of businesses that have both business and private customers and suggest how their services may differ.

Did you know?

One study found that it costs six times more to attract a new customer than it does to keep an old one.

Individuals versus groups or families Some organisations regularly have to think about their customers in terms of groups or family units. Examples include travel companies and hotels, theatres and tourist attractions. They may specialise in offering special terms or discounts to groups and a range of facilities that take into account the needs of different members of a family.

Men versus women The degree to which gender differences need to be considered will depend on the products or services offered by the organisation. At one time many businesses ignored these. It is only in recent years, for example, that many traditional businesses such as car dealers and financial institutions have realised the value of striving to meet the different needs of their male and female customers.

Did you know?

The 5-star Grange City Hotel in London has a woman only floor with female-friendly rooms and female only staff to meet the security needs of women, often travelling alone on business.

Activity

Divide into different gender groups and list your top five needs if you were buying a car. Compare your lists. Then suggest how car manufacturers and sales people should take gender differences into account.

Age differences Businesses who deal with families with young children need to provide distractions, such as a toy box, fish tank or colouring books plus facilities for meeting basic needs, such as nearby toilets, a baby changing room and a drinks machine. Some provide a crèche or play area. The benefit is that if the children are happy, parents don't feel pressurised to leave as quickly as possible.

Many stores, such as Miss Selfridge, adapt their layout, furnishings and the music they play to take into account their target customers.

If you deal with elderly customers, remember that whilst some may be very sharp, others dislike being pressurised to make a decision quickly. They may also need complicated information explaining carefully, particularly if it relates to hi-tech items. Retired customers often have more time and may want to shop around before they buy.

Did you know?

The 'grey pound' (customers aged 50+) is worth over £280 billion (80 per cent of the UK's wealth) so no business can afford to ignore this group. This is why Nintendo advertised its computer game Brain Training *in Saga magazine – written for over-50s.*

Activity

Stereotypes encourage you to categorise people wrongly, so you assume all elderly people are doddery or all blondes are bimbos. Test your prejudices by deciding the likely age, gender, fitness and background of Commander Collins, who piloted the Spaceshuttle Discovery *in 2005. Then check your ideas with your tutor.*

Special needs Customers may have special needs, particularly if they do not speak English very well or if they have a disability. You will always do better dealing with people who are different from you if you are a natural 'people-person' and enjoy trying to understand and help other people. See the table below.

Type of customer	Ways to meet their needs
Foreign customers	*It may only become obvious that someone cannot speak English very well when you try to explain something to them so . . .* Speak relatively slowly Use simple English words (and no slang or local expressions) Use short sentences Write it down for them. Their reading skills may be better than their listening skills Don't shout, be embarrassed, laugh or show impatience Know which of your colleagues speak other languages Ask for help if you need it
Customers who are deaf or hard of hearing	*You cannot tell if someone is deaf by looking at them but some deaf people can lip read so . . .* Look at the person when you are speaking Don't speak too quickly If asked to do so, write down what you want to say Don't shout! Know whether your organisation offers the TypeTalk service to deaf people who make contact by phone
Customers who are blind or visually impaired	*Not all blind people wear dark glasses or carry white sticks but someone with a severe visual impairment may tell you this as they arrive so . . .* Speak to them so that your voice will act as a guide Unless they ask for assistance, don't grab hold of them If you are asked for help, lead them gently Warn them of obstacles and stairs – say how many steps there are and whether these are up or down Tell them if there are Braille buttons on the lift or on other signs
Customers who have mobility problems	*Under the Disability Discrimination Act, all organisations must provide appropriate access and facilities for customers so . . .* Know the facilities that exist in your organisation, such as wheelchair access, disabled toilets and disabled parking spaces Be ready to hold open doors Don't try to rush someone or appear impatient because they are on crutches or in a wheelchair

■ *The special needs of customers*

Ikea was criticised for showing only men assembling furniture in its manuals. Some women were shown – but all were holding panels for men to assemble.

Internal customers are colleagues who work with you and need you to do something.

External customers are outside businesses and individuals who contact your organisation because they require goods or a service.

Special needs are particular requirements a customer may have, often related to a disability.

If you are struggling to communicate with someone who does not speak English, you can empathise by thinking how you would feel if you were abroad, could not speak the language yet had to make yourself understood.

Organisations that provide outstanding customer service usually save money on advertising, make higher profits, have happier customers and more motivated staff.

View 1: The needs of external customers should always take priority because they are more important than internal customers.

View 2: The needs of all customers are equally important. Internal customers have their own external customers to keep happy.

With which viewpoint do you agree – and why?

The benefits of customer service

All organisations benefit from providing excellent customer service. Private sector businesses want to increase the number of orders they receive because this directly affects profits. They know it is cheaper to increase sales through repeat business and by word of mouth recommendations than by advertising. They also know that this can be achieved by giving the customer a superb experience. In the public sector, failure to meet customer service standards may be reflected in league tables or published by the media.

In addition to organisational benefits, it is far pleasanter for employees to work in a business that has high standards and treats its customers well. Customers also gain because they can rely on excellent service all the time and have no need to shop around.

The main benefits experienced are summarised in the table below.

To the customer:

- Goods or services are supplied as promised.
- Fewer problems or reasons to return goods or complain.
- The transaction is completed more quickly.
- The customer feels valued and important.
- The customer looks forward to repeating the experience.
- The customer saves time 'shopping around' in future.

To the organisation:

- Customer enquiries are handled quickly, accurately and professionally. This encourages customer loyalty so repeat orders are gained.
- Word of mouth recommendations by satisfied customers increase business at no cost.
- Obtaining feedback from regular customers provides useful feedback that can help to improve the business.
- Less staff time is spent dealing with complaints and problems.
- There is far less chance of damaging negative publicity.
- The image and reputation of the business is continually enhanced.
- The organisation flourishes as its profits and/or demand for its services increase.

To the employee:

- Working is more enjoyable because staff know they are doing a good job and customers rarely complain.
- All staff know that they can depend on each other for prompt and accurate information.
- Building a positive working relationship with regular customers and working to achieve high standards both contribute to job satisfaction.
- If organisational profits increase and/or service standard targets are achieved there is more likelihood of better pay, bonuses and/or promotion opportunities for individual staff.
- There is greater job security because companies with many satisfied customers are unlikely to go out of business.

■ *Benefits of effective customer service*

Over to you

1 *You are working in your school or college office. Work in groups and prepare a chart, using the format below, to suggest the most likely needs and expectations of the following customers and the ways in which you could meet them. As a guide, refer to the table on page 55, which shows how to help customers with special needs.*

When you have completed your chart, identify one person to present it to the whole group. When all the charts have been presented, draw up a final version which incorporates all the best ideas.

Type of customer	Likely needs and expectations	Ways to meet their needs
A business woman arriving for a meeting		
A mother with a young toddler arriving for an appointment		
A business man phoning for information		
A young couple who have just walked into the building		
An elderly man who has never been before		
A middle-aged woman who worked there until last year		
A group of teenagers looking around		

2 *For each of the following types of businesses, identify two types of customers they are likely to deal with. Then suggest four needs and expectations any of their customers may have that the business will aim to meet.*
To help, check out websites for unfamiliar types of businesses to see the type of services and facilities they offer. When you have finished, compare your ideas with those of other members of your group.

a) *A car hire firm*
b) *A veterinary centre*
c) *An online bookstore*
f) *A Chinese restaurant*
g) *Any business where you have worked, either full-time or part-time.*

3 *The Institute of Customer Services provides a free fact sheet on Setting Customer Service Standards under the headings of Timeliness, Accuracy and Appropriateness. Download this from their website at www.instituteofcustomerservice.com and use this to decide on appropriate standards your friend Kate should adopt under each heading. Kate is a florist who has her own business and employs two assistants.*

Case study Assessment practice

Customers used to require only that their bank kept their money secure. Today expectations are much higher, so banks that do not keep their customers happy may see their profits falling. Many banks reduced their high street services some years ago, expecting everyone to go over to Internet banking. Now they are rethinking that strategy, following customer criticisms and worries about identity theft and online fraud.

NatWest claims to have stopped routing all customer calls to call centres and now advertises bank contact numbers. Barclays has chosen a makeover instead. Rather than black pens, chained to the counter, you will now find free blue pens with logos like 'Take me, I'm yours'. Signs are more informal. 'Reception' has become 'I'd love to help' and 'Please queue here' is 'This way to the counter'.

HSBC has taken a different approach. Following customer complaints about queues in branches at busy times, it now has its own radio station playing music and providing current announcements to distract waiting customers. Nationwide has focused on higher interest rates to attract new business and free withdrawals from cash machines abroad.

Whether these changes will meet customer needs is another matter. When the Henley Centre surveyed different groups of customers about banking it found that more than half in the 18–24 age group wanted text alerts about balances or cash credits and 29 per cent of the 25–44 age group wanted to text requests to their bank. Forty-eight per cent expected a reply within one hour and 28 per cent within half an hour – proof that patience is no longer seen as a virtue by customers.

1(P) Describe the needs and expectations of different types of bank customers by answering the following questions.

- **a)** Identify and describe the main needs and expectations of three different types of bank customer who visit their branch.
- **b)** Identify any additional needs or expectations of customers who use online banking services.
- **c)** Banks deal with both private and business customers. Suggest three ways in which the needs and expectations of these two groups may differ. ***(P1)***

2(M) The Henley Centre surveyed customers in different age groups and according to how technically 'savvy' they were. Explain three ways in which both these factors are likely to influence bank customers' needs and expectations. ***(M1)***

3(D) As a group analyse how effective you think the changes made by these banks will be by identifying the potential benefits for the customer, the organisation and their employees. ***(D2)***

Grading tip

If you are giving an explanation, provide relevant details to support the case you are making.

Analyse means you need to identify each factor that applies and then think about its likely effect.

2.2 Be able to apply appropriate presentation and interpersonal skills in customer service situations

It is pointless for an organisation to provide a wide range of services for customers if staff are scruffy, ill-mannered or cannot answer routine questions. Often the attitude of staff is remembered by customers long after they have forgotten what they wanted at the time. We are all impressed if someone is extremely helpful and can also recall, too, the odd person who was exactly the opposite!

There are three main skills you need to develop to deal with customers effectively: your presentation skills, interpersonal skills and communication skills. You must also be able to apply these in a range of situations.

Presentation skills

These skills relate to you as a person. What do other people see as you approach? Do you attract them or alarm them? Remember, this has nothing to do with good looks but everything to do with a welcoming smile, appropriate clothes and a smart appearance!

Personal presentation

Many businesses – such as airlines and supermarkets – issue uniforms to their 'front line' staff. There are many advantages – employees do not have to worry about what to wear, customers can easily spot the staff and the organisation projects a consistent image. Other businesses provide a dress code or guidelines which tell staff what they can and cannot wear at work. The guidelines should not discriminate against any particular groups of people, such as forbidding women to wear trousers.

In other organisations you will just be expected to use your common sense. This means:

Did you know?

The more your customer service skills improve, the more confidence you will have when you deal with your customers.

Did you know?

Some organisations ban their staff from eating strong foods, like curry or garlic, when they are going to deal with customers.

Fact file

Many organisations have uniforms, a dress code or guidelines to ensure staff project a consistent image to customers. At all times personal freshness, clean clothes and a professional appearance is essential.

Did you know?

Poor personal hygiene isn't the only reason why people smell unpleasant. Someone whose clothes or breath reeks of cigarette smoke is just as bad.

- being clean, tidy and fussy about personal hygiene so that you smell fresh at all times. Remember that your hair, fingernails and shoes are just as important as your hands, face and clothes
- wearing suitable work clothes if there is no uniform. This normally excludes jeans, trainers, Doc Martens, flip flops, crop tops and shorts
- having a relatively conventional hairstyle in terms of style and colour
- if you are female, wearing restrained make-up
- keeping your jewellery subtle.

Body language

Body language is the term given to the messages we transmit by our gestures, facial expressions, posture – and where we position ourselves in relation to other people.

Did you know?

Always remember it is distracting if you wave your arms when you are speaking and, no matter what the provocation, you must ***never*** *use any socially unacceptable gesture at work.*

Gestures are used to communicate with someone who is a distance away (and are usually better than shouting) and to emphasise what you are saying. Gestures often reveal your feelings – you may touch your hair or smooth down your clothes if you are nervous or want to make an impression. Shrugging your shoulders means you don't care, looking around says you are bored, putting your hands on your hips looks aggressive. You clench your fists or show the whites of your knuckles if you are anxious or in pain. And if your customers start tapping a foot or drumming their fingers, it's a sign they are getting impatient.

Facial expressions give away your thoughts and emotions. Unconsciously, you signal surprise, disappointment, joy, boredom, annoyance and even sexual attraction with your eyes and facial expressions. Children are interesting to watch because they have not learned to conceal their emotions. As adults, we are expected to mask any inappropriate feelings, so you should realise that saying the right thing to a customer is useless if you are yawning, raising your eyebrows to a colleague or scowling. Making eye contact is usually seen as a sign of honesty. Although you might be tempted to look down quickly if you are nervous, it tends to make you look shifty to a customer.

Your posture displays your confidence and attitude. Positive people sit, stand and walk tall. They do not slouch or sit in a hunched up position. Folding your arms and/or crossing your legs is a defensive position and you will lower your head if you feel negative or are under attack. Leaning forward means you are interested whereas you lean back when you are relaxed or confident. Sitting upright means you are alert and interested.

Activity

The best way to ensure good presentation is through preparation. Each night, plan what you will wear the next day, check it is clean and pressed and hang it on the outside of your wardrobe. Then allow enough time to get ready next morning. Try this for a week and log your progress.

Your body position tells others about you. The closer people stand to each other the more they know and like each other. If you stand too close to strangers then they will normally move away to keep their distance. You show your interest in someone when you turn your body (including your feet) towards them, tilt your head and maintain eye contact. You show you are empathising when you 'reflect' their body language, such as shaking your head when they do, or nodding to show your agreement.

Fact file

Body language sends out messages all the time. It's no use saying one thing if your body language says the opposite.

Activity

Learn to shake hands properly. Put anything you are carrying in your left hand. Hold out your right hand, grasp the other person's hand positively and shake it firmly once or twice. Strike a balance between gripping too tightly and offering a hand like a limp rag! Practise with someone to get it right.

Working environment, work area and equipment

Your working environment relates to the area you work in – its design, layout, the equipment that is available, the space you have and facilities such as rest rooms, eating and changing areas. Your employer has a legal duty to provide a healthy and safe working environment and you have a legal duty to cooperate with your employer. This means working safely, keeping your own work area and communal areas tidy and following recommended guidelines for using equipment. The following points should help.

- Tidy as you go by putting away items related to one job before you start the next.
- Keep your personal belongings out of the way. There may be rules that these must be kept in a locker in a changing area and never brought into areas that customers use.
- Keep walkways, aisles and areas behind doors completely clear of clutter.
- If you have your own desk, keep paperwork on top to a minimum and tidy the drawers every month.
- Aim to have a place for everything and put everything in its place.
- If you have to leave partly completed work in a communal area for a short time, put a note on identifying yourself as the 'owner' and saying when you will return to move it.
- Tidy up the working area around shared items of equipment, such as a photocopier, before you leave.
- *Never* help yourself to someone else's possessions without agreement.
- *Always* follow the specific instructions for using complex item of equipment and for reporting faults if these occur. Never try to remedy a problem by guessing what to do!

Key terms

Presentation skills are those you need to look and act like a customer service professional.

Body language is the message you communicate by using gestures, facial expressions and posture.

Working environment is the design, layout, facilities, equipment available to staff as well as the ethos of the workplace.

Fact file

If you are a messy worker then you will never look efficient or professional – or be a good colleague.

Did you know?

The quality of your working environment is dependent upon two things: the physical environment and the people within it.

Activity

The Workplace (Health, Safety and Welfare) Regulations covers specific areas at work. Find out what these are by searching online at www.businesslink.gov.uk, www.hse.gov.uk or www.worksmart.org.uk.

Did you know?

Anyone can do the right thing when they feel great. Being professional means doing the right thing even when you feel dreadful.

More broadly, the working environment also includes the way people treat each other in the workplace. Most organisations want their employees to enjoy going to work and take pleasure in achieving their targets. Therefore, the behaviour of employees is also important for a productive working environment.

Interpersonal skills

Your interpersonal skills relate to the way you behave when you are dealing with other people. Even if you are popular with your friends and adored by your family this does not mean you will be great to work with or employ. Neither does it mean that you will automatically be skilled at handling customers. This is because the interpersonal skills you need at work are different from those you use in your private life – and your boss and colleagues will be less forgiving if you behave badly. Your employer pays you to be professional, to treat your colleagues courteously and to show interest in helping your customers all the time, regardless of how you feel personally.

Activity

You are employing someone to help you to run your own business. In pairs, decide on six personal qualities your assistant must possess and six that you would not tolerate for one second. Then compare your lists with other groups and identify ten positive and ten negative attributes that everyone agrees on.

Attitude

Your attitude is influenced by the way you think. If you are depressed you will be negative; if you are fed up then you will be bored. If you enjoy being with other people, you will be friendly. If you enjoy doing your best, you will be focused and motivated. Whilst this is important when you are dealing with customers, many employers think that the most valuable attribute is to be positive. There are several reasons for this.

- People prefer being with others who are positive because they are open, approachable and easy to be with. They make other people feel better!
- Positive people always think 'yes' or 'can do' not 'no', 'can't do' or 'never been done'. They look at problems or difficulties as a challenge and an opportunity to show what they can do.
- If you are positive about your work and your customers then you also give an up-beat image of the organisation. You reflect commitment and interest in every customer.
- Positive people usually have high personal standards and always want to do their best. They also believe they are capable of doing this.

Activity

Are you a naturally positive person? If you are asked to help someone, but this involves doing something you dislike would you answer 'yes' or 'no'? For the next fortnight, check your own responses when someone asks you a favour. If it's usually 'no' then it's time for a rethink!

Behaviour

This is closely linked to attitude because this influences what you do and why you do it.

- If you are a positive person, you will normally behave in a cheerful and friendly way.
- If you enjoy working with people you will normally behave in a courteous and thoughtful way and respect their feelings. You do not indulge in back-biting, being hurtful or misleading people to get your own way.
- If you are committed to doing a good job you would not cheat your employer, tell lies, arrive late, leave early, pretend to be sick when you're not or simply give up if the situation became too difficult.
- If you accept that you are paid to act in a mature and professional way then you will not behave in a childish or irresponsible manner. Neither will you sulk if you cannot get your own way.

Did you know?

Being mature and professional means understanding the impact of your behaviour on other people.

Fact file

Employees are paid to behave in a professional and business-like way at work, no matter how they feel personally.

Activity

In 2006 the Government launched its 'Give respect, get respect' campaign. As a group, decide what you think is meant by 'respect' and how this influences people's behaviour to others.

Did you know?

You only get one chance to make a good first impression!

First impressions and greeting customers

Your interpersonal skills are on show from the moment you greet a customer to the time you say goodbye. Many organisations spend a considerable amount of money on their reception areas and their telephone system to impress external customers – but this has to be matched by the greeting they receive from staff. There may be an official greeting you should use to external customers and there may be rules which state how you should address customers if you do not know their names. If in doubt, it is wise to err on the side of formality and use 'Sir' or 'Madam' – this never offended anyone. And you should already know how to shake hands (see page 61), in case you are introduced to a customer by your boss or another colleague.

Did you know?

Many organisations insist that all staff introduce themselves by giving their name – or wear name badges. This is more friendly but also means customers know who you are if they have a complaint.

Building customer relationships

Building a relationship with a customer involves several interpersonal skills, as you can see in the diagram below.

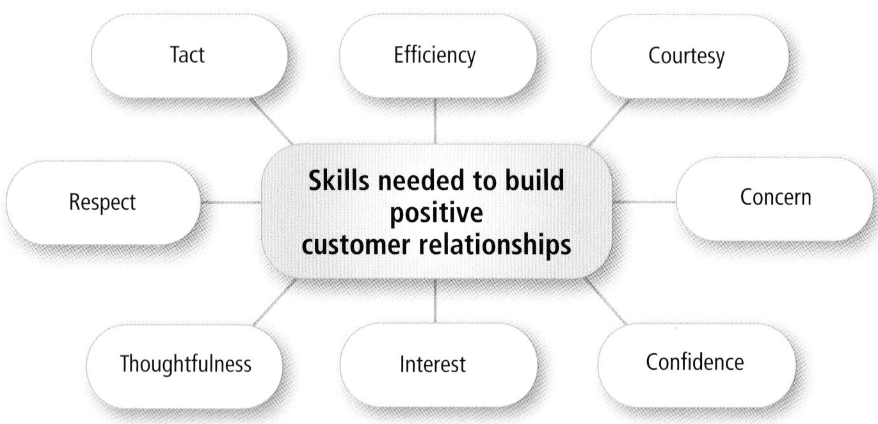

■ *Interpersonal skills and customer relationships*

Activity

Work in small groups to identify examples of customer situations when each of the skills in the diagram would be demonstrated. You can decide on positive or negative examples – or both. Compare your ideas.

If you enjoy dealing with people then you will find it easier to put yourself in your customers' shoes when you are discussing their requirements. You will be naturally interested in what they want and more likely to think carefully about the best way to help them. You will be concerned not to say anything that might cause offence or be hurtful. At the same time, you will realise that you still need to be efficient at your job to meet your customer's needs by:

- listening carefully and noting down any long or complex requests
- asking questions if you do not understand something or need further information
- aiming to give a positive response to their request. If this seems impossible, get help or advice from a more experienced colleague.

Responding to different customer behaviour

Customers display different behaviour for many reasons. They may be in a rush, under stress or be extremely happy with life and have plenty of time to chat. If your customers are in front of you, watch their body language as you listen to their words. You will be better able to respond to their mood as well as to what they are saying.

Be aware that some internal customers may be more sensitive or demanding than external customers – such as a manager who is under pressure on a busy day and reacts badly if you pick the wrong moment to say something (see also page 74). Again being observant and aware of other factors which might influence their behaviour will help you to better gauge what to say and when to say it.

Your challenge is to remain pleasant and courteous even if a customer is boring, annoying, sarcastic or uncommunicative. If you have serious problems in dealing with someone – either because you cannot understand them or because they are being personally insulting or abusive then get help. Otherwise, count to ten under your breath, keep smiling and chat about it later with a close colleague to let off steam!

Did you know?

Tact means thinking of the most diplomatic way to say something, such as 'Could you please state your date of birth?' not *'How old are you?'*

Key term

Interpersonal skills are those you need to relate to other people in a courteous and appropriate way.

Activity

You are working in the new College fitness centre one night a week, greeting and assisting people. As a group, suggest four ways in which being confident would affect the way you approach and handle these customers. Then identify what you would need to know individually to feel confident in this situation.

Communication skills

You have already learned about one method of communicating – body language – on page 60. You obviously need to speak to your customers as well – and how you do this is important. Although you will learn more about oral communications if you study option unit 4, all the following factors influence the effectiveness of your communications with customers.

Fact file

Demonstrating interpersonal skills such as concern, interest, thoughtfulness and respect enables you to respond more effectively to a wide range of customers.

■ *Getting the message across requires several skills*

Did you know?

Your 'tone' signals your emotions – from concern or compassion to irritation or determination. It can soothe or annoy your audience. You know you have made a mistake if someone says: 'Don't use that tone with me!'

The importance of tone

'Tone' is easy to understand if you compare how you speak to your friends, to how you talk to your tutor, and the way you would talk in an interview. Hopefully, there would be a significant difference in relation to the words you would use, your tone of voice and how informal you were. Your tone should vary depending upon the 'message' and your recipient, as follows:

- with a colleague or customer you know well or with someone of your own age, you will want to be friendly
- with an older person, someone senior to you or an external customer you need to be polite as well as friendly
- with someone very important, influential or very senior, you may be polite and slightly deferential
- if you are giving good news then you can usually be rather more informal and friendly. You should be more restrained if you are giving unwelcome news
- if you are giving information that will worry someone, then your 'tone' should reflect your concern. Similarly, if you are in the wrong and apologising, your tone should be conciliatory; if you are asking for a favour it should be persuasive rather than grovelling!

Activity

Try saying 'Who, me?' in three different ways: first to register surprise; second to express delight; third to show annoyance. Then think about the effect on the listener each time.

Speaking clearly

This has nothing to do with sounding 'posh'; it just means that people can understand what you are saying. If you mutter, speak too quietly or miss the endings off words, then anyone who doesn't know you well will have problems.

Aspects to consider include the following.

The pitch of your voice relates to how you sound. A low-pitched voice is deep and gruff: a high-pitched voice easily sounds shrill. Varying your pitch makes you sound more interesting and enables you to hold people's attention better than if you speak in a monotone. If you have to speak to several people at once, pitch your voice so that everyone can hear you. This means lifting your head and speaking more loudly and clearly – without shouting!

Activity

Some organisations greet customers formally: 'Good morning, Atkins and Roberts'. Others are informal 'Hi, my name is Alex, how can I help you?' Suggest reasons for these differences.

The pace relates to the speed at which you speak and should be varied depending upon your audience and the message. Never speak so quickly that your words run together. 'D'yuhknowim?' is unlikely to be intelligible to anyone except your closest friends! Speak more slowly if the information is complicated, if you are talking to several people at once, there are lots of other noises or distractions or if the other person does not speak English very well. But do not speak so slowly that everyone falls asleep or loses interest!

The language you use should be appropriate for your customer.

Technical phrases and jargon are commonplace in all industries. IT staff discuss platforms and motherboards, retailers talk about bogofs and

Did you know?

When the Met Office told its forecasters to use plain English and be more upbeat it thought the change would be welcomed. Some viewers didn't agree and complained the weather reports were now over-simplified.

merchandising. These terms are often gobbledegook to anyone not in the industry and best avoided with external customers. If it's impossible to describe something without using jargon, remember to explain what it means.

Slang includes words used informally– such as 'Hi', or 'See you', 'waste of space', 'cut it out', 'cool', 'chill', 'wicked' and 'slaughtered'. None should be used in business and some organisations even frown upon staff using 'OK' when they are talking to external customers.

Fact file

Choosing the appropriate words to use to a customer and using the right tone are essential if you want to communicate the right message.

Activity

*When you first start work you may be puzzled by expressions known as 'management speak' such as: 'Learning to **think outside the box** is hardly **rocket science** and a **no brainer** for the **movers and shakers** in our business.' Try to interpret the sentence above! Ask your tutor for help if you are stuck. Then suggest what you should do if a manager spoke to you using phrases like that.*

Listening skills

Most people are terrible listeners. Their mind starts wandering almost as soon as someone starts to talk to them and they regularly interrupt people to have their say. Good listeners, on the other hand, can normally repeat back accurately what they have just heard – though surprisingly few people can do that. Good listeners are usually highly prized by their friends, who appreciate having someone they can talk to. For similar reasons, good listening skills are also invaluable in business, particularly in the following situations:

- when a customer is telling you about his or her needs and preferences

Did you know?

Using someone's name at several points during the conversation helps your customer to feel more valued and also helps you to remember their name.

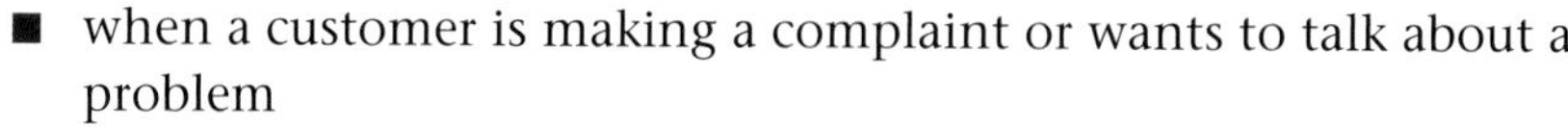

- when a customer is making a complaint or wants to talk about a problem
- when you are receiving instructions. This is particularly important if you are receiving them from a senior member of staff or someone you cannot contact later to check what you heard
- when you are being given a message to pass on to someone else.

You can improve your listening skills through active and reflective listening.

Active listening means concentrating on the speaker so you notice their feelings and whether, for instance, they are nervous, impatient, stressed or worried. This means that you are more likely to respond appropriately.

Reflective listening involves restating what you have heard at points during the conversation to check your understanding.

Fact file

Good listening skills help you to better understand your customer's needs. But if the information is complicated or important, you should also write it down.

Activity

Practise active and reflective listening with a partner. Describe something interesting you have done recently for three or four minutes. Your partner should listen and try to summarise it back accurately without making notes. Then reverse roles.

Appropriate to the customer and the situation

A key attribute of customer service professionals is flexibility because you must always be prepared to adapt your approach to the customer and the situation. You may know that you should not shout when you speak to customers, but if you were trying to talk to a customer in Virgin Megastore on a busy Saturday you might have to make an exception. If you are greeting VIPs at your school or college then the situation is very different. Equally, you should not speak to a senior manager at work in the same way as you would to a colleague of your own age.

Sometimes at work it can be difficult to know exactly what to do and say, because some organisations expect more formality than others. Try to watch more experienced members of staff and follow their example.

Key terms

Tone is the way words are spoken to reflect the speaker's attitude. Tone can also apply to the choice of words in a written communication.

Jargon is terminology or slang which is not universally known or understood.

Customer service situations

Depending upon your job role, the way in which you communicate with customers may vary. In sales, on reception or in a retail environment you will usually meet external customers face to face. In a call centre or an office then you may deal with customers on the telephone. You may also communicate in writing – by sending a note or an email. These situations will affect the way in which you apply your personal skills, as you can see in the table opposite.

Communication	Presentation skills	Interpersonal skills	Communication skills
Face-to-face	Professional appearance essential. Body language denotes manner and attitude.	Good first impression important. Use appropriate greeting, be friendly and interested in meeting customer's needs.	Speak clearly, use appropriate tone of voice and avoid jargon with external customers. Make sure body language gives the same message!
Telephone	Smiling during a conversation shows in the voice and makes you sound friendly.	Use business-like greeting. Attitude and concern is shown by verbal response and tone of voice.	Clear voice and appropriate pace doubly essential as gestures cannot be seen.
In writing	Neatness, clear layout and accurate spelling required.	All written communications must be courteous and tactful and the wording should be appropriate for the situation.	The 'tone' and degree of formality depends upon the person and your reason for writing.
By email	Message style and layout must follow recommended business format.		Business emails should comply with organisational rules and recognised standards.

■ *Applying skills to different types of communications*

The type of situation may also affect the way you should react.

Urgent situations need an appropriate response – from marking an email as 'high priority' to passing on important messages immediately to a supervisor. In a crisis, too, it is important to listen carefully and stay calm.

Difficult situations include awkward customers you cannot handle, problems you cannot solve and occasions when you are under pressure. The golden rule is not to panic, to remember the basics and to get assistance if you need it. No one should blame you for asking for help. This is safer than trying to cope and making a mess, leaving someone else to put matters right.

Fact file

It is important to be able to apply the appropriate customer service skills to a wide range of customer service situations.

Activity

The WOW awards are UK National Customer Service awards and winners are chosen or nominated by members of the public. Find out about some of the winners and how they behaved in customer service situations at www.thewowawards.com.

Talking point

View 1: Call centres help organisations to deal with customers more efficiently and are fine providing that staff have good interpersonal and communication skills.

View 2: Call centres infuriate and lose customers no matter who works there simply because they are so impersonal.

With which viewpoint do you agree – and why?

Over to you

1 *Divide the following examples of body language into two columns, positive and negative. For each one, suggest the message it sends.*
   - **a)** *keeping your head up*
   - **b)** *fidgeting*
   - **c)** *shrugging your shoulders when you are asked a question*
   - **d)** *sitting still*
   - **e)** *giving someone a blank stare as they approach*
   - **f)** *avoiding eye contact*
   - **g)** *staring out of the window when you are being spoken to*
   - **h)** *tilting your head to one side.*

2 *In each of the following cases, state how you could have responded more positively to the customer.*
   - **a)** *'I'm sorry, that's not my job.'*
   - **b)** *'I can't tell you at the moment, we're moving offices and it's chaos here.'*
   - **c)** *'I thought I'd already told you that. Which bit didn't you understand?'*
   - **d)** *'Sorry, it's not my fault – I was just following orders.'*
   - **e)** *'I can hardly help you if you can't remember the order number or the date you sent it, can I?'*
   - **f)** *'Yes, OK, I should be able to get round to it later today.'*

3 *Assess your own skills by doing the quiz below.*

Test your own interpersonal skills!

Choose one option from each of the options below and check your score on page 87. Decide how you can best improve any problem areas.

1 It's Monday, it's raining, you've had an awful weekend. Do you
   - **a)** grouch around all day, grumbling to everyone who will listen
   - **b)** try to put it behind you – after all, it's the start of a new week
   - **c)** refuse to let it get you down and fool around as usual.

2 Your manager asks you to help to unpack some stock, a job you detest. Do you:
   - **a)** make a mess of it, so you won't be asked to do it again
   - **b)** do it as quickly as you can, then you can do something more interesting
   - **c)** complain loudly to anyone who will listen.

3 Out of the corner of your eye you see an elderly male customer approaching you and your colleague. Do you
   - **a)** push your colleague forward and run. You know old people go on and on forever about nothing
   - **b)** smile and walk towards him, to see if you can help
   - **c)** try to avoid eye contact and blank him out if he looks at you.

continued ▶

4 Your boss says that the senior regional director is due any time and asks everyone to let her know the moment he arrives. Do you

a) keep busy elsewhere, so that you don't have the worry of dealing with him

b) ask what he's called and what he looks like so you can recognise him quickly

c) rush to check your appearance – so you can make a better impression on him than your colleagues.

5 A mother with a young child has been asked to wait for a short time, but the child is getting restless and she is struggling to keep him quiet. Do you:

a) disappear for your break, to get out of the way

b) offer her some paper and two highlighter pens so he can draw

c) give her the two catalogues that are on your colleague's desk and watch with amusement as the child rips up the pages.

6 A customer rings to ask when her order will arrive – she has already been waiting two days. You check the record and find out there will be a further delay of about four days. Do you:

a) Tell her they will arrive that afternoon, to get her off your back

b) Apologise that there is a further delay and offer to call her when you know exactly when they will arrive

c) Tell her it's nothing to do with you – she should contact the delivery firm.

7 It's a cold frosty day and you slither in through the front door. Do you

a) Turn up the heating and keep your coat on until you thaw out

b) Find the caretaker and ask that the path is salted immediately

c) Watch through the window to see how many people fall trying to get into the building.

8 A customer fills in a form and enters her date of birth as this year. Do you:

a) Say: 'Unless you were born last week, you've made a mistake.'

b) Say: 'Sorry, could you please correct that for me, I don't think you've put the right year.'

c) Say: 'You might look young but I don't think you look that young!'

9 Your customer needs to collect an envelope in your main office – which is across the road. It's pouring down. Do you:

a) Give her directions and then get on with your own work

b) Tell her to wait and run over and get it for her

c) Offer to lend her your umbrella.

10 A man enters reception complaining about the lack of parking spaces. Do you:

a) Raise your eyebrows to your colleague, then give him two minutes before you ask him what he wants

b) Sympathise and tell him the times of day when it's less busy

c) Tell him it's even worse for the staff, who can't use customer parking spaces.

Assessment practice

The National Consumer Council (NCC) represents the views of consumers. Its report 'The Stupid Company' reported their anger about being misled, patronised and harassed by many businesses. It claimed many businesses focus on making a quick profit rather than developing longer-term customer relationships. They often 'over-promise and under-deliver' which angers and alienates their customers.

Specific gripes include 'robotic' call centres, hard-sell sales pitches, missed appointments, being put on 'hold' for ages or passed from one person to another during a call and being sent a standard letter in answer to an individual enquiry. Misleading advertisements were criticised as well as complex or inaccurate information about what a product can do. Face-to-face service was also considered poor, with consumers claiming that even when firms employ sufficient staff it was almost impossible to attract their attention.

Large companies were claimed to be the worst offenders, particularly financial services, telecoms, utility companies, electrical retailers and garages.

Financial services company Lloyds TSB is keen to improve. Its call centre staff have been told to stop reading from scripts after research showed this angered 90 per cent of customers. Most thought scripts resulted in staff failing to listen or answer questions properly. They also said scripted conversations were impersonal and often went on too long.

1(P) **a)** State why the NCC report alleges some companies are 'stupid'.
b) Identify the complaints which relate to poor communication or customer service skills. ***(P3 part)***

2(M) **a)** Explain why call centre staff need a confident approach when they are dealing with customers.
b) To what extent do you think the use of scripts may affect the confidence of call centre staff – and why?
c) Explain the interpersonal, presentation and communication skills that are important for call centre staff who aim to provide effective customer service. ***(M2)***

3 Practice your customer service skills through the following role play.

Your class has been asked to show around prospective students, parents and local employers at an Open Night and answer any questions they may have.

Divide into two groups.

Group A will prepare for meeting, greeting and showing around the different visitors. Work in small groups to identify the type of presentation, interpersonal and communication skills that you will need to do this efficiently and give a good impression of your school or college.

Group B will take the part of the visitors. Work in small groups to identify the likely needs and expectations of each type of visitor (i.e. the prospective students, their parents and employers) and think of some questions each person may ask. Then assign one of these roles to each person.

Work in pairs from Group A to Group B to role play this scenario. As a group, observe each role play and decide whether each Group A person:

a) Demonstrated the presentation and interpersonal skills required in this situation. ***(P2 part)***

b) Displayed a confident approach to their 'customer'. ***(M1 part)***

c) Anticipated and met the needs of their customer(s) in this situation. ***(D1 part)***

Then reverse groups.

Grading tip

As part of your explanation you must identify the skills that are needed and apply these to the situation.

2.3 Know how consistent and reliable customer service contributes to customer satisfaction

Customers want to be able to rely on consistently high levels of customer service. If you regularly need information from someone else at work to do your own job properly then you will have serious difficulties if they often let you down. And as an external customer, you are unlikely to keep using a supplier that sometimes provides you with shoddy goods or a slapdash service.

Wise businesses are aware of this and take steps to ensure they provide consistent and reliable service to guarantee customer satisfaction.

Consistent and reliable customer service

The National Consumer Council believes that 'smart' businesses should ensure that the same member of staff deals with an individual customer from start to finish. Whilst this is the ideal, it isn't always possible. Therefore, most organisations provide special training to staff to ensure that each person has the same approach with external customers. This is likely to focus on the following aspects of the job.

Scope of job role

Staff should know what they can and cannot do as part of their job and the type of issues they must refer to a supervisor. This should not stop them using their initiative to resolve a straightforward problem quickly, providing they do not overstep the limits of their job role by making arrangements or promises that are outside their authority.

Activity

Talk to your tutor about the job roles of student services staff at your college who handle course enquiries. What limitations are there to their job roles? And what sources of information do they have about the courses on offer?

Knowledge of products/services

It is impossible to provide customers with accurate information or advise them about the best options to suit their needs without a thorough knowledge of the products and/or services available. It is not always possible to memorise these, so it is also important to know where to find the information – such as in a catalogue, brochure or online database.

Type and quality of products/service

Simply knowing the range of goods or services available is fine if you are selling consumable items, such as chocolates. Anyone who sells expensive items or complex services should also be able to give advice on the 'best buys' or most reliable suppliers, based on their own knowledge, feedback from other customers and press reports.

Staff attitude and behaviour

As you saw on pages 62–65, the importance of all staff having a consistently positive attitude and behaving courteously and professionally to customers cannot be underestimated.

Activity

The NCC also thinks 'smart' businesses should be honest about delays or problems. Find out more about what it thinks smart businesses should do at www.ncc.org.uk.

Activity

The phone is ringing, an external customer has arrived in reception, and your boss is urgently beckoning you. You are on your own. Say how you would cope by identifying exactly what you would do first, next and last in this situation.

Did you know?

Some organisations invent slogans to remind staff of the importance of providing a reliable service to customers, such 'Customers are your friends. You don't let friends down.'

Timing

Approaching people at the wrong time, or if they are stressed, upset or busy can get a bad response (see page 65). If you do this by accident, simply apologise and say you will contact them later. Being aware of your timing also means not keeping people waiting unduly; arranging appointments, phone calls and deliveries at your customer's convenience, not yours; and never failing to call people back exactly as you promised.

Accessibility/availability

There is nothing more irritating for customers than to want something and then find they cannot have it for some reason. This can relate to a product they have seen advertised but which has now sold out; an appointment with someone who cannot see them for some time or a room in a hotel which is fully booked. In this situation your job is to sympathise with the customer's disappointment; try to help them if you can (such as by putting their name on a waiting list) and pass on the information to your employer. This is important. If you have received 20 enquiries for the same thing in a day, and disappointed 20 people, the stock levels and/or range of goods and services offered should be reviewed.

Meeting specific customer needs

The skill of meeting customer needs involves identifying these by talking to the customer, and then matching them to the range of goods and services that you can offer, as you saw on pages 46 and 47. Further information is provided in Unit 6, Personal Selling.

Working under pressure

Anyone can be charming to customers on a quiet day. The situation is different at busy times, as anyone who has worked in a retail store at Christmas will tell you. It is also more difficult if lots of things are happening simultaneously and you are trying to do three things at once. The first rule is to stay calm and not to panic. The second is to realise that you can only do one thing at once. The third is to deal with the most urgent/important thing first. The fourth is to work as fast as you can but to stay pleasant at the same time!

Confirming service meets needs and expectations

Sensible businesses do not forget their customers once they have made a purchase or used a service, instead they check that they are satisfied. A useful way to do this is to make 'customer happy calls'. The quick follow-up phone call checks that all of the customer's needs and expectations were met. Some garages do this after a car has been returned following a service or repair.

Dealing with problems

There are many different types of problems you may have to deal with. The golden rules for dealing with customers who are unhappy include:

- letting them talk without interrupting
- checking that you have the facts right

- doing your best to help
- referring the problem to a supervisor if it is serious.

You should also find the guidance in the table below useful.

Type of problem	Suggested response
The customer wants a product or service the organisation doesn't provide.	Suggest appropriate substitutes/refer to sales department/suggest nearest outlet where item is available. This gives a good impression even if a sale isn't made.
The customer's requirements have changed since an order was placed.	Take down the details and check if the customer's request can be met. Refer the request to your supervisor if you are unsure.
The customer is returning a faulty product.	Under the Sale of Goods Acts, if the product is faulty then a full refund must be given (see Unit 7, page 284). It is your job to know your organisation's policies on returned goods.
The customer is returning a product because it is no longer suitable/the customer has changed his/her mind.	There is no legal obligation to give a refund or exchange – refer to your organisation's policies for dealing with returns or ask your supervisor.
The customer has a worry or concern, e.g. ordered goods haven't arrived, the customer thinks he/she has received the wrong information or been charged wrongly.	Take down the details and check if the customer's worries are justified. If so, apologise on behalf of your organisation and then investigate why the problem occurred and get it corrected. If necessary, ask your supervisor for assistance.
The customer is making a complaint.	Apologise on behalf of your employer, take down full details and pass these to your supervisor.

Key term

Consistent means offering the same standard over and over again.

Fact file

Customers expect consistent and reliable customer service. This is essential to achieve customer satisfaction.

Customer satisfaction

Customers are 'satisfied' when they receive the service they expected. Many organisations aim for more than this. They want to 'delight' their customers by exceeding their expectations.

Important factors in this process are given below.

- Customers have **confidence in the service** that has been provided This applies to every aspect of the service, from accurate information to reliable goods and excellent after-sales service if there is a problem.
- Customers believe they have got **value for money**. This doesn't mean that they have bought the cheapest product or service. It means that the whole package – which may include expert help, credit terms, special delivery and installation, guarantees and/or warranties – is considered a good deal.

Key terms

Customer satisfaction is how customers feel when their needs and expectations have been met.

Value for money means that the price paid was fair.

Word of mouth involves customers telling their friends and colleagues about their experiences.

Fact file

The organisation benefits if external customers are satisfied because it gets repeat custom and word-of-mouth advertising. Benefits from internal customer satisfaction include greater job satisfaction and more effective teamwork.

- The organisation then benefits because satisfied customers are far more likely to return again and again. **Repeat custom** has two main benefits. It increases sales without the business having to spend more on advertising and satisfied customers normally tell their friends.
- Satisfied customers tell people about their experiences. This **word of mouth advertising** can rapidly enhance a firm's reputation far more effectively than any other method.
- **Internal customers** who are satisfied because they can rely upon consistently accurate information and good service from their colleagues are more likely to experience job satisfaction and to benefit from working as members of an effective and supportive team.

Did you know?

One firm has as its motto 'customer satisfaction isn't our highest priority, it's our only priority'.

Activity

Good communication helps to achieve customer satisfaction – poor communication has the opposite effect. As a group, suggest the type of problems that could be caused by someone who has poor communication skills (see pages 65–68) or who cannot be bothered to check their facts.

Did you know?

The Research Institution of America found that the average person who has a bad service experience tells at least nine others about it. In comparison people who have an excellent experience tell only three or four others.

Codes of practice

Codes of practice are voluntary guidelines or standards that have been drawn up to identify the standards of service that customers can expect. They usually include advice on what to do if something goes wrong and who to contact in this situation. They are helpful because they provide information and guidance for external customers and for staff who know exactly what type of services they are supposed to provide.

Codes of practice can be drawn up at different levels.

- **Industry codes of practice** relate to issues that affect many different types of organisation, such as advertising or recruitment, or to the organisations that operate in a particular industry such as the water, gas, motor or mobile phone industry.
- **Organisational codes of practice** are written by a business to set out its own standards for customers. Sometimes these are known as Customer Charters, particularly in the public sector.
- **Professional codes of practice** set out minimum standards for professional workers, such as solicitors, accountants, doctors and social workers. They are often drawn up by professional bodies on behalf of their members.

Ethical codes of practice focus on trading fairly with customers and suppliers and taking steps to ensure there are no corrupt or dishonest practices. Some businesses specify the minimum standards they expect of their suppliers and other organisations they work with. The Institute of Business Ethics provides guidance to organisations about devising ethical codes at its website www.ibe.org.uk.

Fact file

***Codes of practice** state standards of service that customers can expect and tell them what to do if something goes wrong.*

Did you know?

Many major supermarkets and food producers have developed ethical codes of practice as a result of worries about additives and other food scares.

Over to you

1. *Identify the customer service training that any members of your group have received as part of their job. Compare the different aspects that were covered to see how these varied between different organisations.*
2. *In small groups, decide the key features of customer service that must be provided consistently and reliably by your college or school librarians and by your refectory staff. Then identify any similarities or differences and the reasons for them.*
3. *Find out how the Institute of Customer Service thinks complaints should be handled by downloading the facts sheet from their website at www.instituteofcustomerservice.com. Then, as a group, compare the recommended methods with those used by any organisations where you or other members of your group have jobs.*
4. *Divide into five groups to investigate codes of practice online and to present and describe examples to the class.*
   - ***Group one:** search under 'industry codes of practice' to find a code written to cover a common issue, such as health and safety, advertising or recruitment.*
   - ***Group two:** search under 'industry codes of practice' to find one code devised and endorsed by a particular industry.*
   - ***Group three:** find out about the school or college Student Charter.*
   - ***Group four:** search for a 'professional code of practice' online.*
   - ***Group five:** find out about ethical codes of practice. One useful website is www.ethicaltrade.org but try to find other examples as well.*

Talking point

View 1: Customers prefer cheap prices to consistent or reliable customer service. Businesses like Ryanair and Ikea have proved this.

View 2: Most people expect superb customer service even if they are paying rock bottom prices. If they don't get it, they go elsewhere.

With which viewpoint do you agree – and why?

Activity

Some organisations have codes of practice for serving customers with special needs. Find out about the service that National Express, the coach firm, offers to customers with special needs at www.nationalexpress.com/why_choose/disabled/practice.cfm.

Case study

Assessment practice

The basic needs and expectations of most travellers usually include a reliable service, a reasonably priced ticket, courteous staff, a clean and preferably spacious seat to name but a few. Yet all too often rail passengers have to wait on dirty, draughty stations for a train that is late and over-crowded. And pay more and more for the privilege.

One company aiming to improve on this is Grand Central Railway, which wants to operate a new service between London and the north east. It promises a personal service, greater accessibility for many communities, 'park and ride' facilities and value for money, and guarantees to refund half the fare in cash to any passenger who has to stand on a long journey, even if a seat later becomes available.

South West Trains has a different approach. It offers seats for as little as £1 on some long-distance journeys to try to fill trains at 'quiet times'. Bookings must be made on the Internet or by phone and a confirmation number is sent by email or text message. Passengers then give this to the guard.

Cheap online fares is a service copied from budget airlines such as Ryanair, which has often been criticised for its casual attitude to customers. One Channel 4 Dispatches programme highlighted several problems including disinterested cabin crews and dirty planes. It argued that Ryanair believes customers will sacrifice anything to travel cheaply, with the exception of safety.

The day after the Dispatches programme Ryanair announced a 3 million free ticket giveaway.

The Skytrax website paints a different picture. Customers record their opinions on airlines and airports and Skytrax awards airlines stars based on product and staff service standards. Look for this next time you are going travelling!

1(P) **a)** Identify four main features of customer service that are important to train passengers.

b) Describe how Grand Central Railway and South West Trains are trying to meet the needs of their passengers.

c) Check passenger opinions on airports or airlines at www.airlinequality.com/index.htm and identify six main services that are important to customers.

d) Use this information to describe how consistent and reliable customer service contributes to the customer satisfaction of anyone travelling by train or air. ***(P3)***

2(M) Explain why the presentation, interpersonal and communication skills of staff are important to train and airline passengers. ***(M2)***

3(D) Analyse how effective customer service by an airline or train company can benefit the customer, the organisation and the staff who work there. ***(D2)***

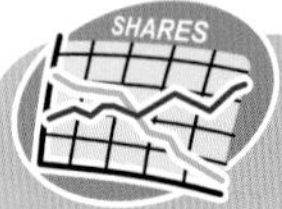

Grading tip

Remember that your explanation must include reasons to support your choice of skills.

Analysing means explaining each factor and saying how it contributes to the topic.

.4 Know how to monitor and evaluate customer service within an organisation

Businesses monitor and evaluate their customer service for one simple reason. If they do not know what their customers think then they cannot remedy problems or introduce improvements because they will not know what is needed. This may be fine if the organisation is the only supplier of a product or service but this is rarely the case today.

Monitoring customer service

Methods used to obtain customer feedback vary between organisations, often depending upon their size and how much money there is available.

Informal customer feedback

When you finish a meal and a waiter asks you if everything was fine, this is a cheap, easy and informal way of getting customer feedback. Other methods include watching customers as they enter and leave and chatting to them. Many retailers do this – noting comments people make, how long they stop and look at certain displays and whether they have made a purchase or not. This technique can be adapted by other organisations – such as watching visitors in reception, checking that they have not been waiting too long and ensuring that receptionists pass important comments on to a manager.

Did you know?

Blogs and online forums are the latest way to capture customer comments, as well as encouraging email feedback. You can email Google at gblog@google.com and chat about iPods at www.ilounge.com.

Did you know?

The IWOOT (I want one of those) customer survey divides its questions into 'boring stuff' and 'less boring stuff' and puts its questions in fun format.

Customer questionnaires/comment cards

Because the waiter may forget to relay your comments back to the chef or the manager, many restaurants prefer to put a comment card on your table and ask you to complete it before you leave. Other businesses do this too. Cards are available in Tesco stores for customers to complete if they have a comment or suggestion to make.

Many businesses want more information than would fit on a comment card so they issue questionnaires for customers to complete. You will often find these in hotel rooms and many travel companies issue them at the end of a package holiday. Questionnaires may be sent more widely – to existing customers and previous customers who have not made a purchase for some time to find out why. This is because, as well as feedback, they also provide useful information about the 'typical' customer. However, asking about salaries or ages must be done tactfully, because many people object to answering these types of questions.

Many organisations send out regular online questionnaires to a representative customer group to check their views. Debenhams is one example. It asks for feedback on a wide range of topics, from store layouts or advertising campaigns to its store cards and credit cards.

The information organisations want to get from these often differs depending on the type of business.

Did you know?

Harley Davidson, the motor cycle manufacturers, expects its managers to ride with customers at least 10 to 15 days a year – to find out what they really think.

Manufacturers and retailers	Service providers
Price Speed of delivery The range of products The product(s) and their features Packaging Catalogue/website information Returns procedure Attitude of staff (retailers only)	Range of services/facilities Prices, for commercial services Speed of service The way in which the service was delivered The attitude of the staff The quality of the finished result

■ *Key components of customer questionnaires*

Staff feedback

Staff feedback is valuable for two reasons. First, many staff deal directly with external customers. They can therefore pass on comments made by customers – both positive and negative. Sales representatives, for example, are usually expected to chat to customers regularly and pass feedback to their manager.

Activity

Many organisations agree that staff questionnaires can be completed anonymously. Can you think why?

Second, staff are internal customers, so their views are also important. If many staff are unhappy and leaving to work elsewhere it is sensible to find out why. For that reason, most organisations regularly assess staff views by issuing questionnaires, by holding meetings with the staff association or group that represents their views and/or by inviting leavers to attend an exit interview.

Mystery customers

Some retailers employ mystery customers to visit their own stores to assess staff. They may also check competitor's stores to compare service levels. They will be interested in factors such as the following:

- speed of service
- the way in which the service was delivered
- the attitude of the staff
- the quality of the finished result.

It is not only retailers that use mystery customers. One health authority has also employed them to visit hospitals to check if doctors and nurses are washing their hands, in its efforts to prevent patients catching the MRSA bug.

Did you know?

Another way of getting staff views is by operating a suggestion scheme and rewarding those who come up with good ideas for improvements.

Did you know?

Focus groups *represent key customer groups and advise organisations on current and proposed products and services. How useful they are is another matter – one BBC focus group rejected the idea of bringing back Dr Who!*

Activities

1. *Find out more about mystery customers at www.mystery-shoppers.co.uk/index.htm. If you're a shopaholic, you might be interested in becoming one!*
2. *E-satisfy Inc specialises in measuring customer satisfaction and loyalty. Find out more at www.e-satisfy.co.uk/. Note that you have to register on the site to read the case studies.*

Complaints and compliment letters

If a customer makes a complaint, either by telephone or letter, this indicates a possible problem area. If several complaints are received about the same thing, there is obviously a serious problem that needs immediate attention. This is why organisations record the complaints they receive and then check them to see if there are any common factors.

Similarly, a card or a letter which thanks the staff for wonderful service or praises a product is to be treasured – which is why many organisations pin these on a notice board or make mention of them in their newsletters.

Fact file

There are many ways of obtaining customer feedback including informal questions, questionnaires and comment cards. Customer service can also be assessed by using mystery shoppers and by analysing complaints and compliment letters.

Evaluate means to review the information and evidence before forming a conclusion.

Evaluate customer service

If a business is receiving marvellous feedback from its customers, then it could be reasonably expected to be thriving. If it isn't then something is obviously wrong. To evaluate customer service it is therefore important to look at key business information which will either confirm or deny this, such as that shown in the table below.

Key information	Trend	Method of investigation
Level of sales	Should be rising for all key product groups	Check sales turnover figures. Analyse by product and by branch.
Repeat customers	Customer loyalty is demonstrated through repeat business	Check customer accounts to find out reorder frequency.
New customers	Numbers should be increasing	Check number of new customer accounts. Should also be reflected in sales turnover.
Level of complaints/ compliments	Complaints should be falling, compliments should be rising	Check complaints records both for overall number received and for any trends. Check compliments received.
Staff turnover	Should be steady or falling.	Check number of people leaving each month. Hold exit interviews to find out reasons.

■ *Methods of evaluating customer service*

As a group, suggest the types of information the departments in your school or college may be able to provide that will confirm whether its customer service is successful or not.

Improvements to customer service

It is obviously pointless obtaining and evaluating customer service if no action is taken to remedy any problems. The evaluation process should identify any areas where improvements are required. This may include any of the following.

Improvements to quality of service

Businesses have to differentiate between general failings that are affecting many consumers and problems which are more specific. As an example, in 2004 Sainsbury's was struggling with an IT problem that affected distribution of supplies, so many of its shelves were empty. Customers complained and sales fell. The company took immediate action to resolve the problem and the improvements it made helped to boost sales.

Consumer pressure can force companies to take rapid action. When the screen on Matthew Peterson's iPod Nano cracked he set up a website, flawedmusic player.com, to tell everyone. His site attracted similar complaints from around the world and forced Apple to take notice.

This presents a different problem to the company than a complaint made about a member of staff who has been rude or negligent. This type of complaint needs to be investigated carefully to find out what actually occurred before any action is taken, in case the complaint is unfounded. If there is a serious problem, the person concerned may need to be retrained and/or disciplined.

'Which' the consumer association reports on unreliable products and services – and bad reports can quickly affect sales.

Reliability

Reliability is essential for consumer confidence. Buying something that fails after a few days will annoy anyone. If several items are reported as unreliable then this is likely to lead to a serious loss of business, profits and reputation.

For this reason, most products undergo reliability testing before they are launched. This takes into account the materials that are used, the manufacturing process and even environmental factors, such as heat. This is done because it costs more to remedy a problem later. If a fault is serious, the company may need to recall the product and make changes to the way it is produced.

1. *Check the products that have recently been recalled in the UK because of problems at www.ukrecallnotice.co.uk/. In small groups investigate one of the ten types of products on the site.*
2. *As a group, identify any products or services you have experienced that have been unreliable, how this has affected your opinion of the supplier and what (if any) action you took as a result.*

Service reliability is also important. A taxi firm that cannot be trusted to arrive is unlikely to stay in business for long and if you were relying on a response from one of the emergency services then service reliability may be crucial to saving lives.

Improvements to the organisation

In 2006 the Royal Mail service was fined £11 million by the regulator Postcomm because 14.6 million letters had either been lost, stolen or substantially delayed during 2004–2005. The aim of the fine was to focus Royal Mail on the need for urgent improvements.

If the Royal Mail is to avoid a fine next year it has to address several organisational problems, including how it recruits and trains staff and how it keeps mail secure from loss, theft or damage. This will be the task of senior managers who are focused on improving performance and have the power to make the required changes.

Other examples of organisational improvements include the following.

Improving service and/or products This may include making improvements to organisational systems, such as IT or distribution, like Sainsbury's did, offering different or new services or concentrating on improving the service given by individual staff. Methods of doing this include increasing training, offering incentives such as bonuses or commission or assessing workloads and reallocating some duties. Customer feedback can also be used to improve existing products or services or to supply new products not currently made or stocked.

Fact file

Monitoring and evaluating customer service may show that improvements are required in product or service quality or reliability.

Keeping staff If staff turnover is increasing then action needs to be taken because losing good, experienced staff costs money. This is because it is expensive to recruit and train new staff. Organisational improvements need to be targeted at improving areas where staff are dissatisfied. These may range from salary levels to lack of training or promotion opportunities.

Attracting new customers This will normally be the task of sales and marketing staff; however, advertising and promotional campaigns cost money and it will be up to senior managers to decide how much to spend.

Increasing sales turnover It is normally cheaper to persuade existing customers to return or to spend more than it is to attract new customers. This is why many organisations operate loyalty schemes or offer rewards in the form of vouchers or points that can be traded for free goods. Identifying the potential for increasing sales will again normally be the task of marketing staff.

Complying with legal obligations The Royal Mail was fined by Postcomm in 2006 for being in 'serious breach' of its licence to deliver mail. This is because the terms of its licence require it to take security measures to prevent mail being lost or stolen. All businesses have to comply with the laws of the land as well as the specific regulations that relate to their type of business. Failure to do so can result in serious penalties as the Royal Mail discovered.

Did you know?

A common method of increasing sales turnover is to persuade the customer to buy 'add-ons' – such as satnav in a new car. You will learn more about this if you study option unit 7, Personal Selling.

Key term

Organisational improvements are improvements that affect the way the organisation operates and are decided by senior managers.

Activity

As a group, suggest the main types of laws with which all businesses have to comply. Then turn to Unit 9, page 375, to see if you were right.

Improvements for employees

All businesses are keen to retain hard-working employees and this is more likely if staff enjoy working for the organisation and feel they are valued and treated fairly. This increases motivation, as you saw in Unit 1 (page 33). Improvements may be required in two main areas.

Job satisfaction A famous study carried out by Frederick Herzberg concluded that the main factors that contribute to job satisfaction are as follows:

- interesting work
- having responsibility
- being praised for doing a good job
- being able to achieve something personally
- personal growth and learning new skills
- opportunities for advancement, such as training to learn new skills and promotion within the organisation.

Working environment This relates to the physical environment and the 'atmosphere' of the workplace. Most employees would reasonably expect good lighting and ventilation, modern furnishings and equipment, adjustable heating, a lack of noise and will work better if there is a restful colour scheme. They will expect all their legal rights to be met and not to be discriminated against, bullied or victimised in any way. You will learn more about this if you study option unit 5, People in Organisations.

Activity

Many organisations hold appraisal or personal development interviews with staff (see also page 223). Check if any group members have experienced these and what happened. Then discuss their role in identifying individual staff concerns and bringing about improvements.

Key term

Job satisfaction is positive feelings related to the job and the workplace.

Fact file

Employee improvements may be needed to promote job satisfaction if staff are bored or feel unappreciated. However, the working environment is important, as well as salary levels.

Talking point

View 1: Using mystery customers to spy on staff is sneaky and underhand and just annoys people. It is especially awful in hospitals.

View 2: Using mystery customers is a good idea. If staff are doing their jobs properly, they have nothing to fear.

With which viewpoint do you agree – and why?

Over to you

1. *Describe three ways in which each of the following organisations could monitor its customer service. In each case give a reason for your choice.*
   a) *A large supermarket*
   b) *An estate agent*
   c) *An educational publisher, such as Heinemann*
   d) *A health centre*

2. *Jon and Jake started their own car valeting service last year. They found that Business Link, which advises entrepreneurs, recommends checking the following information regularly:*
   - *sales renewal rates*
   - *the number of queries or complaints about the product or service*
   - *the number of complaints about staff*
   - *the number of damaged or faulty goods returned*
   - *average time to fulfil an order*
   - *the number of contacts with a customer each month*
   - *the volume of marketing material sent out and the responses.*

   As a group, suggest how they could apply this advice to their business and how **each** *type of information would help them to evaluate their customer service.*

3. *Computer software can be used to capture and evaluate customer feedback so that managers can respond quickly. Find out more at sites such as www.crtsolutions.co.uk and www.respond-uk.co.uk/about. Choose a case study on each of these sites and identify the benefits the business says it has gained as a result.*

4. *Identify the ways in which your school or college obtains feedback from* **all** *its customers, as well as its staff. Then find out how it evaluates this.*
   Work in groups to decide how obtaining and evaluating this can benefit the students, the school or college itself, and the staff. Then compare your ideas.

Case study Assessment practice

Richer Sounds, the high street hi-fi and electrical retailer, believes customer satisfaction is a more important measure of its business success than profits. It believes that it offers a customer friendly environment and that its employees – which it refers to as 'colleagues' – are smart, well informed and friendly. However, it regularly checks that it is right by asking both customers and colleagues for their opinions and employing mystery shoppers to visit and phone its stores.

All customers are given a till questionnaire when they make a purchase and asked to complete and return it to the Freepost address printed on the other side. To encourage customers to do this, every month 50 replies are picked at random and the senders receive £20 in vouchers. Customers can also complete 'We're listening' comment cards in store to give feedback.

Every month the responses are analysed to see what action should be taken or improvements made as a result. These have included introducing a queuing system for busy times and improving phone answering times.

The information is also used to compile a Customer Service Index (CSI) which analyses each sales assistant's personal customer performance that month. The CSI also takes into account any positive and negative letters and 'we're listening' cards received. Staff who receive 'excellent' and 'very good' feedback are rewarded with £3 bonus for each excellent and

continued ▶

Case study *continued*

£1 bonus for a very good. No rewards are given for 'good' feedback because this is the expected minimum standard. A special reward is given to anyone who is consistently highly ranked.

Stores, too, are awarded points on their performance based on information from returned customer questionnaires, mystery shopper visits and phone calls, staff suggestions and store visits. Points are lost for 'avoidable' complaints – like poor service – but not for 'unavoidable' ones which staff cannot control, like lack of car parking. The top stores also win prizes, depending upon their ranking.

To check that colleagues are happy too, Richer Sounds issues an annual Colleague Attitude Survey to find out their opinions. It also encourages contributions through its staff suggestion scheme and its 'listening sessions' when managers and colleagues talk about their ideas for their store and the company as a whole, as well as any concerns they may have. Good ideas the business has adopted have included installing bells at the doorways for disabled customers and redesigning the catalogues.

1(P) **a)** Describe how the views of staff and customers are monitored by Richer Sounds.

b) Suggest three types of business information Richer Sounds could check to evaluate its customer service feedback and the trends it would want to see. ***(P4)***

2(M) Explain how monitoring and evaluating has improved customer service for Richer Sounds itself, its customers and employees. ***(M3)***

3(D) Analyse how providing effective customer service benefits Richer Sounds' customers, its employees and the organisation itself. ***(D2)***

4(D) Practice the customer service skills you would need to demonstrate if you wre working at Richer Sounds. Work in pairs and decide the likely needs and expectations of three different customers who might visit a store. Then take turns to demonstrate your skills in a role play where one of you takes the part of a customer and the other then part of the sales person. ***(D1 part)***

Grading tip

A full explanation includes details, reasons and evidence to support the argument you are making.

Your analysis should look at the different factors involved and the effect each of these has. You may find it helpful to think about what might happen if a factor was absent.

Key to quiz on pages 70–71

Only 'b' answers earn a mark in this quiz. All other responses are likely to alienate or annoy a customer or colleague!

If you scored 9 or 10 then congratulations! You have the right attitude and approach for dealing with your customers.

If you scored 6–8 then you are on the right track but still have some work to do.

If you scored 5 or less then you are seriously out of step with your customers' needs.

3 Investigating financial control

All businesses need money to survive. The revenue they earn must be higher than their costs if they are to make a profit. This unit focuses on the techniques used by businesses to control their finances, record their transactions and minimise fraud or theft.

What you need to learn

- The importance of costs, revenue and profit
- How businesses use break-even analysis
- How to prepare and analyse a cash flow forecast
- How financial transactions are recorded and fraud can be prevented

3.1 Understand costs, revenue and profit for a business

Fact file

Fixed (indirect) costs *have to be paid regardless of how much is produced, for example, rent and rates.*

Variable (direct) costs *are directly related to the amount produced or sold, for example, raw materials, and stock for resale.*

Business costs

There are three main types of business costs.

- **Start-up costs** These are incurred before a business begins to operate, such as the purchase of land, buildings and equipment.
- **Fixed costs** These are incurred once a business is running, no matter how many products it sells or how many customers it has. A car manufacturer has to pay heating bills whether it sells one car a day or a hundred. Fixed costs are also called **indirect costs**.
- **Variable costs** These are also incurred once a business is operating. This time the amount spent directly relates to the number of products sold or the amount of services provided. The number of tyres bought by a car manufacturer depends on the number of cars made. This is why variable costs are also called **direct costs**.

Activity

Identify the variable and fixed costs in your own household by listing those items that still need paying when you are away on holiday.

Key terms

Start-up costs are costs incurred before a business starts or when it is expanding or going into a new venture.

Operating costs are costs a business incurs once it is up and running.

Costs incurred at start-up

The type and amount of start-up costs depends on the type of business. The M6 toll road had to be built before drivers could use it and cost £500 million, so it will be many years before Midland Expressway (who built it) gets its money back. On the other hand, a window cleaning business can be started by anyone with some ladders, a bucket and a few cloths – assuming that they already have transport.

Start-up costs are also incurred when businesses plan to start a new venture or expand. For example, a soft furnishing manufacturer could decide to produce dining furniture – chairs and tables which would need different production machines. A business which makes caravans may wish to take advantage of a growing market by building an extension to its existing factory.

Did you know?

Many people underestimate their start-up costs by forgetting important items or under-estimating how much they will cost.

Activity

As a group, list the start-up items you think you would need if you were opening a sandwich shop.

Operating costs

Variable costs and fixed costs added together are known as **operating** or **running** costs since they are both incurred when a business is running.

Fixed (indirect) costs

Fixed costs have to be paid whether the business is busy or quiet. If your sandwich shop was near a school, in term time you would be busy but during the holidays there would be fewer customers. But you would still have your fixed costs to pay. This is why they are called **fixed** costs.

Variable (direct) costs

Variable costs increase *in direct proportion to* the level of activity. A jeans manufacturer producing 200 pairs of jeans would use twice as much fabric and buttons or zips than one producing 100. Again the type and amounts of money involved can be very different. In some businesses, such as those that make large consumer items like washing machines, most costs are variable. The components are usually 'bought in' and the product is assembled by the business. Others are just the opposite; a tanning salon,for example, has mainly fixed costs such as rates, insurance, wages and heating. The only variable costs would be a small amount of electricity for the sun beds and cleaning materials used to disinfect the equipment in between users.

Did you know?

The easy way to decide if a cost is fixed or variable is to ask yourself:

'If the business sells more of the product will it need more of these items?' If the answer is 'yes', then the cost is variable. If the answer is 'no', it is a fixed cost.

Did you know?

Some businesses have high fixed costs – others do not. Airlines have to pay fixed costs, which include airport fees, salaries of the crew, fuel, maintenance and cleaning, whereas a mobile hairdresser's fixed costs mainly relate to the car or van that is used.

Key terms

Variable (direct) costs are costs that change when the number of products made or sold changes.

Fixed (indirect) costs are costs that never change, regardless of the number of products made or sold.

Total costs are all fixed and all variable costs added together.

Variable costs are calculated in the following way:

Variable cost of each product × number produced

As an example, if an ice cream cone cost 4p and the ice cream filling was 10p then the variable cost for each filled cone sold would be 14p. If a shop sold 200 cones in a day, the total variable cost for that day would be:

14p × 200 = 2800p = £28.00

Activity

As a group, list the operating costs you think you would incur if you opened your sandwich shop. Then divide these into fixed and variable costs.

Total costs

All businesses need to know how much money they are spending altogether, i.e. the total costs. This is the total fixed costs and the total variable costs added together.

Activity

The fillings for your cheese and pickle sandwiches cost 24p. The rolls cost 6p and margarine is 1p. If you sell 50 of these sandwiches today, what are your total variable costs?

Revenue

Revenue is the income received by a business from all sources.

- **Sales** These are the main source of revenue for most organisations because customers pay for the goods or services they buy.
- **Leasing** a part of a building to another business can also provide a source of income. Some businesses specialise in leasing cars or equipment to other organisations.
- **Interest** This is earned when a business has money in an interest-bearing account at the bank.

Businesses may also sell items they no longer need to other firms, such as equipment or vehicles that are being replaced.

Calculating total revenue

To do this you need two items of information:

- the selling price
- the number sold.

You then use the following formula:

Total income = selling price × number sold

Therefore, an ice cream business which prices its cones at £1 and sells 100 will have a total income of £100.

Most businesses sell several products, so the revenue for each product has to be worked out separately and the amounts added together to find the total sales revenue. In our ice cream business, for example, it would add on the revenue from selling its ice lollies, choc ices and drinks, too.

Activity

Calculate the total income of your sandwich shop if you sold 150 sandwiches a day at an average price of £1.40.

Did you know?

Some businesses offer incentives to staff to motivate them to increase sales. Countrywide, a national estate agent, offers sales staff a percentage bonus based on their sales and Richer Sounds, the hi-fi retailer, give each sales person a percentage of their shop's weekly takings.

Calculating gross and net profit

Gross profit

Gross profit is the amount of money remaining from sales income when the cost of materials purchased is deducted. For example, a newsagent might receive £4,000 income in a week from selling papers, magazines, sweets and other items. If it costs her £2,500 to buy these goods then the gross profit for that week is:

£4,000 – £2,500 = £1,500

The amount spent by the newsagent on the papers, sweets and other stock is called **cost of sales**. So the formula for calculating gross profit is

Gross profit = Sales income – Cost of sales

The gross profit figure gives useful information to the business owner because it only includes expenditure that is outside the control of the business. The newsagent cannot control the amounts she pays for her stock. The real test of how well she runs the business is what she spends the rest of her income on.

Fact file

Gross profit is sometimes called operating profit because it is the profit made from the business operations of buying and selling goods.

Net profit

Net profit is calculated by subtracting other expenses from the gross profit. If the newsagent spends £1,000 on operating costs such as business rates, wages for part time staff, heating, rent, business rates etc., the net profit is:

£1,500 – £1,000 = £500

So, the formula for calculating net profit is

Net profit = Gross profit – Operating costs

The net profit is the real measure of how well the business is being run.

Fact file

Business owners must pay tax on their net profit. Sole traders and partners pay income tax; limited companies pay corporation tax.

Key terms

Revenue is the total amount of money going into a business. It is also called ***income*** and sometimes ***sales***.

Gross profit is the amount left over from revenue when the cost of sales is deducted.

Net profit is the amount left when the operating expenses are deducted from the gross profit figure.

Activity

What is the gross and net profit if the revenue from your sandwich shop is £28,000, the bread and fillings you buy (cost of sales) come to £10,000 and your operating costs are £3,500?

Maximising profits

The 'health' of a business is measured by how much profit it makes. High profits mean that the owners, who took a risk by investing in the business, receive a good income *and* have money to reinvest in the business to ensure good profits in years to come. For this reason, good businesses are always looking for ways of improving profits – called **profit maximisation**.

There are two basic ways of improving profits;

- increasing sales income
- reducing running costs.

In most businesses, both of these activities happen all the time.

Did you know?

Net profit is sometimes called 'profit before tax'.

Increasing sales income

There are different ways of trying to achieve this. They all have risks as shown in the chart.

Method	Risk
Increase prices	Sales could fall
Reduce prices to increase sales	Not enough extra sales would be made to compensate
Increase advertising	Extra cost may not be covered by increased sales
Sell new type of product to existing customers	New type of product may not be popular
Increase scale of business and operate in a wider area with same product	Expansion costs money and has its own risks (see Unit 1, page 8) especially if there is stiff competition

■ *Risks associated with trying to increase sales income*

Did you know?

It is harder to increase selling prices without affecting sales if competition for business is fierce, or if people can easily do without your products.

Businesses need to look at all the options and weigh the balance between potential advantages and risks. For example, some products will stand an increase in selling price, such as 'must have' children's toys at Christmas. Others will not. You may know a motorist who will drive miles to save a penny per litre on petrol!

Reducing operating costs

You already know that costs fall into two categories, variable and fixed. Variable costs are mainly materials that go into the product, such as LCD screens for a VDU manufacturer and bricks for house builders. Most businesses have many operating costs, ranging from business rates and utility bills to window cleaning and toner for the photocopier.

When a business carries out a cost-reduction exercise, one of the ways to approach it in a systematic manner is to list all expenditure items for a year in order, starting with the highest. So, for example, a car valeting business could have a list which begins:

Staff wages	£200,000
Property rental	£50,000

and ends with:

Ball pens	£20.00
Paper clips	£4.50

The next stage is to examine the high value items and look for ways of reducing the amount being spent on them.

Methods of reducing costs fall into two main categories:

- minimising usage
- finding the best purchase deal.

The table below gives some ways of achieving this. The middle column suggests how fewer materials can be used. The end column suggests ways in which the purchase price could be reduced.

Item	Use less	Reduce purchase price
Labour	Reduce staff levels by increasing number of automated or computerised operations	Increase productivity Sub-contract work to cheapest bidder
Raw materials	Use fewer materials in product Reduce wastage	Negotiate cheaper deal with supplier Look for a cheaper supplier Purchase large quantities at discounted price Look for alternative, cheaper materials
Gas, water and electricity	Replace older items with energy efficient ones, e.g. energy-saving bulbs, lights which turn off automatically, taps which do the same, more efficient heating system Encourage all staff to be energy conscious	Ask utility companies to design tariff to suit individual business needs, including service Switch utility company if this would reduce costs
Consumable items, e.g. stationery	Send documents by email rather than by post (reduces photocopy and postage costs); photocopy back-to-back; keep print-outs to a minimum	Shop around for cheaper suppliers and investigate online sources

■ *Methods of reducing costs*

Did you know?

If you are spending more than you are earning then you, too, should reduce your operating costs for a while!

Fact file

Businesses will always try to keep costs as low as possible because costs always lower profit.

Productivity is the output in goods or services produced by a person or machine. (See also Unit 1, page 18)

Sub-contract means arranging for someone outside the company to do a job for an agreed price.

A profit and loss account is a table that businesses produce every year giving the figures for income, gross and net profit and income and expenditure.

Re-investment is the amount of money from profits that managers put back into the business to keep up-to-date or expand operations.

Profit maximisation is making as much profit as possible.

Remember that types and amounts of expenditure will be different for every single business. The table simply gives examples to illustrate the principles involved.

The importance of profit

After the tax is paid the business can spend the remaining money in several ways. Obviously, the more profit a business makes, the more options it has.

If the business is a limited company with shareholders, some of the profit will be paid as **dividends**. Dividends are the reward paid to shareholders for investing their money – similar to the interest you earn if you save money in a bank.

- For small businesses, most of the profit is used to pay the owner a wage.
- Profit can be kept in the bank as **reserves** to be used on a future occasion or in an emergency. In this case, it should be placed in a high interest account.
- Profit can be used to expand the business, such as by buying another business.
- Equipment could be upgraded or updated to improve efficiency.
- If the business has taken out a loan, some or all of it could be repaid.

You can see from this list that making a healthy profit is very important for a business.

View 1: Businesses should treat staff as a variable cost by employing them on a temporary basis so that they only have to be paid when work is available.

View 2: Staff need a steady income and should be treated as a fixed cost. In the long term they will work harder and be more loyal.

With which viewpoint do you agree – and why?

Over to you

1 *Tom runs a small garage which repairs and services customers' cars. He employs one mechanic on a permanent basis and another, who is semi-retired and helps out at busy times, on a part-time basis. The list alongside gives some of Tom's costs. Rewrite the list under three headings – start-up costs, fixed costs and variable costs.*

Wages for the full-time mechanic
Heating
Installing MOT equipment
Spare parts for the cars
Business rates
Cash register
Oil for filling engines during servicing
Construction of MOT viewing area
Wages for the part-time mechanic
Tools
Safety signs
Insurance for the premises (paid monthly by direct debit)
Coffee for waiting customers
Sign above door 'Tom's Automotive'

2 *A large car dealer, based in a major city decides to offer a promotion on a new model, the Familycarrier. The sales manager thinks that if he offered the car for sale at £15,000 he would sell 50, but if the price was £14,000 he would sell 100. Calculate the business's income in each case.*

3 a) *Copy out the table below and complete the end two columns by working out the gross and net profit figures.*

Company	Sales Income(£)	Cost of Sales (£)	Operating Expenses (£)	Gross Profit (£)	Net Profit/Loss (£)
A	100,000	80,000	10,000		
B	350,000	57,000	255,000		
C	755,000	574,000	105,000		
D	53,500	4,700	37,500		
E	865,000	601,000	307,000		
F	345,000	171,000	113,000		

4 *Sheena runs a cattery and her expenses for one month are listed alongside. She considers that she is in the top end of the market since she provides high-quality accommodation and food.*
Using the information about Sheena's business, answer the following questions

a) *What were the business's total expenses?*

b) *For each of the items marked * suggest how Sheena might try to reduce her expenditure on the item.*

c) *Suggest two costs which she would probably not be able to reduce. Give reasons for your choice.*

d) *Divide the list of costs into fixed and variable headings and find the total for each.*

e) *If Sheena increased her prices, what might the result be?*

Rent	£400
Business rates	£500
Insurance	£250*
Fresh fish	£800
Heating	£1,000
Fresh meat	£600*
Electricity, water and telephone	£100*
Tinned food	£1,000
Miscellaneous (stationary, cleaning materials etc.)	£50*
Cat biscuits	£300

Case study Assessment practice

The HMV group runs the HMV music chain and also owns Waterstones book stores. In January 2003 the chief executive, Alan Giles, was a happy man. Profits had risen to £6 million and the sales of DVD software, with DVD titles including Lord of the Rings and CDs from bands like Blue and the Red Hot Chili Peppers had combined to give HMV a 'bumper Xmas'. The future looked rosy and, true to predictions, sales rose again the following year.

In January 2006 the picture was very different. Operating profits for 26 weeks to 29 October 2005 fell to £2.8 million – down from £15.7 million in the same period the previous year; pre-tax profits were down to a meagre £200,000, down from £10.5 million the previous year. Over Xmas, sales fell yet again.

What went wrong? Although HMV's new stores performed well, the massive price cutting of books, CDs, DVDs and video games by competitors such as online stores and supermarkets caused serious problems. And although HMV has long sold CDs online it only entered the music download business in 2005. Its appeal is also limited as HMV downloads are not compatible with iPods. HMV has now moved its fulfilment operations for its online store to Guernsey because taxes are lower for Channel Island companies. This means it can sell goods more cheaply and offer free delivery to customers. Despite this, when Alan Giles gave the profit warning he also announced his intention to retire and left his job in December 2005.

1(P) Identify four ways in which the HMV group earns its sales revenue. ***(P1 part)***

2(P) HMV invested £14.3 million in new stores in 2005.
- **a)** What are these types of costs called?
- **b)** Suggest five types of costs incurred in opening a new music store.
- **c)** Identify five other types of costs incurred in running a music store.
- **d)** Describe the importance of costs to a business organisation like HMV. ***(P1 part)***

3(P) **a)** Copy out the following table and complete it with the profit figures for the group:

	26 weeks to 29/10/2005 £	26 weeks to 23/10/2004 £
Operating profit		
Profit before tax		

- **b)** Identify which of your figures represents gross profit and which represents net profit.
- **c)** Explain the difference between gross and net profit.
- **d)** Describe the importance of profit to a business like HMV. ***(P1 part)***

4 **a)** Why does HMV think the problem occurred?
- **b)** What is HMV doing to try to improve the situation?

5 Analyse what might happen in the future if HMV's ideas do not succeed.

Grading tip

Give a full description by stating the effect on a business if revenue, costs or profit increased or decreased. You must think about the factors that apply, decide which are the most important and how they might contribute to the result.

3.2 How businesses use break-even analysis

In the last section you learned that businesses make a profit if their sales income is greater than their total expenditure. If expenditure is greater than income, businesses make a loss. In between these two extremes businesses are said to break even – when income and expenditure are almost the same. Businesses carry out break-even analysis when they are considering making investment decisions, because it helps them to answer important questions.

Did you know?

Unfortunately, Chelsea football team's finances are not as good as its performance on the pitch. In 2006 they reported record losses of £140 million, the biggest in football history. They hope to break even by 2009–2010.

Fact file

Businesses break even when income and expenditure are the same.

There are two ways of finding a break-even point. You can either construct a break-even chart or use a formula. In this section you will do both, using the following case study.

Constructing a break-even chart

Len's lawn mowers

Len runs a successful garden centre. He sells all kinds of plants, shrubs and small trees, in addition to fertilisers, compost and many types of garden tools and accessories. He is wondering about developing his business by selling lawnmowers. Having researched the market, he decides to sell one of the most popular models of mower to see if he can make a profit. If he is successful, he would expand the range of mowers he would sell and even move into other mechanical garden aids, such as strimmers and hedge cutters. For safety and other reasons he needs to add an extension to his existing building and would have to take out a bank loan to pay for this.

Did you know?

*Some business organisations **plan** to break even, e.g. charities and government departments. By law they cannot make a profit and they would get into serious trouble if they made a loss over a long period.*

A break-even chart is a type of graph. It has a horizontal and vertical axis.

Len does some calculations and produces the following figures based on forecasts for the first year of selling mowers:

- cost of each mower from the distributor (the variable cost) = £50
- fixed costs (including loan repayment, additional insurance, business rates, heating etc.) = £2,000

Len decides to draw a break-even chart to see if he could make a profit if he sold the mowers for £80 each. He thinks that the most he would sell in the year is 100 mowers. The following sections take you through the five stages of drawing the chart.

Stage one – drawing and labelling scales for the graph

The first step is to draw and label the axes of the graph. The horizontal axis shows the number of mowers sold. Len has already decided that he will probably sell 100 at most, so the scale goes from 0 to 100. The vertical axis represents both costs and revenue. The easiest way to work the maximum on this scale is to multiply the selling price by the maximum forecast sales. In Len's case this is:

£80 × 100 = £8,000

So the vertical scale goes from zero to £8,000

You can draw a break-even chart on graph paper or create one using a spreadsheet package if you prefer.

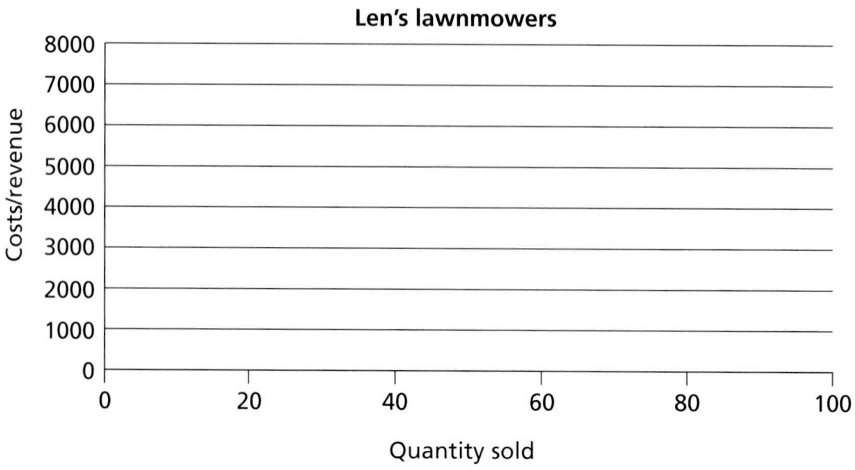

Stage two – plotting the fixed cost line

In Len's case, the fixed costs add up to £2,000. If you look at the next diagram you can see that this has been added to the graph by drawing a horizontal line starting at £2,000 on the vertical scale. The line is horizontal and not sloping because *fixed costs do not change with level of sales*. In this case, if Len sells hardly any lawnmowers, he will still have to pay the loan repayments, business rates etc. Looking at this graph should help you to understand why drawing a break-even chart is so useful, because you can *see* that the fixed costs do not change with the level of sales.

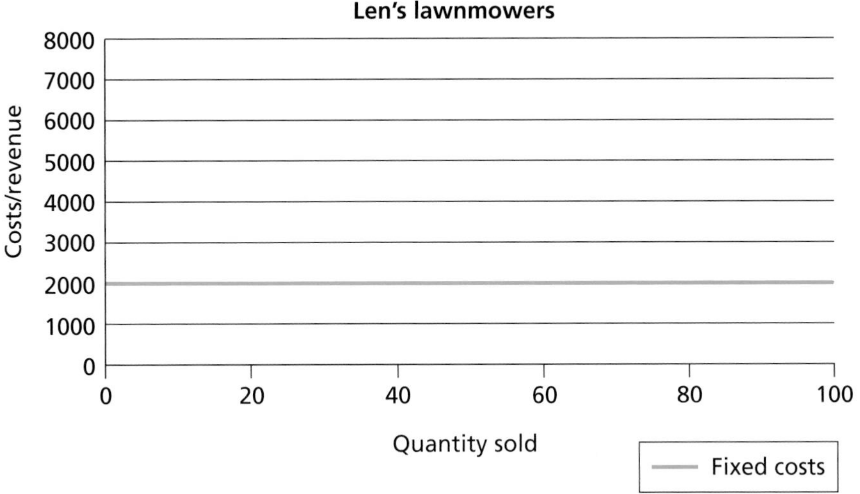

The fixed cost line on the graph is always *horizontal, because fixed costs do not change with the level of sales.*

Stage three – including the total cost line

The variable cost line is now added to the chart. The first step is to calculate the total cost if 100 mowers were sold. The variable cost for each mower is £50 since this is what Len pays for them, so if he sells 100 the total variable cost would be £5,000.

Since the fixed cost line has already been included, the variable cost line begins where the fixed cost line meets the vertical axis and ends at £7,000 for the 100 sales level (£2,000 + £5,000). In other words, if 100 mowers are sold, the total cost is the sum of the variable *and* the fixed costs = £7,000.

The variable cost line always starts at the point where the fixed cost line meets the vertical axis.

Did you know?

If you are careless when you plot the lines on your chart and they are not absolutely accurate, it is highly likely that the figures you read off will also be wrong.

This time the line slopes upwards from left to right, showing that the variable cost amount increases in direct proportion to the number of mowers sold. This line can be used to find the total cost for any level of sales. For instance, if 80 mowers were sold, the total cost would be £6,000. Check this to see if you get the same answer. Ask your tutor for help if you are not sure how to do this.

Stage four – adding the sales revenue line

The next diagram shows the final line added to the break-even chart. The two points used are the bottom left zero point – if there are no sales there is no income. At the other end of the chart when 100 mowers might be sold, the revenue would be 100 x £80 = £8,000. Again the slope is upwards from left to right showing that as sales increase so does the income. The line allows the revenue to be read off for any number of mowers sold. So, for example, if sales were 80, income would be £6,400.

Fact file

The variable cost line and the sales revenue line both slope upwards from left to right because variable costs and sales income increase with the number of sales.

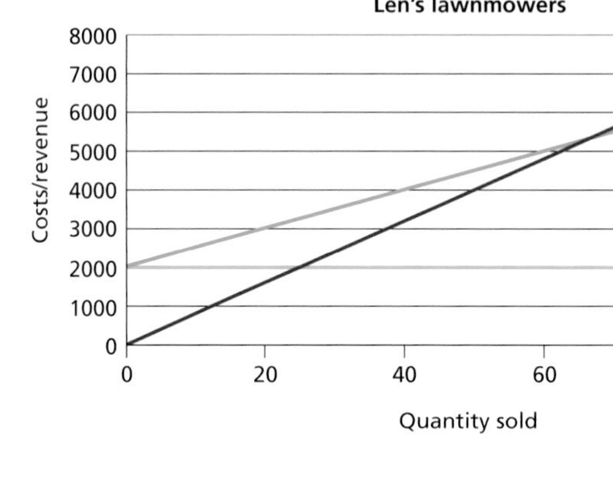

Stage 5 – analysing the chart

The final version of the chart has one additional line and some extra information. First, a line has been drawn from the point where the total cost line and the revenue line intersect. This meets the sales level scale at 67 mowers. This is the **break-even point**. In other words, if Len sells 67 mowers he covers all of his costs (fixed + variable) but does not make a profit or a loss.

Fact file

When the level of sales is above the break-even point on the chart, the business is profitable.

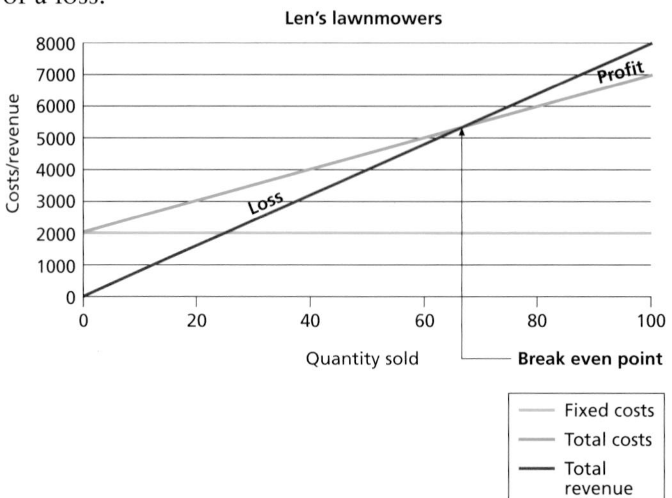

You should note that when you are reading figures from a break-even chart, the answer is only approximate. If complete accuracy is needed, any required figure can be calculated. For example, you will learn later that there is a mathematical formula to calculate the break-even point. This would show that Len would have to sell 66.666666 (recurring) lawnmowers to break even. He might struggle to sell 0.6666 of a machine to a customer! In this case 67 is quite accurate enough.

Above the break-even point, the gap between the total cost line and the sales revenue line above the break-even point shows that Len would make a profit if he sells more than 67 mowers. The gap between these two lines for sales below 67 shows the amount of loss he would make.

Look carefully at the cost and revenue lines if 80 mowers were sold. The cost line intersects at £6,000 and the revenue at £6,400. So the amount of profit Len would make is £400. If you read off the figures for sales of 40 mowers, you find that the total cost figure is £4,000 and the sales revenue is £3,200, so Len would make a loss of £800.

Activity

Using the final break-even chart for Len's lawnmower business, find the following:

a) the sales revenue for sales of 30 and 90 mowers
b) the total cost for sales of 30 and 90 mowers
c) the profit/loss for 40 and 80 mowers
d) the margin of safety if 80 mowers are sold.

Talking point

View 1: Private businesses are wise to plan to break even if they want new business, because they can set their price much lower.

View 2: It is never sensible for private organisations to just break even. They must make a profit to survive.

Which viewpoint do you agree with – why?

Key terms

The ***break-even point*** is the level of sales where the total cost and revenue lines cross on a break-even chart. Because the lines cross, the total income and expenditure figures are the same.

The ***margin of safety*** can be measured when the level of sales is above the break-even point – in other words, the business is profitable. The margin of safety is the number by which sales would have to fall before the break-even point is reached. In Len's case, if sales were 85 then the margin of safety would be 85 – 67 =18.

The ***profit margin per unit*** can be found by subtracting the variable cost per unit from the unit selling price. Len buys his lawnmowers for £50 and sells them for £80, so his profit margin per unit is £80 – £50 = £30.

Using a formula to calculate the break-even point

The formula for finding the break-even point is

$$\text{Sales for break even} = \frac{\text{fixed costs}}{\text{selling price} - \text{variable cost}}$$

The figures used for selling price and variable cost are both per unit. Think back to the example of Len's lawnmower business. Len buys them for £50 (the variable cost) and sells them for £80 each. His fixed costs are £2,000. So these figures would go into the formula as follows:

$$\text{Sales for break even} = \frac{£2{,}000}{£80 - £50} = \frac{£2{,}000}{£30} = 66.666$$

The answer would be rounded to the nearest whole number, 67.

Did you know?

When you have done a division calculation, you can check your result by multiplying your answer by the number on the bottom line. It should give you the figure on the top line.

Activity

Copy out the chart below and complete the last column by calculating the break-even point in each case using the formula. Round your answers to the nearest whole number if necessary.

Business	Total fixed costs (£)	Variable cost/unit (£)	Selling price per unit (£)	Break-even point
A	20	2	4	
B	1,000	50	100	
C	500	21	31	
D	270	18	33	
E	1,050	7	11	
F	2,714	53	107	

Fact file

Break-even analysis involves checking the potential effects of increases or reductions to the selling price, the fixed costs and the variable costs and deciding the best and worst possible outcomes.

The use of break-even analysis

Break-even analysis involves finding out what would happen if there were changes to costs or revenues. Managers ask questions such as:

- Could we increase our prices by 5 per cent and still make a profit if sales fall?
- If we reduce prices by 10 per cent, would we increase sales by enough to survive?

- We are very dependent on one supplier, what would happen if they went out of business and we had to use an alternative source which charges higher prices?
- If we moved to cheaper premises, how would this affect our profits?

Plotting these changes on a chart, or reworking the formula, will give the answer. In addition, managers are also aware that there are other types of risks they must consider relating to these decisions:

- If they decide to reduce the variable costs by using cheaper materials, the quality of the product could suffer and sales could fall.
- If prices are increased, sales could fall to a point where overall profits are reduced.
- If a jeweller's shop moves from a prime town centre location to cheaper premises on a quiet street, the fixed costs will be reduced but the number of customers could also fall.

Did you know?

For most goods there is a link between price and number of sales. The more expensive the goods, the fewer are sold.

Talking point

View 1: Managers should not take break-even calculations too seriously. They should go with their 'gut feeling'.

View 2: Managers should base all their decisions on the precise information given by a break-even calculation.

With which viewpoint do you agree – and why?

Activity

As a group, identify four goods you would not buy if the price went up, and four you would still want to buy, regardless of price. Compare your ideas with other members of your group, then suggest how this difference affects business decisions.

Over to you

1 a) *Construct a break-even chart for Super Smoothie Maker using the information below:*

- *fixed costs £10,000*
- *variable cost per unit £20*
- *selling price £50 per unit*
- *maximum sales 500 units.*

Tip: The horizontal axis should go up to the maximum possible sales – 500.
The vertical axis (costs and revenue) should go up to £25,000 (500 × £50).

b) *When you have completed the chart, label the following items:*

i) *the fixed cost line*
ii) *the total cost line*
iii) *the variable cost for maximum sales*
iv) *the profit area*
v) *the loss area and the break-even point.*

Ask your tutor to check your chart before you move on.

continued ▶

Over to you *continued*

c) *Using the chart, find the following information:*
  i) *the break-even point*
  ii) *the income and expenditure at the break-even point (they should be the same)*
  iii) *the income and total expenditure when the sales are 450 units*
  iv) *profit or loss (say which) when sales are 400 and then 200*
  v) *the profit margin per unit*
  vi) *for ii) to iv) above now calculate the figures to check your results.*

2 *Discuss the following situations in a group. Decide what advice you would give to the business, giving reasons for your answer. Remember to identify any effects on fixed and variable costs, sales revenue, break-even point and profit.*
  a) *A mail order company is thinking about transferring its customer call centre to a country where the labour is far cheaper.*
  b) *A double-glazing window manufacturer has found a cheaper source of the plastic raw material.*
  c) *A school is considering building a new IT block to provide courses for adults.*
  d) *A taxi firm is deciding whether to buy second-hand cars, which would require repairing from time to time, or new cars, which would have warranties but which would cost more to buy.*

3 *Len's lawnmower business has been running for a year and he has now sold 80 machines, making a profit of £400. His costs have remained the same – fixed costs £2,000 and variable costs £50 per unit. He still sells his mowers at £80 each.*

Len is considering spending money on advertising his business. He thinks he could spend £1,000 on 10 weekly advertisements in the local paper during the summer months – that is £100 per week. This amount would have to be added to his fixed costs, since it would be spent even if his sales were not affected.

  a) *Redraw the break-even chart first produced for Len (see page 101) with fixed costs of £3,000. In addition, since Len hopes that sales will increase, you need to increase the maximum sales on the horizontal scale to 200 units. Compare your result with the original chart and answer the following questions.*
    i) *How many mowers would Len now have to sell to break even?*
    ii) *Use the formula to check this result.*
    iii) *How many more mowers than before must he now sell to break even?*
    iv) *Why is the break-even point higher than it was originally?*
    v) *How much revenue would Len receive if he sold 150 mowers? Read this from the chart and then check by calculation.*
    vi) *What profit/loss would he make if he sold 150 mowers?*
    vii) *From the chart, find what Len's profit/loss would be if he still only sold 80 mowers, even after advertising.*
    viii) *Use the figures you have been given at the start of this section to check your answers to vi) and vii).*
  b) *Len looks at the two break-even charts and tries to decide what to do. Should he spend the money on advertising or leave things as they are? In a group, discuss Len's problem and decide what advice you would give him.*

Case study Assessment practice

Ali is a DJ who is tired of working most evenings. He wants to use his knowledge to set up his own music store, but knows that many high street shops are having a tough time. He has therefore decided to specialise in second-hand and out-of-print CDs and vinyl records and sell these online. Because he does not think his IT skills are up to designing a website he investigates setting up an eBay store instead.

Ali has discovered that eBay offers three types of store. He has listed the costs of these, as well as the other expenses involved in running the business, on a notepad. He already has a good computer and printer but will need a better car. Although he wants to buy goods online, he will also go on buying trips to find items to sell.

COSTS

eBay	**Basic store**	**Featured store**	**Anchor store**
Subscription fee	£8 a month	£25 a month	£250 a month

Listing/value fee – paid per item sold. Allow 50p per item for this.

Other costs
Internet connection: £25 a month
Expenses (heating, lighting, phone etc): £200 a month
Car lease: £250 a month
Car fuel: £50
Average cost price for CDs/vinyls = £5.50 (estimated)

NOTE: Postage and packing to be paid by purchaser

■ *Ali's notepad*

1(P) **a)** What items contribute to Ali's fixed costs?
b) What are Ali's total fixed costs per month for each type of store? ***(P2 part)***

2(P) List the items that contribute to Ali's variable costs. ***(P2 part)***

3(P) Ali aims to sell his stock for an average price of £11 per item. Assuming his variable costs average £6 per item, find the break-even point to calculate the approximate number of items he would need to sell each month before he made a profit.

For his first option, draw a break-even chart and allow for maximum sales of 200 items; for his second and third options, use the break-even formula to find the answers:

a) if he had a basic store
b) if he had a featured store
c) if he had an anchor store. ***(P2)***

4(M) Ali has decided to operate an anchor store. Demonstrate how each of the following events would affect his break-even point.

a) Ali buys a box of old vinyl records cheaply in an auction and discovers it contains some very rare items. He reckons that these will increase his average selling price to £15 per item.

b) eBay increases the subscription price of its anchor stores to £300 a month. ***(M1)***

Grading tip

Demonstrate means to provide evidence to support your arguments. In this case reworking a chart or formula would prove the case you are making.

3.3 Preparing a cash flow forecast

Fact file

Cash flow relates to all the money flowing into and out of the business. All businesses want their cash inflows to be greater than their outflows.

What is cash flow?

Cash flow relates to the amount of money received and spent in a given period. Cash flow problems occur when the amount spent is greater than the amount received. You may have cash flow problems from time to time – especially just before pay day – when you are short of cash to buy or do what you want. Unless you want to get into debt you need to reduce your spending until you get more money.

Businesses can also have cash flow problems. This may be because they have spent too much or because some people who owe them money have not paid their bills when they should. The business then does not have enough money in the bank to pay the bills it has received from its suppliers.

Businesses use **cash flow forecasting** to predict how much money they should have in the bank at any particular time, usually at the end of a month. This means listing and adding up all their expected **cash inflows**. This is the money the business expects to receive and pay into its bank account. It then needs to add up its **cash outflows**. This is the money the business expects to pay to other people or businesses. The difference between these two figures is the **cash balance**. Every business will always aim for a positive cash balance, which occurs when inflows are greater than outflows.

Did you know?

Cash flow does not just apply to cash in the form of coins but all types of payments, such as credit or debit card payments, cheques and electronic transfers.

Activity

Two major events in the year cause cash flow problems for most people. What are they and why do they cause problems?

Did you know?

A business that wants to borrow money temporarily may prefer an overdraft rather than a loan. This means it spends more than the balance in its bank account. This must be authorised by the bank in advance, otherwise the interest rate is much higher.

Cash inflows

Cash inflows are money received by the business for a variety of reasons.

Capital

This is the name given to money that the owner puts into the business at the start. It represents savings or borrowings invested to pay for the start-up costs you read about in section 3.1.

The owner may decide to boost the capital by reinvesting some of the profits into the business at the end of the financial year. For that reason, you are only likely to find capital mentioned in a cash flow forecast about once or twice a year.

Sales

Sales to private individuals and/or other firms are the major source of income for all commercial businesses. A voluntary organisation will receive most of its income through donations and most public sector organisations will obtain theirs from government grants or taxation.

Loans

These are amounts of money the business has borrowed, usually from a bank or other financial institution. The business will pay interest on the loan and will want to negotiate a rate that is as low as possible. The repayments as well as the interest must both be taken into account when calculating future cash outflows.

Activity

If you borrowed £5,000 at 8 per cent interest to be repaid in a year, what would be the amount of each monthly repayment?

Activity

Identify the sources of cash inflows received by your school or college and compare these with those of any businesses where members of your group are employed.

Cash outflows

Businesses spend money in many different ways, again depending upon the main purpose of the organisation. Typical payments include the following items.

Key terms

Cash inflows are the sums of money entering a business's bank account.

Cash outflows are the sums of money leaving a business's bank account.

Purchases

Manufacturing businesses will buy raw materials; retail firms will buy stock for resale. All organisations buy consumable items such as office stationery and cleaning materials. Capital items are more expensive goods which are expected to last for much longer, such as computers, business vehicles and production equipment. Business services also need to be paid for, from legal advice to window cleaning.

Loan repayments

These must be included for any loan agreements that have been made.

Wages

The wage bill for the staff must be included in addition to associated costs, such as the employer's contribution to National Insurance payments and any bonuses or commissions that may be paid.

Regular and irregular inflows and outflows

Some inflows and outflows of cash are regular whereas others are not. All businesses prefer regular payments because this makes it much easier to plan and predict cash flow. For this reason, many firms, such as electricity and gas providers, offer customers a discount if they sign up to pay by direct debit – which is a regular payment system – precisely because this gives the firm a regular flow of income.

Activity

As a group, identify some of the cash outflows of your school or college as well as those of any business where members of your group are employed.

Fact file

Some inflows and outflows are regular, others are not. Businesses far prefer regular payments (in or out) because these are easier to predict and plan.

As with inflows, some payments are routine and can easily be forecast. They include routine purchases, regular loan repayments and the monthly wage bill.

In any situation where inflows or outflows are irregular then the timing is critical. A large annual payment or major purchase must be planned in advance or it can cause havoc to cash flow. This is particularly the case if inflows are also irregular, as you will see under seasonal businesses below.

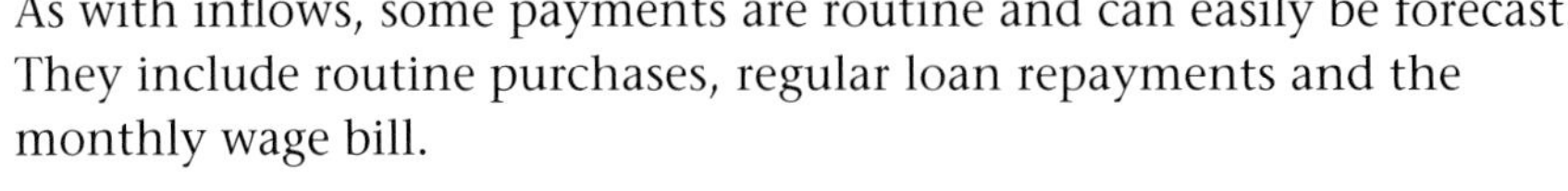

Activity

For your personal cash flow, identify four regular inflows or outflows and four irregular ones. What is the impact of a large unexpected outflow on your cash flow – such as a present for a friend's birthday you nearly forgot?

Did you know?

*A **bad debt** is a debt which is never paid. Some small traders have gone bankrupt because a customer did not pay them a major debt.*

The timing of inflows and outflows

The timing of inflows and outflows is absolutely critical. Even a highly profitable business can struggle if inflows suddenly dip at the same time as a very large bill is received. There are several events which can affect the timing of inflows and outflows. The most common ones are identified below.

Late credit payments

Virtually all businesses offer credit to their business customers. This means that they are allowed to pay for the goods a few weeks after they have received them. The time allowed and the amount of credit may vary depending upon the customer's **credit rating**. This will be higher for customers who regularly place large orders and/or for prompt payers. The usual procedure is to issue an invoice shortly after the goods have been despatched and to expect payment within the next 28 days.

Many customers will pay promptly but some will not. The problem is made worse if some late payers owe large amounts of money. This can leave the business seriously short of cash. Because of this, some firms offer discounts to encourage customers to pay promptly and all businesses send reminders to customers if payments are overdue. They may stop supplies until an outstanding bill is paid. The situation is trickier, however, if the late payer is a large business which the smaller supplier does not want to pressurise in case it loses future orders as a result.

Seasonal businesses

These receive most of their inflows over a short period of time, yet have to make payments all year round. Obvious examples are theme parks such as Alton Towers and Blackpool Pleasure Beach, which are closed during the winter. They still need to find the money to pay business rates and wages to their permanent staff. Strict cash flow management is vital for these types of industries, so that income earned during the busy period is invested for meeting routine bills all year round as well as for capital expenditure (see below).

Activity

As a group, identify six other seasonal businesses whose inflows fluctuate throughout the year.

Capital expenditure

This is spending on large items which are expected to last for some time – such as investments in new rides by Alton Towers. Other examples include production equipment, new vehicles, extending the premises, refitting a retail store or upgrading the computer network. These are 'one-off' large items of expenditure yet most inflows are smaller and more regular. The business must therefore plan which items it can afford, as well as the best time to make the purchase.

Activity

People buy consumable and capital items, too. Identify two expensive capital items you own. How difficult do you find it to save to buy such items?

Cash balances

The cash balance is the amount remaining in the bank account at the end of a specific period, when all payments have been received and all the bills have been paid. You will see how this works by reading about Simon's business, Decorblock.

Income and expenditure per period

Decorblock specialises in laying block paving for pathways and drives. During October Simon has received various payments which he has paid into the bank. These amount to £10,000. Simon has also made several payments for items like raw materials and staff wages. These total £9,000. Simon uses these figures to draw up a simple cash flow statement.

Did you know?

Cheques paid into an account are only 'cleared' for spending when the money has been received from the other person's account, which takes about three working days.

Fact file

*A positive cash flow increases money in the bank, whereas a negative one decreases it. The key to a positive cash flow is the **timing** of payments – both into and out of the business.*

Key terms

The ***opening balance*** is the amount of money in a business's bank account at the start of the period.

The ***closing balance*** is the amount of money in a business's bank account at the end of the period.

Income per period is all the cash inflows during that period.

Expenditure per period is all the cash outflows during that period.

If you subtract the opening bank balance at the start of a cash flow forecast from the closing bank balance at the end, this gives you the forecast profit for the business.

Summary cash flow statement – October

Income for period (cash inflows)	£10,000
Expenditure for period (cash outflow)	£9,000
Net cash flow	£1,000

The figure he has calculated, net cash flow, is found by deducting expenditure from income. In October Simon received £1,000 more than he has paid out and this is called a **positive cash flow**.

Opening and closing balance

Simon must also take account of the money he had in the bank at the beginning of the period – in this case on the first of October. On that day, he had £3,000 in his account. This is called the **opening balance**. Simon then checks the balance on the last day of the month, called the **closing balance**, and sees that it is £4,000 because it now includes the £1,000 net cash flow for October. Finally, he completes his cash flow statement to make sure that all the figures agree.

Completed summary cash flow statement – October

Income for period (cash inflows)	£10,000
Expenditure for period (cash outflows)	£9,000
Net cash flow	£1,000

Monthly summary

Opening bank balance	£3,000
Net cash flow	£1,000
Closing bank balance	£4,000

Simon is pleased because he has more money in the bank at the end of the month than at the beginning. This is because he had a positive cash flow.

View 1: Owners haven't time to constantly watch their cash flow. They should spend their time maintaining and improving the business.

View 2: So long as an owner monitors cash flow, the business will always be healthy.

With which viewpoint do you agree – and why?

Copy Simon's summary layout to produce cash flow statements for four businesses:

1. *Mac's Motors: Opening balance £8,000, income £40,000, expenditure £37,000*
2. *Happy Holidays: Opening balance £50,000, income £200,000, expenditure £180,000*
3. *First Features: Opening balance £22,500, income £164,300, expenditure £158,360*
4. *Creative Works: Opening balance £16,429, income £287,987, expenditure £285,783.*

Cash flow statements

Cash flow statements are normally produced in a little more detail than the summary statements above. Simon's full statement for October is shown below.

The most important figures on a cash flow statement are those on the last line. For that reason you will often hear it referred to as the ***bottom line****. This is the line that financial managers look at first.*

SIMON'S CASH FLOW STATEMENT FOR OCTOBER

	October **£**
Income from sales	10,000
Expenditure	
Blocks	4,000
Sand	1,000
Diesel fuel	500
Wages	3,000
Miscellaneous	500
Subtotal of expenditure	9,000
Net cash flow	1,000
Monthly Summary	
Opening bank balance	3,000
Net cash flow	1,000
Closing bank balance	4,000

■ *Simon's cash flow statement for October*

All the main headings in this statement are identical to the summary. The only difference is that the total expenditure figure has been broken down into various items – such as his purchases and the wages he paid. This expanded version of the statement is useful since Simon has more information to help him understand what is happening. This type of chart is also used to **forecast** cash flow.

Now look at the statement below in which Simon has added his figures for November. You will see that Simon had a negative cash flow. In other words, more money left his business than went in. This was mainly due to a fall in income. However, he also bought more bricks and spent more on wages. He knows that these two increases were due to some extra work which he undertook. Finally, you should see that the closing bank balance for October has become the opening balance for November.

Spreadsheets are an ideal way of constructing cash flow forecasts because you can easily change the figures to see the effects of possible changes in inflows and outflows.

Activity

Create Simon's cash flow statement for December when his income was £7,000 and he spent £3,000 on blocks, £750 on sand, £400 on diesel fuel, £3,000 on wages and £400 on miscellaneous items.

Has his situation improved since November? To what extent do you think Simon's business may be affected by seasonal factors? Give a reason for your answer.

SIMON'S CASH FLOW STATEMENT

	October £	November £
Income from sales	10,000	6,000
Expenditure		
Blocks	4,000	4,500
Sand	1,000	1,000
Diesel fuel	500	500
Wages	3,000	3,500
Miscellaneous	500	500
Subtotal of expenditure	9,000	10,000
Net cash flow	1,000	–4,000
Monthly Summary		
Opening bank balance	3,000	4,000
Net cash flow	1,000	–4,000
Closing bank balance	4,000	0

■ *Simon's cash flow statement for two months*

Cash flow forecasting

Cash flow forecasting means preparing a cash flow statement for the future with predicted inflows and outflows. This is always easier to do for an established business because the managers have more experience and knowledge on which to base their decisions. They also need to consider future demand for their goods and any specific plans for the business.

They can also take appropriate action to try to ensure that all the income is used wisely – such as moving surplus cash balances to an account which pays better interest, or planning for payments of any major capital items to be made at that time.

They can see which periods may be problematic and take appropriate action. This may mean reducing expenditure temporarily, arranging with the bank to operate an overdraft for a short time, or chasing up any outstanding debts that are owed by customers more vigorously.

The business must obviously monitor its cash flow, investigate any differences between the forecast figures and actual inflows and outflows and take prompt action if this is needed.

You can see how this works when Nikita, who runs a business selling shoes and trainers, decides to forecast her cash flow for the first six months of the next year. The Christmas period was good for sales and Nikita plans to re-stock the store room ready for the busy summer period. She sits down with a pen and paper and produces the figures given below.

Did you know?

Cash flow statements are a bit like weather forecasts – the further they are in the future the more likely they are to be wrong! This is because more can happen to change the situation in the meantime.

NIKITA'S CASH FLOW STATEMENT

	January £	February £	March £	April £	May £	June £
Income from sales	50,000	48,000	50,000	55,000	58,000	60,000
Expenditure						
Shoes	45,000	30,000	25,000	20,000	22,000	20,000
Trainers	22,000	20,000	15,000	14,000	14,000	13,000
Wages	5,000	5,000	5,000	5,000	5,000	5,000
Rent	1,000	1,000	1,000	1,000	1,000	1,000
Miscellaneous	500	500	500	500	500	500
Subtotal of expenditure						
Net cash flow						
Monthly Summary						
Opening bank balance	20,000					
Net cash flow						
Closing bank balance						

■ *Nikita's cash flow forecast (1)*

Activity

Produce a cash flow statement using Nikita's figures and calculate her total expenditure and net cash flow. Nikita has an opening bank balance of £20,000 at the start of January. Prepare her monthly summary, identify the months where she has a negative cash flow and suggest the main reasons for this

Fact file

Many businesses produce a cash flow forecast for 12 months into the future. They will amend it from time to time as circumstances change.

Cash flow and problem solving

Nikita has a problem because in some months her closing balances are negative. If she does not take action about these she must obtain a loan or overdraft to cover this amount, or more, to allow for the unexpected. Nikita, however, would prefer not to let her account balance to fall below zero. She therefore decides to reduce her stock purchases in January and February.

Look at the revised forecast below and compare it with Nikita's first attempt. The amounts of money for shoe purchases in January and trainers in February have been reduced. The result of this is that the closing bank balance in January is now positive and in February it is zero. Nikita is much happier with this because she no longer needs to have an overdraft.

Did you know?

An overdraft is normally cheaper than a loan because bank charges are only paid on the actual amount owing on any day.

NIKITA'S CASH FLOW STATEMENT

	January £	February £	March £	April £	May £	June £
Income from sales	50,000	48,000	50,000	55,000	58,000	60,000
Expenditure						
Shoes	35,000	30,000	25,000	20,000	22,000	20,000
Trainers	22,000	18,000	15,000	14,000	14,000	13,000
Wages	5,000	5,000	5,000	5,000	5,000	5,000
Rent	1,000	1,000	1,000	1,000	1,000	1,000
Miscellaneous	500	500	500	500	500	500
Subtotal of expenditure	63,500	54,500	46,500	40,500	42,500	39,500
Net cash flow	–13,500	–6,500	3,500	14,500	15,500	20,500
Monthly Summary						
Opening bank balance	20,000	6,500	0	3,500	18,000	33,500
Net cash flow	–13,500	–6,500	3,500	14,500	15,500	20,500
Closing bank balance	6,500	0	3,500	18,000	33,500	54,000

■ *Nikita's cash flow forecast (2)*

Did you know?

The main cause of business failure is through cash flow problems. Danger areas include:

- *allowing too many customers to owe money*
- *being too dependent upon one or two customers*
- *borrowing too much*
- *buying or spending too much*
- *not forecasting changes that might affect the business.*

Activity

How sensible is Nikita to plan to have a zero balance in February? Suggest two possible problems with this.

Talking point

View 1: If a plumber insists on customers paying only in cash and pays for materials in cash, the business is bound to be profitable.

View 2: If the plumber does this he/she will lose customers who don't want to go to the bank and carry large amounts of cash.

With which viewpoint do you agree – and why?

Over to you

1 a) *Use the following information to produce a cash flow forecast for three months from January to March. The figures are for Garden Features, a small business making garden ornaments.*

Item/month	January £	February £	March £
Sales income	20,000	18,000	22,000
Cement	2,000	3,000	2,500
Sand	1,000	1,000	900
Wages	14,000	15,000	14,000
Paint	500	500	500
Miscellaneous	300	200	200
Opening bank balance	3,000		

■ *Garden Features cash flow forecast*

b) *When you have completed the chart, identify the month in which the cash flow is negative. Then examine the chart and say which figures have caused the problem by comparing them with those for January.*

2 *Tired of city life, Karen and Ken have fulfilled a long-term dream by buying a small hotel in Devon. They have invested money, time and energy in refurbishing this over the last three months and plan to open for business in May. They have now decided to forecast their cash flow for the next twelve months, but haven't much idea how to do this. You have offered to help.*

a) *They have noted down the following items. Put these into the correct order and carry out the required calculations for the first month – May.*

Closing bank balance; income from reservations £8,000; opening bank balance £2,500; expenditure £6,000; net cash flow (appears twice); monthly summary.

b) *Identify for them the main benefits of subdividing expenditure into separate items in a cash flow forecast.*

c) *Why might a small seaside hotel suffer from irregular cash inflows and how might this affect their cash flow over the year?*

d) *Ken seems to think all he needs to do is to record his income and payments and then work out his actual cash flow at the end of every month or two. Is this true? Give a reason for your answer.*

Case study Assessment practice

You learned about Ali's online music business on page 107. Having worked out the break-even figures, Ali is confident that the business can make a reasonable profit.

Ali's next step is to carry out a cash flow forecast, since he knows that the cash flow must be good if he is to be successful. He has jotted some more information onto his notepad.

OPENING BANK BALANCE: £2,000

FORECAST INCOME (per month)
Jan – June: £4,000 July and August: £2,000;
Sept – Dec; £6,000

REGULAR PAYMENTS (per month)
Internet connection £25
Expenses (heating, lighting, phone etc) £200
Car lease £250
Car fuel £50
Purchase of stock (DVDs and vinyls) £2,000 Jan – July
Purchase of stock (" " ") £3,000 Aug – Dec

EXCEPTIONAL PAYMENTS
Pay tax – 31 January and 31 July (£3,000 each time)
Accountant's bill – June (about £400)

WISH LIST
Upgrade own computer system – £2,000 (September?)

■ *Ali's notepad*

1(P) Use Ali's information to prepare his cash flow forecast for 12 months from January to December. At this stage, do not include his computer upgrade. ***(P1)***

2(M) Help Ali to understand the implications of cash inflows and outflows by analysing your forecast and answering the following questions.

- **a)** Give your comments on his cash flow figures for each month, including the main reasons why each one is positive or negative.
- **b)** Calculate the forecast profit for the business for the twelve months.
- **c)** Comment on any trends in his closing bank balance figures.
- **d)** When would you advise Ali to upgrade his computer? Give your reasons for choosing this time.
- **e)** If Ali found that in reality his sales were much lower in summer than predicted but had the potential to be far higher in November and December, if he could supply the stock, what implications would this have for his business? ***(M2)***

3(D) Help Ali to see how cash flows contribute to managing business finances by answering the following questions.

- **a)** In June, Ali has been running his business for six months and his cash flow has been exactly as planned. At the end of the month he receives a phone call from a friend telling him about a private collection of vinyls for sale. The price is £15,000 but Ali thinks that he can sell them for £50,000. What should he do and why?
- **b)** Ali believes businesses are only successful if entrepreneurs take risks and takes advantage of a similar offer in July. When you ask him how this has affected his cash flow he says he has been too busy to update it. Summarise the dangers of Ali's approach by evaluating the role of cash flow in managing business finances. ***(D1 part)***

Grading tip

Your analysis must prove that you understand what the figures mean, as well as how they relate to each other and their implications for the business.

When you evaluate you must form a judgement and then give evidence to support your opinion.

3.4 Ways of recording financial transactions

Financial transactions take place every time a customer buys goods or services, or the business makes a purchase, or pays staff wages. Each transaction affects the amount of money held by the business and the potential profit (or loss) that can be made. It is therefore important to record every financial transaction, so that these can be analysed to give managers up-to-date information on the performance of the business. They can then take immediate action if a problem occurs.

Did you know?

Records of financial transactions are used to calculate actual cash flow, which is then compared to forecasted cash flow.

Business transactions and business documents

On page 110 you learned that most firms allow their business customers a period of credit. In other words, buyers do not pay for goods immediately. This means that the transaction process can take a month or more from start to finish. At each stage a document is involved. It begins with a purchase order being sent from a customer to a supplier and is only completed when the customer's payment arrives in the supplier's bank account.

Activity

You participate in several transactions every week. List six recent ones.

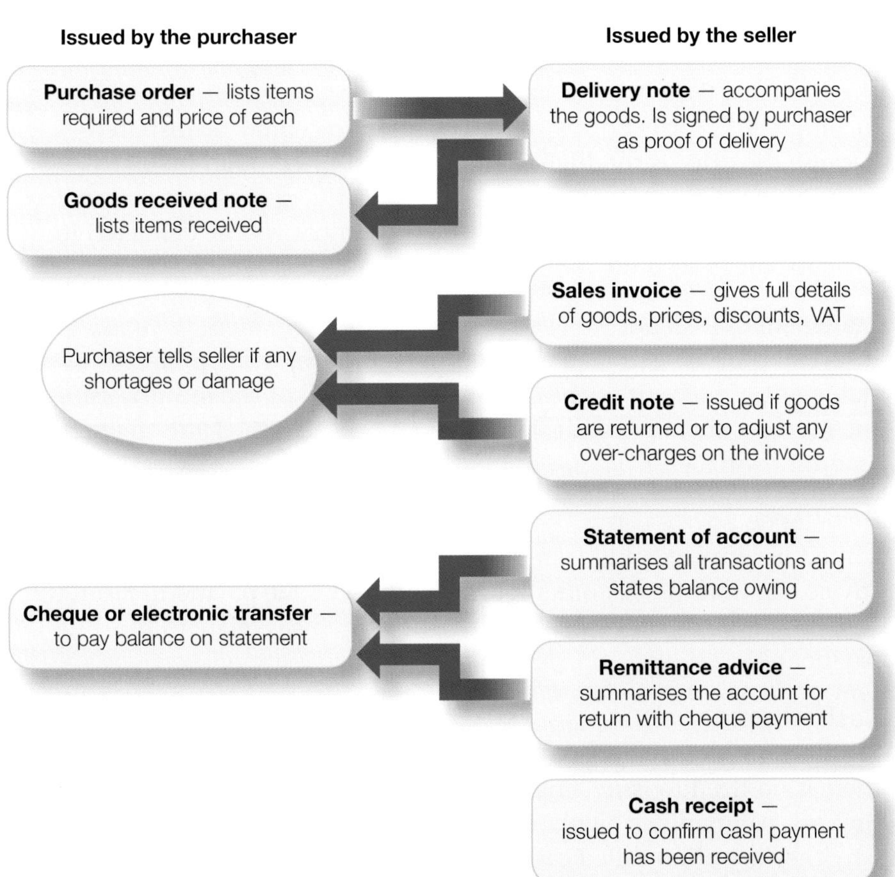

Several documents are used to record the various stages of the process. They are as follows.

Purchase order

In business, every item must be officially ordered and each order must be signed by someone authorised to make purchases for the business. A purchase order is the official order for goods and lists the items required. These may be sent by fax, post or electronically.

Delivery note

The supplier sends the goods to the customer accompanied by a delivery note, which lists the items sent. The customer signs this as proof of delivery and keeps a copy for his or her records.

Goods received note

The person who checks the goods completes a goods received note (GRN), which is sent to the accounts department as proof that the goods have been received. It provides a record of the actual goods received and their condition on arrival.

Did you know?

Cheque use almost halved between 1990 and 2004. APACS, the UK Payments Association, forecasts that by 2014 only 1 in 25 regular bills will be paid by cheque. Since 2001 most businesses pay their trade suppliers by automated payments.

Invoice

The supplier sends an invoice to the customer stating the amount of money owed. This is a bill for payment. When the customer receives the invoice it is checked carefully to make sure that it matches the GRN and the prices match those quoted on the purchase order.

Credit note

Occasionally, there may be a problem because the goods supplied are incomplete, incorrect or damaged. Or an invoice may be disputed because the price is too high. If goods are returned or an invoice is incorrect then a credit note is issued. This is the opposite of an invoice and confirms that the amount on the credit note will be deducted from the customer's account.

Statement of account

If several transactions take place during a month, the supplier sends a statement of account to the customer at the end of the month, listing all the invoices and any credit notes that have been issued and the total amount owing.

Remittance advice slip

Sometimes invoices and statements are accompanied by a remittance advice slip that the customer returns with a cheque payment. From the slip, the supplier can easily identify which invoices relate to the payment.

Activity

Collect six cash receipts you receive over the next few days and list the information they contain.

Cash receipts

Most business customers pay by cheque or electronically. In both cases, there is no need to issue a receipt. These are only given to acknowledge the cash payments, which are rarely made by business customers. This is why they are often called cash receipts.

The content of financial documents

Each financial document records key facts about the transaction. If you compare documents from different organisations, you will often find that although they have similar headings and information, this is in a different order.

Below you can see the main information that is recorded by following the transaction when Speedlink Ltd, a distribution company, buys some office consumables from a local supplier, SuperStat Ltd.

The purchase order form The first stage is for Speedlink staff to complete an official purchase order. This contains the following information:

Speedlink Ltd

Premier Industrial Park LEEDS L19 8JS
Tel: 0113 238 3610 VAT Reg No 846/3822/98
Fax: 0111 238 4567
Website: www.speedlink.co.uk Email: service@speedlink.co.uk

PURCHASE ORDER

To:
SuperStat Ltd
17 Canal Road
Armley
LEEDS
LS12 2JN

Supplier No: 271
Official order no: 05/703
Date: 31 January 200-

Please supply:

Quantity	Description	Item code	Unit price
50 packs	A4 white printer paper	PP1003	£3.80
10	Endys inkjet cartridges – black	ED2839	£21.50
5	Copyrite toner cartridges	CR6028	£135.50

Delivery: As soon as possible

Signed: Keith Smith Designation: Office Manager

Suppliers should note that orders are only valid if signed by a designated executive of the organisation.

A ***purchase order form*** is an official document listing requirements and authorising supplier to provide goods.

A ***delivery note*** is a document sent by supplier with goods, lists quantities but not prices.

A ***goods received note (GRN)*** is completed by some organisations to list deliveries received.

An ***invoice*** is the bill for the goods or services provided.

Details of business transactions involving the buying and selling of goods are recorded on a series of business documents. The first document in the sequence is the official purchase order.

- Speedlink's address, telephone and other contact information – this is needed so that SuperStat knows where to deliver the goods and send the invoice and how to make contact if there are any queries.
- The VAT (value added tax) registration number – which is a legal requirement if the business is VAT registered and sells goods on which VAT is levied. Businesses that sell more than a certain value of goods a year (£60,000 in 2006) must be registered for VAT and add VAT to their bills.
- SuperStat's name and address.
- SuperStat's supplier number. This may be allocated by the computer database to approved suppliers.
- Order number – every order is allocated a unique number, so that each transaction can be identified. This number will also appear on subsequent documents relating to the same transaction.
- Date of order – this is important in case there is a query or dispute later.
- Order details – this gives the quantity, description, item code and price of each item. A 'unit' is the quantity normally supplied as listed in the catalogue (e.g. a pack, box, or single item). The supplier needs to ensure that all product descriptions match the codes and that the prices are correct and up to date.
- Delivery date – this would be important if Speedlink wanted the goods by a specific date.
- Signature and designation – the purchase order commits the business to pay for the goods, so it is important that the order is signed and/or authorised by someone in authority. For large value orders, a senior manager usually has to authorise the purchase.

Did you know?

In many firms, staff can only buy goods from suppliers on a 'preferred list'. These have been approved because of their competitive prices and good service.

Activity

If anyone could make out an order in a company, or people could order from any supplier, what problems could this cause? Discuss your ideas as a group.

Delivery note When the goods are delivered, the driver asks the person who accepts them at Speedlink to sign a delivery note. He leaves one copy and takes the other copies back to SuperStat as proof that the goods have been delivered. The main information recorded on this document is as follows:

- SuperStat's contact details
- the customer number that SuperStat has allocated to Speedlink (again usually linked to the database or accounting system)

- the number of the invoice that will follow
- the method of delivery. This is useful when a delivery service is used. If there are any problems, the carrier may have to be contacted
- the signature of the person who receives the goods. The driver will not wait for the goods to be unpacked and checked before they are signed for, but if the package is damaged then this fact should be noted on the delivery note.

Activity

If you received a damaged package and signed for it, what is the next thing you should do – and why? Discuss your ideas as a group.

SuperStat Ltd

17 Canal Road Armley LEEDS L12 2JN
www.superstat.co.uk
Tel: 0111 238 4567

VAT NUMBER 640 2923 96

DELIVERY NOTE

To:
Speedlink Ltd
Premier Industrial Park
LEEDS
L19 8JS

Delivery address (if different):

Date 5 February 200-

Your order No	Customer Account No	Despatch date	Invoice No	Delivery method
05/703	12704	5 February 200-	16702/06	Own van

Item code	Quantity	Description
PP1003	50 packs	A4 white printer paper
ED2839	10	Endys inkjet cartridges – black
CR6028	5	Copyrite toner cartridges

Thank you for your order. Please retain this delivery note for your records

Received in good condition (or comment here)

Goods OK

Signed H Patel Date 5/2/200-

Please print name HAMID PATEL

White copy: customer
Yellow copy: driver
Pink copy: SuperStat Ltd

Check the GRN against the delivery note on page 123 and identify the differences between these two documents.

Goods received note (GRN) The GRN is similar to the delivery note but this time it is completed by the purchaser. It is the formal record to confirm that the goods have been received. It is only completed after the goods have been unpacked and checked. Any problems or discrepancies are noted on the GRN. The accounts department will check the GRN before they pay for the goods.

If you buy goods online or by mail order then they will arrive with a document enclosed. This may be a delivery note, advice note, parcel summary or invoice – depending upon the firm you have bought from. Some documents include a delivery reference and even the packer's name.

Speedlink Ltd

GOODS RECEIVED NOTE

Supplier: SuperStat Ltd GRN No: 05/91

GRN date: 06/02/200-

Supplier A/c No: 271 Delivery Note date: 05/02/200-

Carrier: SuperStat Van Checker: Jim Howe

Order No	Quantity ordered	Quantity delivered	Description	Tick box or enter details if goods damaged or discrepancy identified
05/703	50 packs	50 packs	A4 white printer paper	✔
"	10	10	Endys inkjet cartridges – black	✔
"	5	5	Copyrite toner cartridges	One cartridge damaged

White copy: Purchases file
Pink copy: Accounts

Invoices The signed delivery note is proof to SuperStat that the goods arrived safely. They then send an invoice to Speedlink requesting payment. This is shown below.

The information on the invoice can be divided into four types as given below.

- Standard information. This includes the names and addresses of the seller and buyer and other contact details.
- Information copied from earlier documents. This includes all the reference numbers, product codes, descriptions and prices.

Fact file

After the seller receives the signed delivery note, the invoice will be sent. This shows the amount now owing by the buyer.

SuperStat Ltd

17 Canal Road Armley LEEDS L12 2JN

www.superstat.co.uk VAT NUMBER 640 2923 96
Tel: 0111 238 4567

INVOICE

To:
Speedlink Ltd
Premier Industrial Park
LEEDS
L19 8JS

Your order No	Customer Account No	Date/tax point	Invoice No
05/703	12704	05/02/200-	16702/06

Item code	Quantity	Description	Item Price £	Net value £
PP1003	50 packs	A4 white printer paper	3.80	190.00
ED2839	10	Endys inkjet cartridges – black	21.50	215.00
CR6028	5	Copyrite toner cartridges	135.50	677.50
			TOTAL	1082.50
			VAT 17.5%	189.44
			TOTAL DUE	1271.94

Terms: 28 days
Carriage paid
E & OE

White copy: customer
Yellow copy: sales
Pink copy: accounts

Did you know?

E & OE on an invoice stands for 'errors and omissions excepted'. This means that if an error is made, such as asking for too little money, the seller still has the right to full payment.

Activity

Check the calculations on the invoice. Are they correct? Do the prices match those on the purchase order? Why do you think businesses make checks like this before they pay invoices?

Did you know?

As a customer, you do not have to accept a credit note if you return faulty goods and can insist on a refund. You do not have this right if a shop agrees to exchange something just because you don't like it!

- The calculations. This is the main difference between the invoice and earlier documents, because this records the amount now owing to SuperStat.
- The 'terms' of the invoice. In this case payment is requested within 28 days of the date of the invoice.

Credit notes Most transactions go smoothly but sometimes problems occur, such as despatch of the wrong goods or goods are damaged in transit. In this case, the goods would be returned and the purchaser would not expect to pay for them. Similarly, an error may mean the customer is over-charged on the invoice in which case an adjustment is required.

SuperStat Ltd

17 Canal Road Armley LEEDS 12 2JN

www.superstat.co.uk VAT NUMBER 640 2923 96
Tel: 0111 238 4567

CREDIT NOTE

To:
Speedlink Ltd
Premier Industrial Park
LEEDS
L19 8JS

Date 12 February 200-

Your returns ref	Customer Account No	Date/tax point	Invoice No	Credit note No
05/703	12704	05/02/200-	16702/06	704

Item code	Quantity	Description	Item Price £	Net value £
CR6028	1	Copyrite toner cartridge	135.50	135.50
			TOTAL	135.50
			VAT 17.5%	23.71
			REFUND DUE	159.21

Reason for return:
Cartridge case damaged.

White copy: customer
Pink copy: sales
Yellow copy: accounts

Businesses do this by issuing a credit note. This records the amount the customer is now owed by the supplier. In the example below you should see that:

- the details relating to the transaction are included, so that the content of the note can be connected with the original order and subsequent invoice
- the reason for the credit is given
- the amount to be credited is calculated and clearly stated.

Activity

Calculate the amount of the credit note if Speedlink had **also** *returned 5 packs of paper, because they were crumpled and unusable.*

Statements of account Business customers do not pay a supplier every time they receive an invoice. Instead, they pay for a series of transactions made over a period, usually once a month. As a reminder, and to summarise the transactions, the supplier sends a statement of account. This lists all invoices and credit notes issued, and any payments made, during that period. An example of a statement is shown opposite. The main information recorded is as follows:

- any money still owing from last month by the customer
- this month's invoices sent to the customer. These are in the debit column
- payments made by the customer during the month and any credit notes issued. These are in the credit column
- the amount now owed by the customer.

A remittance advice form is attached. This is normally returned with cheque payments to enable the recipient to link the payment to the correct account.

Fact file

The statement of account is sent out at the end of the month and summarises all transactions and payments made between buyer and seller during that period.

Activity

The right-hand column of the statement has a running balance that changes every time another entry is made. Check that you agree with the figures in the example.

Did you know?

Remittance advice forms are often sent as email attachments, to tell the recipient about an electronic payment that is being made.

Cash receipt If you pay for goods by cheque, debit or credit card the information is recorded on documents issued by the bank or card company, so you do not need another record. If you pay by cash, the situation is different because the receipt is the only proof that you paid for the goods. In business, receipts are mainly necessary on two occasions:

- when staff need to reclaim the money from their employer (see page 131)
- when staff receive money from a customer and do not have access to a cash register or laptop to record the payment.

Did you know?

Any statement should be checked to make sure it is correct. This includes bank statements and credit card statements that list all purchases and payments made during the month and state the amount now owing.

Activity

Use the cash receipts you collected (see page 120) to identify the key information that is recorded that proves the transaction took place.

Key terms

A ***credit note*** is the opposite of an invoice and is issued to reduce the amount owing because of a fault or discrepancy.

A ***statement of account*** is a summary of the transactions and payments over a period.

A ***remittance advice*** is a notice of payment, either attached to an invoice or sent electronically to accompany payment.

A ***cash receipt*** is a document that confirms receipt of a cash payment.

SuperStat Ltd

17 Canal Road Armley LEEDS L12 2JN

www.superstat.co.uk
Tel: 0111 238 4567

VAT NUMBER 640 2923 96

STATEMENT OF ACCOUNT

To:
Speedlink Ltd
Premier Industrial Park
LEEDS
L19 8JS

Customer A/c No 12704

Credit limit £10,000

Date 28 February 200-

Date	Details	Debit (£)	Credit (£)	Balance (£)
1 Feb	Balance Owing			1502.14
5 Feb	Invoice 16702/06	1271.94		2774.08
10 Feb	Payment received		1502.14	1271.94
12 Feb	Credit Note 704		159.21	1112.73

AMOUNT NOW DUE: £1112.73

REMITTANCE ADVICE

From Speedlink Ltd **Customer A/c No** 12704
Statement date: 28 February 200-

Amount enclosed .... Cheque No ....

Your ref .... Payment date ....

All cheques should be made payable to SuperStat Ltd.

Activity

Compare the purchase and sales documents shown here with those you have at home and those received and issued by your school or college. Your tutor may be able to obtain examples for you to see.

Recording financial transactions

Business documents are one way of recording financial transactions – but they are not the only way. Some businesses – for example, a coffee shop or newsagent – deal mainly with individuals who pay by cash. Others, such as a hotel, may receive mainly debit or credit card payments. They will use different methods of recording the transactions. One basic choice is whether to record the transaction manually or electronically.

Manual and electronic recording

Today, most transactions are recorded electronically because they are processed either by an electronic cash register (see page 133) or by computer. Even people who receive payments in a customer's home – such as service engineers – are now more likely to record the transaction on a laptop than carry a receipt book with them.

The benefit of recording transactions electronically means that any related documents are printed automatically – such as itemised receipts issued by a supermarket. In addition, any electronic system is usually linked to the firm's computer system. This means that the information is immediately entered into the relevant accounts (see page 130) and managers can obtain reports that summarise this information – such as total income, sales or expenditure over a period and profit to date. Additional links to a stock control package mean that new stock levels are calculated every time a sale is made.

Manual records are only kept by businesses that would not find it worthwhile to buy a cash register or use a computer system. An estate agent may act as an agent for rental property, only collect a few rents each month and find it easier to record these manually. A taxi driver will issue manual receipts to passengers who want to reclaim the money from their employer and tradesmen who deal in small cash amounts, such as window cleaners, are also likely to keep manual records.

Even the smallest business has to keep financial records because the owner has to complete a self-assessment tax return for Her Majesty's Revenue and Customs (HMRC). Failure to do this by the required date results in a fine and other penalties.

Activity

HMRC are more likely to be suspicious of traders who deal in cash than those who receive all their payments electronically or by cheque. Can you suggest why?

Day books

Day books are used by some businesses to summarise transactions before the information is transferred to the main accounts (see below). The most common types of day books areas follows.

- **Sales Day Book** – which records all sales made to date from invoices issued by the business.
- **Sales Returns Day Book** – which records any goods returned from customers, again by date. This lists all the credit notes issued by the business.

Day books are useful if there is a query, you need to find a transaction and you do not know the name of the customer. You can search by date and/or amount of payment instead. They record key information in relation to purchases and sales by date.

- **Purchases Day Book** – which records all purchases by date and matches invoices for raw materials or stock received by the business.
- **Purchase Returns Day Book** – which records any goods returned to a supplier (e.g. because of a fault), again by date. This matches any credit notes received by the business.

Below is a sample page from a Sales Day Book which shows that the following information has been recorded:

- the date an invoice is issued
- the name of the customer. Alternatively, the customer account reference could be recorded
- the number of the invoice sent to the customer
- the total amount of the transaction.

Today, most businesses use computer accounting packages which automatically compile day books from the information entered about a transaction. Obtaining a summary total from a day book gives managers important information. For example, the total of sales, less items returned by customers, is the same as total income to date. Similarly, the total of the purchases, less goods returned, gives the value of all the purchases made by the business.

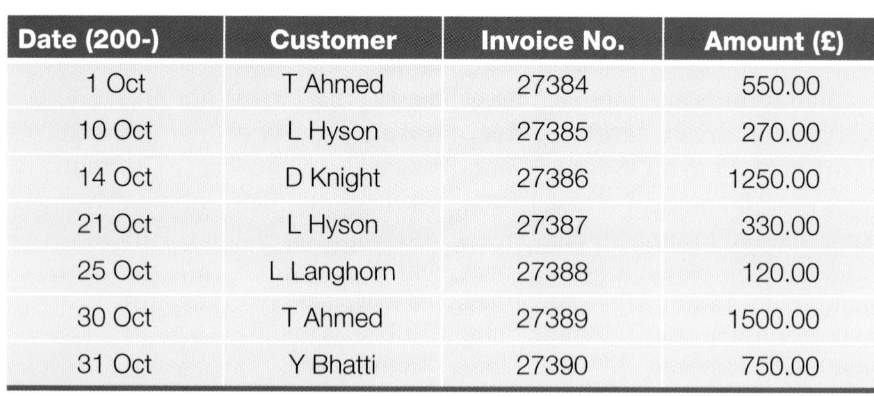

Date (200-)	Customer	Invoice No.	Amount (£)
1 Oct	T Ahmed	27384	550.00
10 Oct	L Hyson	27385	270.00
14 Oct	D Knight	27386	1250.00
21 Oct	L Hyson	27387	330.00
25 Oct	L Langhorn	27388	120.00
30 Oct	T Ahmed	27389	1500.00
31 Oct	Y Bhatti	27390	750.00

■ *An example of a sales day book*

Accounts

Business accounts summarise financial information in different categories, such as sales by customer, purchases by supplier, payments by type of expense, as well as cash in the bank and any cash on the premises. There are several reasons for doing this.

Financial information is recorded against a particular category, so that it is easier to obtain a precise summary; for example, how much has been spent on stock or travel expenses or advertising this year.

Some customers will be good payers, others will not. Recording sales information by customer means that the customer history can be used to determine credit levels and a list of outstanding debts, by customer, can be obtained at any time.

Activity

If you subtracted the total purchases of a business from its total sales, what information does this give you? If you have forgotten, turn back to page 93!

Key terms

Financial accounts use recorded information to prepare statutory accounts, such as the profit and loss account for last year.

Management accounts use recorded information to produce reports for management about financial performance, such as actual cash flow and profit (or loss) to date.

The information in all the accounts is linked because each entry is made twice (hence the term 'double-entry'). This enables accuracy to be checked. For example, paying a supplier's bill of £500 reduces the money held in the bank by the same amount – so two accounts are affected – the supplier's and the bank account. Similarly, receiving money from a customer increases the bank account and reduces the amount the customer owes by the same amount.

Accounts information can be summarised to provide managers with instant information about actual cash flow, potential profit (or loss), debts outstanding, stock levels etc. – which enables them to take action when needed.

The information in the firm's accounts is used to produce **statutory accounts**. These are business accounts required by law, such as the profit and loss account, cash flow statement for the period and balance sheet. All VAT registered businesses must also send regular VAT returns to HMRC.

Did you know?

***Auditors** are external specialists who check the business accounts of large companies and public sector organisations to make sure that they are accurate. VAT inspectors also visit VAT registered businesses to make spot checks.*

Activity

Bank statements do not always show the same amount of money as that recorded in the business 'cash in bank' account on a certain date. As a group, can you suggest why?

Did you know?

Statutory accounts are historic – they only say what has happened in the past. Managers, though, need current information so that they can take prompt action when it is needed.

Petty cash

The petty cash account is used to record small items of expenditure. It links to the main cash account (which records the money kept in the bank). Rather than withdraw money from the bank every time a small purchase is required, an amount is issued to the petty cashier who is responsible for keeping the cash safely, usually in a lockable cash box or a small safe. The cashier also has petty cash vouchers, for each time someone needs to be paid, and an accounts book for recording all petty cash transactions. Alternatively, the transactions may be recorded on a computer.

The money is used to buy small items, particularly when cash is needed to pay for them. Examples include:

- buying stamps for using on emergency postal items when the mailroom is closed
- paying the window cleaner
- paying for a taxi to take a visitor to the train station.

Petty cash is also used to reimburse staff who pay for business items out of their own pocket. The member of staff must obtain a receipt as proof of purchase and then complete a petty cash voucher, like the example shown. The cashier will authorise the voucher, then repay the amount and record the transaction in the petty cash account.

Received £	Date	Details	Voucher no.	Total Payments £	VAT	Item (net)
400.00	1 Feb	Balance				
	1 Feb	Petrol	132	15.00	2.23	12.77
	3 Feb	Coffee	133	3.50	-	3.50
	5 Feb	Petrol	134	45.00	6.70	38.30
	8 Feb	Buffet lunch	135	52.25	-	52.25
	8 Feb	Train ticket	136	85.30	-	85.30
	15 Feb	Tea	137	1.75	-	1.75
	17 Feb	Stationery	138	31.05	4.62	26.43
	19 Feb	Travel expenses	139	20.93	3.12	17.81
	23 Feb	Sandwiches	140	14.75	-	14.75
			Total	269.53	16.67	252.86
			Balance	130.47		
400.00				400.00		
130.47	1 March	Balance				
269.53	1 March	Cash received				

■ *Example of a petty cash book page*

Activity

Staff must usually get permission before they can spend money to reclaim through petty cash. Can you think why?

If you study the sample page from a petty cash book, you will notice that the first amount of money entered is £400.00. This is the amount of cash which was put into the fund at the start of the month. It is known as the **float** or imprest. An entry is made every time petty cash is paid out and these are cross referenced to each petty cash voucher by using the voucher numbers. At the end of the month, the total amount paid out is added up and deducted from the float figure. Also, the balance of money left over from the float is counted. Both of these figures should be the same – in the example shown, £130.47. If everything is in order, the fund is topped up again at the start of the next month.

PETTY CASH VOUCHER No: 139 Date: 18/2/2006

Name: Paul Hawarth Dept: Sales

Purpose (attach all receipts & invoices)	TOTAL (inc. VAT)	VAT (A)	NET (A) (excl. VAT)
Taxi to station	4.00		
Taxi from station	4.00		
Breakfast on train	12.93		
The sum of (in words as far to the left as possible) Twenty pounds -93p	£20.93p	£	£

Approved by: L Whitehead date: 19/2

Received by: P Hawarth date: 19/2

Allocation	
Amount	Account

Cash registers

In a small shop, many items will have a price sticker attached. The sales assistant will read the amount from the label and key this into the cash register. At the press of another button the cash drawer is released. The assistant then takes your money, puts it in the drawer and selects your change. At the same time, the machine records the amount of money spent and issues a receipt.

On electronic machines, the assistant will key in the amount owed, the amount offered and the cash register will display the change owed to you. Other features on these machines include programmable keys so that differences between products or department/operator can be entered, and PLU (price look up) keys which saves the operator from looking up the prices of popular items. One variation is the touch screen cash registers you often see in bars and restaurants.

More advanced are POS (point of sale) systems which include bar code scanners and PC-linked cash registers that are linked with credit card payment systems and stock control software.

Activity

Every day a senior member of staff will check that the money recorded by the cash register is the same as the amount it contains. The two figures should be the same. What reasons might there be for a discrepancy?

Electronic point of sale (EPOS) systems

Rather than link a POS system to a computer, large stores prefer an EPOS system where all their cash registers are linked to a central computer. This allows some or all of the following functions to be performed.

- Bar code readers can identify each product and find the price from the computer. The total spent by each customer is also calculated.
- Stock records can be updated as soon as a product is sold. This also allows low/high turnover stocks to be identified. Stock types which need re-ordering can also be identified.
- Some systems also update delivery requirements sent to a central distribution centre.
- The identity of the sales assistant dealing with every transaction can be recorded. Each assistant who is trained to use the till has his or her own pin number or swipe card. They 'log on' and off each time that they operate the machine.
- Credit/debit card payments can be processed – including authorisation.
- Detailed receipts can be printed which include each item purchased, together with the price. Businesses can also add card details, promotional messages, and its VAT number.
- Some large supermarkets use the data to draw up profiles of regular customers so that they can mail them with information on promotions of their favourite products.

EPOS Electronic point of sale system, where cash registers are linked to the central computer system.

Fraud

Fraud occurs when someone attempts to gain an advantage by deception, so someone who exaggerates their qualifications on a job application is technically committing fraud. Mostly, the word fraud is

Activity

Your friend Emily is a florist. She is setting up her own business and trying to work out what type of cash register to buy. She does not want to spend more than £300. Investigate the options available online and recommend the one you think would be the best for her, with reasons for your choice.

Did you know?

According to the Attorney General, speaking in 2003, fraud costs the UK economy £14 billion a year, or £230 for each member of the population.

Did you know?

***Shrinkage** is the term used by retailers for stock which cannot be sold to customers because it has been stolen. In the UK this is about 1.7 per cent, i.e. £17 out of every £1,000 worth of stock.*

used in connection with financial deception – such as taking money or goods which belong to someone else (which is the same as theft), 'fiddling' the accounts or passing off a stolen credit card as genuine.

Fraud can be carried out by customers, staff or complete strangers in several ways.

- **Stealing goods** This includes taking items of stock from a stock room or off the sales floor or taking office consumables (pens, printer cartridges etc.) without paying for them.
- **Stealing money** Cash is easily accessible in businesses where customers pay in cash, such as leisure centres and shops. It is normally only available as petty cash in other types of businesses. Cash is very tempting to steal because it is difficult to trace. In other words, if someone is carrying a large amount of cash, there is no proof where it came from.
- **Other forms of money theft** This can include gaining unlawful access to a bank account to withdraw money, deliberately entering false figures into accounts to obtain money, or passing an invoice for payment made out by a friend for goods that have not been delivered.
- **'Sweetheart' deals**, where staff and a friend collude. In this case the friend would be given an illegal discount or not charged at all for goods or services.
- **Card fraud** – such as stolen cards offered in payment or 'skimming', where a counterfeit copy of a card is recorded by a special machine and then used to buy goods. 'Chip and pin' cards have reduced these types of fraud because the holder of a stolen card will not know the PIN and there is less opportunity for skimming now that owners do not need to part with their card during a transaction.
- **Identity theft** This is a complex type of fraud. Criminals obtain personal details of an individual and use this information to apply for credit cards.
- **Internet fraud** This can include hacking into a business website (particularly one that takes payments online) to steal card details, or setting up a bogus website to trick shoppers into giving their card number.
- **Embezzlement** Obtaining and using money that rightfully belongs to someone else. To cover their tracks, someone who is embezzling their employer may falsify business accounts.

Managers are concerned about fraud because money lost by the business comes *straight out of profit*. In a small business, profit is the owner's income so fraud means taking money directly out of the owner's pocket. Lower profits mean that there is less money to re-invest in the business and this means that the business could be less profitable in the future. If staff are paid a bonus based on the profits, then fraud is taking money from everyone who works for the organisation.

Fraud also means that a business has to sell more to compensate for the money lost, as well as spend money on security measures. These are additional expenses which must be paid for out of profits. In most cases, however, managers see money spent on prevention measures as an investment which should more than pay for itself.

Activity

A clothes shop buys £500,000 worth of stock a year. How much shrinkage can it expect? If the profit figure without shrinkage would be £24,000, what will it now be?

Prevention measures

There are several measures which managers can take to reduce the risk of this type of fraud taking place. Normally, a combination of measures is taken appropriate to the type of business. Most are designed either to make fraud as difficult as possible or to improve the chances of catching people who steal. They include:

- a thorough staff selection procedure which includes character references
- a clear policy on dealing with fraud. Fraud is normally considered to be 'gross misconduct' for which staff can be dismissed instantly as part of the disciplinary procedure
- an induction programme for new employees, which includes an explanation of the procedures for handling and recording transactions, as well as the support available to them if they have personal financial worries. In addition, the disciplinary procedure should be explained
- restrictions on the staff who have access to cash and valuable items or who are involved in recording payments or making money transfers
- proper accounting procedures, which are the specific responsibility of named staff, to ensure all transactions are recorded and processed promptly and accurately
- a 'whistle-blowing' scheme where staff are rewarded for reporting fraud. The procedure should ensure that information is treated in confidence
- the recruitment of security guards, the placement of security cameras at strategic places and restricted access to areas where large amounts of cash or valuable goods are stored.

Did you know?

Computerised accounting systems record an 'audit trail' which lists every entry made in a day and the name of the person who made it. This can be examined at any time if there is a query about a discrepancy.

Activity

Strict regulations are in place to try to prevent ***money laundering****. Investigate this term online and find out what it means and the type of organisations which must comply with money laundering regulations.*

Management information and control

Managers control activities when they find out what is actually happening and compare this with what they expect to be happening. If they are not satisfied with what is going on, they take corrective action. This applies both to taking action to control fraud and managing business finances. In both cases, a key aspect is obtaining *information* and then analysing this to check if it matches forecast or expected results.

Controlling fraud The type of management information and control required to prevent fraud will depend upon the kind of business. In a retail store, the amount of cash in a till is checked at least once a day and

Activity

eBay is very aware of the dangers of fraud to users of its site. Research online to find out the precautions that it takes and the recommendations it makes to buyers and sellers to help to prevent problems.

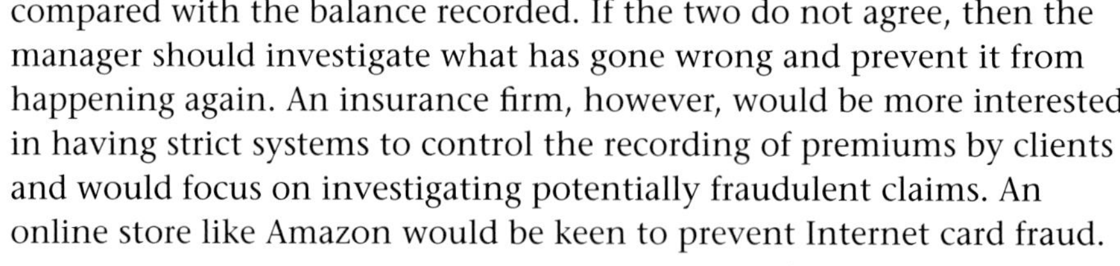

compared with the balance recorded. If the two do not agree, then the manager should investigate what has gone wrong and prevent it from happening again. An insurance firm, however, would be more interested in having strict systems to control the recording of premiums by clients and would focus on investigating potentially fraudulent claims. An online store like Amazon would be keen to prevent Internet card fraud.

For that reason, the manager needs to focus on the types of possible fraud that may occur in that business, the information that is needed to detect this and the corrective action that would then be needed. Additional examples are shown below.

Type of fraud	Information required	Corrective action/ control
Shoplifting	Amount of stock in relation to amount purchased	Regular stock-taking
Falsifying accounts	Details of accounts matched against sales and purchase documents	Employing independent auditors to examine accounts
Internet fraud	Details of payments online compared to sales income received	Increase security precautions on website
Pilferage of stock from manufacturing firm	Quantities of stock in relation to amount produced	Weighing lorries arriving and leaving site Right to stop and search employees if theft suspected
Falsifying claims	Additional details of claim with supportive evidence	Checking expense claims against receipts Insurance companies employing assessors who visit claimants

Fact file

Fraud means obtaining something by deception. The term is commonly used in relation to money.

Did you know?

Fraud, embezzlement and computer crimes are sometimes called 'white collar crime' because they are most likely to be carried out by office staff or managers.

Managing business finances This requires information of a different type. In this unit you have learned that businesses need to spend less than they earn in income to make a profit. You have learned that they can use techniques such as break even to help them to plan what actions to take and how forecasting cash flow will help them to stay solvent. None of this is much use if managers focus on forecasting and forget to check what is really happening. And this can only be done if every financial transaction is recorded promptly and accurately in the most appropriate way. Day-to-day figures are then available which inform management decisions of the actions that must be taken to prevent disasters occurring.

Over to you

1 *Suggest the most likely method each business would use to record the following transactions. In each case give a reason for your answer.*
   a) *The sale of a coat at Next.*
   b) *The payment of a fee to your dentist for doing a filling.*
   c) *The payment of a year's season ticket at a major football club.*
   d) *The purchase of a scarf at the same club.*
   e) *A packet of jiffy bags bought by a member of staff who now wants his money back.*
   f) *All the purchases made by an organisation in a week.*

2 *Samira works for a small vet's practice in the town.*
   a) *Write down eight different types of business transactions with which the practice could be involved, bearing in mind the practice will be both a customer and a supplier.*
   b) *Samira is responsible for recording all transactions on the computer system. The partners who own the practice insist that this is done every day.*
      i) *Explain three ways in which this information will be used.*
      ii) *Explain why the partners are so insistent that it is kept up to date.*
   c) *Suggest three preventative measures the partners could take to reduce the likelihood of fraud by any of the staff.*

3 *As a group, it is likely that several members work – or have worked – in businesses where payments are received. Divide into small groups and try to ensure that each group includes at least one person with this type of experience. Alternatively, find out if your tutor can arrange for you to talk to a member of the college or school staff who is involved in recording and monitoring payments, or to a local business person who would discuss it with you. Your aim is to find answers to the following questions.*
   a) *What precautions does the business take to restrict the number/type of people handling cash?*
   b) *What precautions are taken to check and monitor the way payments are received and recorded?*
   c) *What precautions are taken to prevent unauthorised people ordering goods or making payments?*
   d) *What other precautions are in place to prevent fraud?*
   e) *How do the financial recording systems in the business help managers to monitor and control the business finances?*

Talking point

View 1: Staff will be less tempted to defraud their employer if they are paid fair wages, receive staff discounts, feel valued and are given support if they have a personal financial worry.

View 2: Even if an employer isn't generous and supportive there is still no excuse for fraud. Change job if you don't like it there.

With which viewpoint do you agree – and why?

Case study: Assessment practice

In 2004, John Forster, a lawyer, was jailed for six-and-a-half years after defrauding his clients out of nearly £700,000. Unfortunately, this is not an isolated case. Solicitors handle vast amounts of money on behalf of their clients, and for a small minority the temptation to help themselves is too great. This is why the Law Society (the professional association for solicitors in England and Wales) lays down specific regulations about the way law firms must operate as well as operating a compensation fund, which exists to help anyone who suffers a financial loss because of a solicitor's dishonesty.

One important regulation is the Solicitors' Accounts Rules. These specify that money held on behalf of clients must be kept separate from money relating to the legal practice itself. It must be kept in individual client accounts and can only be used for expenditure related to the client. Solicitors must also pay the client interest if they hold large amounts of their money for any length of time.

Solicitors must also abide by money laundering regulations. They must check the identity of a potential new client by asking for their passport or photocard driving licence, as well as a recent utility bill to verify their address. If everything is in order a new client account is opened in their name, to hold money the solicitor receives on their behalf. This must be in the form of a cheque or electronic transfer – cash is not accepted by most legal practices.

The office account is used to record income and expenditure relating to the business, such as expenses and wages. Petty cash is used for paying the milkman and for reimbursing staff who have entertained clients and paid for coffee or a meal out of their own pocket. Purchases such as office consumables can only be made by the Office Manager.

Payments from a client's account, such as to buy a property or pay out an inheritance, must always be sanctioned by a senior partner. Large sums usually need the authorisation of more than one partner. The annual accounts for the practice are prepared by a firm of accountants and checked by auditors.

1(P) Describe simple ways of recording financial transactions and preventing fraud in a legal practice by answering the following questions.

- **a)** Why does the Law Society regulate the way legal practices operate?
- **b)** A client's house is sold for £200,000 and the solicitor holds the money for two months before it is required to pay for a new property. Do you think the client should receive interest? Give a reason for your answer.
- **c)** Explain the difference between client accounts and the office account and say why these are kept separate.
- **d)** Identify the main measures taken by legal practices to try to prevent fraud. ***(P4)***

2(D) Evaluate how the financial recording systems used by legal practices help the partners to manage and control the business finances. ***(D1 part)***

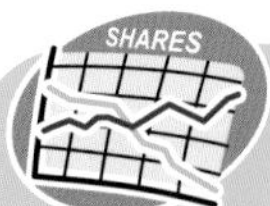

Grading tip

When you evaluate, start by identifying the recording systems used and then identify the role of each. Remember that as well as including benefits to support your argument you may also wish to include the disadvantages or consequences of doing exactly the opposite.

4 Business communication

Good communication skills are essential for anyone who wants to work in business because all businesses need to communicate promptly and accurately with a wide range of people to function effectively. In this unit you will develop your own understanding of business communications and see how these are used in a range of situations.

What you need to learn

- The purpose of communications in different business contexts
- How to use oral communications in business contexts
- How to complete and use written business documents
- How to use interpersonal and non-verbal business communication skills

4.1 Understanding the purpose of communications in business contexts

The purpose of business communication

People constantly communicate in every type of organisation. They talk on the telephone, write letters, send emails and hold discussions in meetings. Every time they communicate they do so for a reason. The most common ones are shown below.

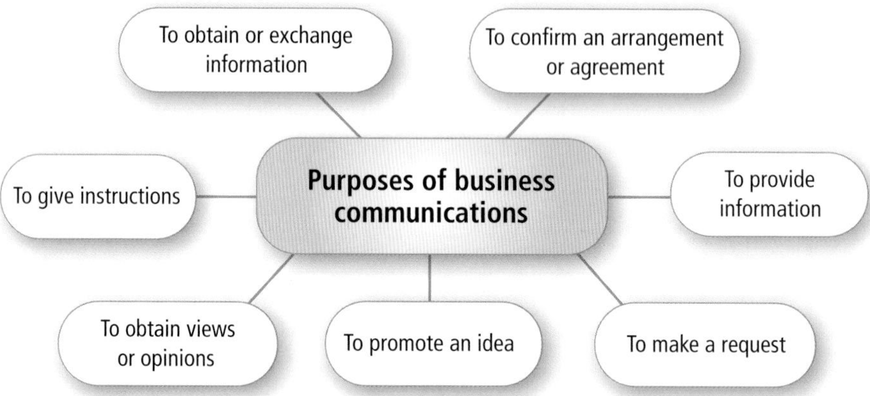

■ *The purposes of business communications*

Activity

As a group, identify reasons why you communicated with different people yesterday. See how many you can list.

Both the **business context** and the **business environment** can affect the purpose of the communication.

The business context

Jacqui works for a solicitor. Her elder brother Jake works in the finance department of a large manufacturing company. Her younger brother Tom is employed by a mobile phone retailer. All three work in different business environments so the purposes of their communications are often different.

The business context also affects communications. This relates to the situation or conditions that the communicator needs to take into account, such as the degree of formality that is required, the status of the recipient and other factors – as you will see below.

Activity

As a group, suggest reasons why Jacqui, Jake and Tom may need to telephone their customers or clients, bearing in mind their jobs and the business environments in which they work.

Formal and informal communication

Jacqui works in a context where many communications are formal, unlike Tom, so she is likely to be rather more formal with her clients. She will be more likely to put information in writing and will address most clients by their formal titles.

Communication in large organisations is often more formal than in small ones. Firstly, because staff will often communicate with colleagues they hardly know – whereas in a small business everyone knows everyone else. Secondly, because the business may be accountable to its shareholders or to the public and must therefore keep records in case actions are queried. This is why schools keep records of their governors' meetings and copies of information sent to parents. Many small businesses communicate with customers more informally and may only have written documents relating to buying and selling goods.

You will find out more about using the telephone and meetings if you study option unit 6.

Formality influences both the style and method of communication. If your tutor sent you a letter, this is more formal than a quick chat after class.

	Used when . . .	Examples
Formal	The matter is important or serious You do not know the recipient very well You want a written record	Business letters, memos and reports Job interviews Important meetings
Informal	People know each other well People are in frequent contact	Email Telephone Face-to-face discussion

■ *Formal and informal methods of communication*

As a group, identify the purposes of communications you receive at school, or college, and compare these with the purposes of those that any of your group receives at work. Suggest reasons for any differences you find.

Telephone contacts are usually informal and invaluable when something is urgent or you need a quick response. It is also easier to discuss something by phone than email. Because there is no written record, though, it is not the best method if you need proof of what was agreed. It is also unsuitable if you are giving long or complex information that your recipient would struggle to understand.

Meetings Meetings can be formal or informal. Large meetings are more formal and are mainly held to give information or instructions. In this case, people sit and listen – such as at college 'welcome' meetings held for all the students. A team meeting is held for a different reason, usually to talk about matters of common interest. This is more informal and everyone can contribute to the discussion. The topics discussed will depend upon the type of organisation, the department and/or main purpose why the group meets.

One-way communication *is when you can only listen but not contribute, such as a large formal meeting or watching television.* ***Two-way communication*** *is when you can put your views forward too.*

Technical enquiries Technical enquiries can range from written requests for estimates or complex quotations, from one business to another, to phone enquiries about courses at a college, or face-to-face questions asked in a retail store. Many of these are informal but some are not – such as business enquiries about the supply and installation of expensive equipment. The response will be in writing to avoid any confusion or

Activity

Suggest the types of technical enquiries Jacqui, Jake and Tom may each receive and how they would deal with these.

Did you know?

Most organisations today have an ***Intranet****. This holds information that can only be accessed by staff and is therefore different from the information held on the website, which is available to anyone.*

Activity

Sam has written a note to a close colleague. Convert this into language appropriate for a) his supervisor, b) a senior manager.

'Need the Jenkins' file urgently!' Bet you've lost it!! It'd be cool if I could have it before 12. Sam.'

misunderstandings. If the request is urgent then a fax or email attachment may be sent, rather than a letter. Any complex or technical information given verbally should be confirmed in writing to prevent misunderstandings.

Communicating with your supervisor, colleagues and customers

You will communicate with people for many different purposes. You may be responding to a communication you have received or initiating a communication yourself. The purpose will influence the method you use and the type of recipient should also influence the words you use and your 'tone', as you saw in Unit 2, page 66.

	Sent to	Examples
Internal communications	Supervisor or colleagues	emails, memos, telephone calls, team briefings and discussions in staff meetings
External communications	Customers and suppliers	emails, business letters, telephone calls, fax messages, purchase orders, invoices, external meetings

■ *Internal and external communications*

Complaints

In retail stores customers may call in to complain about a purchase. If the complaint is valid, they will expect a refund or may wish to exchange the item. This may be noted in a complaints log. More serious complaints will be dealt with differently and many organisations, particularly in the public sector, have a specific procedure that staff must follow. This may say that all complaints must be in writing, or recorded on an official complaints form and written records kept of the action taken. This is essential if the complaint could result in legal action if it cannot be resolved amicably.

Activity

Find out the procedure used in your school or college to deal with complaints and what type of records are kept.

Presentations

Presentations are a special type of business context. They are used to give information to a group of people and are more formal than having a chat or discussion. The purpose can vary considerably. A health and safety manager may give presentations to new staff to tell them what to do in an emergency, whereas sales staff will prepare presentations to promote the firm's products or services to potential customers.

Confidentiality

In this context, you would be dealing with information that is sensitive, and which the organisation does not want to be made public, or your own manager does not want broadcast around the business. It is important to know the type of information that is confidential and how this should affect your communications. You will learn more about this on page 176.

Over to you

1 *All businesses use both oral and written methods of communicating. The choice often depends upon the purpose of the communication, as well as the business context.*
Decide whether you would communicate orally or in writing, in each of the following situations, and give a reason for your answer:
   a) *to provide a customer with detailed information about a product*
   b) *to check the layout of a document with a colleague in the next office*
   c) *to arrange an appointment at the dentist*
   d) *to ask your boss if you can leave early on Friday*
   e) *to state how a customer was injured in reception*
   f) *to provide information on travel arrangements.*

2 *Saira works in the admin office of a college; her friend Julie works for a small hi-tech company which sells and maintains specialist software to large organisations.*
   a) *Describe the main purpose(s) of Saira's business communications in the following business contexts:*
      i) *telephoning a stationery supplier*
      ii) *contacting a member of staff about a timetable change*
      iii) *having a discussion with the senior administrator.*
      iv) *preparing a presentation for a governors' meeting*

continued ▸

Did you know?

Large commercial organisations and those in the public sector have official complaints procedures that all staff must follow.

Key term

Business context The setting or situation that applies and which must be taken into consideration when communicating.

Talking point

View 1: Most business communications have two purposes: those to customers to persuade them to part with their money and those to staff give instructions about work.

View 2: Business communications are sent for a wide range of purposes both to customers and staff.

With which viewpoint do you agree – and why?

Over to you *continued*

v) *responding to a student enquiry*
vi) *responding to a student complaint about a faulty vending machine.*

b) *Julie is involved in preparing a presentation; she has also just received a complaint and must respond to an enquiry. Suggest how the purpose of her communications is likely to differ from Saira's because of the different environment in which she works.*

Case study

Assessment practice

Mark was struggling. He had just changed jobs from a small engineering firm, owned by two brothers, to working in the planning department of his local authority. In his first job, the brothers regularly walked around the workshop, checking on progress and giving instructions to staff. The only written documents that Mark saw were purchase orders and invoices, which it was his job to check. Only office staff used email so this did not help Mark, who often needed information from the workshop. The best way was to go and talk to people or ring them up. The brothers often held discussions with the workshop manager about whether orders were being completed on time and how to solve any problems that could cause delays.

At the town hall it was very different. Mark's job involved receiving and recording planning applications. Some came by post and others were brought in by callers. All were noted in a log and given a reference number. Mark then sent a pre-printed letter acknowledging the application and enclosed a receipt for the fee paid. Neighbours and anyone else who might be affected were informed of the plans in writing and their responses were noted. Planning officers often made site visits and wrote a formal report afterwards. The planning and development committee then received all the papers and considered the application at a formal planning meeting. The agenda, which listed the matters to be discussed, was sent out beforehand and minutes were taken so there was a record of the meeting. Mark then sent out the decision notices to applicants, together with information on their rights to appeal.

The difference between the two places was so stark that it was taking Mark time to adjust. He had been in trouble twice recently – once for not writing down a complaint he received over the telephone and then for repeating what a planning officer had said about a site visit when two callers were present.

1(P) Identify three informal and three formal business communications mentioned in the case study. ***(P1 part)***

2(P) Describe the purpose of each of the following business communications:

- **a)** Mark talking to workshop staff
- **b)** the brothers talking to workshop staff
- **c)** the brothers meeting the workshop manager
- **d)** Mark sending pre-printed letters and receipts to applicants
- **e)** Mark sending letters to neighbours
- **f)** the planning officers writing reports
- **g)** meetings of the planning and development committee. ***(P1 part)***

3(P) Mark was in trouble because he had not taken account of how the business context should affect his communications. For both mistakes he made, explain what he should have done and why. ***(P1 part)***

4(P) Explain how the contrasting business environments have affected the way Mark is expected to communicate. Suggest reasons for this. ***(P1 part)***

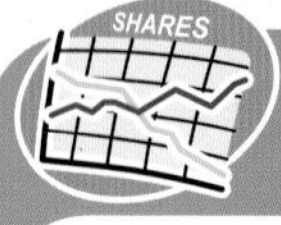

Grading tip

If you are asked to explain something, it can often help to give an example to show what you mean.

4.2 Be able to use oral communication in business contexts

There are a number of ways of communicating orally in business. To use any of these methods effectively, you need three main skills. You need to be a good listener, to be capable of speaking clearly to other people and be able to participate effectively in discussions and meetings as a member of a group.

Oral methods of communication
Telephone
Voicemail
Answering machine
Telephone conference call
Video conference
Mobile phone
Private radio
Face-to-face conversation
Discussion group
Meeting
Team briefing
Interview
Presentation

Activity

Check that you know what is meant by each term used in the list opposite. If any of them are a mystery, ask your tutor to explain them.

Did you know?

In Australia, ABC radio had to apologise when it misheard the word 'lawyers' for 'lies' and wrongly reported a legal firm as being at fault in a legal case.

Listening skills

Listen and understand instructions given verbally

Listening skills were first covered in Unit 2 (page 67), where you learnt that good listeners do not interrupt to talk about their own ideas, nor do they 'switch off' if they have been listening to someone for more than a few minutes.

There are several hazards at work if you do not listen properly. You will frequently be given verbal instructions, sometimes by people in a hurry, or by people using jargon or technical terms you may not understand. In this case, even a *good* listener may struggle to cope. A poor one has no chance of following the instructions. If you have to resort to guesswork then you may make several mistakes or cause a few problems.

Fact file

Everyone's concentration wavers when they are listening. It takes effort to stay focused on what is being said.

Most people will know at least one horror story which comes from not listening. The aim is to ensure that the next time a gaffe is made where you work, you are not the reason for your colleagues' hilarity and your boss's fury.

Did you know?

Researchers have found it takes 50 per cent more effort to listen than to speak. This is because you need to concentrate when you are listening, whereas many people talk without much thought.

Everyone's listening ability fluctuates, particularly if a conversation is lengthy, they are not interested in the topic or are distracted for some reason. This is why you will find your mind wandering if you are bored but will become alert if someone mentions that the office syndicate won the lottery last night!

You can improve your own listening skills by :

- **Stopping what you are doing**. You cannot write and listen, surf the net and listen, or read and listen! If you pick up a pen, it should be for writing notes, not doodling.
- **Noting when you are 'switching off'** and deliberately switching yourself on again.
- **Concentrating on the main topic** of the conversation and not interrupting. If you have to interrupt to clarify something, then focus back on the main topic immediately afterwards; for example, 'I'm sorry – you were just talking about the Scottish visitors next week.'
- **Watching people when they are talking to you** and assessing their body language (see Unit 2, page 60). This will help you to ascertain the speaker's emotions and state of mind.
- **Thinking about what the person is saying** – not about your own reaction or comments you can make.

Did you know?

You give feedback to a speaker by your body language. Nod or smile to show you understand what is being said. If something puzzles you then it is better to look mystified than to scowl.

Interpret instructions and task requirements correctly

Tasks – and instructions – can be simple or complex. Information can be given to you slowly and in a logical order – or rapidly and in a muddle. The worst type of situation requires several skills to cope, including the ability to listen, confidence in yourself (so that you are not scared to stop someone who is talking too fast or using words you do not understand) plus patience and concentration so that you are not easily distracted.

With any task there are normally six important items you need to know, summarised in the following rhyme:

> *I have six honest working men, they taught me all I knew*
>
> *Their names are **what** and **why** and **when** and **how** and **where** and **who**.*

Did you know?

If you struggle to remember what you must say next unless you speak immediately, it helps to jot down a 'prompt' word so that you will not forget.

This means checking that you know and understand:

- **What** – exactly what you are being asked to do.
- **Why** – the work is required, so that you understand what you are doing and how you should do it. For example, if the reason is because an important customer wants it in half an hour, you should realise the task is both urgent and important and the quality must be good!

- **When** – this tells you the overall deadline when the work is required and also the timescale, i.e. how long you have to do the work.
- **How** – this relates to the way in which the work must be done, the standard required and the equipment or supplies you can use.
- **Where** – you need to know where to obtain any supplies you need and where to take or send the work when it is finished.
- **Who** – you need to know who the work is for, who to liaise with and who to see if you have a problem.

Make notes

The aim of making notes is to make sure you have written down the key facts relating to a task. Do not try to do this and talk at the same time. Write as neatly as you can and space out your notes – they will be clearer, if you do. At the end, read them back to the speaker to check they are accurate.

Confirm understanding

It is in everyone's interests that you understand what you have been told. Therefore, if there is any word or term you do not understand, query this when you are repeating your notes back to the speaker. You should now be in a position to carry out your instructions.

Seek clarification where appropriate

Sometimes you may need to seek clarification when someone is giving you instructions. The aim is to avoid misunderstandings which can cause unnecessary work or mistakes. If you are fortunate you will spot potential problems at the outset, when the task is being explained to you. However, sometimes you may only realise there is a problem after you have started work. You therefore need contact details for the person who gave you the job – so that you can obtain advice if you have a problem later.

Did you know?

An AA mechanic was sent on a 300-mile round trip because the control centre operator sent him to Claggan, near the Isle of Mull and not Laggan, near Fort William. It took him four hours to reach the motorist and the AA had to pay for his overnight stay – even though the fault only needed a £12 part to repair!

Times to seek clarification

- If you are not sure how to contact the speaker again if you have a problem.
- If a technical word or specialist term has been used that you have never heard before.
- If you have never done this type of task before.
- If you are not sure whether you are allowed to do this type of task.
- If you do not know the deadline for the task.
- If you will need special help from someone and do not know how to obtain it.
- If you cannot – hand on heart – say you totally understand what you have been told.

Did you know?

Many people are worried they will look silly if they ask a question. In reality, they look a lot more foolish if they have to guess and get it wrong, or keep having to go back to ask questions to fill in the gaps!

Fact file

Listening skills are important, especially when you are being given information for a task. You also need to note down what you have to do and check that you understand your instructions.

Activity

Work in pairs for this activity. Talk about a film you have seen recently and describe what happened. Explain this while your partner takes notes, checks the details and clarifies anything doubtful. Then reverse roles. Both of you should be able to give a clear description of the film the other person saw to your tutor.

One-to-one communication

In this situation you are talking to one other person. This may be your supervisor, a colleague or an external customer or contact. The occasion may be very informal – such as a chat with your colleague at the next desk, or formal – such as a performance review or an interview for a job.

Methods of conveying messages or series of instructions

Face-to-face communications Ideally, in a one-to-one communication you can both concentrate on what each other is saying. This is not the case if there are lots of distractions, so important or complex information is best communicated in private without any disturbances. This is why interviews are scheduled in advance and the interviewer will leave instructions not to be interrupted.

Fact file

One-to-one communications include face-to-face talks and discussions and telephone calls. Additional skills may be required to understand messages received by telephone.

This type of privacy is not possible for many routine messages and instructions that are constantly communicated in business. This is why your listening and concentration skills are so important. You cannot 'shush' everyone in sight whenever you answer the telephone or listen to a voicemail message. You may also receive messages or instructions in front of other people, when you are in the middle of another job and even when you are walking down a corridor. Some people at work carry notepads with them all the time, just for this purpose.

Telephone callers Additional skills are often required to correctly interpret important information given over the telephone – especially if you do not know the caller or much about the topic being discussed. Always start by asking for the caller's name and then find out what the call is about. If the line is poor, it is sensible to arrange to call back. If someone's accent is very strong, or you are having problems understanding what is said, ask the caller to spell out words and then check them using the phonetic alphabet if you know it, for example, 'Did you say C for Charlie and D for Delta?' Listen, too, for verbal cues (such as a sigh) that tell you how the person is reacting to what you are saying. You may also experience problems if you are not given the information in a sensible order. Telephone callers can often be divided into three types.

- those who miss out several important facts needed to make sense of the information, so you need to ask for the additional details you need
- those who give clear, succinct messages – sometimes with the information in the right order, too. These are often professional business people but they might unnerve you if they are very curt
- those who like to chat and include many completely irrelevant details – from the weather to their plans for the rest of this week! In this case you have to select the information you need and discard the rest.

Did you know?

The advantage of voicemail is that people can leave messages at any time. The disadvantage is that they may miss out important information when they do.

Activity

Go to www.dynamoo.com/technical/phonetic.htm and print out a copy of the phonetic alphabet. Memorise useful letters, like your initials, those in your family name and those in your postcode. Then, in pairs, practise spelling out your name and address to each other.

Language and expressions that will be understood by the recipient

Jargon and technical terms are often used in business. You understand the terms 'BTEC First' and 'assessments' because of the scheme you are following, but to someone else these may be meaningless.

For this reason, you should avoid using jargon with external customers if you can. If you have no option then you should explain what the term means. Similarly, if you work in a department that uses specific terms connected to its work (IT is an obvious example) then be aware that colleagues who work in other areas may be just as puzzled if you use these during a conversation.

Activity

The use of jargon and technical terms was covered in Unit 2. Turn back to pages 66 and 67 now and refresh your memory.

Did you know?

You will learn a lot – and show more initiative – if you always ask a speaker to explain a word, term or statement you've never heard before.

Messages to suit different situations

When the police have to give bad news to a family they always make a personal visit, usually with an officer trained for this type of situation. Obviously, a quick phone call would be inappropriate and so would an insensitive approach. Although this is an extreme example, it shows that the type of information you are communicating and the situation will affect two things: the method to choose and the words and tone you use.

The type of message and the recipient should determine whether you communicate with someone face-to-face, or by phone, and the language, expressions and tone you use.

The method you choose Your main choice is between speaking to someone in person or phoning them. The main factors which should affect your decision are given below.

Communicate face-to-face if	Communicate by telephone if
The information is confidential or personal	You are very busy and it will take a lot of your time to see them in person
The matter is urgent and you see the person regularly	The matter is urgent and the person isn't present
You are giving very bad news	You need a rapid answer to a query
You need to have a discussion	The information is quite straightforward
You want someone to do you a favour	

The words and 'tone' you use Both your manner and your words should reflect the situation. If you are telling a customer that the earliest appointment available is weeks away, or that you no longer stock the item required, it is unwise to sound pleased about it! Equally, if you are passing on exciting news it will ruin the effect completely if you look or sound miserable when you do it.

Did you know?

According to the Wireless World Forum, many people under the age of 24 mainly communicate by text message because they prefer to text than talk. Is this you?

Activity

Next time you are watching a soap on TV, turn down the sound. Then see if you can 'read' someone's feelings by watching their expressions and their posture when they are speaking. This is even better if you are watching a recording, because you can play it back with sound to see if you are right.

Working in a group situation

Most people in business work in a group or team. They may meet to discuss joint tasks or projects, to obtain information that is of common interest or to talk through ideas or forthcoming events. Your aim is to be a good communicator in all these situations.

Making a relevant contribution to a discussion about business tasks

Some people are super to involve in discussions, whilst others are just a nuisance. What separates these two groups? Some responsibility obviously falls upon the leader of the discussion to keep everyone focused, but this also needs the combined cooperation of everyone present, as you can see from the table below.

Remember that that your body language should reflect the words you are using (see Unit 2, page 60).

Do	Don't . . .
Think about positive suggestions you can make. You may have good ideas from work you have done before	Sit there silently and then grumble afterwards because you do not like what was agreed
Arrive on time if you have been given previous notice about the time the discussion will take place	Arrive late – unless it's absolutely unavoidable, in which case you need to start by apologising
Listen to the main point of the discussion, when this is outlined, so your contributions will be relevant	Have fixed opinions at the start that you will not change, no matter what
Listen to other people's viewpoints and make notes of other people's ideas, so that you can refer to them later if you need to	'Switch off' when other people are speaking so you do not know what was said
Speak clearly when it's your turn and keep your contribution relevant to the topic under discussion	Speak for too long or use the opportunity to raise lots of other issues you have just thought about
Signal the leader of the discussion to get attention when you have a relevant point to make	Interrupt whenever you have a bright idea or a comment to make
Support other people if you think they have made a good point	Pick holes in everything other people suggest
Be prepared to moderate or change your own ideas as the discussion progresses	Stick to your opinions like glue, no matter what
Make suggestions that build on what has been agreed already	Tell people what to do
Watch people's body language throughout to gauge their reactions	Use negative body language yourself – such as sighing heavily
Question things you are unsure about – tactfully	Tell people straight when you think they are talking rubbish
Expect the outcome to be a mixture of different contributions	Predict doom and gloom or sulk if you don't get your own way

Key terms

Business discussions are informal debates between a group of people to reach a joint agreement.

Business meetings are arrangements for people to meet, often on a regular basis, to talk about specific business issues.

Team briefings are regular meetings with a group of staff to give information relevant to them and their work.

Did you know?

People who are difficult during discussions at work often find that meetings are held at times when they cannot attend. Then they have no choice but to do what everyone agreed in their absence!

Meetings

There are several important differences between a staff discussion and some types of meetings that are held in business. Your role will depend upon the reason for holding the meeting. If it is just to give information to a large group of people, then you would only participate if you had a question to ask. However, this is rare. Most meetings are held with smaller groups to exchange information, obtain ideas and opinions, solve problems or coordinate activities being undertaken by different people. In all these cases, you would be expected to participate. You may even have a specific role or area of expertise, linked to the type of work you do or skills you have.

Did you know?

One study found that many business people spend up to 65 per cent of their working week in meetings and another found some people can spend up to two years of their working lives in meetings. This is a lot of time wasted if the meetings are not effective.

Meetings are an excellent way for communicating with a group, providing that they are effective. Unfortunately, this is not always the case. A meeting that is badly organised can waste everyone's time. So can a meeting at which the participants are unhelpful, negative, argumentative or uninterested in the proceedings. So when you attend a meeting, you are partially responsible for its effectiveness. The skills needed to make a useful contribution are similar to those needed to join in a discussion – such as preparing in advance, treating other people's ideas and suggestions courteously and making positive suggestions yourself.

Some meetings are informal and similar to a discussion. Others are more formal and there is some basic etiquette you must follow, such as always speaking to the **chairperson**, who is running the meeting, rather than directly to other people present. Whilst this may seem strange at first, it does prevent several conversations going on at once and also means the chairperson is always in control of the discussion.

Did you know?

Team briefings provide ideal opportunities for staff to make their views known to their supervisor but can be ruined if people whinge and moan or use it as a talking shop.

At a more formal meeting, too, there is usually an 'order of business' that is followed. This is listed in an **agenda** which is issued in advance. Afterwards the discussions and agreed actions are summarised in the notes, or **minutes**, of the meeting. You will find out more about this in the next section.

Team briefings

Team briefings are informal sessions run by a team leader to pass on and discuss information of relevance to the team and its work. Many organisations use these to pass information downwards from senior

management to junior levels. Each team leader customises the information for his or her particular team. The advantages of face-to-face sessions are that queries can be clarified and sensitive information discussed, which the team leader may prefer not to put in writing.

Because the information may be given quite rapidly, it is sensible to take a notebook with you and to write down the points that are mentioned. This means you do not have to pester people for information afterwards because you cannot remember what was said.

Occasionally, you may be asked to contribute to a team briefing by telling other people about an area of work with which you have been involved. If you are given advance notice, jot down the key points, in a logical order, so that you are well prepared. If you are expected to think on your feet and are struggling, give a brief summary and suggest that you provide more details at the next team briefing or send everyone an email with the information instead.

Fact file

Discussions, meetings and team briefings in business all need the positive cooperation of their members to be effective.

Respond appropriately to others

Ironically, most people are extremely polite with strangers or people they hardly know and then, particularly when they are stressed or under pressure, they forget the basic courtesies with people they know well. Not saying 'please' and 'thank you' are two obvious examples.

If you find yourself doing this, take a step back and remember that you are likely to get treated casually yourself if you do this – or given a dressing down if you try it with your boss.

Did you know?

At work, it is not wise to treat your colleagues quite dismissively and expect them to put up with it – even if you sometimes do this with your family.

In Unit 2, you learned how to respond to customers. Below are some hints and tips for responding to your supervisor and your colleagues.

To your boss or team leader	To your colleagues
Be cooperative Appreciate their priorities Accept their decisions gracefully – and look for the plus points Understand the stress or pressure they may be under Respect their seniority and status Report problems and difficulties accurately and promptly Do not make a drama out of a crisis	Be fair and treat everyone equally Be loyal and never disclose confidences Be tactful and diplomatic so that you do not hurt them unnecessarily Show extra consideration if they are under pressure or having a bad day Be open minded and listen to different views – you may learn something Give praise when it's due and thank people who help you Be honest and admit your mistakes Be a prompt, accurate and reliable communicator, no matter what the message

Moving a discussion forward

It is always easy to reach agreement with people when you all think the same way. Yet often when a group of people are discussing something they are unable to reach agreement. This may be because the issue is particularly difficult or because people hold very different views. Unless something is done a decision will never be reached and, in business, this is not an option.

It is important to be able to ***negotiate*** *when you work in a group. You will do this more easily if you focus on the best solution possible for everyone.*

The problem will be worse if:

- one person is very dominant and always shouts everyone else down
- the team bicker and squabble between themselves
- the leader is unable to keep order
- people are allowed to trade insults with each other.

It is easier to move a discussion forward if people do not see it as a contest that they have to win. The best approach is to treat the problem as a challenge to the team as a whole, so that everyone tries to reach the best solution possible. Often, in this way, a simple suggestion by one person can be refined or improved by the others, so that the end result is better than anyone would have thought of on their own.

You will help to move the discussion forward if you are prepared to:

- respect other people's views and opinions
- focus on solving the problem so everyone benefits

- build on suggestions that have been made previously
- use persuasiveness, rather than aggression, if you are trying to win people over to your way of thinking.

If there is still deadlock then a group vote may be the only option to decide the best way forward. You will then have to abide by the wishes of the majority with good grace – and not complain about it afterwards!

Fact file

The best group decision is often a mixture of a variety of contributions, rather than the ideas of any one person.

Activity

As a group, you have been asked to discuss a possible timetable change. You can either start one hour later each day or finish one hour earlier. Negotiate the solution you would prefer. Your tutor will give feedback on your performance afterwards.

Talking point

View 1: Because of text messaging and email, many people are now hopeless at communicating face to face.

View 2: Text messaging and emails have no effect whatsoever on people's ability to communicate verbally.

With which viewpoint do you agree – and why?

Over to you

1 *Rizwana has been given the following instructions. In each case identify the additional information she needs to do the task properly.*

- **a)** *Find out about train times to Glasgow next week, will you?*
- **b)** *Send a brochure to everyone who came to the meeting.*
- **c)** *Order some more printer cartridges, will you?*
- **d)** *Sort out some sandwiches for Friday's meeting, please.*
- **e)** *Phone John Smith and see if you can rearrange tomorrow's meeting for next Wednesday.*
- **f)** *Ring Asif in IT services and tell him my computer is playing up and needs fixing.*

2 *Your school or college wants to give each new student a welcome pack next year. Your group has been asked to suggest the content.*

Work in groups of three or four and decide on a team response. Your decision should be reached by means of discussion and negotiation, so that each person feels that his or her views have been heard and considered.

Case study Assessment practice

Ailsa wasn't looking forward to tomorrow's discussion. Joanna, their team leader, had just announced a forthcoming visit by some important foreign customers. At tomorrow's discussion they would agree on and allocate the jobs that had to be done. Ailsa could imagine the scene now.

Gareth would sit there silently. No matter what was suggested he would just nod, rather than say anything. Ruth would write everything down, then spend ages arguing about minor details. Parveen would only half-listen then make lots of irrelevant or outlandish suggestions that distracted everyone. Sayed would agree with everything Joanna said – and suggest even more complicated things everyone could do – before finding some excuse to offload his jobs onto someone else. And her? Ailsa knew that she sometimes found herself staring out of the window, day dreaming, which had sometimes caused problems when she misheard what was said.

In her defence, Ailsa reckoned that this wasn't always her fault. Last time Joanna had gabbled information to her over the phone before she rushed off to a management meeting to discuss the latest sales figures, and Ailsa hadn't dare to interrupt her! Ailsa's job had been to photocopy and staple a set of brochures and to send them out. She was convinced Joanna had said 70 copies, even though it turned out only 20 were needed and nothing had been said about sending them urgently, she was sure. Otherwise, she would not have used second class post. And it wasn't her fault they went to Bradford instead of Brighton, given the noise going on the office at the time.

Ailsa knew Joanna was now watching her carefully and would raise the issue at her next review meeting. And she wasn't looking forward to that any more than she was looking forward to tomorrow's discussion.

1(P) Prove you would respond better than Ailsa to verbal instructions to carry out a task by role playing this situation. Divide into pairs – one person giving a series of instructions and the other person making notes. Check the notes accurately and clearly summarise what is required before reversing roles. ***(P2)***

2(P) **a)** Describe in turn how each person in Ailsa's group could make a more positive contribution to group discussions.

b) Then role play this situation in small groups by deciding on the type of jobs that would need to be done and how these should be allocated. For the person you have been asked to play, demonstrate how you would make an individual contribution to the discussions. ***(P3)***

3(M) Identify four methods of oral communication used in Ailsa's office and explain why each is used. ***(M1)***

4(D) Analyse the effectiveness of the discussions held by Joanna to allocate work and suggest ways in which these could be improved. ***(D1 part)***

Grading tip

At merit level, an explanation should provide full details and evidence to support your opinion.

To provide an analysis you need to consider each factor or piece of evidence separately and decide how these contribute to the topic as a whole.

4.3 Be able to complete and use written business documents

Every day millions of documents are sent and received by businesses, from formal, lengthy reports to informal emails between colleagues. They include messages, letters, faxes, leaflets, invoices and application forms, sent electronically and by post to other businesses and to private individuals. They all have two things in common:

- they provide information which the recipient must be able to understand
- they all give an impression of the business and the writer – and for that reason must be correct in every respect.

This section looks at the key aspects that you must observe to ensure that your written business communications are of an appropriate standard.

Business documents

Different documents have different features, which means that some are more appropriate for certain purposes than others. Whichever type you prepare, you need to be aware of the correct layout to use and the standards of presentation and writing that are normally expected.

Did you know?

Although the design of many standard documents, such as purchase orders and invoices varies from one business to another, the type of information they contain is almost identical.

Type of document	Sent to	Features
Business letter	External contacts	Formal, slower than electronic methods, impersonal, provides permanent written record
Email	Internal and external contacts	Informal, rapid, other documents can be attached, can be sent worldwide very easily
Fax	External contacts or branch offices	Fast, useful for order confirmations on official paper
Form (for completion)	Internal and external contacts	Used to collect information in a systematic manner. All sections must be completed accurately
Telephone message or note	Internal contacts	Short and informal. Usually left on recipient's desk unless absent or on holiday
Memo	Internal contacts	More formal than email, provides permanent record if filed
Report (informal)	Internal contacts	Gives clear account of an event or investigation under separate headings
Report (formal)	External contacts	Provides a detailed account of an event or inquiry under specific headings
Agenda	People entitled to attend a meeting	Provides list of items to be discussed in order
Minutes of a meeting	People who attended and those entitled to attend but absent	Summarises what was discussed, often with action to be taken and by whom
Discussion summary	Those who attended the discussion and others affected by the outcome	A record of the main items discussed and/or answers to questions asked
Purchase order	An external supplier	Provides official authority for the supplier to provide the goods listed at the quoted price
Invoice	A customer	Includes details of the items purchased, the unit price, the VAT payable and the total price

■ *Types of written documents and their features*

*The layout and style of a business document must be fit for its purpose, as well as appropriate for the task and the audience. The document **must also** be completely accurate, as well as legible and consistent.*

Appropriate layouts

Most business documents have fairly standard layouts and formats that have been designed with the following criteria in mind.

Fitness for purpose

The type of information in a document and the way it is set out must take account of its main purpose. A letter provides continuous information; an invoice summarises financial details relating to a purchase; and an agenda lists items to be discussed at a meeting. The layout must ensure that the key information is clearly seen.

Appropriate to the task and the audience

Some documents serve a similar purpose – both purchase orders and invoices relate to financial transactions. However, the layout is different because one is concerned with obtaining goods whilst the other aims to obtain payment. Similarly, letters and memos both provide information but they are written for different audiences. A letter is written to provide information to external contacts but memos are only sent internally. This affects the layout as you will see on pages 162 and 163.

Use of different formats and styles

'Format' is simply another word for design. Some organisations have a specific **house style** that specifies how documents should be set out. There may even be a model set on the firm's Intranet and/or templates that can be downloaded. The instructions may include the type and size of font that can be used, as well as the style of headings, how pages should be numbered (paginated), and what headers or footers should be used.

Activity

1 *On the word processing package you normally use, find out the different font styles and sizes available, the methods of numbering documents and how to insert headers and/or footers on a document.*

2 *There are many online sites you can use to help to improve your written English skills, such as www.bbc.co.uk/skillswise/ and www.spellzone.com. Or your school or college Intranet may have a useful guide. Find out which ones suit you best!*

Writing documents for business

Writing acceptable business documents is different from sending a note to a friend. Quite apart from accurate spelling, punctuation and the correct grammar you also need to be able to do the following.

Use relevant technical language

As you already know, technical language or jargon is often used to describe particular aspects of a business. Some people argue that jargon enables staff to describe something technical in the shortest way possible. Others claim that jargon forms an 'exclusive group' that excludes outsiders who don't understand the terms used. Many staff find this applies when they are talking to colleagues in their IT department!

Did you know?

Images in business documents are more often tables, charts or diagrams than graphical images or pictures.

Key terms

Format is the design and layout of a document.

Legibility is when a document is clearly written and easy to read.

Consistency is when the format is the same throughout the document in relation to typeface, style of heading, spacing etc.

Conventions are basic principles which relate to the way certain documents are written.

Did you know?

According to an Abbey National survey, 74 per cent of customers believe that businesses use jargon deliberately to confuse and deceive them; 56 per cent think that jargon is used as a 'cover' by staff who do not know what they are talking about, but 31 per cent admit to using it themselves to impress their own customers and clients.

The main point to remember is only to use technical language if you are communicating with someone who will understand it *unless* you clearly explain what it means. This normally means restricting it to internal communications. And never use a term you do not understand yourself, just to impress someone.

Did you know?

The KISS principle *stands for* ***K****eep* ***I****t* ***S****hort and* ***S****imple. This should apply to* ***all*** *your written communications. Never use long words just because you think they will sound impressive. They won't.*

Drafting and redrafting to ensure accuracy

Whilst you may be able to write a quick note or an email to a friend in five seconds flat, this is unwise if you are preparing a business document. Not only do you need to check your spelling, punctuation and grammar, but you also need to make sure that your information is in a logical order, that nothing has been missed out, that the 'tone' is right and that your reader will understand it easily. This is likely to take a few attempts before you get it right.

Legibility and consistency

Although you are unlikely to handwrite many communications, those you do prepare must be legible. Jotting a note that tells your boss to urgently ring a customer whose name or number is unintelligible is unlikely to make you very popular!

Consistency refers to the way the document is set out *and* to the words you use. If you decide to use one blank space between paragraphs, which is normal, this must be the same throughout the document. If you refer to yourself in the plural 'We will be pleased...' then you must not change to the singular 'I would like' later on.

One of the main hazards of email is that it is all too easy to press 'send'! It is much safer to store a first attempt in your drafts folder until you have checked it properly.

Conventions

There are several conventions you must observe, usually relating to the type of document you are preparing, as you will see on pages 161–170.

Checking for accuracy, consistency and fitness for purpose

The ability to proofread your work carefully to check for accuracy and to put yourself in the shoes of the recipient when you do this is very important. Far too many people think they can simply run a spell check and that is sufficient, but it is not. Spell checkers miss any errors where the result is another 'real' word: for example, form/from; too/two; stationery/stationary, pin/pine. Checking means reading through your work carefully and asking someone else for advice if you are not sure about anything.

It is not wise to have total faith in electronic grammar checkers any more than you can trust your spell checker. If the suggestion it gives you seems weird, check it with a more experienced colleague.

Meeting deadlines

No matter how many checks you need to make, the document must be despatched by the agreed deadline. If you are struggling to finish or check a document in time, ask for help. Don't flounder and then make a mess of it or miss the deadline without warning anyone.

Layouts and conventions for specific documents

Below are examples of a business letter, memo and report, together with guidance on how to write them. Business emails are covered in Unit 6 (page 245) and purchase orders and invoices were illustrated in Unit 3 (pages 121 and 125). Agendas, minutes and discussion notes are discussed in section 4.4.

Did you know?

You will make a better job of checking your work if you let it 'go cold' before reading it through because you then see it through the eyes of a recipient, rather than as the writer, and errors are more obvious.

Activity

The formats for a business letter, memo and report are shown on pages 162–166. Check these and note the main conventions, which are shown on each one.

Business letters

All business letters are written on headed paper. This gives key information about the organisation, such as its name, address, telephone and fax number, website address and often the address of the registered office. A standard layout is shown below.

Other points to note:

- slang and abbreviated words, such as don't or can't are never used in a letter
- the style and tone should suit the purpose: so a sales letter is upbeat, one making a complaint should be factual and one responding to a justified complaint should be apologetic
- letters must be polite – use the word 'please' if you want something. Avoid its overuse by switching to other phrases such as 'we would be grateful if . . .' or 'it would help us if . . .'
- a letter should never end with 'thank you' on its own. Instead use a more business-like phrase such as 'We appreciate your help in this matter'.

Did you know?

Many businesses use ***open punctuation*** *– where commas are inserted only in the body of the letter to help understanding but are not used in abbreviations, or at the end of address or date lines.*

It is easier to write a letter if you know some of the standard phrases to use.

The opening paragraph focuses on the reason for writing and introduces the main topic, such as in the examples below.

- We would like to invite you to our Open Day on Wednesday, 10 May.
- Thank you for your letter of 6 May informing us about your new range of wool carpets.
- I refer to your recent telephone conversation with a member of our staff about our landscaping service.

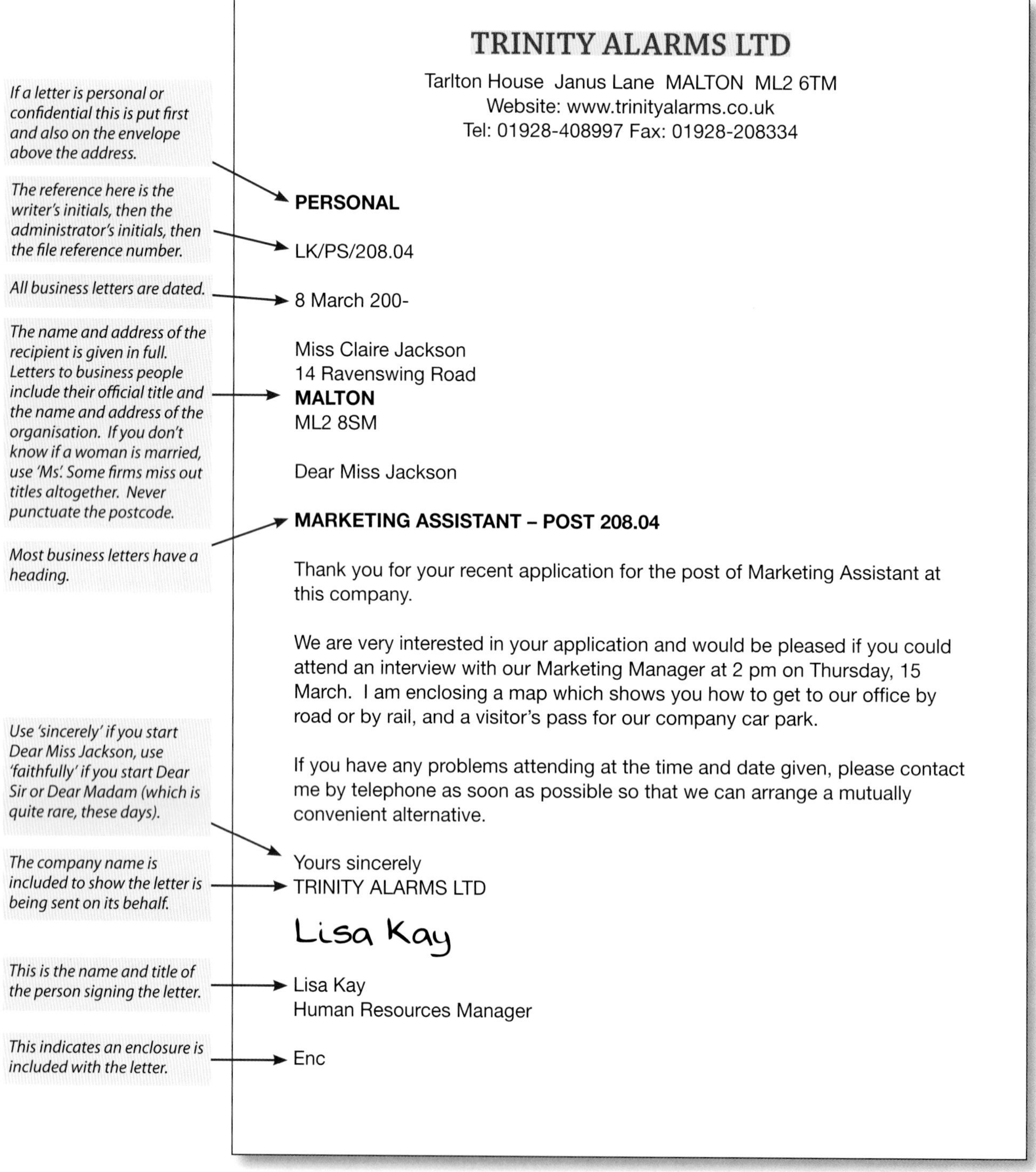

TRINITY ALARMS LTD

Tarlton House Janus Lane MALTON ML2 6TM
Website: www.trinityalarms.co.uk
Tel: 01928-408997 Fax: 01928-208334

PERSONAL

LK/PS/208.04

8 March 200-

Miss Claire Jackson
14 Ravenswing Road
MALTON
ML2 8SM

Dear Miss Jackson

MARKETING ASSISTANT – POST 208.04

Thank you for your recent application for the post of Marketing Assistant at this company.

We are very interested in your application and would be pleased if you could attend an interview with our Marketing Manager at 2 pm on Thursday, 15 March. I am enclosing a map which shows you how to get to our office by road or by rail, and a visitor's pass for our company car park.

If you have any problems attending at the time and date given, please contact me by telephone as soon as possible so that we can arrange a mutually convenient alternative.

Yours sincerely
TRINITY ALARMS LTD

Lisa Kay

Lisa Kay
Human Resources Manager

Enc

The second paragraph goes into more detail about the information introduced at the start. If there is a lot of information, it is better split into two or more paragraphs.

- The Open Day is being held to enable all prospective students and their parents to visit the college. There will be displays of work, refreshments prepared by the catering students . . .

- We are particularly interested in the Appleby Range which has been treated to be stain resistant . . .
- We offer a wide range of services including . . .

The closing paragraph is often just a simple, appropriate ending that relates to what will happen or the action now expected.

- We very much hope you will be able to attend.
- We look forward to hearing from you.
- Please let us know if you require any further information.

Memos

Memos are internal documents sent between members of staff. Although they are less common today because of email, they are still sometimes used for more complex or less urgent internal communications – and to send information to staff who do not have email. They are also used when it is useful to have a printed record for future reference. The most usual layout is shown below.

MEMO

TO John Barnes cc Bill Scott

FROM Lisa Kay

DATE 16 March 200-

REF KJ/PB

SUBJECT NEW PHOTOCOPIER

At our last team meeting, several members of staff reported problems they were having with the new photocopier which I thought you should know about.

- The room in which the copier has been placed is very small and staff are struggling to work in this area. Bill Scott has mentioned there is also an issue relating to safety regulations here.
- There is no suitable fire extinguisher in that room for tackling electrical fires.
- The paper is continually jamming in the machine. The service engineer has informed us that the type we use is unsuitable and has recommended a different brand which is slightly more expensive.

When you have had time to consider these points, I would be grateful if we could meet to discuss the situation early next week.

LK

Anyone who is receiving a copy is listed after the 'cc'.

Name of recipient

Sender's name

No addresses are required in a memo because it's an internal document. There is also no salutation or complimentary close.

Sometimes memos are initialled. They are not usually signed.

You are friends with Claire, who tells you that she has just accepted another job, so she needs to write to Trinity Alarms to tell them she is no longer interested in the vacancy. Draft the letter she could write in reply, using an appropriate layout.

If you are sending a memo to a group of staff, you can put a general title at the top, for example 'All staff' or 'Sales team'.

Did you know?

It is always clearer to divide up lengthy information into separate paragraphs or numbered or bulleted points. Bullets are better when there is no specific order.

The formality of a memo will depend upon the recipient and the subject matter. A memo about a social event will be worded very differently to one about a serious customer complaint.

Slang expressions should be avoided but abbreviated words are often used, for example 'thanks', 'I'll' or 'haven't'.

Reports

Business reports are often written as the result of an investigation, or to provide information on a topic, particularly after research has been carried out. For example, a report could be written that said whether complaints have increased or decreased (with reasons), or on staff retention rates saying why staff have left over the past 12 months.

Reports can be informal or formal. Informal reports are more common and you are more likely to be asked to write an informal report at this stage of your career. The main differences are shown below.

Activity

Write a memo to your tutor asking if you can be excused from class next Friday afternoon. Explain that you have a part-time job and that you have been asked to help out because of staff shortages. Reassure your tutor this is an exceptional case and that you will catch up with any work you miss if he or she agrees.

Informal report	Formal report
Usually for internal/departmental use	May be prepared for senior managers or external audience
May be prepared on plain paper or on a memo	Usually prepared on plain paper. May be bound rather than stapled
Report title **Introduction** – reason for writing the report **Body of report** – information obtained **Conclusion** – sums up information and says whether action is needed or not **Recommendations** – own suggestions for action (if you're asked for these). Name of writer and date added at foot of report if on plain paper	**Report title** **Terms of reference** – scope of the report/what the writer was asked to do **Procedure** – methods used to find information **Findings** – facts found out **Conclusions** – basically answer the questions set in the Terms of reference **Recommendations** – writer's suggestions for action (if requested) Additional items may include **Appendices** (additional items attached) and **Bibliography** (list of references)

Activity

Compare the two different designs for Rachel's report that folllow, illustrating the formal and informal style. As a group, see how many differences you can find.

Two examples of reports, illustrating each style, are shown below. These were written when Rachel Bryne was asked by Lisa Kay, the HR Manager, to find out why the department was suddenly spending twice as much on paper and to see if introducing 'green policies' may help to reduce usage. She was asked not to add her recommendations at this stage.

MEMO

TO Lisa Kay

FROM Rachel Bryne

DATE 5 March 200-

REPORT ON COST OF PRINTER SUPPLIES

Introduction

Last week you asked me to investigate the use of A4 paper in the department as the cost has nearly doubled over the last two months and to find out whether introducing 'green' policies would help to make staff more aware of wastage.

Staff interviews

According to the staff I spoke to, the main reasons for increased use are as follows.

1 Several additional documents were required last month, particularly for the sales conference and the presentation to the Australian visitors.

2 Draft documents are often returned with amendments or corrections.

Paper stocks and supplies

I checked how we purchase paper and the cost, as well as how we store and issue it.

1 We buy our paper from a local company, H Bryson. We like them because they will deliver at short notice. However, their prices are higher than those charged by many other suppliers, particularly online.

2 Some of the paper in the stock room is not stored properly and it is not issued in strict rotation. When old stock becomes discoloured or damaged it is then unusable.

Green policies

I asked staff for their views on green policies.

Most staff thought green policies would be a good idea and suggested recycling spoiled papers and buying recycled paper as well as photocopying documents back-to-back to save paper.

Conclusions

My conclusions are as follows.

1 Although there has been an increase in demand for paper recently we could do more to reduce the amount we use.

2 Introducing green policies would also help and most staff would support this idea.

■ *Example of an informal report*

REPORT ON COST OF PRINTER SUPPLIES

1 **Terms of reference**
Last week I was asked to investigate the use of A4 paper in the department as the cost of this has nearly doubled over the last two months and to find out whether introducing 'green' policies would help to make staff more aware of wastage.

2 **Procedure**
To find this information I undertook the following investigations.
- 2.1 I talked to the staff about paper use.
- 2.2 I investigated how we purchase paper and the price we pay.
- 2.3 I checked the way paper is stored and issued.
- 2.4 I asked staff for their opinions on green policies such as recycling.

3 **Findings**
As a result of my investigations I obtained the following information.
- 3.1 Several additional documents were required last month, particularly for the sales conference and the presentation to the Australian visitors.
- 3.2 Draft documents are often returned with amendments or corrections.
- 3.3 We buy our paper from a local company, H Bryson. They are preferred because they will deliver at short notice but the price is higher than that charged by many national or online suppliers.
- 3.4 Paper is not stored properly and is often not issued in strict rotation. Older stocks often become discoloured or damaged and are then unusable.
- 3.5 Most staff would welcome green policies, such as recycling spoiled papers and buying recycled paper. They also suggested photocopying documents back-to-back to save paper.

4 **Conclusions**
My conclusions are as follows.
- 4.1 There has been a genuine increase in demand for paper recently but more could be done to reduce the amount we spend.

Rachel Bryne

5 March 200-

■ *Example of a formal report*

Whether reports are formal or informal the headings and spacing must be consistent and no slang or abbreviated words must be used. In formal reports, standard headings are used.

Before you attempt any type of report there is a certain amount of preparation to be done – including checking whether you are writing a formal or an informal report.

- **Consider the aim** – why have you been asked to write it? Who is it for? What do they want to know?
- **Draft the introduction or terms of reference** – this is the easiest part. You simply say who asked you for the report and why.
- **Organise your information** – put your facts into a logical order and then decide how to separate them to keep them clear.
- **Decide appropriate recommendations** – if you are asked for these, make sure that they are sensible and relevant given the rest of your report.

Did you know?

A report should be objective. This means that you report the facts and not your opinions, unless you are specifically asked for these.

Activity

Lisa now wants Rachel to add a final section headed 'Recommendations' and to say what action she thinks should now be taken. As a group, decide on five appropriate recommendations that Rachel could make. Then write these for both the informal and the formal report.

Recording and reporting

Notes are often taken during conversations or discussions and typed up afterwards, so that there is evidence of what was said and/or agreed. If you are involved in preparing these types of records, then you will need to develop rather different skills to those you use to compose letters or memos.

Did you know?

Both in court and in Parliament a verbatim (word for word) record is made of the whole proceedings. Find out more at www.parliament.uk/hansard/hansard.cfm.

Type of record

The main types of written records of conversations in business are:

- messages taken on behalf of other members of staff
- summary of a discussion
- minutes of a meeting – often with actions to be taken and by whom.

These are not the only types, of course. Sometimes reports are written to summarise a conversation. The police write a report every time they interview someone and business representatives often do this following a visit to a customer.

Keeping accurate and complete records

Whether you are recording a conversation you have had on the 'phone, jotting down notes or writing the minutes of a meeting, it is important that the record is both accurate and complete. You will be relieved to know that this does not mean writing down every word – which would be impossible for most people. It does mean that the information is correct and nothing important has been omitted.

Accurate and concise reporting in sufficient detail

The trick is to decide which information must be included and which can safely be left out and then to write the essential points clearly and concisely. It may take several attempts before you can do this easily.

Preparing messages

Ideally, you will use a printed form which will prompt you to obtain all the important information relating to the caller, otherwise you will have to write or type out the message on plain paper. Use the following tips to help.

Activity

As a group, suggest some of the consequences of recording incorrect information or missing out important details. Start by thinking about names, phone numbers, dates and times.

TAKING A MESSAGE

1 Write out the message as you are listening, *then* redraft it into a final message for the recipient. This enables you to identify the key information and put it in the right order.

2 Listen carefully. Ask a rapid speaker to repeat anything you do not hear properly or understand.

3 Check you have all the **key facts** you need. These usually include:
- the name of the person (check the spelling if you are unsure)
- the name of the person's organisation or his or her private address
- the caller's telephone number and local dialling code
- the main points relating to the message, e.g.
  - the reason for the call
  - details of any information requested
  - details of any information given to you
  - action to be taken.

This may mean asking a few questions to obtain all the information you need.

4 **Double-check** information about dates, times, place names, product names or codes, prices, quantities – or any other numbers. You cannot guess these afterwards!

5 If the message is long or complicated read it back to the caller to check you have understood everything correctly.

6 Write out the message promptly, using simple, straightforward words that cannot be misunderstood. Include all the key facts in a logical order, even if the caller gave you the information in a random way. Be specific about days and dates and give *both* to be on the safe side. Never say 'today' or 'tomorrow' in case the message is read on a different day to that on which it was written.

7 Leave out personal details or irrelevant information that does not directly relate to the message.

8 Put **your own name** on the message and the **date and time of the call**.

9 If the message is urgent, pass it on *immediately*. If the intended recipient is not available, give the message to a manager or supervisor.

Preparing a summary of a discussion

Talks and discussions are often summarised, so that a written record is available. Perhaps an expert is visiting to talk to a group or answer questions on a topic; or your team may discuss how to split up a task so that the workload is shared. Simply trying to remember what was said is very risky and can lead to many arguments about what was actually said or agreed – and by whom.

The format of a discussion summary should vary, depending upon the main purpose. If you are summarising a question and answer session, it is easier to put each question as a heading then put the reply beneath. If it is a discussion to allocate work, it is important to list each task, any important points made, the name of the person who will do the task and any agreed deadline. An example is shown below. Marie Kemp has signed it to confirm she has read and agreed that the notes are correct.

TRINITY ALARMS

PREPARATIONS FOR ANNUAL SALES CONFERENCE TO BE HELD ON 5 MAY 200-

SUMMARY OF DISCUSSION HELD 25 MARCH 200-

Marie Kemp announced that the large meeting room at the Swan Hotel has been reserved, together with overnight accommodation for those travelling more than 25 miles.

It was agreed that the preparations would be carried out by the team and a follow-up meeting would take place on Tuesday, 15 April to check on progress.

Accommodation and meals Deadline: 20 April

Claire agreed to make a list of those attending and identify those who would need overnight accommodation. She would also check if anyone has special dietary requirements, agree appropriate menus with Marie and inform the Swan.

PowerPoint presentation Deadline: 20 April

Damian will liaise with John Evans, Sales Manager, and prepare this in time for the rehearsal on 21 April.

Catalogues and leaflets Deadline: 25 April

Fatima will order additional copies from the printers immediately because they take three weeks to arrive.

Handouts Deadline: 20 April

Fatima and Claire will prepare these together. Claire will check with John Evans to find out the format he prefers.

Any problems to be reported to Marie Kemp.

MKemp

26 March 200-

Activity

Work in pairs for this activity. Decide on a message you want to give your tutor. Then tell your partner who must write it down to pass on. It is up to you whether you give the information in the right or wrong order – or deliberately omit something important. Then change roles.

Did you know?

It is better to err on the safe side if you are unsure of whether some information should be included rather than miss out something that matters.

Preparing meetings documents How to prepare an agenda or write the minutes of a meeting – together with the formats to use – is explained in Unit 6, pages 258–265.

Did you know?

You are in danger of forgetting to do a routine job – like writing out a message properly – if you do not do it straightaway.

Working within given deadlines and timeframes

If a document is required urgently then you must give it top priority. It is no use taking an urgent telephone message for someone and then only writing it out a day later! Similarly, people who attend a discussion often wait for the notes to appear before they start doing what they promised. Whenever you have meeting or discussion notes to produce, it is sensible to agree a deadline and then plan your work to take account of the timeframe and your other jobs. If you take an important message then hopefully you can be trusted to use your own initiative to deal with it promptly.

Did you know?

The appropriate person to tell about an issue is normally the person who asked you to do the work or your supervisor. Until you have notified this person that there is an issue, they will assume that everything is going to plan.

Reporting issues as they arise to the appropriate person

Problems or issues can arise for a number of reasons. A task may be more complicated or difficult than you first thought; you may be held up waiting for information from someone; you may not be able to understand scribbled notes you have made or the job may be taking much longer than you thought it would, so you cannot achieve the agreed deadline.

Early in your career it can be difficult to achieve the right balance between keeping someone informed about important issues and not panicking unnecessarily every time there is a slight hiccup. Although you will not want anyone to think you cannot cope on your own, it is important to tell someone promptly if an issue could cause a serious problem. The best way to assess this is to think about the consequences that might occur if it is not solved promptly. The worse these are, the more important it is that you tell someone in time for them to take the appropriate action.

Fact file

There are many occasions when it is important to keep a record of conversations or discussions in business, from telephone messages to minutes of meetings.

Over to you

1 *Use the chart on page 158 to decide which type of document would be most suitable to use for each of the following business purposes. Give reasons for your choice and describe the layout you think would be most suitable.*

   a) *A manager is informing a supplier about a series of faults that have occurred on a new expensive machine.*
   b) *An administrator has to inform all the staff that the car park will be closed for resurfacing on Monday.*
   c) *You are working in the office alone when an important customer rings to speak to your boss.*
   d) *An administrator wants to obtain a further supply of printer paper.*

continued ▶

Over to you *continued*

2 *Each of the phrases below is inappropriate in a business letter. In each case identify the reason why it is unsuitable and then suggest an appropriate alternative.*

a) *Hope to hear from you.*
b) *Thanks for getting back to us.*
c) *With reference to your recent letter.*
d) *Is there any chance you could pop in to see us next week?*
e) *Looking forward to seeing you.*
f) *We are really fed up with the poor service we are getting.*

3 *Your student council has recently discussed the range of food and drinks that is supplied by the refectory and whether this could be improved. The student services manager has asked for the matter to be investigated and for a short informal report to be prepared, giving the council's conclusions and recommendations.*

As a group, take the part of the student council. Discuss the range of meals and snacks that you can buy in your college refectory and decide whether you think this can be improved. Then use the comments that are made to prepare the report that is required.

Talking point

View 1: It's perfectly possible to be successful in business without good written communication skills. Dozens of people have done it.

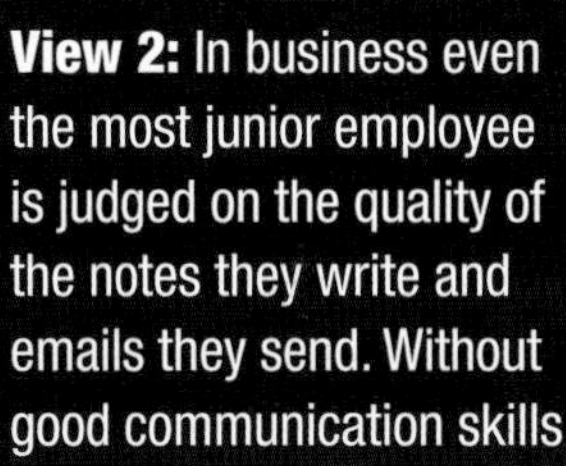

View 2: In business even the most junior employee is judged on the quality of the notes they write and emails they send. Without good communication skills they'll never get on.

With which viewpoint do you agree – and why?

Case study – Assessment practice

Jemma Scott is thrilled. She has just been promoted from customer service assistant to trainee marketing officer. She won the promotion on the basis of her excellent verbal communication skills with customers. Now she needs to prove that she can produce written documents to the same standard.

Craig Eccles, Jemma's boss, is a bit of a stickler, and Jemma wants to make a good impression. On her second day she attends a team briefing, where Craig is talking about their spring campaign. Craig asks her to take notes. Phil, who heads the creative group, will come up with ideas for the theme; Saddiq will investigate the cost of print advertising; Julie will look at different types of online advertising; and Paula will look at possible promotional methods. Craig wants the whole team to come back with their ideas by this time next week.

After the meeting Craig passes Jemma a copy of a new magazine, *Online Marketing Today,* and asks her to find out how to take out a subscription. The publishers have a special offer for businesses at the moment, which Craig thinks is a good deal as he has heard good reports about the publication. Jemma phones the number given and speaks to Rizwana Asghar in the sales department who tells her that the easiest way is to write a letter on her firm's headed paper and enclose a cheque for £116.

When Jemma goes to check that Craig is happy about this, he hands her a note he has received from Shaun Baxter, a new member of staff, and says: 'Ask Shaun to come and translate this, will you, when he's got a minute?' Craig then leaves to go to another meeting.

Jemma goes back to her desk to start work. She starts to compose the letter. After three attempts she is getting desperate. When the phone rings she takes a message for Craig and writes that out. She is no happier with that either. When you see her she is getting visibly upset.

continued ▸

Case study *continued*

Ms Rizwana Asghar
Sales Department
Online Marketing Today
14 Walpole Street
LONDON
NW4 8DL

Dear Rizwana

Thanks for being so helpful when I rang.

We are really keen to subscribe to your magazine, especially with the reduced offer at the moment that we think is a really good deal. We have wanted to try it for some time but thought it was too expensive. With the cheaper rate it's now much better.

I am enclosing a cheque for £116, as you requested, and really look forward to seeing our first copy.

Yours faithfully

FROM THE DESK OF . . .

Shaun Baxter

Craig:

I told my mate Brian about your home wireless network and he says you're only secure if you set up a WEP key and for this you need to know the IE address to talk to your router. Then you'll be ok!

All best

Shaun

continued ▸

Case study *continued*

MESSAGE

URGENT/NON URGENT

TO: Craig Eccles DEPT: marketing

DATE: 9 march TIME: 11.15 am

CALLER'S NAME: Gavin ORGANISATION He didn't say

TEL NO: 07792394839 EXT NO

Message:
He rang this morning about the photos you want for the brochure and the website. He said you would know what he means. He says he could of started work this week if he'd known sooner but can now start next week, if that's OK. He will start in reception at 10 and wants about four people to be there to be like visitors. He then wants to go to sales and production. He wants to know if he should visit some customers, too, and says he will if you ring him back and tell him who. He also said something about outside shots if you want them.

Taken by: Jemma

1(P) Help Jemma by rewriting both the letter and the telephone message so that they would be acceptable for Craig. ***(P4 part)***

2(M) Prepare notes for the team briefing that Jemma attended using an appropriate layout. Then give reasons for the layout you have chosen. ***(M2 part)***

3(M) Explain why the publishers wanted Jemma to write them a letter, rather than send a fax or email. ***(M2 part)***

4(D) Analyse the effectiveness of each of the written communications Jemma prepared, and Shaun's note. Then do the same for the written communications you prepared yourself for question 1. ***(D1)***

Grading tip

Explain by giving reasons to support the points you are making.

Analyse by identifying, and commenting upon, the separate factors that influence whether each communication is effective or not.

4.4 Be able to use interpersonal and non-verbal business communication skills

In Unit 2 you first read about the importance of appropriate presentation and interpersonal skills (see pages 59–71). You also learned about body language. All these aspects are important because the way you look, act and behave also communicate information to the people you deal with.

Conveying a professional image

If you walk into a top hotel or business organisation you expect to be greeted by someone who is smartly dressed, well-groomed, speaks clearly and is sitting – or standing – behind a tidy reception desk. You do not expect a scruffy individual with a nose stud to peer at you from behind a mound of paper and ask you what you want.

Whilst this may seem obvious, it is amazing how many people think they can work in business without considering how they appear to other people – or whether they would appear professional or not. Conveying a professional image includes all the following aspects.

Appropriate dress or uniform and excellent personal hygiene

The dress code for an organisation will depend upon several factors, including the type of industry and the overall style of the organisation. You are more likely to be expected to wear a uniform if you regularly deal with customers than if you do not. There may be a specific dress code, which regulates what you must wear, or there may just be guidelines you have to follow.

Even if there are no guidelines, common sense should tell you that certain outfits are appropriate for business and others are not. You should also realise that dressing appropriately does not just mean wearing suitable clothes that are clean and pressed but also ensuring that you are always nice to be near.

Activity

The importance of excellent personal hygiene, how to dress and the way you should present yourself to other people at work was covered in detail in Unit 2, pages 59–65. Turn back to those pages now and refresh your memory.

Sound organisational skills

Some people are 'naturals' at being well organised. This is usually because they are good at:

- writing down anything they may otherwise forget
- making realistic plans which take into account the priority levels of different jobs
- being self-disciplined and keeping to schedules
- storing information so that it can be easily found
- keeping their belongings neat, tidy and in working order
- breaking down long or complex tasks into smaller, more manageable chunks they can complete in an agreed timescale
- monitoring their progress and letting people know if there is a problem.

Did you know?

Major benefits of being well-organised include working more quickly, making fewer mistakes, being less stressed and keeping your belongings in tip-top condition.

Activity

Check out your organisational skills. How quickly can you find a handout you were given last week, a pencil and a pen? What condition are they in? If the handout is crumpled (or punched in three places), the pencil is blunt and the end of the pen is chewed then you have failed, even though you found them.

Good time management

Time management means being self-disciplined about the use of your time so that you do not waste time doing unnecessary things. Good time managers are normally able to achieve far more in the course of the average working day. This is because they do jobs when they are scheduled to be done, rather than when they feel like it! They are also firm about interruptions. They discourage people from distracting them when they are busy and are equally sensitive enough not to disturb anyone else at the wrong time, either.

Did you know?

***Displacement activities** are things we do to put off starting a job we do not want to do – such as getting a cup of coffee, checking if new emails have arrived or sending an instant message to your friend in the next office. Which ones do you use?*

Professional and business-like manner when dealing with staff and customers

Most people can easily identify the type of behaviour that is not professional – but find it harder to say what is. Chewing gum, running down a corridor, being late, using bad language, making personal calls or sending personal emails at work – all of these are 'unprofessional'. So what type of behaviour do you expect from a professional?

Did you know?

Acting in a business-like manner obviously includes using appropriate body language when you are communicating with staff and customers. If you have forgotten about this, turn back to Unit 2, page 60 to refresh your memory.

Most importantly, professionals have a good knowledge of their job and what they can do and cannot do. This means you can rely on their judgement and know they will seek assistance if they need it. You will also expect them to have all the necessary skills to do their job effectively – someone fumbling with a till, jabbing one finger at a keyboard or struggling to understand their computer screen is not a professional.

You will also expect them to be confident, approachable, friendly, courteous *and* to give you their full attention during a conversation. You will expect them to be truthful, to do accurate work, to take responsibility for their decisions and to fulfil their promises. Finally, you will expect them to show self-control, particularly if things are going wrong. Someone who acts like a 10-year-old if something goes wrong, or who responds aggressively to a perceived (or real) criticism is neither professional, nor business like. There are times when every business professional has had to bite their tongue or count to ten before replying to someone!

Fact file

Excellent presentation and organisational skills are needed to give professional image. Being well organised also means managing time effectively.

Dealing with confidential matters

Many types of information handled by businesses can be confidential. All organisations have a responsibility to keep personal or sensitive information on individuals secure and to dispose of it effectively or they will be acting against the requirements of the Data Protection Act. Beyond that, there is commercially sensitive information that they would not wish to fall into the hands of their competitors or the press.

Using appropriate methods of communication to convey confidential messages

Confidential messages can be conveyed quite safely in a number of ways providing sensible precautions are taken:

- Only convey confidential messages verbally when you know you cannot be overheard.
- Be wary about what you say over the telephone, even to a caller you know. You cannot be sure who is listening in at the other end.
- If you are preparing a confidential message on computer, position the screen so that it cannot be read by someone approaching your desk. Then start a second document and quickly switch windows by pressing Alt+Tab if someone approaches.
- If you have confidential documents on your computer, *always* log out when you leave your desk.
- Never stay logged into email when you are away from your desk.
- Distribute any written messages in a sealed envelope, clearly labelled 'confidential' and do not leave copies on your desk or on the photocopier!

The IT policy of many organisations forbids the transmission of confidential information by email unless it is encrypted.

- Only agree to send a confidential message by fax if the recipient is waiting to receive it *or* if their machine can be specially programmed to store the message in memory until a password is entered.
- Destroy any draft copies in a shredder.

Find out the precautions taken by your school or college to ensure that confidential communications are conveyed securely.

Sensitivity in dealing with confidential issues

Being sensitive about confidential issues means that you use your own common sense and do not need someone standing over you all the time because you are impervious to what is happening around you. In business it is quite possible that someone will try to get you to divulge confidential information, because they think you are gullible enough to tell them what they want to know. This could be a colleague from another department asking you what happened at your last team briefing or a rep trying to get an edge on the competition.

- Be careful about the information you divulge over the telephone, no matter how charming or persuasive the caller. It could be a competitor trying to find out more about your existing customers or your charges.
- Never 'gossip' with a customer or give away internal information unnecessarily. Keep your explanations brief and focused on the topic. Do not be led astray by flattery, shared confidences or sympathy for your heavy workload.
- If you are not sure if you should disclose information, simply say you do not have it and will have to find out. This saves having to explain why you will not tell. Then refer the request to your supervisor.
- When you are photocopying sensitive documents, check you have not left a copy on the glass before you leave.
- Keep a folder in your desk so that you can always put sensitive documents inside if you have an unexpected visitor. Lock away all work-in-progress papers relating to anything confidential in this folder every night.
- Follow all the systems and procedures in your organisation that relate to security – whether you agree with them or not.
- If you identify any security lapses or flaws, report them promptly to your supervisor.

If you are discreet then you will rarely have a problem with confidentiality. This is because people who are discreet opt to say very little, rather than a lot, in situations where they are uncertain how much they should disclose.

Understanding of material that might be confidential

All types of material may be confidential, but usually the following types of information are the most sensitive:

- personal details about staff which they would not wish other people to know

Dealing with confidential matters properly involves handling sensitive information appropriately as well as being discreet.

Did you know?

Many second-hand computers are sold with hard drives that still contain personal information because just 'deleting' it still leaves it recoverable. The National High-Tech Crime Unit recommend removing the hard drive, smashing it up and disposing of the bits in an environmentally friendly way, before selling the computer.

Talking point

View 1: It is better to be open and honest with people, so you don't mislead them.

View 2: In business, the less said the better. That way you can't say the wrong thing.

With which viewpoint do you agree – and why?

- new product developments or lists of customers, both of which would interest competitors
- financial information or employee negotiations which would result in unfavourable publicity for the organisation if it was given to the media
- internal plans which have not yet been agreed and which managers want to keep secret
- passwords or access codes that would be invaluable to a hacker or thief.

Some material may contain a combination of these. For example, if sensitive talks on a possible sale of the business were leaked to the press there may be banner headlines about possible redundancies, which would be dreadful for the staff and may be totally untrue.

Over to you

1 *Suggest a more tactful way to make each of the following remarks to a colleague.*

a) *'You must be joking!'*
b) *'I haven't had time yet, have I?*
c) *'Can't you do anything on your own?'*
d) *'I do wish you'd shut up. I can't concentrate.'*
e) *'Don't you ever listen?'*

2 *You work for the manager of a small company that designs websites for businesses. The company deals with a considerable amount of privileged information about its clients, which must never be disclosed to anyone. From the following situations, decide which information you can disclose and which you cannot. Then say what you would do in the cases where the information is sensitive.*

a) *An external customer wants the mobile phone number of your boss, because he has lost the business card on which it was printed.*
b) *An external customer says that she thinks the quote given for their site to be redesigned is too high. She knows your firm recently updated another firm's site and asks how much they were charged.*
c) *A colleague in another office asks if you know whether your boss has approved a pay rise for everyone yet this year.*
d) *An external customer asks if the rumours are true that your company is cutting back on staff because of financial problems.*
e) *A prospective customer asks you which website design awards your company won last year.*
f) *An external customer asks you for a colleague's home address because he wants to send her a birthday card.*

Case study — Assessment practice

Nadia was bored. She was also cross. She had only volunteered to help on the stand at the careers exhibition thinking it would be fun and an excuse to get out for a bit. Her timing had been a bit awry – it had taken ages to get her hair right, so she had arrived at the last minute and she had a horrible feeling she had forgotten some of the leaflets for the display.

Now to make matters worse, she was stuck here with that awful Sajid. He had spent the last half hour swaggering around, chatting up other exhibitors whilst it was quiet. They had already had one row, just because she had wanted to go outside for a cigarette. He had accused her of smelling like an ashtray. She retorted that it was better than reeking of aftershave. He then said that her skirt was too short and they had not spoken since. Nadia stared around, picking off flakes of nail varnish at the same time.

Thankfully, the hall started to get busier. Several groups approached the stand. Out of the corner of her eye she spotted Sajid, smoothing down his hair and straightening his tie. Nadia raised her eyes heavenwards in despair.

She soon forgot her irritation when she was talking about careers in the industry and started to enjoy being the centre of attention. She had already decided that her real work sounded a bit dull and had started spicing things up a little. As the group moved away, Sajid turned to her and asked 'What was that rubbish you were spouting – about earning £35,000 and travelling to the States twice a year?'

Nadia felt herself going hot and cold but stood her ground. 'That wasn't rubbish, it's true.'

'No, it's not. Neither of us are on anything like that. And what were you saying about the firm moving to Brigsteer next year? At the staff meeting we were asked to keep it quiet for the time being.'

Nadia turned on him. 'Oh, do give it a rest, Saj. I was telling them about Paul, not me, and I said it was my boss's salary, not mine. And for another thing, he shouldn't hold a staff meeting and tell everyone if the information is secret. So just get off my case, will you?'

'I'm sure Paul will be delighted that half the town knows how much he earns,' remarked Sajid, acidly. 'In future, I think it would be best if you just tidy up the leaflets. I'll talk to visitors.'

'How dare you? Who on earth do you think you are . . .' Nadia said, when she was interrupted by a cough. They turned to see Paul Hughes, their boss, standing behind them. Neither of them knew how long he had been there. 'Did I hear my name mentioned?', he asked. 'Perhaps we should talk more about this when we get back to the office.'

1(P) If you were attending a careers exhibition and representing your school or college, list the main interpersonal and non-verbal skills you would be expected to demonstrate. ***(P5 part)***

continued ▶

Case study *continued*

2(M) Explain the interpersonal and non-verbal communication skills that Nadia and Sajid need to demonstrate to support effective verbal communications to visitors. ***(M3)***

3(D) Evaluate the performance of both Nadia *and* Sajid at the event. Then explain the importance of effective interpersonal and non-verbal communication skills in this situation. ***(D2)***

4(P) Prove you can do better than Nadia and Sajid. You are attending a careers exhibition and representing your school or college. In pairs, one person plays the volunteer and the other person the visitor.

As the volunteer demonstrate the interpersonal and non-verbal skills you identified were important in Q1. Then reverse roles. ***(P5)***.

Grading tip

Your explanation should give reasons and link these to the essential communication skills required.

When you evaluate you should review all the information you have; then bring it together to form a conclusion, based on the evidence.

5 People in organisations

All organisations aim to employ people with the right skills and attitude. They need hard-working, committed staff to operate successfully. This unit focuses on aspects of employment that will be useful to you no matter where you work in the future.

What you need to learn

- How to prepare for employment
- The terms and conditions of employment
- How working practices are developed
- How to plan your career development

5.1 Know how to prepare for employment

Many people struggle when they are faced with the task of applying for a job. Some think they have no chance of succeeding at all, and are defeated before they start. Others over-estimate their abilities – and get a nasty shock when they do not get very far in the selection process. The answer to these problems lies in the preparation – and this starts with a little self-analysis.

Personal audit

Carrying out a personal audit is the first stage in preparing for employment. It involves assessing your knowledge and skills now, identifying areas where you are strong and areas you need to develop. You can then match your knowledge and skills better to appropriate job opportunities and improve other areas to increase the range of opportunities available to you.

It is always better to have evidence for knowledge or skills you possess because then your claim is indisputable. Obvious examples are exam certificates, references and school or college reports. But other people's views and the experience you have gained away from school, college or work are also invaluable. So are your own opinions – although you will usually need to give specific examples to support your claims to convince other people these are more than wishful thinking.

Your school or college may issue a form on which you should carry out a personal or skills audit. The example on page 183 also shows a common way of doing this.

Did you know?

One study found that both business entrepreneurs and job applicants often over-estimate their abilities. Experts believe this is why over 60 per cent of new businesses fail within five years and many job applicants are continually disappointed because they do not get an interview or fail to receive a job offer.

Did you know?

Even if you aim to continue studying full time, it is useful to pause regularly to assess and record your progress. This enables you to benefit from opportunities to improve your skills or learn new ones.

Activity

An American survey found that 70 per cent of students thought they had 'above average' leadership skills and only 2 per cent thought they were below average. Over 85 per cent said they had no problems getting on with other people. What would your score be? Do you think English survey results would be different and if so, why?

Did you know?

Many employers consider practical and interpersonal skills to be the most valuable because they say specific technical skills can be taught on the job.

PERSONAL AUDIT

Name .... Date ....

KNOWLEDGE

(List your qualifications here then identify knowledge you have gained from other sources, such as hobbies, interests or work experience – e.g. first aid or how to do stock-taking for a retail firm.)

Knowledge gained **Evidence**

SKILLS

For each skill listed below score yourself from 1 – 5 where 1 = I am very good at this skill, 2 = I am good but it could be improved, 3 = I definitely need to improve this skill, 4 = I would have to work hard to develop this skill, 5 = I have never had the chance yet to develop this skill.

Communication skills

Speaking to people face to face
Listening carefully
Joining in a group discussion
Using correct punctuation and spelling
Writing clearly and concisely
Speaking clearly on the telephone
Expressing my ideas and opinions
Persuading other people
Writing neatly
Composing business documents

Technical skills

Using ICT equipment
Using a range of software
Keyboarding
Using office equipment
Using the Internet
Producing professional documents

Practical and work skills

Working accurately
Finding and correcting own mistakes
Organisational ability
Being punctual
Solving problems
Thinking up new ideas
Accepting responsibility
Working with details
Tidiness
Meeting deadlines
Planning how to do a job
Making decisions
Dealing with numbers
Using own initiative

Interpersonal skills

Helping other people
Working as a member of a team
Being sensitive to the needs of others
Respecting the opinions of others
Dealing with customers
Being tactful and discreet
Being even-tempered
Being reliable

Activity

Carry out a personal audit, using the format shown opposite. Then discuss your conclusions with your tutor.

Key term

Personal audit is a review of the knowledge, skills and attributes you have gained to date.

Fact file

Carrying out a personal audit, then identifying the knowledge and skills listed in job adverts that appeal to you will enable you to work out which areas you need to develop to be successful.

Did you know?

*The term **casual workers** is used to describe employees who have flexible hours, which are normally specified by the employer. Casual workers are only offered work when they are needed, which may not be on a regular basis.*

Matching your knowledge and skills to job opportunities

On a business course, the knowledge and skills you learn will enable you to apply for several jobs in the business world – but not all of them. Whilst this may seem obvious, some people do make inappropriate applications simply because they do not have the necessary experience or qualifications for the job.

All good job advertisements clearly state the **essential** knowledge, skills and experience required (see page 194). They then include the **desirable** attributes, which are optional. Whilst you would need to possess all the essential attributes to be offered an interview, you may be successful without the desirable ones if you could persuade the interviewer that you are keen to develop these areas.

Finding examples of suitable job opportunities enables you to identify the knowledge and skills that are usually considered as essential for jobs you would like to do. You can then compare these with your personal audit to identify the areas you need to develop to give yourself the best chance of success.

Types of employment

If you are a full-time student then you may already be working part-time. During the holidays you may ask for extra hours or take on another job, working on a temporary or seasonal basis. All these are different types of employment and this variety suits everyone. Employers benefit because there is increased flexibility, and employees can find work which suits their current circumstances and family commitments.

Full-time employees These are contracted to work for the standard operating hours of the company. These may vary from 37 to 42 hours a week, but can be more.

Part-time employees These work for less than the standard operating hours but each individual contract may be different. One employee may be contracted to work 15 hours a week and another only 5 hours.

Permanent employees These work for a set number of hours per week from a specified start date. They will continue to work until the contract is terminated because the employee leaves, retires or is dismissed.

Temporary employees These are employed for a fixed term, such as employees covering for someone on maternity leave, those employed short-term because the firm is very busy or hired for a specific project. The final date of the contract may be stated if this is appropriate.

Seasonal employees These are also temporary and employed to work until the end of a specific 'season' – such as the summer season for jobs in tourist resorts and the Christmas season for many retail jobs.

Paid work In this situation employees receive a regular salary as stated in their contract of employment.

Voluntary work In this situation people work for no payment. They volunteer their assistance for a special cause or charity, such as helping at a local hospice or working in a charity shop.

Sources of information and advice

Many business students have little idea of the wide range of jobs and careers that are open to them – let alone information on other types of occupations that might be a possibility. Indeed, far too many people 'drift' into jobs without making much attempt to search for one that might suit them better.

Try to avoid this if you can. Obtaining information and advice from a variety of sources not only gives you a better choice but might even reveal some types of work that you never knew about before.

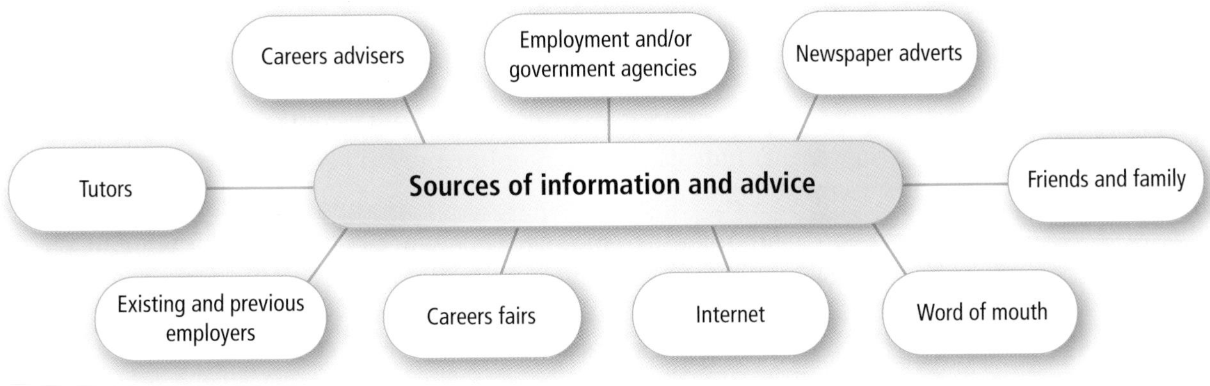

Fact file

There are several different types of employment relating to the number of hours worked, whether the job is permanent or temporary, paid or unpaid.

Did you know?

If you buy a copy of the **Big Issue** *you support a valuable cause and can also read adverts for voluntary work. Some may provide interesting opportunities for you in your spare time or holidays to add to your knowledge and experience.*

Did you know?

More and more companies are advertising vacancies online. Carphone Warehouse now uses its website for almost all its recruitment purposes.

Activity

Check out the Jobs4U Careers database at www.connexions-direct.com. Use the advanced search option if you are not sure what type of job you want to do.

Did you know?

If you are aged 17 or 18 many jobs on offer will be Apprenticeships, where you have time off to study for an NVQ qualification whilst you gain experience at work.

Did you know?

***Networking** is the term used for making professional contacts. In some industries, such as the media, this is a major way of finding out about new job opportunities.*

Obtaining information and advice about jobs

Careers advisers and the Connexions resource area in your school or college Use this area, and talk to the staff, to find information about the wide variety of careers in business – such as jobs in marketing, HR and finance, which are all very different!

Government agencies such as Connexions or the JobCentre Connexions provides advice if you are under 19, or if you are under 25 and have learning difficulties or disabilities. You do not have to visit a Connexions centre; you can find out about different careers and vacancies in your area online instead. JobCentres are for anyone of working age and again you can search for jobs and information online at www.jobcentreplus.gov.uk.

Word of mouth You may hear about a vacancy from someone you know – a neighbour, friend, relative or your tutor. Or you may be able to find out more about a particular type of work because you or your family know someone who works in this area.

Advertisements in your local newspaper Most newspapers have specific 'jobs nights'. Knowing about these saves you the cost of buying a paper on other nights. Alternatively you can check whether your local newspaper puts its vacancies online or is linked to a website, such as www.fish4jobs.co.uk.

Local recruitment or employment agencies Find those in your area by checking in your local *Yellow Pages* or online. Agencies normally do not charge applicants for finding them a job but will charge for several other services, such as helping with an application or CV.

Job boards online Today many companies post their job vacancies online. It is sensible to check the websites of companies in your area that you would like to work for.

Careers fairs These are held throughout the year and are invaluable because you can walk around and chat to people on the different stalls.

Existing and previous employers Both can be useful sources of information and advice on careers in their area of work. These may give you good ideas or, conversely, confirm the type of jobs you would not like to do on a full-time basis.

Your tutors Your personal tutor should be your first contact and is probably best placed to give you advice about the type of jobs that link to your own strengths. Other tutors, too, may be able to provide useful information, particularly if they have an interesting or varied career history themselves.

Your friends and family It is easy to overlook one of the most obvious sources of information and advice because they are under your nose. If you are talking to people check, too, who *they* know who might help you.

Did you know?

Going round a careers fair in a group is not a good idea. You will learn more if you go with one close friend or a parent and focus your search on areas that interest you.

Did you know?

A good question to keep asking yourself is: 'Who else could I talk to who could help me with this?'

Activity

Sketch all your possible contacts by putting your own name in a circle in the middle of a page and then surrounding yourself with the names of people you know. Extend this by adding people that each of your contacts knows, and so on. If anyone has experience in a certain type of job, make a note of this too.

Applying for jobs

At some stage, you will make your first formal job application. You may already have a part-time job and/or have visited at least one organisation on work experience. You may have had to complete official forms, or attend a short interview, in either of these situations. However, when you apply for a permanent job, you are likely to find that the procedure will be more formal. This is because the organisation is making a much greater commitment if it employs you. You will also normally find that there is far more competition for the job – so everything about your application is extremely important if you want to stand a chance of success.

The more you know about the job, the easier it is to target your application effectively. Employers know this, which is why many of them send a copy of the job description and the person specification to anyone who asks for an application form.

Fact file

There are many sources of information and advice on jobs. Investigating these improves your chances of finding a job you will enjoy.

Did you know?

To apply for jobs effectively you must be able to match your strengths to the employer's list of required skills and qualities.

Job descriptions

Job descriptions summarise all the basic facts about a particular job and the role of the job holder. Many organisations prepare or revise this when a vacancy is created and before it is advertised. If you receive a copy, this helps you to understand exactly what type of work you will be asked to do. It also states the salary level. An example of a job description is shown below.

Key terms

A ***job description*** is a statement which lists the main elements of a job and the duties of the job holder.

A ***person specification*** links to the job description and states the skills and abilities needed to do the job effectively.

Curriculum vitae is a summary of a person's education, skills and experience.

PERIVALE SERVICES LTD

JOB DESCRIPTION

Department:	Marketing
Job Title:	Trainee Marketing Assistant
Hours of work:	37.5 per week, normally 9 am – 5.30 pm Monday to Friday with one hour lunch, but some flexibility required
Salary scale:	£11,500 – £14,500
Responsible to:	Marketing Manager
Responsible for:	Not applicable
Job purpose:	To provide general support for the marketing team, to prepare marketing materials, to keep the website up to date and monitor online responses.

Duties and responsibilities

1 Receive telephone calls, deal with general enquiries and take messages for other team members as necessary.

2 Assist in the monthly update of the product brochure by writing basic product descriptions and obtaining artwork as necessary.

3 Keep the customer database up to date.

4 Assist in the preparation and distribution of mail shots to customers.

5 Update the marketing section of the company website with new product details or special offers as requested.

6 Monitor website activity and produce a monthly report for the marketing manager.

7 Ensure all customer email enquiries receive prompt responses, referring these to a more senior member of staff for resolution, if necessary.

8 Attend any training course or team events that may be considered appropriate by the Marketing Manager.

9 Maintain confidentiality about future projects and customer information at all times and be aware that breach of this could lead to instant dismissal.

10 Undertake any other relevant duties which may be identified.

This job description is not intended to be fully prescriptive and will be the subject of regular review and possible amendment. The post holder may be required to undertake related tasks which are not specifically mentioned above.

August 2006

■ *Job description*

Did you know?

No job description can include every task you might have to do. This is why there is often a 'catch all 'phrase at the bottom.

Person specification

This lists the essential and desirable qualifications, skills and attributes of the person required. Preparing this document enables the employer to think about the best type of person for the job and means that it is easier to highlight the essential and desirable qualities clearly in the advertisement. Applications are compared and the applicants chosen for interview are normally those who have all the essential requirements and several of the desirable ones as well.

An example of a person specification to match the job description for the Marketing Assistant is shown below.

PERIVALE SERVICES LTD

PERSON SPECIFICATION

Department: Marketing

Job Title: Trainee Marketing Assistant

Vacancy No: 509

Personal attributes	***Essential***	***Desirable***
Qualifications	4 GCSEs grade C or above, including English or equivalent business qualification	CLAIT or e-skills qualification
Experience	Some experience of dealing with customers in part-time or full-time employment	Previous experience of working in a team in a business environment
Skills and abilities	Verbal communication skills Neat handwriting	Use of Microsoft Office Webpage updating
Personal attributes	Keen interest in working in Marketing Willing to undertake further study Neat and tidy appearance	Friendly and outgoing personality Creative abilities

■ *Person specification*

Did you know?

You can find vacancies and download job descriptions and person specifications at the NHS jobs website at www.jobs.nhsuk. Use search terms such as 'finance', 'clerical', 'administration' to find jobs that are non-medical.

Fact file

Obtaining the job description shows you what the job entails, whereas the person specification enables you to check that you meet the essential criteria.

Did you know?

Many organisations ask you to phone or email for an application pack. Be aware that your skills may be monitored from this stage onwards, so your phone manner or email must be totally professional.

Did you know?

You can often save an online application form before you send it. You can then ask someone to check it with you first.

Application forms

Many organisations send standard application forms to applicants and some make these available online. Job applicants frequently make silly mistakes when filling in application forms – from scruffy writing to using a 'blobby' pen or forgetting to complete every section. This often eliminates them right at the start of the selection process.

The main dos and don'ts related to completing application forms are shown below.

DO . . .	DON'T . . .
Photocopy the form and practise on this copy	Complete the original form until you are sure your practice form is as good as it possibly can be
Read the form through first	Try to do it in a rush or if you are distracted
Collect all the relevant information, e.g. examination results, before you start	Guess anything important, such as grades or dates
Check what type of pen you must use	Change the type of pen half-way through. If a disaster occurs use another one with the same colour of ink and texture as the first
Check where you should use block capitals	Write the postcode in the wrong place. Check carefully where it should go
Write neatly and think about what you are doing	Put the current year for your date of birth
Check if you need to include names of referees	Include the name of a referee without asking his or her permission first
Think about your answers in relation to the space you are allowed	Make any spelling errors
Check where you need to sign and date the form	Complete any section marked 'for official use only'
Ask someone whose advice you respect to check your form for you	Sulk if they criticise parts of it
Complete the original form slowly and carefully	Cross out an error you make. Use a tiny amount of brand new correction fluid
Take a photocopy before you post it	Attend an interview without reminding yourself what you wrote

■ *Dos and don'ts of completing application forms*

Did you know?

Many application forms contain a special section where you have to say why you want the job. This is similar to the type of information you would put in a job application letter (see page 192).

Activity

Check out online recruitment at www.careersatcarphone.com/vacancies.htm. Find and compare current vacancies. Applicants who complete an online application form and attach their CV receive email confirmation of its receipt.

Curriculum vitae

A CV, or curriculum vitae, is a summary about you and your achievements. It is your advert, about yourself, to an employer. It must therefore look professional, so you should create it on a word processor and only send an original document, not a photocopy.

A CV is normally divided into sections under clear headings to include the following information:

Your personal details Your name, address and phone number are crucial. Most people put their date of birth and include their email address. Other personal details are normally unnecessary, such as marital status or nationality.

Your education This is normally in date order with the most recent course first. Include the school or college, dates attended, qualifications obtained, examinations taken where you are still awaiting the result.

Employment details This should also be in date order, with the most recent job first. In each case, give a brief example of what you did. If you are still a full-time student, include part-time, temporary or Saturday jobs you have undertaken.

Other useful information This section can often make all the difference. Include:

- any positions of responsibility you have held
- details of hobbies, interests, sports or voluntary work you have done
- details of any organisations to which you belong
- any other useful, relevant information, such as a clean driving licence or fluency in a language.

Referees It is usual to give two names. One should be a current tutor who knows your work well. Ideally, your other referee will know how you work in business, so could be your employer if you work part-time, or a work experience supervisor. Always ask a person's permission before you include their name on your CV.

Activity

Some people put their name at the top, as a main heading, on their CV and then write a brief paragraph about themselves in a box underneath. As a group, discuss the advantages and disadvantages of doing this.

Did you know?

Employers often have to wade through dozens of CVs so those that are short and focused are often the only ones that are read through to the end. One page is therefore better than two and anything over two is too many.

Did you know?

If you lie about your skills or qualifications in your application and your employer finds out, you can be dismissed as a result.

Did you know?

It is not wise to give the name of a family member as a referee. Most organisations would naturally think that such a person would be biased towards you.

Did you know?

If you are sending an application form and/or your CV, some employers specifically state that you must not send a letter as well – so check carefully.

Letters of application

There are different types of job application letters.

A brief covering letter If you are sending your CV, it is usual to attach a short letter that simply explains why you are sending it. This must be set out properly with your home address at the top and be addressed to the right person. It should also include any reference numbers given in the advert and be signed by you.

A letter justifying your application This is a harder letter to compose because you are trying to 'sell yourself' to your prospective employer. This type of letter is expected if you see the words 'apply in writing' or 'apply in writing attaching your CV' at the end of an advertisement. The main points to note are listed below.

- The letter should be fairly short and use the standard format for a business letter (see page 196).
- There must be no spelling, punctuation or grammatical errors.
- It will normally have three or four paragraphs.
- The *first* paragraph should say where you saw the advertisement (or found out about the job) and state that you would like to apply for the position.
- The *second* paragraph should give general background information about yourself at school, college or work. If you are enclosing your CV then refer to it. Otherwise you will need to go into more detail in the letter about your qualifications and the work you have done.
- The *third* paragraph should say why you want the job or would like to work for this organisation – or anything else to make your application different and interesting.
- The *final* paragraph should say that you are available for interview at any time or state when you are not available.

Did you know?

Most application letters can be prepared on a computer these days. Rarely are people asked to apply in handwriting – but double-check the advert, just in case.

Making an application special

Most people find it difficult to talk positively about themselves. Yet this is essential if you want your application to stand out. You may need to do this:

- on an application form, if there is a special section asking you why you want the job
- in an application letter, to convince the reader you are keen to get the job
- on a CV, if you decide to put a brief personal statement about yourself at the top.

The important point is that this statement should be changed for each application – so that it is tailored to the essential and desirable requirements of the advertisement. This is also where your personal audit comes in useful, because it should help you to identify your strengths in different areas and focus on your skills and achievements.

Activity

As a group, go through the adverts in one edition of your local paper and find out how many different ways are specified to apply for different jobs.

Fact file

There are many different ways to apply for jobs. Some employers send out application packs with the job description, person specification and application form. Others ask for CVs and a covering letter, or for applications to be made in writing.

Over to you

1 *Add to the personal audit you carried out on page 183 by carrying out the following activities.*

a) *List all your achievements, both in and out of school or college. Write down everything at this stage – you can revise your list later so that it only includes the most relevant ones.*

b) *List all your interests. Make these specific, rather than general, e.g. playing 5-a-side football (rather than 'sports').*

c) *List any other facts about yourself that other people might find interesting – from voluntary work you have done to running in a local charity event or visiting relatives abroad.*

d) *Highlight five positive characteristics that apply to you, e.g. friendly, loyal, patient, enthusiastic, kind, tactful, hardworking. Then ask one or two of your friends to do the same. Then make three lists. The first has those which you have both identified. The second has those that your friends have put down and you have not. The third is for those you have identified but others haven't spotted. Then suggest the reason for these differences.*

e) *Arrange a tutorial when you can talk through your lists and findings with your tutor – and refine your personal audit as a result.*

2 a) *Use at least four sources of information and advice listed on pages 185–187 to obtain details of job opportunities and careers in which you would be interested.*

b) *As a result of your investigations, either online or from your local paper find a job advertisement that interests you. Using the personal audit you carried out and the information you obtained in question 1 above, write a short paragraph that you could include in a form or letter in support of your application.*

Talking point

View 1: Many firms don't acknowledge applications sent in by applicants who don't make the shortlist. This is sensible because if there are hundreds of applications it would be too expensive.

View 2: There is no excuse for not responding to job applications these days. To save postage, a quick email could be sent instead.

With which viewpoint do you agree – and why?

Case study

Assessment practice

Gareth Cooper has seen a job which appeals to him in his local newspaper, the *Westbury Gazette*. This is shown opposite.

Gareth telephoned Perivale Services to obtain more information and received the job description and person specification shown on pages 188 and 189. He has now prepared a CV and a covering letter, as instructed. These are shown on pages 195 and 196.

PERIVALE SERVICES LTD

TRAINEE MARKETING ASSISTANT

We are looking for a keen, well-organised person to join our dynamic marketing team. Duties will include assisting with direct mail, updating the customer database and marketing administration.

You will need to possess a minimum of 4 GCSEs at grade C or above, including English, or have an equivalent business qualification, as well as some experience of dealing with customers in a working environment. Ideally, you will also have basic IT skills and be familiar with Microsoft Office. You should have worked in a team in a business environment and will be able to demonstrate that you can deal with customers in a clear and professional manner.

We expect the successful candidate to be eager to learn about all aspects of marketing and develop sound marketing communication skills and to be keen to study for higher level qualifications.

Hours: 9 am – 5.30 pm. Salary negotiable depending upon age and experience.

For further details of the vacancy telephone 03781 809823.

Please apply in writing, enclosing your CV and a brief letter which says what interests you about the job to Rachel James, Human Resources Manager.

Closing date: 26 August.

Perivale Services Ltd, Abbeydale Road, Westbury, WT4 BR9

Perivale Services is an equal opportunities employer and applications are welcome from all minority groups.

1(P) Describe how obtaining the job description and person specification will have helped Gareth. ***(P1 part)***

2(P) Assess how well Gareth meets the essential and desirable requirements for the job. ***(P1 part)***

3(P) Identify the extent to which Gareth has matched his current knowledge and skills to this particular job in his application. Do this by identifying statements that make it obvious to Perivale Services that Gareth has tailored his application for this particular vacancy. ***(P1 part)***

4(P) Refer to your own personal audit and assess whether your current knowledge and skills would enable you to apply for the job at Perivale Services. ***(P1 part)***

5(P) *Either* apply for the job at Perivale or select an appropriate job opportunity from your local paper or online and prepare your own CV and letter of application. ***(P2)***

Grading tip

Make your assessment by matching Gareth's knowledge and skills to the requirements of the job.

Assess yourself by matching your own current knowledge and skills to the requirements of the job.

Remember that your application must be accurate and complete in every respect.

GARETH COOPER

Address:	14 Chester Road, Westbury, WT8 6PT
Telephone:	03781 683737
Nationality:	British
Date of birth:	12 June 1989
Marital status:	Single
Email address:	garethcooper@athome.com

EDUCATION

2005 – present	Westbury College, business and IT (ECDL) course
1999 – 2005	Jackson High School, studying for GCSEs

QUALIFICATIONS OBTAINED

June 2006	BTEC First Diploma in business (merit grade). Key skills award in Communications, Use of Number and IT.
June 2005	GCSEs English (B) Maths (D) Applied ICT (Double Award) (DD) Science (Double Award) (DD)

EMPLOYMENT AND WORK EXPERIENCE

July 2005 – present	Part-time sales assistant at Everysports store.
March 2005	Two weeks' work experience in the sales and marketing department at Piplax Ltd where I helped to prepare and distribute newsletters to customers using the customer database.
March 2004	One week's work experience for Capital Housing where I carried out general office duties.

ADDITIONAL INFORMATION

During College holidays I have always been offered additional hours at Everysports because I am used to helping and serving customers. I am currently doing a summer ECDL course to improve my career prospects as I know good IT skills will be very important. My hobbies include playing 5-a-side football – I play for a local charity team – and going to the cinema. I am also learning to drive.

REFEREES

Mrs J Brookes, Tutor, Westbury College, Newby Road, Westbury, WT1 3SL
- telephone 03781 - 382798
Mr T Harper, Manager, Everysports, Swan Street, Westbury, WT5KS
- telephone 03781 – 603982

14 Chester Road
WESTBURY
WT8 6PT
Tel: 03781 683737
Email: garethcooper@athome.com

16 August 2006

Ms Rachel James
Human Resources Manager
Perivale Services Ltd
Abbeydale Road
WESTBURY
WT4 BR9

Dear Ms James

TRAINEE MARKETING ASSISTANT

I would like to be considered for the position of Trainee Marketing Assistant which was advertised in the Westbury Gazette last Friday.

I successfully completed a BTEC First business course at Westbury College last month and since then have been working at the local Everysports store, as well as taking a summer course to improve my IT skills by achieving an ECDL award. I am attaching my CV, which gives full details of the qualifications I have taken and my results to date.

I would very much like to be considered for this job for several reasons. I am always been very interested in marketing and really enjoyed working in the sales and marketing department at Piplax when I was on work experience. I used their customer database and helped with their customer mail shot. I also like dealing with customers at Everysports and contributing to team meetings, when we discuss new ways of attracting customers to the store and meeting their needs when they visit. I would really enjoy learning more about marketing and would welcome the opportunity to obtain higher level qualifications. I am very familiar with the range of products made by your company, which are excellent quality and value for money. I also know your organisation has an excellent reputation for training staff.

I am an enthusiastic and conscientious worker. I am also used to working in a team – both at Everysports and as a member of a local charity football team.

I can attend for interview at any time.

Yours sincerely

Gareth Cooper

Gareth Cooper

Enc

5.2 Understand terms and conditions of employment

Wherever you work and whatever you do there will be certain conditions attached to your job, both for you and for your employer. This is because there are laws that cover most aspects of employment in the UK. These affect the terms and conditions related to any job.

Statutory employment laws are passed by Parliament and affect everyone in the country. Everyone must abide by these. For example, all employees have the right to be paid at or above the national minimum wage rate for their age and to receive statutory sick pay (SSP) if they are ill for at least four consecutive days. Some of the main laws relating to employment are given on pages 204–205.

Contractual employment terms are additional rights and conditions which are contained in a contract of employment. These affect just that job holder. For example, many people are paid above the minimum wage rate and their starting salary will be shown in their contract. Similarly, many employees benefit from a company sick pay scheme if they are ill, which pays more than SSP.

Contracts of employment define your terms and conditions of employment and the actions that you and your employer can and cannot take.

Terms and conditions for employment

Anyone who works for an employer for more than one month must be given details of their terms and conditions of employment in writing. The document must be sent within two months of the date when their employment started. The information may be given in an offer letter or in a more formal document, called a **contract of employment**. Many documents just summarise the **main terms of employment** and state where other essential information can be found.

Key items in a contract of employment

The letter, contract or statement of main terms must contain certain specific items. Other essential items can be included in a separate document and the employee must be told where to find them. Whatever type of document you receive you will be instructed to read it, sign one copy and return it as proof that you accept and agree to the conditions. It is therefore important to check that you understand them.

Within the contract must be the following information:

- your job title
- your hours of work
- your place of work
- the main terms and conditions of your employment
- your pay and other benefits, e.g. sick pay and holiday pay

A ***contract of employment*** is a written document containing the terms and conditions of employment relating to a particular person and their job.

Express terms are terms that are clearly stated in the contract.

Implied terms are terms that are not written down because they are considered obvious.

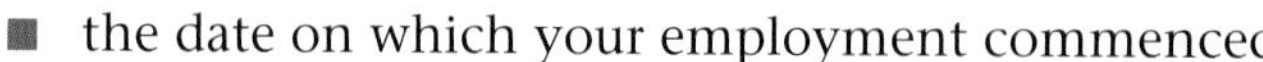

All paid employees must receive written information on their terms and conditions if they are employed for longer than a month. They must receive this within two months of starting work and essential information includes the hours and place of work, salary and other benefits and main terms and conditions.

- the date on which your employment commenced
- the name of your employer
- your name.

Additional information that can be given in a separate document is as follows:

- in some cases, if the job is temporary, the date on which the job will end
- details of any trade union agreements which relate to you
- details of your employer's grievance and appeals procedure (see page 200).

Further information to which you must have access is:

- details about sickness benefits and sickness entitlement if you are ill
- pension scheme details
- how much notice you must give if you want to leave the job
- details of your employer's disciplinary rules and procedures (see below).

An example of a Statement of the Main Terms of Employment is shown on page 199 for Perivale Services.

Terms and conditions within a contract

All contracts are slightly different because the exact terms and conditions of the jobs are unlikely to be the same. As long as the employer includes all the essential items and does not include anything which is against the law, this is quite acceptable. Types of information to look out for are given below.

Payment terms Your contract will state your salary, how often you will be paid and the method of payment. Details of any bonus or commission schemes will also be included in addition to information on sick pay.

Probation Many employees start on a probationary period – from three months to a year. During this period they may be paid a lower salary and less notice will be required on either side to end the employment. So if you normally had to give a month's notice or more, this may be reduced to a week when you are on probation; and your employer may only need to give you a day or two. During this period your performance is continually assessed. If it is satisfactory then you become a 'full' employee when it is over. If there are minor problems the probationary period may be extended for a short time. If there are serious problems the employee will either be demoted or dismissed.

Disciplinary procedures state what action the employer will take if there is a problem with an employee. They are used if the employee breaches the contract, fails to comply with disciplinary or organisational rules or does not fulfil his or her responsibilities.

There is no law that says your employer must pay you sick pay, but many do pay for a maximum number of days at the employee's normal rate. The number of days varies between organisations.

During a trial period, both job-related skills and personal skills are assessed, such as time-keeping, attendance and ability to work with others.

STATEMENT OF MAIN TERMS OF EMPLOYMENT

This statement, together with the Employee Handbook, forms part of your Contract of Employment and sets out the main terms of your employment with Perivale Services Ltd.

Name: Gareth Cooper

Job Title: Trainee Marketing Assistant

Place of work: Perivale Services Ltd, Abbeydale Road, Westbury, WT4 BR9

Date of commencement of employment: 20 September 2006

Salary: £11,500 per annum on salary scale 2. On this scale your salary will increase by £500 each year to a maximum of £14,500. Salaries are paid on the 28th day of the month by BACS credit transfer.

Hours of work: 37.5 hours each week over 5 days, Monday to Friday.

Holidays: Annual holiday entitlement and holiday pay is calculated on the basis of 24 days for each full calendar year of employment plus 8 statutory public/bank holidays. The annual entitlement increases with length of service, details of which are provided separately. The holiday year runs from 1 April to 31 March and unused holiday entitlement may not be carried forward from one year to the next.

Holiday pay: Normal rate for all holidays including statutory public/bank holidays.

Sick pay entitlement: The scale of the company sick pay scheme is as follows. Up to 8 weeks' service: Nil; After 8 weeks service: Up to 2 weeks at full pay and 3 weeks at 50% pay in any 12 month period. You may also qualify for statutory sick pay.

Absence from work: Your supervisor's permission must always be obtained in advance for planned absence. Unexpected absences must be notified to your supervisor by 10 am on the first day whenever possible. To qualify for statutory sick pay and payment from the company's sick pay scheme, you must complete a self-certificate when your absence lasts from 0.5 to 7 days, including Saturday or Sunday. A doctor's or hospital certificate must be produced for all absences exceeding 7 days.

Health and safety at work: All employees must comply with the company's health and safety policy and with all the rules laid down by the Health and Safety at Work Act and all other relevant regulations. A copy of the health and safety policy and the relevant requirements will be issued during your induction period.

Notice: A minimum period of 4 weeks' notice is required. The minimum notice you are entitled to receive from the employer is: Between 4 weeks and 4 years service – 4 weeks' notice from the company. This increases by 1 week for each additional year's service up to a maximum of 12 weeks from the company.

Disciplinary rules and disciplinary procedures: The disciplinary rules and procedures are fully explained in the employee handbook.

Grievances and grievance procedure: The company grievance procedure is described fully in the staff handbook, available from the HR department.

Monitoring of employees: The company reserves the right to monitor and record staff telephone calls, email and Internet use. Full details are given in the company's IT policy as set out in the staff handbook.

Date of issue of this document: 20 September 2006

I acknowledge receipt of my Statement of Main Terms and the Staff Handbook and confirm that I have read and understand these documents. I understand that any amendments to this statement will be agreed with me and confirmed in writing within one month.

Signed .... (Employee)

Signed .... (Employer)

This contract is subject to the information submitted on your application form being correct. The company reserves the right to withdraw any offer of employment or to terminate your employment without notice if any information provided by you is found to be false or misleading.

Did you know?

The Employment Act 2002 (Dispute Resolution) Regulations 2004 specify the exact procedures that must be followed by both employees and employers in the case of a grievance or if disciplinary action is being taken.

Activity

Find out the first step you could take if you had a grievance by going to http://www.dti.gov.uk/employment/Resolving_disputes/index.html. Find out too, the first step your employer would take if you were being disciplined for some reason.

Did you know?

In the UK, there is no automatic legal right to time off on a Bank Holiday, unless this is stated in your contract. Nor does the law relating to annual leave apply to students on work placements or work experience. It does, however, cover students employed during the holidays.

Grievance procedures tell employees what action to take if a dispute cannot be resolved informally and if the employee feels there is a legitimate complaint. Most grievances are individual but a collective grievance can be pursued by a group of employees.

Annual leave All full-time employees have the legal right to a minimum of 20 days' paid holidays a year – often referred to as 'annual leave'. Part-time and temporary employees must, by law, be treated in the same way as full-time employees, so their holidays must be comparable on a pro rata basis (i.e. adjusted in relation to the number of hours worked). Therefore if all full-time employees receive 20 days' paid holiday a year, then part-time or temporary employees working 50 per cent of hours must receive 10 days' paid holiday.

Some employers may be more generous and this would be stated in the contract, together with any restrictions on holidays. For example, if your employer is very busy at a certain time of the year, holidays may not be allowed then except by special agreement with a senior manager.

Leave arrangements include the following:

- **Maternity leave** Pregnant women automatically qualify for maternity leave for a minimum of 26 weeks. Many have the right to receive a minimum level of pay during this time and those who have worked for longer with an employer can take additional unpaid leave. During this time the woman's terms and conditions must remain the same and she must be allowed to return to her old job afterwards, or suitable alternative work if the job she did has ceased to exist. If she is sacked or made redundant then this would automatically be classed as unfair dismissal.
- **Paternity leave** Most working fathers can take up to two weeks' paid leave following the birth of their partner's baby.
- **Adoptive leave** This gives similar rights to a couple who are adopting a child as to those who are expecting a baby.

- **Parental leave** All parents are entitled to 13 weeks' unpaid parental leave after one year's continuous service with an employer. They can take this normally until the child's fifth birthday; if the child is disabled up to 18 weeks' unpaid leave can be taken until the child's 18th birthday.
- **Dependants and urgent personal leave** Employees can take reasonable time off to resolve an emergency concerning a dependant.

Notice and termination of contract There is a minimum amount of notice that you, or your employer, has to provide if the contract is terminated. This is to allow you to find another job, or for your employer to replace you. Some employers extend this, particularly for senior staff, who may be harder to replace.

Redundancy Redundancy is a situation where a person is dismissed because there is no work for them to do. In law, redundancy must be fair – an employer cannot pick and choose which employees to make redundant and must consult fully over the criteria for selection with the trade union and follow an agreed process. If there is a staff association, it must be consulted when more than 20 jobs will be affected. Employees who have worked for the employer for more than two years must receive redundancy pay at, or above, a minimum legal level based on their age, length of service and weekly pay up to a specified amount. They must also be offered free counselling or retraining and given time off to go for interviews for a new job.

Right to trade union membership If a trade union is recognised by the employer, then all employees have the right to join – or the right to refuse. This is a statutory right so may not be stated in a contract. However, you must be told about any union agreements that relate to you. Employers do not have to recognise a trade union, but many are prepared to do so if the majority of employees would prefer this.

Compliance with company policies/codes of behaviour Most organisations have specific policies and rules on aspects of work, such as discrimination, bullying, harassment, the use of IT equipment, health and safety and security. Some staff may also have to comply with a company dress code or codes of behaviour relating to confidentiality and/or dealing with customers.

Representing the organisation All organisations are keen to safeguard their good name and their reputation. They may therefore include a specific term in their contracts for employees to uphold the standards, values and beliefs of the business in their dealings with their external contacts.

Ethical behaviour This relates to treating people honestly, fairly and openly. It means not misleading customers to make a sale, not trying to avoid paying tax, not exaggerating the benefits of a product – or doing any other type of sneaky trick. Many organisations have a code of ethics that all employees have to abide by and this requirement may be included in their contract of employment.

Did you know?

The Work and Families Bill, published In October 2005, included plans to extend maternity and paternity leave and provide leave for workers caring for sick or elderly relatives.

Fact file

A contract of employment defines the legal relationship between employee and employer. When both have signed it, it is binding and both employer and employee have to obey and observe its terms unless they mutually agree to change these.

Did you know?

You may think that how you behave outside work has nothing to do with your employer. But it depends what you are doing and how this relates to your job. An RSPCA inspector was found guilty of neglecting his own dog – and was dismissed because this brought the employer's name into disrepute.

Activity

Responsible newspapers insist that their journalists conform to the paper's code of ethics. You can see how this affects their behaviour by reading the Guardian's editorial code at http://image.guardian.co.uk/sys-files/Guardian/documents/2005/02/25/code2005.pdf.

Contract fulfilment Because a contract of employment is a legal document, it is legally binding. Both parties must abide by its terms. If they do not, then they are in breach of the contract and there are legal repercussions. An employee who breaches the contract can be disciplined and may be dismissed. If an employer breaches the contract, then the law is on the side of the employee who may decide to take legal action.

Express and implied terms

A contract of employment contains **express terms** that you must not breach. But there are other things you and your employer must and must not do that are supposed to be so obvious they do not need to be written down. These are known as **implied terms** of employment and are summarised below.

IMPLIED TERMS OF EMPLOYMENT

The employee

All employees have the following responsibilities, even if they are not expressly stated in the contract of employment.

- Comply with all the terms of the contract
- Follow health and safety regulations
- Comply with other laws related to their work, e.g. not drinking and driving.

In addition, the employer can expect the employee to:

- be reasonably competent and possess the skills claimed at the interview
- be 'ready and willing' to work and do what any 'reasonable' employee would do in a situation
- take reasonable care of the employer's property
- work towards the objectives of the organisation
- carry out reasonable instructions and requests
- be honest
- not disclose confidential information
- behave responsibly towards other people at work
- be prepared to change when the job changes, e.g. when new technology is introduced into the workplace.

The employer

All employers have the following responsibilities.

- Meet all the terms of the contract and notify employees of any changes within one month of these being made
- Comply with all statutory employment law and regulations
- Provide a safe working environment.
- Provide appropriate training
- Allow employees to join a trade union or staff association
- Allow employees access to confidential records kept on them.

The employee can also expect the employer to:

- treat them reasonably
- give them the opportunity to participate in and be consulted on company matters that would directly affect them
- never ask them to do anything that is illegal.

Activity

1 *Find out more about contracts of employment and what happens if your employer wants to change it at www.direct.gov.uk/Employment/Employees/EmploymentContractsAndConditions/fs/en.*

2 *As a group, suggest actions that an employee who is unaware of the implied terms of employment might unwittingly take at work.*

Legal framework for employment

On page 197, you saw that all employees also have statutory legal rights because of laws passed by Parliament. Understanding the main ones helps you to understand your own rights and responsibilities better and also to see the reason for many company policies on equal opportunities, parental leave, health and safety and other related areas.

The law on discrimination

Discrimination basically means treating someone differently and unfairly because of a reason unrelated to their job. It can occur at any stage of the employment process, such as during an interview, or when offering opportunities for training, or access to staff benefits.

Discrimination is often divided into two types:

- **direct discrimination** is where one group is obviously excluded, such as 'Only men considered' or 'Only white applicants need apply'
- **indirect discrimination** is where a condition makes it more difficult to one group to comply, such as 'All applicants must be over 1.8 metres tall' or 'Only those with English as a first language need apply.'

To prevent discrimination and related problems, such as bullying, victimisation and harassment, which are also illegal, many companies have policies on **equal opportunities policies** and **diversity** to promote good workplace relations and help to protect the employer against claims relating to discrimination in the workplace.

There are several laws to protect employees (see page 204).

Key terms

Discrimination is treating someone differently and unfairly because of a reason unrelated to their job.

Bullying is when one person is singled out for unfair treatment by a person or group.

Victimisation is treating someone unfairly particularly after complaining about a discrimination issue.

Harassment is unwelcome behaviour that offends, frightens or upsets someone.

Fact file

Discrimination, bullying, harassment and victimisation are all illegal in the workplace and employers must take action to stop them.

The law	What it says
The Sex Discrimination Act 1975 (as amended)	This Act makes it illegal for anyone to be directly or indirectly discriminated against or harassed on grounds of gender (or gender reassignment). It applies to all aspects of employment, e.g. recruitment and selection for jobs and promotion, training, treatment at work, dismissal and redundancy. There are some exceptions, such as acting and live-in jobs, but these are rare.
The Race Relations Act 1976 (as amended)	This Act makes it unlawful for anyone to be discriminated against or harassed on grounds of colour, race, nationality or ethnic origin. Again both direct and indirect discrimination apply – although the definition of the latter is broader. It covers employment, education, vocational training, access to goods and services and social protection. Again there are a few special circumstances under which discrimination may be justified (such as some restaurants, for authenticity).
The Employment Equality (Sexual Orientation) Regulations 2003	These Regulations make it unlawful to harass, victimise or discriminate against any workers because of their sexual orientation, whether they are bisexual, lesbian, gay or heterosexual. This includes employees, agency workers and vocational trainees.
The Employment Equality (Religion or Belief) Regulations 2003	These Regulations make it unlawful to discriminate, harass or victimise anyone on the grounds of their religion or belief. This does not, however, include political beliefs. They relate to issues such as the provision of a 'quiet room' for prayer, time off for special religious events, choice of menu in worker canteens, social events (at which non-alcoholic drinks must be available) and dress codes.
The Disability Discrimination Act 1995 (as amended)	This Act protects people with disability against discrimination in employment, when obtaining goods and services, buying/renting land or property and gaining access to business premises. Employers must make reasonable adjustments to the workplace to enable a disabled person to do the job. Public bodies must have policies and action plans to tackle discrimination and no employer must treat a disabled person less favourably than able-bodied people without justification. Discrimination is not divided into 'direct' or 'indirect' but is based on the grounds that less favourable treatment cannot be justified.
The Gender Recognition Act 2004	This Act gives transsexual people the legal right to live and work in their new gender.
The Employment Equality (Age) Regulations 2006	These Regulations outlaw discrimination on grounds of age (either young or old) so that firms are banned from using age as a basis for recruitment, promotion or training. They cannot force people to retire below the age of 65 and give employees the right to ask to carry on working after this age. They also give employees over 65 the same dismissal and redundancy rights as younger workers.

■ *Laws on discrimination*

The law and equal pay

Before 1970 women could be paid a lower rate of pay than men even if they were doing the same job. **The Equal Pay Act 1970** and **Equal Pay (Amendment) Regulations 1983** aimed to stop this. Nowadays, if a woman believes that she is being paid less than a man she can make a claim in certain situations:

- if she is doing **like work**, i.e. the same work in the same organisation and there are no significant differences (such as the man working antisocial hours, having extra responsibility or working in less pleasant conditions)
- if her work is **rated as equivalent** in a job evaluation scheme
- if she does **work of equal value** so the value of each job is the same. This helps women who do assembly work or cleaning and catering where there may not be a man doing the same job.

Did you know?

In 2006 the Women and Work Commission found that women in the UK still earn less than men and the pay gap is the worst in Europe.

Your other statutory employment rights

There are a large number of employment laws that give you rights at work. The main ones are given in the table below.

The law	What it says
The Employment Rights Act 1996	This Act gave all employees the right to a written contract within two months of starting work, maternity leave, the right to 'opt out' of Sunday working, the right to a minimum period of notice depending upon length of employment and the right to redundancy pay after two years' continuous employment.
The Employment Relations Act 1999	This Act improved maternity leave, introduced parental and family leave in the case of an emergency. Under this Act employers must consult employees about key decisions and changes that will affect them.
The Employment Act 2002	This Act introduced 'family friendly policies' and the right to request flexible hours, outlawed discrimination against temporary workers and also covered the ways in which disputes should be resolved at work. (See also page 200).
National Minimum Wage Act 1998	All employers must pay a minimum hourly wage to workers over the age of 18 regardless of where they work, the size of the firm or the worker's occupation. From 1 October 2004 the national minimum wage was extended to workers aged 16 and 17 but this does not include apprentices aged 16–18. Apprentices aged 19 and above qualify for the minimum wage after the first twelve months of their apprenticeship.
Working Time Regulations 1998	Under these Regulations employees can only be asked to work a maximum of 48 working hours per week, averaged over a 17-week period, unless they are in an exempt occupation; 16–18-year-olds are limited to 40 hours a week and night work is not allowed. Under these Regulations, too, most workers have a statutory right to four weeks' paid holiday.

Activity

Check out the latest minimum wage for different age groups on the DTI website at www.dti.gov.uk/er/nmw/index.htm and also download the Short Guide for Young Workers which gives more details for workers aged 16–21.

Statutory employment laws provide minimum legal protection for all employees. These rights cannot be reduced by the employer, but can be enhanced in the contract of employment.

The law and health and safety

All employers and employees have legal duties relating to health and safety and these are defined in the Health and Safety at Work etc. Act 1974. This Act applies to all work premises in the UK and to anyone who is there. This includes employees, visitors and external contracted workers, such as plumbers or builders.

Businesses with more than five employees must draw up a written safety policy and have safety procedures that everyone must follow in an emergency, if an accident occurs, or if they are doing certain types of work. Businesses must monitor the risks in the workplace and take action to eliminate or reduce these as much as possible. They must also follow up employee concerns and investigate any accidents.

The Act is enforced by the Health and Safety Executive (HSE). HSE inspectors can visit any industrial premises without warning to investigate an accident or complaint, or to carry out a random inspection. Offices and shops are inspected by an environmental health officer employed by the local authority.

The main provisions of the Act are shown below.

THE HEALTH AND SAFETY AT WORK ACT 1974

1 Applies to all work premises. Anyone on the premises is covered by and has responsibilities under the Act, whether employees, supervisors, directors or visitors.

2 Requires all employers to:
- 'as far as is reasonably practicable' ensure the health, safety and welfare at work of their employees. This particularly relates to aspects such as
  - safe entry and exit routes
  - safe working environment
  - well-maintained, safe equipment
  - safe storage of articles and substances
  - provision of protective clothing
  - information on health and safety
  - appropriate training and supervision
- prepare and continually update a written statement on the health and safety policy of the company and circulate this to all employees (where there are five or more of them)
- allow for the appointment of safety representatives selected by a recognised trade union. Safety representatives must be allowed to investigate accidents or potential hazards, follow up employee complaints and have paid time off to carry out their duties.

3 Requires all employees to:
- take reasonable care of their own health and safety and that of others who may be affected by their activities
- cooperate with their employer and anyone acting on his or her behalf to meet health and safety requirements
- not interfere with or misuse anything provided for health, safety or welfare.

Many other Regulations have been passed to keep health and safety laws up to date. These include The Workplace (Health, Safety and Welfare) Regulations that you first met in Unit 2 (see page 62).

Activity

All businesses must display the main terms of the Health and Safety at Work etc. Act in a notice for employees to read, or provide them with a leaflet summarising the law. Find out if a copy is displayed in your school or college and read it.

Fact file

All employees have a legal responsibility to cooperate with their employer on health and safety issues. This is often stressed in their contract of employment.

Over to you

1 *If you work part-time as a student you can check your own legal rights at work by downloading the booklet on student rights at work from the TUC at www.tuc.org.uk/tuc/rights_student.cfm. This tells you what you can expect now, as a student and part-time employee.*

2 *If you have (or have had) a contract of employment from a part-time job, see if you can find a copy. Or see if you have a friend or close relative who will let you look at their contract.*
- **a)** *Identify four express terms that relate to the job.*
- **b)** *Compare your list with those made by other members of your group.*
- **c)** *As a group, decide the implications of these differences for the job holder.*
- **d)** *Identify four implied terms that they all must observe.*

3 *Worksmart is the TUC site which aims to answer questions about employment issues. As a group, decide upon four questions you would like answered on the following topics. Then divide into six groups to research the answers and report back to the rest of the class. You can find the information you need at www.worksmart.org.uk but you might also like to find out more on employment law at www.dti.gov.uk/er as well as in your college library.*
- **a)** *Employer and employee responsibilities in relation to health and safety law.*
- **b)** *Working life and family policies.*
- **c)** *Discrimination and harassment.*
- **d)** *Discipline, rules, regulations and policies.*
- **e)** *Pay and contracts of employment.*
- **f)** *Working hours, holiday breaks and leave.*

Talking point

View 1: Women are paid less than men because they often choose low paid jobs that are traditionally 'women's work'. Better careers guidance is needed in schools and colleges.

View 2: Women are paid less than men because employers know they can get away with it. Firms should be made to carry out regular equal pay audits to check there is no discrimination.

With which viewpoint do you agree – and why?

Case study Assessment practice

Gareth has been working at Perivale for two weeks when his sister's friend, Rehana, announces that she, too, is changing her job. She is going to work in a hotel in the town centre. Rehana tells him that she has just received details of the job in writing, although she doesn't see much point, because she was told all about it at the interview.

Gareth disagrees. He stresses that written information is important and offers to look at it with her. He suggests they compare her document with the one he received to identify the differences in their job roles and discuss what these might mean.

1(P) Rehana asks Gareth to describe the terms and conditions of his employment at Perivale Services. Do this by referring to the Statement of Main Terms he received on page 199 and answering her questions.

- **a)** Will Gareth work fixed hours every day (e.g. 9 am to 5 pm) or more flexible hours? According to the contract, which is more likely to be correct?
- **b)** How many days holiday will he get each year and can he save up his holidays to take more next year?
- **c)** What must he do if he wakes up feeling ill?
- **d)** How much he will be earning in two years' time?
- **e)** Why won't he get company sick pay, if he is ill, right from the start of his employment?
- **f)** How much notice will he have to give if he finds a better job?
- **g)** What other rules he must abide by? ***(P3)***

2(M) Gareth has told Rehana that written terms and conditions of employment are important. She asks him to tell her why. Provide an explanation that will convince her. ***(M1)***

3(D) Extracts from Rehana's Main Terms of Employment are shown on page 209. Analyse this document and suggest the implications for Rehana when she is at work. Do this by identifying the main differences between the terms and conditions of her job and those at Gareth's place of work. ***(D1)***

Grading tip

A convincing explanation will include appropriate examples to support the argument you are making.

Analyse the document by identifying the separate factors that are relevant. Then explain how each one relates to the topic.

MAIN TERMS OF EMPLOYMENT

The Employer: Westbury Hotel Group

Job title: Receptionist/Administrator

Place of work: Your normal place of work is at Westbury Hotel, 14 High Street, Westbury. The Employer also owns the Princess Hotel, 16 Castle Walk, Westbury and you may be required to work at this location on a temporary basis from time to time.

Salary: Your initial salary is £11,000 per annum. Your salary will be regularly reviewed but will not necessarily increase as a result of the review. Salaries are paid monthly, on the 22nd day of the month by credit transfer to a named bank account.

Hours of work: Your normal working hours are 38 hours per week to be worked at such times as the Employer reasonably requires between the hours of 8 am and 10 pm over seven days a week.

Holidays: The Employer's holiday year runs from 1 January to 31 December inclusive. Annual holiday entitlement and holiday pay is calculated on the basis of 20 days per annum plus 8 statutory public/bank holidays. The right to take normal statutory days may be varied to suit the needs of the Employer. Unused holiday entitlement may not be carried forward into the next holiday year and the Employer will not make any payment in lieu of holidays not taken. You must obtain authorisation from the Employer before making any holiday arrangements.

Sickness: The Employer does not operate a sick pay scheme other than Statutory Sick Pay. Full details of the employer's requirements for reporting and certifying absence for Statutory Sick Pay purposes are given in the Employee Handbook. Failure to comply with these may result in disciplinary action.

Probationary period: Your employment is subject to a probationary period of 2 months from the commencement date. The length of your probationary period may be extended if the Employer considers it appropriate. During your probationary period this Contract can be terminated by either party giving to the other not less than one day's written notice.

Notice period: Following the end of the probationary period, and subject to the statutory minimum notice requirements, this Contract can be terminated by either party giving the other not less than one month's notice.

Dress code: All employees are required to abide by the terms of the hotel's dress code and uniform policy. Full details are given in the staff handbook.

Right of search: Where reasonable evidence of theft exists, the Employer reserves the right to search any employee, their personal belongings, locker, bags and vehicles.

■ *Extract from Rehana's main terms and conditions*

5.3 Know how working practices are developed

Did you know?

At work you may hear the expression ***custom and practice****. This refers to working practices that have been in place for many years. Sometimes they will have arisen through trial and error, at other times by joint agreement between staff and managers.*

If you have already studied Unit 1, you will know that all organisations have a reason or purpose for their existence. They decide on their main aims and then plan how to achieve them.

Achieving these plans needs the combined talents and efforts of all the staff and is only possible if the organisation has developed appropriate working practices. This includes an organisational structure that enables everyone to contribute to achieving identified targets plus effective team working and staff who understand their own role and contribution to the enterprise.

Activity

Organisational aims vary depending upon the sector. If you have studied Unit 1 but have forgotten about these turn back to pages 21 and 23 and refresh your memory.

Organisational structures and job roles

All organisations need some type of structure to operate productively. Even a small firm will have specific job roles for the staff, so there may be a general manager, along with technical experts and/or others responsible for sales and accounts. In a car dealership, for example, there may be a manager who oversees four sales staff, three mechanics and an office administrator.

Did you know?

In management terms, the number of staff for whom a manager is responsible is known as their ***span of control****. The typical number is between 8 and 12 but it depends upon the jobs people do. It is easier to supervise large numbers of staff doing routine operations, such as checkout operators, than those doing complex work.*

Large organisations employ more staff and organise them into different groups. The number of groups and how they are organised often varies, depending upon the size of the enterprise and its main business activities.

Flat structure is an organisation with only one or two levels of employees.

Hierarchical structure is an organisation with several levels of employees.

Matrix structure is a structure that combines functional management with project specialists.

Flat organisational structures

An organisation which only has two or three levels of staff is said to have a flat structure. This is the case for many small businesses, such as the car dealership above. Another example would be a local travel agent with a branch manager and several travel advisers.

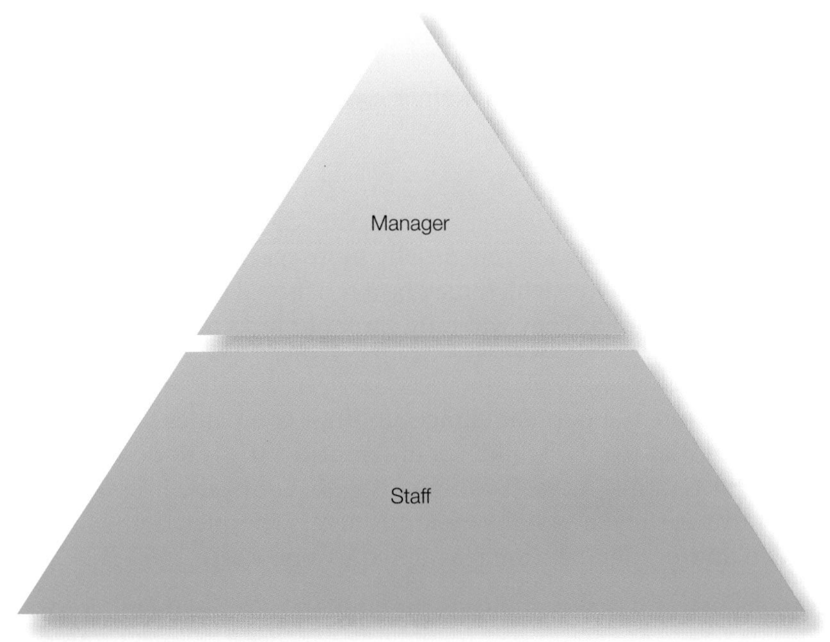

Organisational structures are normally shown as a pyramid because there is usually only one person at the top and far more at each lower level.

As the organisation grows and more people are employed then it becomes impossible for one manager to control everyone for whom he or she is responsible. Before this happens, it is usual to employ another manager, or a deputy, to help to share the management role. Recruiting a deputy will increase the number of levels to three.

Over time, the same problem is likely to recur, as even more staff are recruited. At this point, another level of managers may be introduced, and so on.

*Any combination of levels or job titles in an organisation is possible, depending upon the preferences of the person at the top. Sometimes organisations are **restructured** if it is thought that a change would help to improve performance.*

Hierarchical structures

If you looked at the structure of a large car manufacturer then you would see a rather different picture to the small local dealership. You would see several levels of staff – from the managing director at the top, through various levels of managers and supervisors, to the staff at the bottom. In this case, you would be looking at a hierarchical structure. The number of levels varies. Some large organisations may have as many as seven or eight levels.

Activity

Identify how many levels there are in any organisation where members of your group work part-time. Then identify the number of levels that exist in your school or college and draw a pyramid with job roles at each level.

In a hierarchical structure jobs are usually more specialised. Staff are allocated to a specific area which may be a functional area, division or department (see below). They will only carry out tasks related to this area.

Matrix structures

A matrix structure is a popular choice amongst companies and consultancies that regularly 'bid' for different contracts to do work for outside organisations. As each contract is won, a project group is put in charge of this particular work. When this task is completed, the team is disbanded and/or members are reassigned to a new task.

Each project group, however, needs the support of other members of staff (or departments) who provide the key operations – such as finance, marketing and human resources. This leads to a matrix structure, as illustrated below.

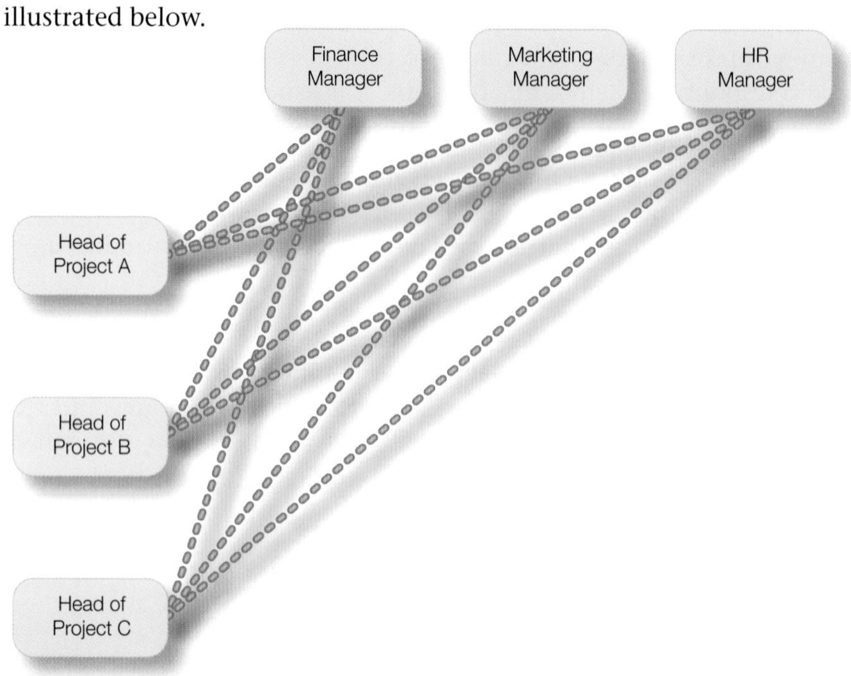

Did you know?

Examples of large companies that use matrix structures include construction firms like Balfour Beatty and defence companies such as BAE Systems.

Other variations

In Unit 1, you learned that many organisations are structured into **functional areas** (see pages 27–42). These are the main areas of work (or functions) of a business, e.g. finance, production, distribution, marketing and sales. However, there are some variations.

- **Functional areas** may have different names – and roles – because of the type of work carried out by the organisation.
  - hospitals have departments such as Radiography, Physiotherapy and Pathology
  - large legal firms divide their operations into different areas of law such as employment, property and probate
  - your local council will name its departments after the services it offers, e.g. Education, Planning and Social Services
  - a charitable organisation may have a Supporter Relations department and a Campaigns department rather than a Customer Service or Sales department.
- The business may be structured into separate **divisions** which reflect either the type of customers or the geographical area.
  - Banks have separate divisions for private accounts and business (corporate) customers. They may separate these even further, into small businesses and large corporate customers.
  - International companies, such as Ford Motors, which has its headquarters in the USA also has a European division. Most large banks, too, have international divisions.

Fact file

The types of organisational structure must be appropriate for the size of the organisation and type of work carried out. For this reason, the structure may change as an organisation develops or expands.

Activity

List the names of the functional areas at your school or college and identify how the names are influenced by the type of work carried out there.

Organisational policies on behaviour and conduct

In a small firm there may be little need for formal rules or policies because the manager can talk to staff individually if there is a problem. As the firm grows in size this becomes impossible. At some stage, it is essential that some rules are drawn up so that there are common standards that relate to everyone.

There may not be one over-arching policy that covers everything. Instead, there may be a general code of conduct which specifies acceptable staff conduct. Other aspects may be covered in additional policies, such as the IT or Communications policy, which tells staff what is and is not allowable when they are using computers and telephones in the workplace.

In general, the main aspects covered by organisational policies are those in the table on page 214.

Did you know?

Information about organisational policies relating to behaviour must be given in the contract of employment – or the employee told where these can be found – for them to be legally binding.

Activity

Compare the codes of conduct and/or policies in your school or college that specify standards of student behaviour with the list on page 214. How many are different and how many are similar? Suggest reasons for any differences.

Did you know?

Aims and objectives say ***what*** *must be done. Organisational policies say* ***how*** *it must be done.*

Key term

Organisational policies are courses of action, beliefs and principles set out by the business that must be followed by its employees.

Topic or policy	Typical content
Staff behaviour towards one another	Treating others politely and with respect, showing sensitivity, being fair and courteous, valuing the opinions of others, not discriminating or harassing another employee and reporting situations where this is witnessed
Alcohol, smoking and illegal drugs.	Whether the consumption of alcohol during working hours is allowed, company policy on smoking outside the building and taking 'smoking breaks', the penalty for being under the influence of illegal drugs (normally instant dismissal)
Dress code and appearance	Whether a uniform has to be worn, staff responsibility for keeping this clean, other requirements relating to hair or jewellery and the wearing of name or ID badges
Ethical behaviour to customers and suppliers	Not misleading customers, ensuring they know the price and terms of sale, not accepting gifts from suppliers
Confidentiality and data protection	Understand the type of information that is confidential, not disclosing information obtained at work to other people, not taking home company documents
Intellectual Property and Copyright	Understanding that documents and products created in the workplace belong to the company and must not be taken from, sold or used by employees as if their own
Use of company equipment and resources	Use of company equipment and resources by employees both in and outside the workplace (such as laptops). Returning company items when employment ends
Expenses	Company rules on reclaiming expenses including which items are allowable and how to claim
Conflicts of interest	Reporting these to a manager, e.g. a friend applying for a job, a personal connection with a customer or supplier
Competitors	Not to have any dealings with competitor organisations during the period of employment
Other employment	If full-time, not taking another job without permission. If part-time, obtaining manager's agreement before accepting other work
Conduct outside work	This may include the types of activities undertaken or groups that can be joined, as well as behaviour at firm's social events
Criminal convictions	Reporting these to a manager, e.g. for a driving offence
Computer use	Restricting personal use of the Internet to acceptable levels, not surfing offensive sites, observing all IT security rules
Health and safety	Observing all health and safety regulations and not endangering self or colleagues

■ *Organisational policies relating to behaviour and conduct*

Roles within departmental structures

In a small firm, the job roles of staff may be extremely varied with many people expected to help out in a variety of ways, particularly at busy times. Some specialist jobs may be contracted out – such as market research, advertising and the preparation of end-of-year accounts. A large organisation will employ more specialists so these tasks are more likely to be undertaken within the organisation.

Job roles vary in two ways – by level and by area of work.

By level In a hierarchical structure there are various levels of staff. Each has different types of responsibilities.

- **Senior managers** are responsible for the total enterprise. Their major role is deciding the main purpose and future aims of the organisation and defining its objectives. They also represent the business to the outside world and are involved in all complex or important negotiations. Examples of job titles include the chairman, the managing director and individual directors, e.g. the sales director or a regional director.
- **Middle managers** support the top managers by converting the objectives into tasks that can be carried out by their staff. They must be able to communicate well with their own managers and with their staff. Examples of job titles include the sales manager or a branch manager.
- **First line management** is so called because it is the 'first rung' of the management ladder. These staff need good technical skills to solve problems quickly and good people skills to motivate their own workers. Job titles include team leader and supervisor.

By area of work Job roles obviously differ depending upon the area or department in which staff work. The main activities carried out by different functional areas were covered in Unit 1 (see pages 27–42). Some typical job titles in a large organisation and the type of job roles and functions carried out by staff in the main functional areas are shown on page 216.

Activity

In groups, identify four job roles of different staff in your school or college or in any other organisation you know well. Identify the function and responsibility of each person. Try to ensure that these cover at least two different levels of staff and at least two different functional areas. Then compare your ideas with other groups.

Did you know?

*Many agencies and marketing departments employ **account managers** who do not manage other staff. Instead, they look after important customer accounts by keeping in touch with them and trying to generate new business.*

Activity

As a group, suggest how the job role of a manager would be different if he or she owned the business and employed only seven staff rather than managed a department in a large organisation.

Did you know?

*Many firms **outsource** specialist roles to external organisations, such as employing a firm of accountants to prepare the annual accounts, or paying a payroll bureau to prepare the wages, because this is more cost-effective than employing someone to do it.*

Department	Typical job titles	Function and responsibilities
Human resources	HR manager, Recruitment officer, Staff development officer, Personnel/staffing officer, Health and safety manager	Recruiting and selecting staff, organising training and staff development, keeping staff records and monitoring staff welfare. Staff/industrial relations. Monitoring disciplinary and grievance procedures
Finance	Financial manager, Chief accountant, Management accountant, Credit controller, Chief cashier, Payroll supervisor, Ledger clerks, Credit control clerks	Recording transactions, preparing statutory and management accounts, checking the credit status of new customers and chasing up overdue payments, banking cash received, preparing wages and salaries
ICT	IT manager, Network administrator, Webmaster, Computer staff	Maintaining IT equipment and the computer network, maintaining IT security, maintaining/updating the company website and Intranet, helping computer users
Production	Production/Operations manager, Purchasing manager, Buyers/order clerks, Stores staff, Chief engineer, Chief designer, Production planner, Production controller, Foremen and women, Production operatives	Responsible for obtaining, storing and issuing raw materials, producing or assembling goods to the quality required and meeting production targets, maintaining production equipment
Distribution	Distribution manager, Shipping manager, Shipping/despatch clerks, Packers	Responsible for the distribution of finished goods both in the UK and overseas, preparing relevant paperwork and packing goods securely for despatch
Marketing and sales	Marketing/Sales manager, Export manager, Advertising manager, Market researchers, Sales coordinator, Sales representatives, Account managers, Telephone sales staff	Responsible for marketing and selling goods/services and meeting sales targets in the UK and overseas
Customer services	Customer services manager and staff, Technical services manager and staff	Responsible for responding to customer enquiries, concerns and complaints and/or for providing technical help and assistance to customers who have purchased complex services or equipment

■ *Job roles and job titles*

Activity

Check the job titles in the table above and find out the meaning of any that are new to you.

Contribution of the individual to achieving business purposes

At the start of your career, it may be difficult to see how your job fits into the scheme of things. If you are a professional footballer, or a sales representative, it is fairly obvious. If a football team does not perform well there are obvious consequences. If a sales representative secures a huge order it is likely that company profits will be higher next year.

However, in other jobs, what you are doing and why may be less clear. Generally, however, everything you are asked to do as part of your job role will contribute towards the main purposes of the business – even if no one has time to explain it there and then. This is because there is a direct link between the specific tasks carried out by individuals and the aims of the business. This is shown in the diagram below.

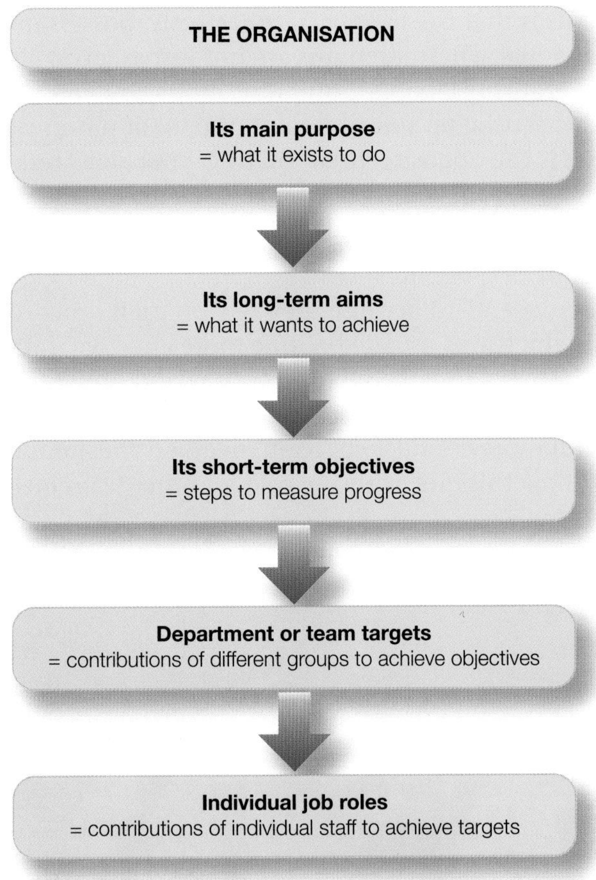

In a well-organised business, all the job roles combined should cover all the key activities needed to achieve the firm's aims and objectives without any overlap of tasks or responsibilities.

Team working

If you associate teams more with sporting activities than business then you are not alone. Originally, this was true, but today the benefits of teamwork are so great that many organisations group their staff into teams, as you will see by reading many job advertisements. Sometimes the ability to be a 'good team player' is considered more important than high-level qualifications.

Teamwork also benefits the members themselves because each person feels a key part of a small group, rather than one individual working alone or lost in a huge department.

A definition of a team is a group of people who possess complementary skills and who work together to accomplish a common goal.

The importance of team working

If you watch a good team in action – from the flight crew in a cockpit to a sporting team – you should be able to note various aspects about the way it operates. Each person knows his or her own role and how it fits in with the others. The teams have complementary skills and work in harmony. They do not get in each other's way or hold each other up. They work to achieve a common objective as quickly and professionally as possible.

A famous writer about teams, Dr Meredith Belbin, argued that a major benefit of teams is that the members, collectively, possess more strengths than one individual. These strengths are not just as job skills but other skills, such as problem solving, communications and an eye for detail. If you are good at setting up spreadsheets but poor at proofreading, and your colleague is the opposite, then 'sharing' your skills brings you both mutual benefits. A team simply does this on a larger scale.

The England football team has been criticised in the past because its members do not play together enough to develop as a team. This means they play as eleven individuals instead.

Interdependence of group members

Teams are interdependent because they rely on each other to get a good result. This is why teams usually become more effective if they work together regularly because the members know and understand each other's strengths and weaknesses. This enables them to depend upon each other with more confidence. Team members must understand their own role and how this 'fits' with the roles of other team members.

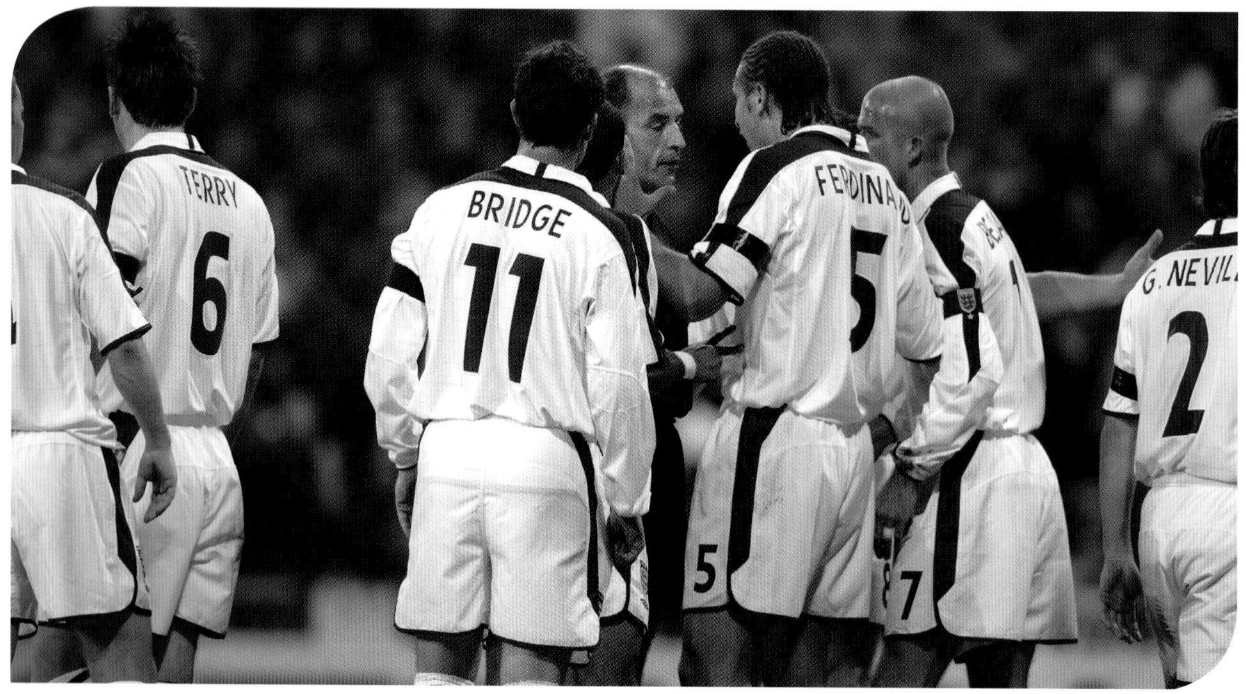

Group responsibility

The critical point about a team is that its members must be willing to put the team's aims above their personal ambitions. This often means readjusting the way you work to fit in with other people, using other people's strengths effectively and supporting them if there are any weaknesses.

Collective responsibility means that the whole group is at fault if something goes wrong. Blaming one or two members is not the answer, because the team should have recognised the problem earlier and sorted it out. Key aspects that influence team effectiveness are summarised below.

All team members ...	
fully understand the target and are committed to achieving it	✔
are willing to put the team's aims above personal aims	✔
understand their own role in the team and how this 'fits with those of other members'	✔
take collective responsibility for the work produced or undertaken	✔
feel they have equal status with other team members	✔
respect the views of other team members, even though they may not agree with them	✔
are reliable and dependable	✔
feel their own contribution to the team is useful and valued	✔

■ *Factors that influence team effectiveness*

Activity

As a group, identify examples of high-performing teams and poor ones. These can be sporting teams or teams you have worked in. Then suggest reasons for the difference.

Personal attributes

In the last section you learned about contracts of employment. You also found out that there are both express (written) and implied (unwritten) terms (see page 202). Many of the implied terms involve the personal attributes of an employee – such as honesty, behaving responsibly and observing confidentiality. These are so important that many organisations also include them in express clauses too, to make sure there are no misunderstandings.

Fact file

Employees at all levels contribute to the work of an organisation through effective team work and positive personal attributes.

The main attributes that a business will expect its employees to have are shown in the diagram below.

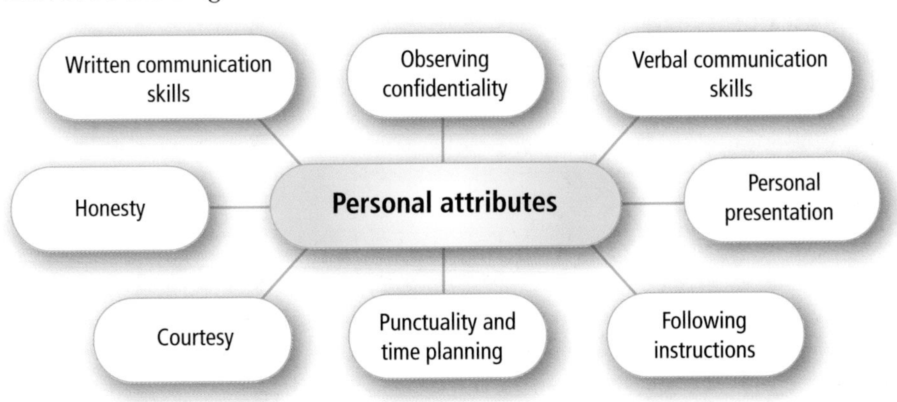

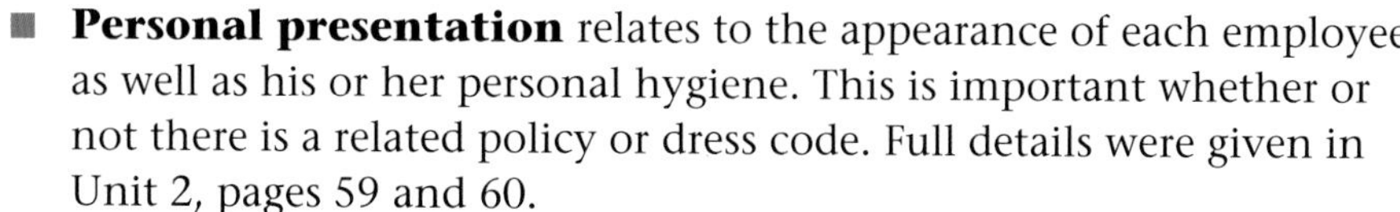

- **Personal presentation** relates to the appearance of each employee as well as his or her personal hygiene. This is important whether or not there is a related policy or dress code. Full details were given in Unit 2, pages 59 and 60.
- **Verbal communication skill**s are important because every employee needs to speak to other people – from senior managers to their own colleagues within the organisation, as well as external customers and contacts.
- **Written communication skills** must be good so that messages can be clearly understood, emails are not full of spelling or grammatical errors and all communications sent externally give a good impression of the organisation.
- **Following instructions** is an implied term of your contract, so long as the instructions are reasonable and no one asks you to do anything illegal.
- **Punctuality and time planning** means turning up on time each day; it also means being able to schedule your time appropriately by thinking ahead. This way you use your time effectively and always do the most important and urgent tasks first.
- **Courtesy** to other people, both your colleagues and external contacts is vital. This is often a stated condition of a code of conduct, as you saw on page 214.
- **Honesty** does not just mean not stealing money. It also means not saying one thing to someone's face and another behind their back, taking a box of CDs from the stationery cupboard or stealing time from your employer by coming back late from breaks or taking a 'sickie' whenever you feel like an extra day off.
- **Observing confidentiality** is an implied term of your contract and is often included as an express term as well as being part of a code of conduct – as you saw on page 214.

Did you know?

Body language is also important if you are to communicate effectively. This must match the words you are saying.

Talking point

View 1: Working for a small firm is better because everyone knows one another and jobs are more varied.

View 2: Working for a large firm is better because it will be better organised and there will be more promotion prospects.

With which viewpoint do you agree – and why?

Activity

Personal presentation, verbal communication skills and interpersonal skills were covered in Unit 2, pages 59–60. Turn back to those pages now and refresh your memory. You can also find out more about verbal and written communication skills on pages 145–170.

Over to you

1 *Kelly works for a small firm of accountants. There is a senior partner, three department heads and the staff. She has now applied for a job in the finance department of a large firm and will report to the accounts supervisor. This person reports to the head of accounts, whose boss is the finance manager – who reports to the finance director.*

- **a)** *How many 'levels' are there in the small firm?*
- **b)** *What type of structure exists at her new company?*
- **c)** *Suggest differences in working practices that Kelly is likely to find, given the differences in size and structure of the two firms.*

2 *Charan is nervous because, after several years of working as a member of the customer service team, she has the opportunity to become team leader. Explain how Charan's job role is likely to change as a result.*

3 *Identify which of the following groups work as a team and which do not. In each case give a reason for your opinion:*

- **a)** *a band of musicians*
- **b)** *check-out operators in a superstore*
- **c)** *surgical staff in an operating theatre*
- **d)** *air traffic controllers in a control tower.*

4 *Work in small teams to prepare a presentation on the benefits of teamwork for the individual and an organisation. Do this by:*

- **a)** *researching some of the work on team roles by Dr Meredith Belbin in your library or online*
- **b)** *as a team, identify each member's strengths and the weak areas of the team as a whole. This means deciding if your strengths complement one another and whether the weaknesses mean there are skills that no member is particularly good at*
- **c)** *as a team, decide how your weaknesses could be minimised, e.g. by people working together on difficult problems*
- **d)** *give your presentation to your tutor. Then, with your tutor present, evaluate the contribution of each person as a team member bearing in mind, too, the personal attributes of each person.*

Case study | Assessment practice

Ashraf, Andrea and Rob started their business, Andromeda, in 2002, designing and building websites for clients. Ashraf was the computer expert, Andrea had good creative skills and Rob was the salesman. A year later they had hired more IT staff and by 2003 they had 12 employees. They also employed another manager – Amina – to organise the financial side of the business, which they all found difficult.

The company continued to expand and staff numbers increased. Ashraf suggested promoting four IT staff into project leaders. Each would run a team and report to him. This would allow him more time to focus on new developments rather than supervising staff all the time. Rob also suggested appointing three account managers to look after their existing customers.

By 2006 Andromeda employed 24 people, but instead of the happy working relations they were used to, a few problems had surfaced. Rob had always been laid back about time-keeping because he trusted staff to be honest and committed but now started to suspect that some people were taking advantage of this. Then some staff complained their project leaders were unfair. One was a stickler for appearance and had sent someone home to change when he arrived wearing shorts.

continued ▶

Case study *continued*

Another lost her temper when a team member argued about instructions he was given for an urgent job and they traded insults for at least ten minutes. When Ashraf tackled the project leader, Julie, she said that in the absence of official guidelines she had just tried to do her best. The final straw came yesterday when Rob found out that confidential information about a current project had been given to someone who rang in with an enquiry.

Rob and Andrea suggested making some staff into deputy project leaders. Amina disagreed. She said employing an HR expert to solve the problems, and perhaps a change of structure, would be better. In her last job she had worked for a large college where staff teams regularly went on team building courses. Amina also thought they should introduce a code of conduct and other policies. Although the college had over 200 employees, everyone had known exactly what they could and couldn't do at work.

1(P) Describe how working practices have developed at Andromeda, since it first started, with reference to its organisational structure, the job roles, team working and personal attributes of staff. ***(P4)***

2(M) a) Compare and contrast the current organisational structure that exists at Andromeda with that of your own school or college.

b) Compare and contrast the main job roles that exist at Andromeda with those at your own school or college. ***(M2 part)***

3(M) a) To what extent do you think the original team of Ashraf, Andrea and Rob worked effectively? Give a reason for your opinion.

b) Explain why the effectiveness of the project teams and the personal attributes of staff are important for Andromeda to continue to be successful. ***(M3 part)***

4(D) Identify the type of personal attributes that are needed by staff working at Andromeda and evaluate the extent to which these, and effective team working, are important to the future development of the business. ***(D2)***

Grading tip

Compare and contrast means explaining the main factors that apply in both situations and then identifying the similarities and differences.

When you are giving an explanation, remember to give reasons to support your opinion.

When you evaluate you assess the value of something and give your opinion. Do this by reviewing the information and giving evidence to support the conclusion you reach.

5.4 Be able to plan career development

Most people like to move forwards in life. They have their own plans and dreams and want to take action to make some of them come true. There are two aspects to this. The first is to have some idea of how you are currently performing and what you need to improve to achieve your goals. The second is to have some idea of what you want to achieve in the long-term. No matter what type of job you first start to do, once you have mastered it you will normally need a new challenge to keep you focused and interested. This means that you will need to acquire more skills and gain enough experience to move upwards and onwards in the future.

An ***appraisal*** is a formal review of an employee's performance which also identifies future areas for development.

Reviewing performance

There are various ways in which you will obtain information on your performance. Some of these are informal, others are more formal. If you are sensible you will take account of all of these. This is because other people's opinions matter when you are at work – whether or not you agree with them.

A performance review should result in an action plan which identifies the targets you have already achieved and those you have to concentrate on next.

Performance at work, school or college

It is quite likely that you are used to regular reviews about your performance. At school or college, formal reports are likely to focus on subject-related achievements and results. Key behaviours such as punctuality and attendance may be included, as well as comments about your organisational skills and whether you can work effectively in a team.

Although end-of-year reports provide useful feedback, by the time you receive them it is too late to influence the result. This is why regular tutorials are more valuable because you receive feedback in time to take action to resolve any problems.

Activity

Search through folders and cupboards at home to find any reports on your performance. Add to this any informal feedback you have received. Then, in your own words, summarise the main message and see if your tutor agrees.

At work, it is doubtful that your boss will regularly take you on one side for a personal self-development chat. You should therefore watch for other signals that give you feedback, such as a smile and a nod when you make a suggestion (rather than a grimace!), praise when you do a good job or being asked to show someone else what to do. If you do not have a clue about what your boss thinks of your performance at work, it is not wise to assume that just because you are still employed you must be doing fine. It might be better to request a formal or an informal review to check your assumptions are correct.

Formal performance appraisal

An appraisal is a confidential interview between a member of staff and, normally, his or her immediate manager. These discussions normally take place once or twice a year and cover:

- the work the employee has done well since the last appraisal – including areas the employee wishes to highlight. This will include targets that were identified on the last action plan or personal development plan (PDP) and have been achieved

- any areas where the employee feels less confident or has performed less well (including targets not achieved), with suggestions for how these problems can be overcome
- the type of work (or jobs) the employee would like to do in the future
- any other areas of personal and professional development the employee would like to discuss.

Did you know?

In some companies appraisals are called ***performance reviews*** *because the employee's performance since the last review is discussed.*

The aims are:

- to enable an employee and manager to discuss current and future performance in confidence. If this is done well, it can encourage and motivate employees
- to identify the employee's future ambitions and link these to the business objectives
- to assist the employee to create a personal development plan for the next period and set key targets for achievement
- to identify training and development requirements for that employee
- to assess future potential or suitability for promotion
- to help the employee to plan his or her career.

Did you know?

A successful appraisal should result in an employee feeling more motivated and in control of his or her future. It should also result in an action plan which lists the targets to be achieved before the next review.

Preparing for a review session

If you attend an appraisal or performance review you will normally be given the opportunity to plan in advance. There may be a form that you complete and hand in ahead of the session, which identifies the areas you wish to discuss.

- Think carefully about your work and the aspects that you are good at. Try to think of examples to support your opinion.

- Which work areas worry or concern you? Why? Is this because you have never been shown properly, or because you have always been weak at this type of work? What help do you need to improve at these tasks? How long do you think it would take before you would be satisfied with your performance?
- Which areas would you like to develop in the future? What additional skills would you need? How would this fit in with the work you currently do, your future plans and those of your employer?

At the session, your strengths and weaknesses will be discussed, as well as areas you should concentrate on improving and developing. There may be suggestions and ideas you had never thought of – such as taking on new responsibilities or learning new skills. Or talk of future opportunities, providing that you put some agreed improvements into practice first. These improvements should therefore be summarised in terms of the specific targets you need to achieve before the next review session.

Did you know?

360 degree appraisals *involve opinions on an employee's performance being obtained from other colleagues at all levels, plus customers and external contacts, as well as the person's manager.*

Activity

Find out if any of the group have had an appraisal at work, how much notice they had to prepare, what documents they received and what happened at the interview.

Informal reviews from peers and colleagues

Your peers and colleagues are the most likely to give you regular, honest feedback – especially if you make a bad mistake that affects them. If you are working in a team, you should be able to assess if everyone is happy with your performance by their body language – and by verbally asking a direct question: 'I think this is OK – but what do you think?'

Sometimes you may be involved in a 'peer review'. This simply means that people evaluate each other's contribution to something – as you did if you prepared the presentation on page 221. As you may already know, there are advantages and disadvantages to this type of activity. The aim is not to make someone miserable or to nitpick – yet this often happens. It needs a good team leader to run such a session successfully.

Fact file

There are several methods used by managers to evaluate an employee's contribution to the work of the organisation. These include formal appraisals and performance reviews, as well as informal reviews and feedback.

Career development

Today, most organisations expect their employees to take personal responsibility for their own development. They will offer help, advice and support but they know that a highly skilled and competent employee may choose to go and work somewhere else eventually. For that reason, you will be expected to have a personal interest in mapping out your own career development plan and to look for development opportunities yourself if these are not available at work.

Aspects to bear in mind include the following.

Some organisations regularly carry out a ***training needs analysis****. This identifies the needs of individual employees and matches them to the needs of the business.*

Induction programmes

These are held by all colleges and most large firms. The aim is to enable new recruits to become familiar with the layout, policies and working practices of an organisation so that they can operate effectively as quickly as possible. During induction, opportunities for further training and career development may be discussed.

Training needs

These may be identified by individual staff or their managers during performance reviews or appraisals. Certain staff may want (or need) to improve existing skills or learn new ones so that they can undertake more varied or responsible jobs. Managers may encourage staff to learn new skills because these are needed by the organisation.

Many young employees mistakenly think that all training should be free, organised by the employer and only take place during working hours. Bright, creative and ambitious young employees look around for other opportunities and are less dependent on their employer for their own development.

Development plans

These are usually the result of performance reviews or appraisals. They should comprise an action plan, which gives specific areas of development over the next few months, and identify how the plan will be achieved, for example by attending training courses and/or learning from someone more skilled in the workplace.

Performance targets

These must be met if an organisation is to achieve its objectives. Staff will normally be encouraged to learn and develop skills that will help the successful achievement of targets.

Certificated training

This relates to official courses, usually away from the workplace. These may last only a day or several months. At the end of the course a certificate or diploma confirms that a person met a certain minimum standard. This type of training is useful because certificates convince future employers of continuous learning and development.

Uncertificated training

This can include many 'in-house courses', such as those held on health and safety, as well as informal learning opportunities, such as finding out how equipment functions or watching someone else demonstrate how to do a complicated job.

Personal development

This refers to any activities that increase knowledge, skills or experience – whether job-related or not. It could include working in another department or learning a foreign language. Some organisations actively encourage their employees to learn new things all the time – no matter what they are.

Flexible working

This is an implied term of an employment contract. All organisations need to change and adapt to survive – as do the staff who work there. This provides opportunities to learn new skills and to stay up to date.

Progression opportunities

These are normally greater in a large, hierarchical organisation because you can plan to move up a level. In a small firm this may not be possible and the only way to progress your career may be to move sideways to learn new skills or to move to another organisation.

Did you know?

Other opportunities to learn more include work shadowing someone to see how they do their job, swopping work roles with someone for a short time and volunteering to help out if someone is absent.

Did you know?

Multi-skilled *staff can do a variety of tasks well. This normally means their jobs are more varied and enjoyable.*

Over to you

1 a) *Identify all the ways in which you currently receive feedback at college and/or work and explain the type of information they give you. Then say whether you think the feedback you receive matches your own perception of yourself.*

b) *If verbal feedback wasn't forthcoming, suggest how you could assess your own performance at work.*

2 *Perdita, Kate, Aziz and Dom work together. They are all having performance reviews with their supervisor, Helen.*

- *Perdita comes out of the office in floods of tears because Helen mentioned that her time-keeping and organisational skills needed improvement.*
- *Kate comes out boasting about how Helen said she had a rosy future.*
- *Aziz comes out, shrugs, and just says it went OK.*
- *Dom comes out chuckling, saying that he and Helen had a good laugh.*

a) *As Perdita's friend, what would you say to her?*

b) *What do you think the others think of Kate and Dom – and why?*

c) *Do you think Aziz was right to keep quiet? Give a reason for your answer.*

d) *You are due to talk to Helen tomorrow. What will you do to prepare for your review?*

continued ▶

Talking point

View 1: Preparing a career plan is a waste of time when you are young because you will probably keep changing your mind.

View 2: Preparing a career plan is a good idea because it helps you focus on areas to develop which will be useful no matter what you do.

With which viewpoint do you agree – and why?

Fact file

Creating a personal development plan involves looking at the outcomes of performance reviews and identifying opportunities for future development.

Over to you *continued*

3 *Carry out a training needs analysis on yourself. Do this as follows:*

a) *List the skills you have now.*

b) *Find out those you will need for a job you want in the future by looking at job advertisements for this type of job.*

c) *Identify the skills you will need to acquire to bridge this gap.*

d) *Suggest how you might achieve each of these bearing in mind the opportunities likely to be available to you.*

Case study Assessment practice

Yasmin signed her name with a flourish. Her form was done and checked and she was looking forward to her performance review the next day – unlike four years ago, when she had hated going to work.

Yasmin knew that she had only had herself to blame. After completing a one-year business course Yasmin had not known whether to continue as a full-time student, join an Apprentice programme or look for a job. In November, long after most courses had started, she still had not decided. Then the manager of the card shop where she worked each Saturday offered her extra hours. Yasmin accepted, both for the money and for something to do.

Before long she knew she had made a mistake. Everyone was very friendly but Yasmin was bored. She knew she should do something about it – but what?

In February, when she was clearing away unsold Valentine's Day cards, she had turned to find one of her past tutors in front of her. After five minutes of chatting about her job they agreed to meet to talk about her career prospects. Yasmin arrived for the meeting concerned that her only option would be to return to full-time study. To her surprise, several ideas were discussed – all linked to her tutor's records and her own views about her strengths, weaknesses and preferences. One of these was an admin job at the College where Yasmin would also deal with members of the public. This would be ideal as it would enable her to practise and improve her community languages.

Yasmin worked for the college for two years, before successfully applying for a higher grade job in the Education offices of her local authority. Now after twelve months in the job, Yasmin hopes to convince her boss that she should become a team leader in the near future. No wonder she was looking forward to tomorrow's review!

1 Identify the consequences of Yasmin not bothering about a personal development plan when she was studying at College.

2 Identify the factors that were taken into consideration when Yasmin returned to discuss her career prospects.

3(P) Soon after starting work at the college, Yasmin was asked to complete a career development plan. This is shown below.

a) To what extent do you think Yasmin was committed to her own career development at the college? Give a reason for your answer.

b) Using a similar format, or a form issued by your school or college, produce your own plan using information from your performance reviews to date. ***(P5)***

continued ▶

Case study *continued*

CAREER DEVELOPMENT PLAN

Name: Yasmin Hassan **Current job role:** Student services admin assistant

Date of plan: July 2004 **Review date:** December 2004

Career aim: (1 year) To become a fully qualified administrator

Career aim: (3 years) To become a careers adviser

Current strengths/areas of work I enjoy/would like to develop (and evidence)

IT – word processing and databases – data entry (speed/quality commented on by supervisor)

Dealing with a variety of people. Would like to learn sign language (discussed in first review on 12/5)

Current weaknesses/areas of work I don't enjoy but need to develop (and evidence)

Routine tasks such as filing – often lose concentration and make mistakes (discussed in first review on 12/5)

Spreadsheets – slow at producing these and sometimes enter wrong formulas (feedback from supervisor)

Improve spelling (emails have been criticised)

Work area	Strengths	Weaknesses
Quality of work	Generally good	
Quantity of work		Sometimes miss deadlines
Knowledge and skills	WP and databases Community languages	Spreadsheets Spelling
Personal attributes	Helpfulness Hard worker	Impatience
Interpersonal skills	Listening skills Verbal communications	Not always tactful

Action plan

Development activity	**Target date**	**Progress at next review**
Learn sign language	September	Started 10/9/04
Do time management training	October	Delayed until January*
Take admin qualification	Start September	Started 17/9/04
Do short course on spreadsheets	October	Completed 30/10

*Course not running again until 2005

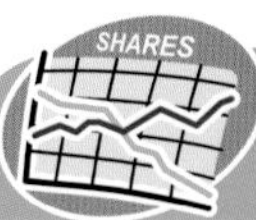

Grading tip

A good plan will show that you have used information from your performance reviews appropriately and positively.

6 Providing business and administration support

Effective business and administration support is crucial for all organisations. This unit introduces you to the main reasons why this is needed and helps you to develop your own skills by understanding and carrying out a range of appropriate tasks yourself.

What you need to learn

- The purpose of providing business and administration support
- How to operate office systems and equipment
- How to organise and produce administrative support for meetings
- How to demonstrate the procedures needed to process, retrieve and archive information

6.1 Understand the purpose of providing business and administration support

In 2006, a secretarial salary survey carried out by recruitment company Michael Page International found that PAs in London and the South East are paid from £24,000 a year by public sector organisations up to £50,000 by financial services companies, such as investment banks. A similar survey by Elizabeth Hunt Recruitment identified salary ranges from £18,000–£40,000 in London and from £9,000–£30,000 in the north of England.

Activity

Check out recent salary surveys for your region at www.hays.com/officesupport/salary-survey.aspx or at www.morganspencer.co.uk/shell/salary-survey.aspx.

Both organisations also reported a shortage of good, skilled support staff. The rapid progression for well-qualified staff into senior jobs has increased the demand for good candidates at more junior levels. As a result, it is likely that salaries will continue to rise.

If you thought that administrators just answer the telephone or file a few papers, it might surprise you to learn that they get paid as much as they do for their services. In this section you will find out why this happens, as you learn about the purpose of business and administration support and the wide range of tasks these staff undertake.

Did you know?

Ninety-seven per cent of businesses surveyed by the Council for Administration (CfA) agreed that the admin function is critical to the effectiveness of their organisation.

The purpose of business and admin support

Business and admin support is often described as the lifeblood of the enterprise, because it keeps the business running smoothly. This is just as important in a small business as it is in a large enterprise for the following reasons.

To ensure consistency

Support tasks should be carried out in the same way, and to the same high standards, no matter who does the job. This is essential if organisations are to take advantage of new business opportunities and continue to satisfy their existing customers.

To make effective use of time

In any thriving business there are many tasks to do in a limited amount of time. Some will be urgent, some important, a few will be both. Others will be less pressing but will become critical in days to come. When tasks are prioritised and carried out by support staff, this frees up other staff to concentrate on meeting the priorities in their own jobs.

Did you know?

Managers who frequently travel as part of their job consider their PA or administrator the key link person between themselves and the rest of the staff.

To support managers

Managers in a business are focused on their own jobs and responsibilities. They cannot concentrate on achieving targets, or running their own areas efficiently, if they are distracted by administrative worries. They will do a far better job if they can rely upon support staff for the assistance they need.

To support departmental functions

In a large organisation most administrators work within specific departments, such as HR, sales or finance. They will then assist with and specialise in the type of work carried out there – from organising recruitment interviews in HR or updating the customer database in sales to checking expense claims in finance.

Did you know?

In many firms, administrators work as a member of a departmental team and are expected to learn more about that area of work. They may then progress by specialising in that area rather than in administration.

Type of support

Admin staff support managers at all levels in an organisation and operate at different levels themselves – from trainee administrators to office managers or PAs at the top of the tree. Although the amount of responsibility and the exact job content differs between organisations and different levels of jobs, the work usually includes a combination of routine and non-routine tasks, which adds up to a considerable amount of variety!

The following types of support are provided by most business and admin staff, no matter where they work.

- **Supporting meetings**, including preparing meetings documents, booking and preparing the room and arranging for refreshments.
- **Producing documents**, such as letters, emails and reports, using word processing, spreadsheet and presentation packages.
- **Arranging events/travel/accommodation**, including assisting with the arrangements of special events such as sales conferences or visits by VIPS, as well as making travel arrangements and hotel reservations.
- **Managing diaries**, by arranging, agreeing and entering details of appointments in either a manual or electronic diary system.
- **Handling data**, by researching, obtaining, recording, storing and retrieving information into manual and computerised systems.
- **Processing expenses**, by checking expense claims and arranging for these to be approved and paid.

All these tasks – and many others, support the work of both managers and the business as you can see in the table opposite.

Did you know?

In a CfA survey in 2006, 95 per cent of administrators said their job was enjoyable, 85 per cent said it was challenging and 96 per cent said it was important to the success of the business.

Activities

1 James and Luigi set up their IT business a year ago, helping small business owners who need IT support or assistance. They are both busy and frequently out of the office. As a group, suggest the benefits they would gain by employing an administrator and the type of jobs the job holder would do.

2 Find out more about admin careers at the CfA website www.breakinto.biz.

Fact file

Support staff help a business to run more efficiently and effectively because they enable other staff to concentrate on their own jobs, safe in the knowledge that important administrative tasks have been carried out promptly and well.

Talking point

View 1: Admin work is more interesting in a large firm because you can work with different departments and find out what they do.

View 2: Admin work is better in a small firm where you make an important contribution and can do lots of different jobs.

With which viewpoint do you agree – and why?

Admin task	Support for the business
Preparing and despatching external documents, e.g. letters, emails, reports, sales literature	Provides a high-quality prompt response which gives a good impression and maintains the business image
Preparing and despatching internal documents, e.g. emails, reports, minutes of meeting	Provides important information promptly within the business to those who need it
Photocopying and distributing documents	Enables staff to receive prompt information on issues that affect them
Supporting meetings	Helps managers to ensure meetings run smoothly and a reliable record is kept
Storing and retrieving documents	Enables all staff to access records quickly and easily so that decisions are based on the latest available information
Maintaining diary systems	Enables activities and resources to be coordinated efficiently and effectively
Using electronic communication systems	Enables rapid responses to be made in important situations without sacrificing courtesy or quality

■ *The purposes of providing specific types of business and admin support*

Over to you

1 *Find out about the activities undertaken by administrative staff in your school or college. Then, as a group, identify how these support the main functions of the organisation.*

2 *Extend the table above by working in small groups to suggest the main purpose behind each of the following administrative activities, in relation to its support for the business. Then compare your ideas.*
   - **a)** *Making/receiving telephone calls and taking messages.*
   - **b)** *Greeting and dealing with external visitors and callers.*
   - **c)** *Making travel arrangements and hotel reservations.*
   - **d)** *Researching information on the Internet.*
   - **e)** *Distributing incoming mail and despatching outgoing mail.*
   - **f)** *Processing staff expense claims.*

Case study

Assessment practice

According to the Council for Administration, the skills needed by administrators are changing. In 2003, junior administrators needed good communication skills, to be able to work as a member of a team and answer queries. Today, the most important requirement is excellent IT skills. Good communication skills are still essential but other requirements include organising and planning, supervising an office, literacy, people management, problem solving and the ability to handle mail.

The variety of skills and attributes required is reflected in job advertisements for administrative staff at all levels. Examples range from a 'well-spoken first jobber with excellent typing and Excel skills' to the 'estate agent requires office administrator to support busy/friendly team of high achievers' to the ultimate 'high powered chief exec needs PA to organise busy schedule including overseas trips and complicated diary arrangements'. All you need is the enthusiasm and the will to learn, it would seem, to make yourself invaluable to the business of your choice!

Whoever said office work was dull?

1(P) Describe five different types of support undertaken by administrative staff and the skills they will need to carry out these tasks. ***(P1 part)***

2(P) Suggest the support that the applicants to each job advertisement in the case study will provide to each business. ***(P1 part)***

3(P) Find two administrative job adverts that interest you, either online or from your local paper. Identify the types of support the job holder will do and the main purpose(s) of the job. ***(P1 part)***

4(P) Describe the main purposes why business and admin support is needed by organisations. ***(P1 part)***

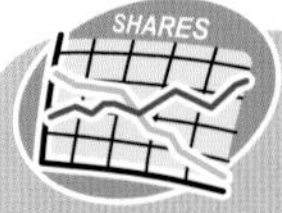

Grading tip

Remember that a good description is often said to be 'painting a picture in words'. This is because it includes all the relevant points or features.

6.2 Know how to operate office systems and equipment

The best known diary or calendar software is Microsoft Outlook. This also has an email function. You can find out how to use it at http://office.microsoft.com/training.

Some appointment systems include the ability to send automatic text reminders to customers.

A range of systems and equipment are used in every office. Providing effective support involves understanding how to use and operate these correctly. In this section you will learn about diary, telephone and electronic communication systems and certain types of office equipment.

Diary systems

The diary system is any method of planning and scheduling future events. These can be divided into two types:

- **traditional paper-based systems**, such as pre-printed desk or pocket diaries or appointment books
- **electronic systems**, such as diary or calendar software, PDAs (personal digital assistants) and electronic appointment systems.

Today, many businesses prefer the flexibility and ease of an electronic system though some traditionalists still like a paper-based diary to carry around with them. A summary of the advantages and disadvantages of both systems is given below.

Paper and electronic diary systems

System	Advantages	Disadvantages
Pre-printed desk diary	Portable Easy to find and enter information by date/time Useful supplementary information (e.g. holiday dates) Specialist versions available, e.g. academic year diaries	Easily lost Difficult to read if too many entries per day/writing is poor Movements of manager not known if diary taken out of office Pre-printed time slots may not match requirements Time-consuming to search for information if date of activity not known Not easy to change entries neatly
Electronic diary systems	Information can be shared over a computer network Entries can be any length and viewed by day, week, month or year Entries can be searched for and edited easily	Computer failure means diary not available Possible data corruption means back-up copy essential If stored on office pc, not portable unless user has online access from laptop or PDA

continued ▶

System	Advantages	Disadvantages
	Automatic reminders can be set to give alerts before an activity The diary can be uploaded onto some PDAs (and vice versa) and/or pages printed out The diary cannot be lost Pre-programmed features prevent basic errors being made (e.g. making an appointment for a past date) If accessible over the Internet, users have access away from the office Access can be restricted so only free time slots are visible, not activities Meetings can be booked electronically using the diary to find a free time for attendees and invitations sent by email Resources set up in the system can be booked by users online or by an administrator who controls which requests are acceptable	To work effectively as a shared facility, all members of staff need to use the system Mistakes and out-of-date information is on view to all who can access the system May be some resistance from staff not used to using computers or who do not have regular access to computer

Activity

Check out www.appointment-plus.com/index.php to find out the features of an electronic system.

The purpose of diary systems

Diary systems are used for two main reasons.

To plan and coordinate activities such as business meetings, appointments with customers, training events, dates of sales trips, interview arrangements and many others.

To schedule the use of shared resources, such as a meeting room, special equipment (e.g. a laptop and projector for PowerPoint presentations) or company vehicles. The time slots show who has booked the item and for how long.

Staff holiday leave can be recorded in a diary system to ensure that too many people are never absent at any one time.

Recording information

Any diary system is only as good as the user. Unless information is entered accurately, completely and – in a paper-based system, legibly – it is worse than useless; it is a positive hazard.

Crucial information needed to make an entry includes the following.

The purpose of the entry This may be to record a new appointment, to arrange a meeting or to reserve a particular resource.

The people involved You need their full name(s) and a contact number. A mobile number is useful in case an arrangement has to be changed at the last minute.

Start and finish times In a paper-based system it is usual to block out any intervening times for a long appointment.

The date Double-check this is correct by always confirming *both* the day and the date of arrangements.

The location If this is out of the office, you may need to include directions.

Did you know?

In some organisations, staff are expected to check their own electronic diary on a regular basis to see whether their managers have made arrangements on their behalf. In others, admin staff notify individuals of additions or changes to their schedules.

Communicating diary information

Most electronic diary systems are operated over a computer network and information is shared between users. If the system is accessible over the Internet, users can view it when they are away from the office. Every time you schedule an appointment for someone, this shows on their diary or calendar.

If you use a paper-based system then you need to tell people about arrangements made on their behalf. The method of communication must be appropriate for the urgency of the situation. It is no use notifying someone by email that you have made an appointment for them in half an hour – and trusting to luck they will read it. In this case, you would need to pick up the telephone or go and find them. When you are giving information about an arrangement, remember to include all the relevant details.

Key terms

A ***PDA (Personal Digital Assistant)*** is a handheld device with several features including a diary/calendar. Many can upload/download information from a central electronic diary system.

An ***electronic diary system*** is software that enables users to schedule appointments and other types of bookings.

Currency of information

Information in a diary must be up to date and accurate, so that users can rely on it to be correct. Some of the biggest problems for admin staff are caused by managers who enter arrangements in a pocket diary or PDA and then do not transfer this information to the main system.

Useful techniques for ensuring that diaries you maintain are up to date include the following.

Writing down entries or amendments you are asked to make, making the changes promptly and ticking them off as you go.

Never guessing information. Make a note if you need to check something or if some details are missing – or 'flag' the entry in an electronic system.

Having liaison meetings with people who regularly make appointments when they are away from the office to keep your information up to date.

A paper diary is less messy if you enter provisional appointments in pencil and only ink them in when they are confirmed.

Changes to entries

It is often necessary to change a previous entry by adding information, amending existing information or changing the date or time.

In a paper-based diary, cross out a changed appointment clearly and re-enter the information under the new date/time. Make sure amendments are clear. If there is insufficient space, add the information nearby, circle it and then link it to the main entry with a clear arrow. In an electronic system, you usually double-click on the entry to bring up the associated appointment card, change the date, make any other amendments and then resave it.

*If you are amending an entry it is always important to check that you are **changing** an existing entry and not adding another one, otherwise you are in danger of duplicating the appointment or booking.*

Implications of changes/new entries

Sometimes a change or a new entry may not be straightforward. You may try to change the time or date of a meeting and find that several people can no longer attend, or the room you need is already booked. You may be asked to change an appointment and find that the person the customer wants to see is out of the office that day – and so on.

At this point, you must obviously look for other solutions, such as holding a meeting with fewer people, at a different time, in a different place or asking someone else to see a customer. In the meantime, the important point to remember is that you ought not to confirm a change is possible, or a new entry has been made, until you have obtained all the information you need and checked the implications for existing entries.

Sometimes one change will have a knock-on effect for other arrangements. If this would be complicated it is sensible to ask a supervisor for approval before you start making lots of major changes.

Prioritising diary entries

Prioritising diary entries is essential if you have two conflicting requests because it means you give precedence to the most urgent and important one. Do this by assessing the following.

The urgency or importance of each type of event or activity. In most businesses arrangements involving external people, especially customers, are given priority over internal events.

The status of the person making the request. A senior manager will normally outrank a junior employee. If both people have equal status it is sensible to ask them politely to decide between them.

Activity

Find out what happens in your school or college if two or three people want to use the same meeting room, or the same shared equipment, at the same time.

Did you know?

In health centres and doctors' practices, space is usually left in the diary each day for emergency appointments. These time slots cannot be given to a patient unless someone senior has agreed that their symptoms need urgent attention.

The order in which you received the requests. If there is no difference in importance between both events and the people involved, the general rule is 'first come, first served'. This normally saves any further arguments.

Negotiating alternative arrangements

Telling people that you cannot do what they want is never easy. They may get exasperated or even angry. It will never help if you sound as if you do not care at all when you tell them, rather than suggesting bright ideas to try to solve the problem.

You negotiate when you consider the individual needs of everyone involved and try to meet these as much as you can. You make suggestions to try to solve the problem – and listen to their ideas, too. Mostly, this will work. If you find you are having serious problems reaching an agreement with someone, refer the matter to a supervisor for his or her decision.

Problems

The worst problem for anyone who uses an electronic diary is computer failure or data corruption that means it is inoperable. For this reason, a back-up copy is usually kept, so that the data can be restored easily, and many administrators take a paper copy of the next day's appointments each evening on a 'just-in-case' basis.

You will also encounter problems if key people are not available for an arrangement your boss wants you to make, there is insufficient time in the diary for a requested activity, or shared resources are already booked for a time or date you need.

More basic problems include not being able to read a written entry in a paper-based system, finding that some important information about a customer is missing, duplicating an entry, putting it under the wrong day or time or finding you have booked several arrangements for a bank holiday by mistake.

The worst problem with a paper system is that the diary or appointment book goes missing altogether – which is why some security precautions are essential.

Activity

As a group, for each of the problems listed opposite (apart from computer failure), suggest the best action to take in that situation.

Security and confidentiality

Many diaries contain information that must be kept confidential, such as the names of some external callers or the reasons for appointments.

In an electronic diary system, this is dealt with by allocating different access rights to users. These control the type of information they can view and the action they can take (i.e. whether they can only read the diary or also make and change entries). If you are recording sensitive information when visitors are around, angle your screen away from them. Always make sure you log out of the system before leaving your desk.

Paper-based diaries should never be left open where they can be read by visitors and should be stored in a locked drawer or cupboard at the end of a day. Very sensitive information should never be entered in case the diary is misplaced or lost.

Of course, all these safeguards are useless if those who make the entries are indiscreet. Never answer questions about arrangements unless you know the questioner has the right to know – just refer them to someone else for assistance.

Did you know?

Many register offices still use a paper-based diary for recording planned weddings. It is kept in a fireproof vault for security; there is restricted access for staff and no details are ever discussed with other people. You might want to think about the consequences if it ever went missing.

Telephone systems

There is a wide range of telephone systems for business users. In most large firms a designated person operates a switchboard or screen-based console, which is often the first point of contact for callers. In a smaller firm, all incoming calls may be routed direct to extensions, so that they can be answered from any phone.

Telephone features

The best way to learn about a particular telephone system is to understand the type of features you are likely to find; then check which ones you have. These are given in the handbook for the system. The main ones are shown in the table on page 242.

Fact file

Diary systems support business purposes by coordinating people's activities, so that events and arrangements take place as planned. They also help to coordinate the use of shared resources.

All fax machines include a telephone. A very small business may have a shared line for both phone calls and fax messages but most firms have dedicated fax lines, separate from the telephone system.

Find out the features available on your school or college telephone system and/or any other business system you use.

Main features of business telephone systems	
Callback	Enables you to recall an engaged extension automatically when it is free
Caller display	Shows the caller's number plus the name and company, if linked to an address book feature
Conference calls	Allows you to speak to several people at once, either extension holders and/or outside callers
Discriminating ringing	The ring tone for external calls and internal calls is different, so that you know which is which
Divert or call forwarding	Allows calls to be redirected from an extension to another phone – useful if someone will be out of their office for some time, yet still wants to receive calls
Do not disturb	Blocks calls to an extension whilst it is set
Hands free/Listen on hold	Enables you to replace the handset and listen and/or talk through a speaker
Interrupt	Indicates a waiting call, usually by a bleep on the line
Last number redial	Automatically redials the last number you called
Message waiting	A light or bleep shows that a voicemail message is waiting. On a computerised system, the message pops-up on screen
On hold/reminder call holding	Enables incoming calls to be held whilst the correct person is found to deal with the call/gives a prompt that the caller is still waiting to be connected
Transfer	Enables calls to be rerouted to another internal extension and on some systems to external numbers too
Redirect	Enables a transferred call to be rerouted if the call has to be redirected yet again
Secrecy button	Depressing this means the caller cannot hear anything you say to a colleague (and is far better than covering the mouthpiece with your hand!)
Speed dialling	Allows abbreviated dialling for long numbers plus abbreviated numbers for calls made frequently
Voicemail	An individual answering service for each person. Callers leave voice messages in individual mailboxes when people are away or engaged on another call. Messages can be retrieved from an extension or external phone

Using features appropriately

The features on your phone system, and how to use them, are explained in the system handbook. Most are quite straightforward and those that you use frequently quickly become second nature.

The one that most often goes wrong – and is the most infuriating for callers – is the inability to transfer a call successfully to another extension. All too often the caller is subjected to silence – or music on hold – for several minutes without explanation, only to end up listening to the dialling tone again. Or they are passed from one extension to another, continually repeating their request to one person after another. In either case, the caller has every reason to take a very dim view of the organisation and the staff who work there.

Making and receiving calls

If you prepare properly, making a business call is easier than receiving one because you are in control of the situation – or should be. You know why you are ringing and what you want to achieve. You should also have some idea about the type of reaction you might receive and how you can respond to it. When you receive a call, you have no idea what the caller might want or what type of questions you might be asked. For that reason, a good way to develop your telephone skills is to start by making a few simple calls.

Never forget, though, that your manner should always be more formal and professional during a business call than when you are talking on your mobile or home phone. Other hints and tips are given in the table below.

To transfer a call to another extension properly you need to know how to do it using your system ***and*** *how to retrieve the caller if necessary. You also need to explain what you are doing and why – to both the caller* ***and*** *your colleague on the other extension.*

Activity

Find out how to transfer a call on your school or college phone system and practise doing this to get it right.

Making a business call	Receiving a business call
Make sure you understand the aim of the call – i.e. the reason for making it Make sure you clearly understand the information you have to give or find out List the points you have to make, or questions you need to ask before you start, so you do not forget anything Introduce yourself clearly and explain why you are ringing Do not speak too quickly or use slang or jargon Speak naturally but clearly – there's no need to try to sound 'posh'! Ask the person you are calling to slow down if they are speaking too quickly Ask people to explain terms you do not understand and spell important words, such as their name, if it is unusual Make notes of important points Check your notes are correct before you ring off Conclude the call by thanking the person, if appropriate, and saying 'Goodbye'	Answer promptly with an appropriate greeting. Remember to identify yourself and the organisation or department Always answer with a pen and paper to hand and automatically start to make a written note Find out the caller's name and write this at the top of your note in capital letters. Check the spelling if you are unsure about it Find out the reason for the call – and write this down If you cannot help the caller yourself, either pass or transfer the call to a colleague or take a message If you can help the caller yourself, then do so. But remember that any information you give must be accurate and up to date. Don't guess! If you need to phone back, make sure you have the caller's phone number (and dialling code) before you ring off If you promise to ring back, do so! Conclude the call by saying 'thank you for calling'

Activity

Greetings vary from the formal: 'Good morning, Tate and Green. How may I help you?' to the informal: 'Hi, Petersen Software, Rizwana speaking. What can I do for you?' As a group suggest other versions you might hear and the reason for these differences.

Telephone technique

Although telephone technique is something you develop with practice, a few key pointers will help to get you off to a good start. Some of these were given in the table on page 243, but the following hints and tips are also useful.

- Never answer the telephone when you are chewing.
- Use a person's name during the conversation, if you know it. It makes them feel important and helps you to remember who you are speaking to!
- Avoid slang, no matter what the temptation. This includes 'OK'.
- Say figures in *pairs* – they are easier to understand.
- Don't try to rush your calls. You may have to allow the other person thinking time to consider what you have said.
- Let the person who made the call conclude it, if you can.

Activity

In pairs, role play making and receiving calls. Devise your own scenario – a college office, travel agent, opticians, etc. One person decides their query and the other person 'receives' the call. Then change places. Sit back to back if you cannot do this using a practice phone system.

Did you know?

If you smile during a telephone conversation this shows in your voice and helps you to sound friendlier and nicer to deal with.

Message systems

Messages are often essential because the person the caller wants is not available. There are several methods in use in business.

Paper messages are the traditional method. They may be written on a printed form that includes headings for the key facts to include, or they may be typed on a computer and/or sent as emails.

Voicemail enables an extension holder to leave a message for a caller who can listen to this and then, if need be, leave his or her own message. There is normally the option to speak to someone who is instantly available, for example, '. . .or press zero to speak to our switchboard'.

Answering machines were once a common feature but are now declining in popularity. Where they are used it is important that someone listens to the messages every morning and after lunch if the office has been closed.

1571 is an answering service which, for a small fee, can be customised with a personal message. This is useful for a small business that can check the messages, as well as the numbers of callers who rang but left no message.

Answering services are organisations that will receive calls, take messages and provide a daily summary, which they will fax or email to their clients. They are mainly used by small businesses, where the key person is frequently away and needs to rely on a professional response to queries.

Communication skills

Making and receiving telephone calls – and writing messages – all require good communication skills. You can also find out more about communicating on the telephone and writing appropriate messages in Unit 3 on pages 149 and 168.

Fact file

Telephone systems vary in terms of their features. All staff need to know how to use these properly, as well as displaying an appropriate telephone manner.

Activity

Find out more about writing messages on page 168 and then extend your role play by giving each other information to write up as a message. Then ask your tutor to check that the message is clear, complete and easy to understand.

Did you know?

Some businesses use Instant Messaging as well as email – such as the medical consultant who sends an IM to his secretary as a patient leaves his office, to tell her when to make the next appointment and how much to charge.

Electronic communication systems

In business, the most popular type of electronic communication system is email. This has replaced fax messages because it is so quick and easy to use. Even original documents – such as a copy of a passport picture or an official order form – can now be sent by email by scanning them into the computer system and then attaching them to an email message.

Communicating effectively using email

There are four aspects to sending business emails:

- the technical aspect – you must know how to use your email system
- your communications – can you send literate, accurate emails that are appropriately worded for the purpose and the recipient?
- email conventions – often known as 'netiquette'!
- the security aspect – which is normally spelled out in the organisation's IT policy.

Did you know?

Your email screen will comprise a reading pane for reading and composing messages, as well as a menu bar at the top, a toolbar with shortcuts and, normally to the left, a navigation pane containing a number of folders.

Activity

Check that you understand the layout of your email screen, where incoming messages arrive and how to identify unread messages.

Email etiquette

There are several conventions you should follow when you are using email at work. The main points, plus some other useful dos and don'ts, are given in the table below.

DO	DON'T
Reply promptly to emails you receive Check the style of salutations and complimentary closes used on emails where you work (if any) and follow this Structure your emails into proper sentences and paragraphs and use correct English (i.e. normal spelling, grammar and punctuation) Be concise and get to the point. People usually read emails quickly Keep your sentences relatively short Use bullets or numbered points for a list of items Send separate emails if you are communicating on different topics Carry out a spell check and then check it yourself for words that spellcheckers miss (e.g. form/from; draft/daft!) Double-check your email through to check it makes sense and has no errors *before* you send it Add 'thanks' at the end if you want someone to do you a favour Check the recipient's name carefully in the 'To: box' before you click on 'Send' Check you have included any attachments you have promised *before* you press 'Send'	Use the same phrases you would use in a social email to a friend Include confidential information SHOUT by using all capitals Use emoticons ☺ or ☹ or informal abbreviations such as LOL (laugh out loud) Use 'Reply to All' unless it's absolutely necessary Forward and copy emails you receive to people unnecessarily – particularly those that include external contacts' email addresses Use technical words or jargon your recipient would not understand Delete the message thread – some people like to look back over this quickly to refresh their memory Print out messages (especially those with a long 'thread') unless it is really necessary Reply to spam Forward chainmail or virus hoax emails Ask for a delivery receipt (it's annoying and can be ignored anyway) Assume all your emails will be dealt with quickly. If you don't receive a response to an urgent message don't send another, pick up the phone instead!

■ *Email dos and don'ts*

Using email functions correctly and appropriately

You must know how to carry out basic functions on your email system. These relate to the operations you can carry out, in addition to writing a message.

Email headers are normally set up by the software package and include:

- **the sender's name** – your name is normally inserted automatically on emails you send
- **the recipient's name** – this is inserted automatically when you reply to an email. If you are selecting a recipient from your address book the name will AutoComplete (which can cause problems – see page 247)
- **the date and time** – again these are inserted automatically
- **the subject** – you must choose a brief title which summarises the content.

Copying You can copy an email you write to other people. There are two types of copies:

- **cc copies** include the name(s) of the recipient(s) at the top so they can all see who has received a copy
- **bcc copies** are *blind* copies. Other recipients will not know that you have included a copy to this person.

Forwarding You can forward an email you have received to another person (or other people) of your choice.

Attaching You can attach other files to an email. These can contain text, graphics, sound clips or other images. You can include documents that you have prepared using different packages, for example, Word or Excel or copies of original documents you have scanned into your system.

High priority You can include a high priority level for important emails. Only use this for important and/or urgent emails or people will start to ignore it.

Did you know?

The abbreviation 'cc' stands for carbon copies – and was introduced when copies of documents were made using carbon paper.

Did you know?

If an attachment is very large, it is normal to compress or 'zip' it, using a package such as WinZip. This makes it smaller and quicker to transmit.

Other features of email

All email packages contain several other features that are extremely useful for users.

A contacts list or address book summarises your frequent contacts and key information about them. If you click on someone's name from your contacts list then this is automatically put in the 'To:' part of a new email message. If you start to enter the name yourself, the system AutoCompletes it for you. This may sound useful but can be hazardous as the system 'guesses' the name from the first letters you enter.

Activity

Suggest the problems that could occur if you accidentally sent a message to Dave Bates (an important customer) instead of Dave Brown (your soul mate at the next desk).

The folders in your email system are normally listed in the shortcut pane on the left of the screen – such as the 'drafts' folder for storing emails on a temporary basis. Adding your own folders enables you to save your emails in an organised and methodical way. Set up folders (and sub-folders) that reflect your main areas of work.

Groups of people can be given a group name or identified in a distribution list. Then, when you enter the name of the group in the 'To:' box, each member of the group automatically receives a copy.

Activity

Practise creating and deleting new folders and sub-folders in your system. Then find out how to set up a group or distribution list.

A ***contact list*** contains details about people frequently contacted.

A ***hacker*** is a person who gains unauthorised access to a computer system with the aim of causing harm.

Zipped files are attachments which have been compressed to increase the download speed.

Email risks

Emails can cause several security problems for various reasons:

- downloading documents and software, and opening attachments from unknown senders, can introduce viruses into the system or network
- spam emails can clog up mailboxes with unwanted offers or offensive material
- chainmails and other circulated emails can use up vast amounts of computer memory if they are allowed to go unchecked
- personal and private information can be passed on very easily
- email users can break copyright law (e.g. by copying or forwarding copyright material, such as illegal music downloads) or libel or harass a colleague by writing something scandalous about them that is untrue.

Workplace computer networks have sophisticated security systems installed to block potentially dangerous or offensive content, block specific types of files and restrict the activities of computer users. This is essential to prevent the system being disabled by hackers, or a virus, and to fulfil organisational responsibility in relation to the use/misuse of the computer system and security of personal information under the Data Protection Act. This is why virtually all businesses have an Internet and email policy for employees. Whilst one aim may be to prevent staff wasting time surfing the net or sending personal emails, the main reason is to minimise risks to data security.

Electronic communication systems enable support staff to pass on information quickly and easily.

Activity

Identify the precautions taken to protect your school or college email system, firstly by finding out about the security systems installed on the network, and secondly by reading the IT policy.

Office equipment

A wide range of equipment is used in offices to undertake many tasks quickly and effectively. Many items of equipment relate to document production – from computer printers and document scanners to the ever-present photocopier. A list of those you are most likely to use and their main purpose is given opposite.

Equipment	Main purpose
Computer printers – inkjet and laser	Produce hard (paper) copies of documents created or stored on computer
Photocopiers	Make copies of documents, such as items received in the mail or stored in the file. Many also collate and staple multi-page documents automatically
Document and image scanners	Convert documents and other images (e.g. photos) into file formats that can be stored on a computer and then saved, emailed or printed as needed
Hole punches	Punch holes in documents for binding or filing. Heavy duty punches are needed for thick documents
Binders	Fasten a multi-page document together, often inside a printed cover for a professional finish
Staplers	Fasten pages with a metal staple. May be manual or electric. Heavy duty staplers are needed for thick documents
Guillotines or paper trimmers	Cut or trim a document to size
Laminators	Put a thin protective plastic film over documents that are to be pinned up or handled frequently
Shredders	Destroy sensitive or confidential documents so that they cannot be read. Cross-cut shredders are best as they slice in two directions, not one

■ *Types of office equipment and their purpose*

Multifunction devices *combine several operations in one machine, such as printing, photocopying, scanning and faxing. They are popular with small businesses but can cause havoc if they break down.*

Types of equipment, their features and functions

The precise equipment required by an organisation will depend upon the work carried out there and the volume. Many small firms cope quite adequately with a desk jet printer and basic photocopier. Very different equipment will be found in an office where thousands of high-quality documents are produced each day.

The features and functions on different machines vary hugely. Photocopiers, for example, can range from small desktop models, which just make basic copies in black and white, to digital machines, which can receive documents sent electronically from computer users to be faxed or printed.

The table on page 250 shows the potential features and functions you may find on an office photocopier.

If your photocopier has a finishing unit then you will find it easy to create and fasten multi-page documents. If not, then you may have to collate and staple these by hand, which is more tedious.

Feature	Meaning/variations
Copying speed	Can range from as slow as 15 pages a minute to over 100
Duplexing	Two-sided copying may not be available, may be a manual operation or may be automatic with different options
Finishing unit	This may collate multi-page documents, hole-punch or staple as required
Image density and other adjustments	Adjusts exposure for light/dark text or dirty backgrounds (e.g. newspapers). Adjustments may also be available for photographs, pale originals etc. to improve copy clarity
Image rotation	Enables image to be rotated to adjust crooked image or to print on differently orientated paper (e.g. portrait to landscape)
Interrupt facility	Enables a long job to be temporarily stopped whilst an urgent job is done
Memory	Pages are scanned into memory before printing; routine jobs can be programmed into the machine and recalled as required
Mono or colour	Whether the copier only produces black and white copies or whether colour copies are an option. Digital colour copiers are expensive and printing in colour is slower than in mono
Networkable	Means it can be linked to several computers
Paper trays and capacity	Can range from one small A4 paper try to two paper trays – one large capacity and the other adjustable for A3 paper. There may also be a bypass tray for labels or transparencies
Reduce/Enlarge	Enables copies to be reduced or enlarged to fixed pre-set ratios. The best ratio is chosen automatically on some machines
Sample copy	Enables a test copy to be made automatically
Stack	This is the opposite of collate. Multiple pages are inserted but each is copied and stacked separately
User ID/counter	Enables usage per user to be logged. Users must enter PIN to gain access to machine
Zoom	Allows reproduction ratio to be set in 1 percentage steps for more precise reduction/enlargement

■ *Potential main features of photocopiers*

Stapling multi-page documents is normally only appropriate for routine internal items. Formal documents and those being sent externally are normally bound instead and for this you need a binding machine. There are four types:

- **thermal binders** use heat to seal the pages to the spine
- **comb binding machines** incorporate a punch to make holes in the paper. They then open a plastic comb over which the pages are inserted. The comb is then closed. Combs can be cut to fit but the depth selected must be appropriate to the papers used
- **wire binders** operate in a similar way, but the binding is made of wire, not plastic
- **slide binders** literally slide over the left-hand edge of the pages. They are cheap but there is a disadvantage because the pages will not open flat

Activity

Check out the different types of binding machines available from an online supplier, such as www.euroffice.co.uk.

Did you know?

There is a right way and a wrong way to use even the most basic items. Stapling so that you obscure the print is unprofessional – so is punching holes that are not aligned. Use the ruler, or gently fold and crease the papers in half and align with the arrow on the punch instead of guessing.

Instruction manuals

All office equipment, apart from the most basic items, is sold complete with instructions. This explains all the features and functions available and also includes other information the manufacturer thought you should know. For that reason it is not wise to ignore the book and just guess what to do. You can easily make a mess of a job, or damage something, and may even do something that is dangerous if you are using electrical equipment.

Activity

Divide into groups to investigate the features and functions on selected items of equipment available in your school or college, chosen from the list on page 249, and agreed with your tutor. Then report back your findings to the whole class.

Training in usage

The best way to learn how to use an item of equipment is to be trained properly by someone who knows how to use it. This is why many photocopier dealers offer a demonstration or training session as part of the package when they supply a new machine.

Economic and efficient usage

Anyone who uses equipment carelessly, or without knowing what they are doing, is likely to waste a considerable amount of time and resources. This can be as minor as stapling four pages in the wrong place, so that the print is obscured, to producing 500 crooked photocopies that are unusable.

An expert can always make a difficult job seem easy. Next time you are watching a demonstration make notes so that you can refer to these when you do the job yourself.

Did you know?

Although it may seem efficient to switch off equipment when you have finished, this does not apply to photocopiers, which are left on all day.

The main points to note are listed in the table below.

For economic and efficient equipment use . . .	
Check you understand your instructions before you start work	✔
Make sure the equipment is clean and ready for use. On a photocopier, the most important part of the machine is the document glass. If this is dirty, your copies will be, too	✔
Make sure your originals are in good condition and repair them or obtain a new copy if they are not	✔
Enter any settings carefully and double-check these	✔
Take and check a test copy before you make any multiple copies	✔
Use duplex mode to make double-sided copies whenever you can	✔
Reuse waste paper where you can, such as by making scrap pads, and recycle it when you cannot.	✔

Problem solving

For most people, the most valuable pages of an instruction manual are the 'trouble shooting' pages which say what to do in an emergency. The manual also tells you which faults need to be reported, particularly if the equipment is leased or rented under a service contract. Never ignore these instructions because even if the equipment is still operational you could be causing further damage and may even invalidate any warranty that was supplied. You could also put yourself in danger if there is an electrical fault.

Most organisations have procedures to restrict the type of actions individuals can take to resolve problems on their own unless they have received specific training. For example, there may be one nominated person only who is allowed to remedy paper jams in the photocopier.

Activity

As a group, decide the ***minimum*** *standards that would be expected of any printed or photocopied document that is produced within an organisation. Think in terms of content, layout, clarity and overall production.*

Ensuring outcomes meet appropriate requirements or standards

The requirements of a job are the specific instructions you receive, for example, 'Copy this ten-page booklet. Make back-to-back copies and staple it.' Work standards refer to the *quality* of work you are expected to produce. You may be tempted to think that if you are producing work that will be used only internally, that quality does not matter. This is a dangerous strategy because anyone who sees it will think you are sloppy, unreliable or both. In addition, the work will have to be redone if someone suddenly decides to send it outside the organisation.

Fact file

All office equipment is chosen to meet specific business requirements, often relating to the production of professional-looking documents.

Working to appropriate timescales or deadlines

This refers to the deadlines in which you must produce work. You should always plan your work so that you achieve a deadline that you have agreed.

If you are asked to meet an impossible deadline, or if something goes wrong that will hold you up so you may miss the deadline, then you need to see the person who gave you the work immediately, either to get help, or to negotiate a more realistic completion date.

Over to you

1 *Your sister is a beauty therapist and is considering changing her paper-based diary system to an electronic one. Each of the following is an example of a software package that she could use. Investigate at least two online and then decide which one you think she should use. Give reasons for your decision.*
   - ***a)*** *Niche appointments at www.niche-technologies.co.uk – then click on 'Products'*
   - ***b)*** *Padtech at www.padtech.co.uk*
   - ***c)*** *Multicalendar at www.multicalendar.com*
   - ***d)*** *Athyrium at www.athyrium.com*

2 *You work for a small firm of architects. When you return from lunch you find the following message on the answering machine, timed at 12.30 pm.*

   'Hi, it's Phil Bryant here from The Brightstone Gazette. We're planning a special 12-page property feature for next month with a special article on designing and building your own home. We would like to talk to you about including a couple of projects your firm has carried out, with the owner's permission, of course. We also think it would be a great opportunity to advertise and can offer you a special rate, linked to the article. I'll ring again to talk about it further tomorrow. Alternatively, please phone me any time on 01294 447282. Thanks.'

   It is common practice in your firm for messages typed up by administrators to be sent to the partners as an email. Assuming your tutor is the senior partner in the firm, carry out this task.

3 *Check you understand the description of all the equipment given on page 249. If there is any type of equipment that you are unsure about, find out more at http://www.euroffice.co.uk/tab_machines.asp.*

Talking point

View 1: If you are pushed for time, it is better to do sub-standard work on time than keep someone waiting.

View 2: If you are pushed for time, it is better to slow down to get it right, even if this means it might take a little longer.

With which viewpoint do you agree – and why?

Case study Assessment practice

Jo Gibbons is the office administrator in a primary school. She enjoys the work because it is varied and busy and she deals with a wide range of people, from young children and their parents to the numerous visitors to the school.

One of Jo's tasks is to use a diary to record the head's appointments and schedule the use of all the shared resources in the school, from TVs, laminators and laptops to musical keyboards and other instruments. She sometimes has a problem allocating scarce but popular resources. Rooms can be a problem because visitors, such as nurses arriving to carry out vision tests and teachers who need to do PPA (planning, preparation and assessment) need a room in which to work. In a crisis, she prioritises the needs of external visitors and will use any vacant room, including the head's study when she is away.

The school office uses a wide range of equipment. The fax machine is a critical item because any pupils who are absent without reason are tracked by faxing their names and pupil numbers to an agency. Before that, of course, the parents may have telephoned with an explanation.

continued ▸

Case study *continued*

Jo takes messages for teachers so that they are not disturbed in class, although she can transfer calls to the head's study or to the staffroom if necessary. Alternatively, she can email the head or members of staff via the school computer network.

Jo considers her computer and photocopier to be her most essential items. Her printer also doubles as a scanner, which is useful when she wants to include artwork in a document to make it clearer for the children. Jo also has a document trimmer and a comb binder, which is useful for producing multi-page booklets and programmes, as well as a sturdy shredder next to her desk.

1(P) **a)** Describe how the diary system is used to support the operations at the school.

b) Demonstrate how you would operate a diary system. Work in pairs to identify 12 entries Jo may make in a diary over a week, then exchange your lists. Then make the entries for each day either on a photocopied paper diary page or in Microsoft Outlook. ***(P2)***

2(P) **a)** Suggest the features that will be useful on a telephone system at the school.

b) Jo speaks to a wide range of people on the telephone. Describe the type of techniques and communication skills you think she will need.

c) Demonstrate how you would use the telephone system with which you are familiar to answer a call and transfer it to another extension. ***(P3 part)***

3(P) Describe how the office equipment she uses meets the requirements of the school. ***(P4)***

4(M) Jo is wondering whether to change over to an electronic diary system from the paper system she currently uses.

Compare and contrast both systems to identify the potential benefits she may gain and any possible disadvantages. ***(M1)***

5(M) **a)** To save money, Jo uses a Risograph, rather than a photocopier, for long print runs. Research this type of equipment online and then explain how the features and functions on this machine will suit her purposes.

b) Jo's brother works for a firm of consultants. He is frequently involved in preparing sophisticated multi-page reports for clients. Suggest how the equipment he will need to do this will differ from the equipment that Jo uses. ***(M2)***

6(D) For Jo's school, analyse the contribution that the office systems and equipment make to the provision of business and administration support there. ***(D1)***

Grading tip

Remember that to compare and contrast you need to identify both the similarities and differences – or advantages and disadvantages – of both systems and apply these to that particular situation.

Analyse by identifying the different systems and equipment used, what they do, and how this links to the requirements of the organisation.

6.3 Be able to organise and produce administrative support for meetings

Meetings are held in all types of organisations every day of the week because they usually get results. Well-prepared, properly organised meetings save time, improve communications and help to generate new ideas and solve problems.

However, not all meetings are effective. You may hear people grumble that a meeting has been a waste of time or that nothing ever gets done as a result.

The difference usually relates to the way the meeting has been organised and supported. Both are key roles for administrative staff and both are the focus of this section.

Meetings organisation

The idea of making preparations for a meeting can be very worrying if you have little idea about what is likely to be needed. Knowing more about business meetings is therefore the first step in understanding the organisational arrangements that might be needed.

Type of meeting

There are many different types of meeting. Some are very formal, with specific rules and procedures. Others are so informal you would hardly recognise them as a meeting. Some are held just once or twice, for a particular reason, whereas others are held at regular intervals. Some meetings will only involve staff, others may include external delegates.

Did you know?

An Annual General Meeting is a legal requirement for all public limited companies. All shareholders must be invited to attend.

The type of meeting will affect every aspect of the organisational arrangements, from the likely length to the number of participants, where and when it will be held, and how long it will last.

The table below gives some examples.

Types of meetings

Informal

- **Regular meetings** – held by small groups of staff, normally chaired by the team leader or manager
- **Briefing meetings** – where staff are given information by a manager or expert, such as the health and safety officer
- **Progress meetings** – where staff working on a project meet to check how things are going
- **Working parties** – set up for a particular reason, such as to organise the move to new premises, and ended when the job is finished

Formal

- **Meetings of the board of directors**, board of governors or other senior executives
- **Committee and sub-committee meetings**, e.g. the planning committee of a local authority
- **Annual general meetings**

Main features

Regardless of the type of meeting there are certain common features.

- **There is a reason for holding it** Otherwise there is no point in having it.
- **People will be invited to attend** It is hard to have a meeting by yourself!
- **Someone will be in charge** In formal meetings the leader is normally called the chairperson.
- **Someone is responsible for organising it** and/or taking notes.
- **There are items to be discussed** These may be written down in an agenda.
- **There is an end result,** such as a decision taken or jobs allocated.
- **There is a record of what happened** – either a formal set of minutes or a more informal summary.
- **The proceedings are normally orderly** Meetings are not a free for all! There is normally a specific order of business (see page 258) and formal meetings have certain rules and conventions that apply.

Did you know?

In all meetings people should address their remarks to the chairperson rather than to each other. This is common sense, really, because otherwise the chairperson would not know what was happening and everyone could be speaking at once!

Meeting brief

All meetings are held with the aim of achieving a specific outcome. For example, an HR manager may want to give staff information about a new pension scheme. She then has to decide whether to call a full staff meeting one lunch-time, or visit small groups of staff one by one to chat to them more informally. Her decision will affect many aspects of the arrangements, including the size of the room(s), the number of rooms required, the timing of the event(s) and the refreshments required – as well as the numbers of leaflets needed at any one time. For this reason, unless you know the brief you could quite easily make a mess of the arrangements, quite unintentionally. Some of the main questions to ask are listed below.

Activity

Find out the types of meetings routinely held in your school or college and divide them into those which are formal and those which are informal. Then find out how the main features listed above apply in each case.

Establishing the meeting brief – questions to ask
Why is the meeting being held?
What paperwork will be required?
Who should attend?
How long is it likely to last? What time will it start and end?
Where should it be held?
Is anyone coming from outside the organisation? If so, do any special arrangements need to be made for them?
Are refreshments required?
Will any special equipment be needed?
What other facilities might be required, e.g. car parking, access to telephones etc.?
Are you expected to organise the meeting and/or attend as well? If so, will you be expected to take notes?

Meeting venue

Any meeting can be a disaster if the room is unsuitable or the facilities are poor. For that reason, basic considerations such as space, heating, lighting, ventilation and sound-proofing are all important. The room must also be clean and tidy and not cluttered with dirty cups and spoiled papers from the previous meeting.

Most informal meetings are held within the organisation, either in the boss's office or in a special room set aside for meetings. Large organisations have a board room or committee rooms. Your school or college will probably have specific meeting rooms – although larger groups may meet in classrooms or other areas.

If you visit a board room or meetings room then you may find it is furnished quite luxuriously, with a large table and comfortable chairs. There may be side tables for refreshments and special facilities for presentations. If audio/visual equipment is routinely used then there will be blackout blinds or curtains.

On certain occasions external venues may be required, such as for a very large meeting to which delegates are invited. This may be at a hotel, an educational establishment or a conference centre. In this case, additional facilities may be required, such as seminar rooms for group discussions, special equipment or accommodation for overnight guests.

Suitable equipment

Some equipment is required at most meetings. People may want to record decisions or ideas on a whiteboard or flipchart and anyone giving a formal presentation may request specific equipment. This can include an overhead projector; a laptop/PC and projector, so that PowerPoint can be used; an interactive whiteboard or even a video link to an external location.

Did you know?

Senior managers in an organisation often have a meetings table and chairs in their office, which means that they can host a small meeting without having to book a special room.

Did you know?

A radio mike enables the speaker to move around easily. Remote mousing means that the speaker can control a PowerPoint presentation from a distance, too.

Activity

Find out the type of equipment used in your school or college during meetings and the requirements for booking or reserving these items.

Did you know?

It is important to ensure that refreshments take account of any religious, cultural, vegetarian and other preferences of staff or guests.

It is important to check exactly what is needed, especially if you are looking for an appropriate external venue. If internal equipment is a shared resource then it is important to book this early and to check that it is working properly beforehand. Even the best equipment is no good if some people cannot see the flip chart or screen properly, so you need to check how it looks from different parts of the room *and* that the lights can be dimmed if necessary.

Catering requirements

The requirements will depend upon the length and type of event and the time of day when it is held.

A hot drink is often provided at the start and is particularly welcome if people are arriving from a distance or over a period of time.

Water and/or other soft drinks, with glasses, are normally provided on the table for lengthy meetings.

A working breakfast or working lunch meeting shouldn't mean talking and eating a three-course meal simultaneously! Finger food is always best, from bacon sandwiches, or toast, to a lunch-time buffet or sandwiches.

Notice and agenda

Some meetings are so informal that everyone might just be invited by phone to attend. Even then it is better if they know about the topic in advance, especially if they are expected to make sensible contributions. Other meetings are so formal that specific information must be sent out a number of days in advance to comply with the rules.

Most business meetings fall in-between these two extremes. Those who are invited receive written notification in advance, together with a list of the topics. This is done by issuing a notice and agenda. These may be sent separately or as one combined document, for ease. For internal meetings, it is often sent by email. It is important to ask people to reply to say if they are going to attend, otherwise you will not know how many to expect.

Did you know?

It is important that agendas are not too crowded and that urgent items are dealt with first. It is then a good idea to vary items so that intense discussions are interspersed with lighter matters.

The agenda is normally decided by the chairperson. There are certain standard items usually included and, for regular meetings, other topics may have been suggested at the last meeting. One of the first jobs for the administrator is to agree the agenda with the chairperson; then it can be prepared and issued in good time. Because the agenda lists the topics in the order they will be discussed, this also means that if someone can only attend for a short time they can estimate when an item will be raised, in which they are particularly interested, or where they will be expected to contribute.

An example of a combined notice and agenda is shown opposite. The standard items, found on all agendas, are items, 1, 2, 3, 7 and 8.

MARTON COLLEGE

NOTICE OF MEETING

14 April 200-

The next meeting of the Student Council will be held in the Library Meeting Room at 1200 hours on Thursday, 25 April. A sandwich lunch will be provided.

Please contact me on extension 1234 if you cannot attend.

AGENDA

1 Apologies for absence ← *1 Lists the names of those who cannot attend*

2 Minutes of the previous meeting ← *2 Gives people the chance to correct any mistakes in the previous minutes*

3 Matters arising ← *3 Enables people to give updates or report on action taken following discussions at the last meeting*

4 Report on student charity ← *Items 4 – 6 are the main business of the meeting*

5 Proposed changes to college IT policy

6 Appointment of new Council Secretary

7 Any other business ← *7 For minor items people want to raise*

8 Date and time of next meeting

Paula Singleton

Council Secretary

Meeting papers and spare copies

Other information that is required will depend upon the type of meeting being held and the topics under discussion. This can be done in two ways.

Papers can be sent out with the agenda. The advantage is that people can read them in advance and think about their responses. The disadvantages are that lengthy documents can be off-putting and people may not read them. They may also forget to bring them to the meeting.

All good administrators take spare sets of all the documents to the meeting, to give to those who have forgotten to bring their copy with them.

Papers can be 'tabled'. This means giving them out at the meeting itself. The advantage is that everyone gets a copy. The disadvantage is that it can take time for people to read them if they are long or complex and there is no 'thinking time'.

Delegates/delegate list

The term 'delegates' is used to describe people outside the organisation who are invited to attend a meeting – such as members of a professional association or a trades union. In this case, each person who is entitled to attend *must* be invited. The same applies to shareholders of a company who are entitled to attend the AGM.

It is important to check the delegate list with the chairperson in advance, so that no one is accidentally omitted.

Confirmation of attendance

For any meeting, you need to know the numbers attending because this affects many other requirements – the number of refreshments, size of room, copies of documents, etc. For a formal event, there may be name badges and special information packs to prepare.

The secret to being well organised is to list the names of everyone who has been invited. Then tick these off as you receive each reply. Chase up any outstanding responses; then prepare two lists. The first contains the names of those who are going to attend. The second is a list of those who have sent their apologies or declined the invitation.

Meeting delegate needs and special requirements

All delegates have certain universal needs. These include the following.

Appropriate information which states:

- the practical arrangements, i.e. the date, time and place of the meeting, how to get there, where to park etc.
- what type of meeting it is and how long it will last
- what refreshments will be provided
- the facilities available.

Did you know?

In some large organisations, members of staff are appointed to check every arrangement before a major meeting to ensure that it meets the needs of disabled visitors. This includes 'walking the route' to spot any problems.

Facilities to meet their personal needs. These may include:

- vegetarian or other food options to comply with religious or cultural beliefs
- a loop hearing system for anyone who cannot hear very well or a signer present if any members are deaf
- paperwork printed in large type for anyone who has a visual impairment
- wheelchair access for anyone who is disabled.

The normal method of establishing these requirements is to include space on the form sent to delegates to enable them to indicate any special facilities they need.

Collating/dispatching papers

Papers that have to be sent out in advance may be collated and sent out with the agenda, or sent out later. For a large meeting, which will include external delegates, it is important to check whether you need to send a set to everyone who is entitled to attend, or only to those who have accepted.

Working within agreed timescales

Making organisational arrangements for a meeting is not a job you can put off because there is obviously a strict deadline. Moreover, there are other consequences of doing things later rather than sooner. Fewer people are likely to attend, for one thing, because they will have made other arrangements on the date. Your chances of booking the best venue will be reduced and even the most flexible catering staff are unlikely to be able to produce dozens of sandwiches at five minutes' notice.

For all these reasons it is important that you list the jobs to be done at the outset, and the timescale in which they have to be completed. Tick them off as you go and never put anything off until tomorrow that you could get done today. Use the checklist below as a guide.

CHECKLIST FOR MEETING PREPARATIONS

Venue
Decide and book appropriate meetings room
Check furniture and layout required

Facilities and equipment
Check equipment required, e.g. flipchart, data projector etc.
Check any overnight accommodation requirements

Food
Check refreshments/meals required and order
Confirm exact number required the day before the meeting

Documentation
Send notice of meeting to participants
Distribute agenda
Prepare/photocopy documents for circulation
Prepare/photocopy documents to be tabled at the meeting

Other
List apologies received from those who cannot attend
Check room immediately before event
Ensure spare copies of documentation available in case some participants have forgotten them

If external visitors involved
Book car parking spaces
Prepare visitors' badges
Send location maps/email confirming details

Did you know?

In many organisations, you will have to follow specific procedures to book refreshments and this will include a reasonable amount of notice for the catering staff.

Activity

Find out how refreshments are booked for meetings in your school or college and the budget restrictions that apply.

Did you know?

It is important not to forget health and safety requirements at the planning stage. This means the equipment and furniture is arranged safely; there are no trailing cables, and fire exits are clearly marked.

Layout of room

The preferred layout of the room will depend upon the type of meeting and the number of people attending. This needs to be discussed with the chairperson beforehand so that you can make the appropriate arrangements. In your school or college, this would mean asking the caretakers; for an external venue, it means notifying the manager.

Your choices are as follows:

- boardroom style, where all participants sit around a table
- classroom – each person has their own desk and chair
- u-shaped – where the table consists of a top section and two legs. If the top table is wide, seating can be placed at both sides of each leg
- hollow square – where participants face the centre
- discussion groups – where groups sit around separate tables
- theatre style – where participants sit in rows. This is the most economical arrangement for seating large numbers for a presentation.

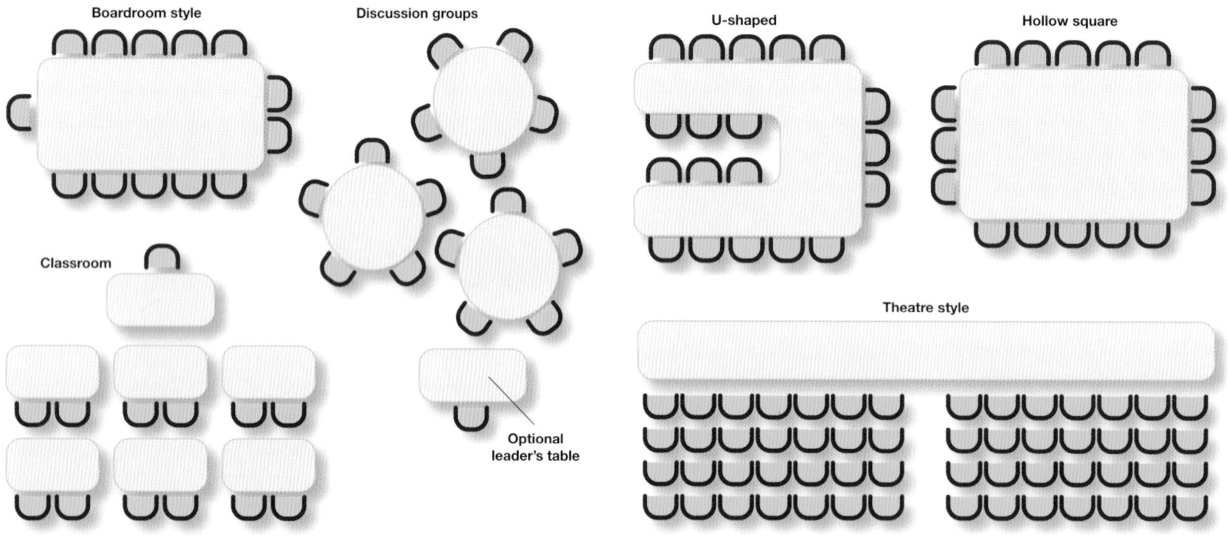

Fact file

The secret to running efficient meetings lies in good planning, which requires liaison between the chairperson and the organiser.

Internal meeting support

This relates to the support that you may be expected to provide for meetings arranged by your own organisation, whether they are held on the premises or at an external venue.

Documentation for delegates

You can expect to be involved in the preparation of documents that will be sent to delegates ahead of the meeting, as well as those that are tabled at the actual event. Remember to have spare copies of absolutely everything, because attendees often forget to bring important documents with them.

Attendance list

It is vital that you know who has arrived. In a small meeting, it is easy to check who is there and apologies should have been received from anyone who is unable to attend. If quite a few people are present and you do not know their names, issue a sheet of paper and ask for it to be passed around the table, for people to print their names on it.

If you report apologies at a small meeting, it is usual to give the reason if this has been provided.

At a very large meeting it is more difficult. One way around this is to greet delegates as they arrive, check off their names on the delegate list and issue them with their name badge and information pack. Your checked-off list then becomes your attendance list.

Information and support needed

You may need to provide information and support to the chairperson and to the delegates themselves. This can include:

- spare copies of documents already issued
- information on the 'housekeeping' arrangements. These include the whereabouts of the nearest toilets as well as emergency procedures
- answering queries relating to previous meetings – which may mean referring back to previous minutes or documents
- emergency contact arrangements through reception
- additional refreshments if the meeting goes on longer than expected
- being a point of reference for external visitors who get lost, have problems parking or any other queries.

The secret is to be well prepared, to have reference sources with you and not to panic if you are besieged with queries. Simply make sure you know where to get help yourself if you need it.

Minutes or record of meeting

It is normal to keep some record of what was said at a meeting, no matter how informal it may, be for three reasons:

- to ensure that the important points discussed are circulated to those who need this information as soon as possible
- to enable the minutes or notes to be agreed as correct at the next meeting
- to remind people what they have agreed to do.

If you are using an agenda then your job is easier because you will normally make a note under each agenda heading. This is also the system used for minutes of a meeting. An example is shown below.

MARTON COLLEGE

MINUTES OF MEETING
A meeting of the Student Council was held in the Library Meeting Room at 1200 hours on Thursday, 25 April 200-.

PRESENT
Mohammed Hussein (Chair)
Tim Brennan
Sara Charlton
Bushra Iqbal
Emma Masters
Tom Shepherd
Paula Singleton

		Action
1	**Apologies for absence** Apologies were received from Salma Khan.	
2	**Minutes of previous meeting** These were agreed as a true and correct record and signed by the Chairperson.	
3	**Matters arising** Sara Charlton said that the IT Centres would stay open later each evening from 4 May. From Monday to Thursday they would remain open until 21.30 hours. This would help students who needed to finish their assignments.	
4	**Report on student charity** Bushra Iqbal reported that the total now raised was £1,250. The presentation ceremony to the Animal Sanctuary staff had been arranged for Tuesday, 18 June at 2 pm. Further details would be given nearer the time.	BI
5	**Proposed changes to college IT policy** The proposed new IT policy had been circulated before the meeting. Members had several queries and it was agreed that Emma Masters would clarify these with a member of the IT staff before the next meeting.	EM
6	**Appointment of new council secretary** A replacement for Paula was required as she was unable to attend any future meetings. It was agreed that Tim Brennan would be ideal in the role because of his interest and previous experience. The Chairperson thanked Paula for all her hard work over the past year.	
7	**Any other business** The Chairperson said that the College Principal had asked that two council representatives attend a governors' meeting on 10 May to talk about the work of the council. It was agreed that the Chairperson and Tom Shepherd would be present.	MH/TS
8	**Date and time of next meeting** The next meeting will be held at 1200 hours on Thursday, 16 May, 200-.	

Signed ....(Chairperson) Date ....

Whatever type of record you make, the important information to include is:

- the name of the organisation
- date of the meeting
- names of those present
- names of those who could not attend
- notes of what has been discussed or decided
- date and time of the next meeting.

Approval of minutes or record

The last thing you want is an argument at the next meeting because no one agrees with your minutes. The best way to prevent this is to work closely with the chairperson. Prepare everything in draft form first and ask for approval before sending out the final version.

However, it is a bit dangerous to assume that during a long meeting the chairperson can remember everything that happened. It is therefore helpful to mark any points where you have queries or think there could be a problem. This is important if you have written something a little controversial. It may be better to agree the wording with the chairperson, rather than risk offending anyone.

Amendments

At the start of the next meeting, those present will be asked to approve the meetings under the agenda item 'Minutes of last meeting'. Any errors and amendments will be noted under this item. Only when the minutes have been agreed as correct should they be signed and dated by the chairperson.

Circulation

The notes or minutes of a meeting are circulated not just to those who attended but to those who could not attend as well, to keep them up to date with developments for the next meeting.

Activity

Find out if you can see two or three past agendas, related minutes and meeting papers issued at school or college meetings – preferably in a sequence. In groups, discuss the contents and find out how those who attended responded to the different agenda items.

External meeting support

This relates to the support you are expected to provide if your manager is attending an external meeting. It may include:

- entering the event in his or her diary

Key terms

An ***agenda*** is a list of items to be discussed at a meeting.

The ***chairperson*** is the leader of a meeting.

A ***meeting brief*** is a summary of the main requirements for a meeting.

The ***minutes*** are a record of decisions made and agreed at a meeting.

Did you know?

Notes of formal meetings may be used as evidence in legal proceedings. Normally, once they have been agreed as correct it is difficult to challenge them in court.

Did you know?

For many routine meetings, where documents are sent by mail, the minutes are sent out together with the notice and agenda for the next meeting, to save on postage costs.

Activity

Find out the types of external meetings your tutor or other staff attend and the support that they would find helpful.

Fact file

Admin staff provide support for their managers at internal meetings, such as by taking notes, and to help them attend external meetings, for example, by arranging travel and accommodation.

Talking point

View 1: The formalities surrounding many meetings are sensible and help to make sure they are run efficiently.

View 2: The formalities surrounding many meetings are unnecessary and outdated. It would be better if all meetings were informal.

With which viewpoint do you agree – and why?

- collecting all the relevant paperwork and putting it into a file or folder
- obtaining information about directions or car parking
- making travel arrangements and obtaining a rail or airline ticket
- arranging appropriate accommodation. This may be provided by the organisers or you may have to make the reservation
- completing any appropriate forms and making sure the organisers know if your manager has any special needs or requirements
- recording the amount your manager spends on an expenses form, attaching receipts and arranging for reimbursement.

Over to you

1 *Your friend is Treasurer for a local charity which holds quite formal meetings once a month. He has asked if you could help by providing administrative support before, during and after the meeting.*

As a group, identify the duties this would probably entail under the headings: ***before***, ***during*** *and* ***after***.

2 *Salma has just prepared a notice and agenda for the first time for the weekly staff meeting. When you look at it you can see a number of problems. Identify these and then prepare a 'model' version for her.*

Jackson Holdings Ltd

20 February

Staff meeting

This will be on 22nd Feb to discuss the following things.

- The holiday rota
- Temporary closure of the car park
- The new database

See you there!

Salma

3 *Dave Parker is Sales Manager at Jackson Holdings. He wants to hold a half-day meeting at an external venue for all the sales staff, including the regional reps, to outline the new product range and associated advertising campaign. He wants the meeting to start with a buffet lunch at 12 noon and end with dinner in the evening.*

a) *As a group, suggest the type of facilities and equipment that are likely to be required.*

b) *In small groups, investigate and suggest two possible venues in your area and give reasons for your choice. Compare your ideas.*

Case study Assessment practice

Emily Sykes was not pleased when she overheard a member of staff saying that he would rather go to the dentist than attend one of her meetings, even though she knew there were sometimes problems.

As team leader, there was often so much to tell everyone. Last week there had been 15 items on the agenda – and they had got bogged down almost immediately when Sam Philips talked at length about the fact that he still had not received the minutes from two weeks ago, which he used as an excuse for not doing the jobs he had promised to do. Then there had been an argument about whose turn it was to take the notes and, for the sake of peace, Emily had done them herself. As usual after an hour they were only half way down the list of items. Perhaps she should ask everyone to come in earlier – or stay later – to get through everything. Perhaps having a breakfast meeting would help, though she couldn't imagine they would be any more efficient if everyone was trying to eat and drink at the same time.

Emily also needed better admin support. Four documents that should have been sent out in advance had been so delayed she had given them out instead, which held things up. One document had gone out ahead but only one person remembered to bring it and Emily did not have any spares.

There had also been confusion about which room to use. This week the large meetings room had been double-booked so they had been crammed into the smaller one, which had been left in a mess by the marketing group who had used it earlier. Emily sighed. Perhaps the new administrator, due to start next week, would be the answer to her prayers.

1(M) Explain the type of organisation and administrative support Emily will require the new administrator to provide for her meetings. ***(M3)***

2(D) Analyse the organisation and administrative support provided for Emily's meeting and recommend the improvements that are needed. ***(D2 part)***

3(P) Organise your own meeting to discuss a day out for your group. Ask your tutor if this has to be an educational trip linked to your course, or whether it can be an 'end of term' fun day out!

Decide on the date, time and location for your meeting. Also find out whether you can afford refreshments and, if so, book these.

Select a chairperson and agree the agenda (e.g. possible destinations, cost, date etc.) and prepare a notice and agenda. Remember that as this is your first meeting you will not need to include 'minutes of previous meeting' or 'matters arising'. Prepare any related documents (e.g. information on possible destinations) and either circulate them in advance or agree to table them.

Select someone to take the minutes or agree that each person will write up their own version and then you can compare the results. ***(P5)***

4(D) Afterwards, analyse your organisation and admin support to see if you did better than Emily. Recommend any improvements that you would introduce if you held a follow-up meeting. ***(D2 part)***

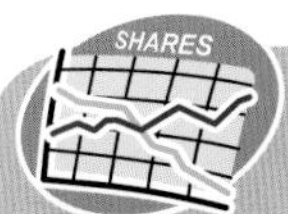

Grading tip

A good explanation will include reasons to support your choices.

Your analysis should show that you have identified the level of support required and where the absence of support is causing problems. Your recommendations should suggest how to solve these.

6.4 Be able to demonstrate the procedures needed to process, retrieve and archive information

Did you know?

You use electronic storage whenever you save a document you have created on computer. You process it when you decide on the title and best folder to store it in, so that you can find it again without difficulty.

Did you know?

In some organisations staff put a 'release mark' (usually a small tick or cross) on documents to be filed to prevent current paperwork being filed by mistake.

Every organisation needs to store information safely and accurately so that it can be retrieved quickly and easily whenever it is needed. Because many people do these tasks, there are normally procedures in place to ensure that they do them in the same way. Otherwise, important information could easily be lost or mislaid. Information that must be kept but is no longer required regularly is normally archived to free up storage space. Again there will be procedures to ensure that this is done correctly.

Processing information

This relates to the way information is handled when it is received and stored. The process will depend upon whether information is stored in a paper-based or electronic system:

- **paper-based or manual systems** contain paper documents
- **electronic systems** contain documents which have been scanned into the system or created on computer.

Information required

The first step is to understand which documents are ready for processing and which are not. Few managers would be pleased to find that several documents they currently need have suddenly disappeared from their desks into the files.

In a paper-based system documents for filing may be placed in a special filing basket or tray near the filing cabinets or collected from filing trays on staff desks.

In an electronic system you are likely to receive a batch of original documents to scan into the system and there will be specific procedures which state what you must do with these afterwards. Often they are stored for a short period in case of queries, before being shredded.

You then need to know how to **classify** and/or **index** each document, which will depend on how the files are stored (see page 270).

Procedures

Filing procedures are required to ensure that everyone does the job in the same way. They are likely to include:

- the general rules of filing
- how to cross-reference a document which could go in either one of two places
- how to control the lending of files and how to trace these if they are overdue
- how long to retain documents and files
- how to deal with confidential documents
- how to archive files
- what to do if a problem occurs.

Activity

Yellow Pages *provides an excellent example of cross-referencing. Look inside to see what happens if you look for an entry in the wrong place.*

Did you know?

In an electronic system, confidentiality is controlled through different access levels allocated to users.

Security and confidentiality

All organisations have legal responsibilities to keep personal and confidential information secure. Policies and procedures control:

- who can access this type of information
- where and how it is stored
- the destruction of confidential papers (usually by cross-shredding)
- the disposal of CD-Roms that contain confidential information.

Did you know?

If you work in a business that keeps sensitive information on individuals you are likely to find a clause in your contract of employment to prevent you talking about this outside the workplace.

Activity

Under the Data Protection Act data must be accurate, secure and not kept for longer than is necessary. Find out more at the website of the Information Commissioner at www.ico.gov.uk.

Legislation issues

The main legal considerations relating to processing information are as given below.

The Data Protection Act 1998 regulates the activities of all organisations storing data on individuals.

Retention periods relate to the length of time that records may be held. In some cases there are specific legal requirements. For example, accident reports must be kept for three years, tax documents for six years and payroll records for seven years.

Storage of information

In a paper-based system information may be stored alphabetically, numerically or chronologically. The difference is shown in the table below.

Did you know?

If files are kept by subject, there is often a master index to prevent people duplicating files by accident, for example IT training or computer training.

Method	Variations	Main use	Examples
Alphabetical	By name	When *the name* of the person or organisation is the most important factor	Customer files Staff records
	By location	When *the place* is the most important factor	Branch office files Overseas contacts
	By subject	When *the topic* is the most important aspect	A manager's personal files Purchasing files (by product)
Numerical	By sequence	When the files *are linked* to a unique reference number (often allocated by a database)	Customer files in a large organisation
	Alpha-numerical	When *letter codes* as well as numbers are allocated, e.g. S = Sales, then S1, S2 etc.	Departmental files in a large organisation
Chronological		When *the date* is the most important factor	Exam results Travel files

Did you know?

In an electronic system the software helps to index the document. This can be done using keywords, customer numbers, the date and other types of data.

Activity

Find out how electronic filing works at www.falcondocumentmanagement.co.uk.

Alphabetical filing Alphabetical files are *direct* – if you know the name you can go straight to the file. However, it is not quite as easy as just knowing your alphabet. There are rules so that everyone knows what to do if people or organisations have the same or similar names, if a name comprises only initials or includes numbers as well as names. You can see how this works in the table below.

Alphabetical filing	
Rule to follow	**Example of filing order**
PEOPLE	
Surname first	Clark, Peter
Short names before long	Clark, Peter Clarkson, Peter
For identical names, follow first name(s) or initial	Clarkson, Peter Antony Clarkson, Peter Michael
Nothing always comes before something	Naveed, H Naveed, Hussein
Treat Mac and Mc as Mac and file before 'M'	MacDonald T McNulty J Marsden F
Ignore apostrophes	Oliver T O'Sullivan B
ORGANISATIONS	
Ignore the word 'The'	Security Store, The
Treat numbers as words	Seven Mile Garage Six Steps Nursery
If names are identical use street or town to decide the order	Top Shop, Martin Way Top Shop, Westminster Parade
Initials come before full names (ignore 'and' and '&')	SB Animal Feeds S & J Upholstery SRA Associates Sainsbury's J plc
Treat Saint and St as Saint	St John Ambulance Salisbury College
File public bodies under name, or town/city if the names are identical	Maidstone Borough Council Medway Council Magistrates' Court Service, Bath Magistrates' Court Service, Bootle Ministry of Defence

The main problem with an alphabetical filing system is that those files beginning with popular letters quickly get crowded.

Numerical filing This system is easier to expand than an alphabetical system so is often used for large numbers of files. The problem is that it is *indirect*. Unless you know the file number you need to refer to an index first.

Indexes are always in alphabetical order. Look for the name then read off the number alongside. Never remove a card from a manual system in case it gets lost. Write down the number instead.

Today many indexes are created and maintained on computer, although some small firms still use card indexes. The type of information an index contains is shown below.

Reference number	Name
72609	Jacqui Ashworth
72610	Karen Bishop
72611	Julie Mitchell
72612	Feroz Daud
72613	Fatima Iqbal
72614	Petra Oswarski

The three main systems of manual filing are alphabetical, numerical and chronological.

Chronological filing This is only used for specific types of documents such as bank statements or petty cash vouchers. The identifying feature here is the date. In a computer system the date must be entered using the same format each time, for example 24/10/2006 or 24.10.06.

Approved locations

Paper-based files may be kept in a number of places, using a variety of different storage systems.

Vertical filing cabinets have between two and five large drawers; they are lockable and fitted with a safety mechanism to prevent more than one drawer being opened at once. Inside are usually suspension pockets. Each has a tab at the front which shows the name of the file.

Papers are usually placed in file folders in date order, with the most recent on top. In some organisations the papers are fastened into the folders, in others they are not.

Lateral filing cabinets are like large open cupboards with a sliding door or blind that can be pulled down when the cabinet is not in use. Inside there are rows of suspended pockets, each with a tab at the side.

Rotary filing systems are like rotating display stands seen in shops. They hold A4 lever arch or box files and spin to give all round access.

Lateral or horizontal cabinets are used for very large documents or those that must not be hole-punched, such as maps or photographs.

Find examples of all the different storage systems listed above in your school or college or online at www.bisley.com and then check out the automated systems at www.kardex.co.uk.

Updating

Information must be processed regularly (preferably daily) and correctly to keep files up to date.

In a paper-based system:

- check the document has been released for filing
- check multi-page documents are complete and in the right order. Then remove any paper-clips and staple the pages
- repair any torn papers with transparent sticky tape
- pre-sort the documents into alphabetical or numerical order, depending upon your system
- punch papers centrally, using the ruler on the punch or the central arrow as a guide
- locate the file you need and remove it carefully. Do not tug at the tab or it is likely to break
- double-check that you have the right file
- put it on a stable surface and insert the new documents with the most recent on the top
- replace the folder in the right place.

In an electronic system:

- scan each document into the system
- check the image is readable on screen. Otherwise enhance it using the methods available on your system
- enter the correct key indexing words, so the document can be easily found
- add the required protection if access rights are restricted
- process the paper document as instructed.

Retrieving information

In this case you are obtaining information from a file. In an electronic system, users who have access rights may retrieve information themselves, but this does not mean that you will never be asked to find anything.

Confirming/identifying information for retrieval

Check that you understand exactly what information is required. The more details you have the better, particularly if you are looking for one document rather than a complete file. Ideally, you need the name, subject and approximate date before you start.

Procedures for locating/retrieving information

In a manual system you may not be allowed to remove individual papers but must take the whole file and record this in an 'absent' system. This tells other users who have taken the file, in case they need it urgently.

Access levels control who can access, amend, change or archive files in an electronic system.

Archiving involves keeping inactive papers safely away from the main system.

Culling involves reducing a file by throwing away unnecessary or duplicated papers.

Document management software is software that converts paper files into an electronic image and indexes documents at the same time.

An ***index*** is an alphabetical system to guide users to files stored numerically.

Retention periods are the lengths of time for which files must be kept.

Activity

Practice keeping files up to date at school, college or on work experience.

Practice retrieving files and documents at school, college or on work experience.

Alternatively, you can usually photocopy the document unless it is confidential.

Accuracy

When you think you have found the correct file or document, check to make sure you are right. This is particularly important in a paper-based system if there are several files with similar names.

The more details you have about a file or document the easier it is to find it. Always check, too, the timescale and the format required.

Accessing information system

You will not be allowed access to confidential documents without permission and in an electronic system can only find documents to which you have access. If you have a problem, refer back to the person who gave you the task.

Format for providing information

Check if the whole file or just a photocopy of one document is required. In an electronic system, check if you should take a hard (paper) copy or email the document.

Agreed timescales

Always check if the information is needed urgently or not.

If all files are stored in an electronic system there is usually no need to archive them because storage space isn't an issue.

Some organisations arrange for archived files to be scanned into an electronic system either on or off the premises. This reduces the storage space required.

Problems

Problems that can occur include:

- the file or document is missing from the system
- all your key words (in an electronic system) draw a blank.

In either case use your initiative before you panic. This means checking if a paper file has been borrowed or misfiled, or if a missing document is still waiting to be filed or scanned into the system. Then recheck if your instructions were correct before asking for help.

Archiving information

Over time, paper-based files start to become full. Unless something is done there would eventually be a need for more cabinets and more space every year. For this reason, the system should be regularly reviewed. Some files can be destroyed, because they will never be needed again. Some papers can be destroyed, because they are unimportant or duplicated. Some files will be archived because although they are inactive, they need to be kept. They are therefore put into long-term storage in another area, such as the basement.

Paper-based files need reviewing regularly to save space. Some may be culled or destroyed. Others will be archived because they may be needed again.

Procedures for archiving information

Specific procedures control when archiving can take place and who can decide which files can be moved and where to. This is always done by senior staff who must consider the organisation's legal responsibilities and statutory retention periods.

Confirming/identifying information for archiving

You need to know exactly which files can be archived so that none are archived by mistake. As a safety precaution, it is usual to remove the files first and then have these checked by a supervisor before going any further.

Accuracy and records

The normal procedure is to write the date the file is closed on the front of the folder, then affix an archive label before placing it into a special archive box. The name or number of the file is then written on the box label. It is important that the name or number is written accurately so that it can be found easily.

Agreed timescales

Archiving is normally done on a regular basis, such as once every year. The next review should be entered into the main diary as a reminder.

Retrieval from archive

This is easy if the box labels have been written correctly, the boxes are in a sensible order and still in a relatively accessible area. Otherwise you may need assistance.

Talking point

View 1: Updating files is something to be done when you've got enough time and haven't any other pressing jobs to do.

View 2: Updating files is an essential routine task that must be done all the time, no matter how busy you are.

With which viewpoint do you agree – and why?

Activity

Find out which types of files are archived in your school or college and where they are kept.

Over to you

1. **a)** *As a group, discuss how you would control the lending and return of files for which you are responsible.*
   b) *How would you amend these ideas to cope with confidential files and documents?*
2. *Rearrange the following list twice. Firstly, put it into numerical order to show the order the files would be stored in a filing cabinet. Then put it into alphabetical order to show the order in which the index cards would be filed.*

Bryant M	*381972*	*McDonald S*	*323749*
Cunningham J	*324973*	*Chambers B*	*312938*
Jalucci K	*323492*	*Jackson S*	*343982*
Ashton P	*324528*	*Mason P*	*312393*
Chambers T	*325927*	*Monk J*	*342394*

3. *As a group, suggest five safety precautions you should take when you are storing, retrieving or archiving files.*

Case study Assessment practice

Jill has just started work in the office of a small local garage, which carries out car servicing and MOT tests. She is horrified to find that the filing system is completely chaotic. Files are overfull and stuffed into six old cabinets. There are many outdated documents in the files and the whole system is a mess. The owner, Steve, has agreed a totally fresh start is needed.

Jill can see that there are files for customers and supplier files for car parts and accessories. Often the same parts are available from several different suppliers and it would be useful to be able to compare prices easily. There are also Steve's own business files, which include his tax returns and payroll files for the three staff he employs. Finally, there are copies of MOT certificates which Steve keeps so that he can remind customers when their MOT tests are due.

1(P) Bearing in mind Steve's paperwork, suggest the classification systems that would be useful for his files and give reasons for your choices. ***(P6)***

2(P) Write a short account for Steve which describes the main procedures you think are needed to process, retrieve and archive the information properly. ***(P6)***

7 Personal selling

Making sales is crucial for all businesses that supply goods and services and the talents of expert sales staff have a direct influence on profits. This unit focuses on the knowledge you need to develop your own personal selling skills.

What you need to learn

- The purpose of sales personnel
- How to prepare for personal selling
- How to demonstrate personal selling skills and processes
- How to identify customers' objections and closing sales techniques

7.1 Understand the purpose of sales personnel

If you have ever watched the TV series *The Apprentice*, in which candidates compete to be offered a job with a six-figure salary by Sir Alan Sugar, you should have noticed that the emphasis of the task has usually been on personal selling. Without this skill, no candidate lasts very long. This should give you some idea of the importance of sales to most business organisations!

However, there are limits to the type of promises that can be made to secure a sale without breaking the law. In this section you will learn about the purpose of sales personnel and the skills and knowledge needed, including the legislation which applies.

The purpose of sales personnel

Sales personnel are a feature of many businesses – from high street shops and travel agents to specialist producers selling to other businesses. They are employed for a number of reasons.

Key terms

Cross-selling is suggesting related items to a customer (to increase overall sales).

Up-selling is promoting a more profitable item to increase the value of sales.

Increasing business sales

The obvious reason for employing sales staff is that they generate additional revenue for the business because more goods are sold. In addition to basic sales, staff can also **cross-sell** by promoting related items (such as shoe cleaner for a new pair of shoes or a printer to go with a new computer) which increases overall sales. They will also be trained to **up-sell**. This means suggesting more exclusive (and profitable) items to a customer – such as a higher specification computer or a more powerful car – which will increase the value of sales.

Helping businesses to remain competitive

Providing excellent service can give a company a competitive advantage over its rivals. This occurs if customers choose a supplier on the basis of its service and/or knowledgeable and helpful salespeople. All sales staff should aim to provide a better service than the customer would receive from any of the firm's competitors.

Heinemann sales consultants visit schools and colleges to talk to staff and students about their preferences relating to new books they would like.

Providing information and services to customers

Frequently private customers 'shop around' for what they want. Without intervention by a sales person, many people would leave without making a purchase, either because they are not sure what they want or because they cannot decide what to buy. Providing information and advice about the best product to meet a customer's needs results usually encourages customers to buy.

Developing customer care

You first learned about customer care in Unit 2 because it is part of the customer service requirement. Customers want quality products, value for money *and* customer care. Sales staff are the first point for demonstrating customer care and can recommend ways in which this can be developed and enhanced to attract new customers and retain customer loyalty.

The purpose of sales staff is to increase business sales and help businesses to remain competitive. They also provide information and services to customers, develop customer care and obtain useful feedback. Ideally, everyone benefits as a result.

Gathering feedback

The information that sales staff obtain from customers and potential customers can be invaluable because it enables the business to respond directly to customer comments. This allows it to develop new products and/or services or adapt existing ones to meet customer needs better.

Benefits

Personal selling provides benefits in several ways:

- **the organisation** gains because it is more likely to meet its objectives – as both sales and the number of customers will increase
- **the employees** gain because they can be motivated to work hard and do well – both in terms of personal achievements and financial rewards for meeting sales targets
- **the customers** gain because they can rely on professional assistance and advice which will help them to obtain the best goods or services that they require.

Knowledge and skills

Can anyone be a good sales person? Several American studies have shown that not everyone has the personal qualities to sell successfully. Only when potential salespeople possess certain important attributes – such as being keen and eager to succeed – is it possible for them to learn and develop the skills that are required. These are shown in the diagram below.

Did you know?

Sales staff employed to sell industrial products to business customers are usually technical experts – such as engineers or designers.

Did you know?

***Resilience** is an important attribute for all sales people. Unless you can cope with rejection and not take it personally, you will find selling very hard work.*

Did you know?

The Internet has changed the way customers buy. Many people now research products online before they go shopping and good salespeople have changed their approach to allow for this.

Sound product knowledge

Expertise makes selling much easier. If you are talking to an expert – your doctor, a solicitor, even your hairdresser – you are more likely to be convinced by their arguments. This is why good sales people always have excellent product knowledge. They should also be interested in what they are selling and, ideally, have some relevant experience. It is far harder to sell cameras if you have never taken a photograph and almost impossible to sell cars if you cannot drive. Sales people should know enough about the range of products or services on offer to be able to match other aspects – such as features, performance and price – to the individual needs of each customer.

Inwardly motivated to sell

Top sales staff are highly driven people and very keen to achieve. They are passionate about their work and get a 'buzz' by solving customer problems. This motivates them to work hard to understand their customers' individual needs (see pages 293 and 296). They are also quick thinkers and inventive at suggesting ways to satisfy these.

Ability to close sales

This ability differentiates the professional from the amateur and is an important topic in virtually all sales training courses. A sales encounter goes through several stages, by which time the salesperson should be in a position to get the customer to commit to buying (see page 314). Otherwise, the negotiations could last for hours, with no result.

Keeps up to date

Good sales people are up to date in three ways. They know the most recent products and services being offered by their organisation (and what is 'coming soon'); they know what their competitors are offering and they know what the latest trends are. This enables them to stay ahead of the game and use their ability to forecast and meet the customer's future needs as a key selling point.

Promotes good selling techniques

Good salespeople know how to make a sale without resorting to cheap tricks or dishonesty. They also know how to move through each stage of the sales process effectively, continually focusing on meeting the customer's needs. A summary of these stages is given below. You will learn more about each one as you progress through this unit.

Stages in the sales process		
1	Planning and preparing to sell	See 7.2 page 291
2	Meeting and greeting the customer	See 7.3 page 305
3	Developing a relationship/attracting interest	See 7.3 page 305
4	Identifying the customer's needs	See 7.3 page 306
5	Presenting, demonstrating and providing information	See 7.3 page 306
6	Responding to objections	See 7.4 page 312
7	Closing the sale	See 7.4 page 314
8	Following up the sale	See 7.4 page 315

***Ethical selling** means not misleading the customer in any way. This contributes to gaining and keeping customer trust which is a key way to increase sales over time.*

Good sales habits

Some of these are just common sense – such as dealing with customers promptly, listening to what they are saying and knowing the product range – but you would be surprised how many salespeople fail to demonstrate them. Below is a list of good sales habits which will be discussed in more detail throughout this unit.

Good sales habits	
Greet, contact or respond to every customer positively and promptly	✔
Do not say 'Can I help you' because the customer can easily answer 'no'. Try 'Good morning/afternoon' with a smile instead!	✔
Observe customer body language to see the type of products they are interested in.	✔
Check if a customer is likely to be a serious buyer before you spend lots of time with them.	✔
Ask questions to find out what they want – don't assume you know!	✔
Listen to the reply. If there isn't a positive response to something then move on.	✔
Keep explanations clear and simple but be honest. Do not mislead or lie to a customer to make a sale.	✔
Sell the benefits to the customer, rather than the features of a product.	✔
Believe in what you are selling so that you are enthusiastic and passionate about it.	✔

continued ▶

The revenue earned by sales staff must be higher than the cost of their salaries or the business would lose money. This is why many are paid a basic rate and then commission is based on sales made. In addition to motivating sales staff to work harder the cost to the business is then always proportionate to the income from sales.

Have a fallback plan so that you can offer something else if your first suggestions are rejected.	✔
Upsell or cross-sell when you can – this improves profits.	✔
Use feedback from customers to suggest improvements.	✔
Change what you do if it obviously doesn't work.	✔
Know when to back off – don't badger, pester or contradict the customer.	✔
Don't make promises you cannot keep.	✔
Keep up to date – don't rely on old information or paperwork.	✔
Close the encounter in a friendly way, even if a sale hasn't been made. Then the customer may be tempted to return.	✔
Record customer details and follow up promptly if appropriate.	✔

Did you know?

Finding out how serious a customer is, before you spend lots of time with them, is often known as ***qualifying a sale****.*

Activity

As a group, match up the sales habits above to the different stages of the sales process (see page 281).

Activity

Find out more about the type of incentives offered to sales staff at www.getactive.co.uk. Check, too, if any members of your group have been employed to sell and, if so, what rewards they received.

Rewarding and motivating sales staff

Sales people who feel that they are appreciated and well rewarded for their efforts are more likely to be enthusiastic about their job and keen to sell more. Businesses are well aware of this and therefore have a number of ways of motivating sales staff.

Commissions and bonuses These are additional payments linked to the achievement of sales targets.

Sales incentives These are rewards, such as vouchers, product discounts, a day out or even a holiday, given to sales staff who do well.

Career development Even the best salesperson may not want to remain at that level forever. Many organisations offer career progression to management level, which can include responsibility for other sales personnel on a local or regional basis.

Legislation affecting personal selling

When you buy something you enter into a contract of sale with the seller. This does not need to be in writing. If you offer to buy an item (e.g. by picking it up and offering money) and the seller accepts your offer (e.g. by wrapping it up and taking your money) then this is a contract – just the same as if you had made a written offer (e.g. by completing an order form) and received confirmation in writing.

The contract is ended in three ways:

- **by performance** – you accept the goods, pay for them and now legally own them

Sales staff must know their product well, stay up to date, be able to use good sales habits and techniques and know how to close a sale. They must be inwardly motivated to sell. This can also be encouraged through financial rewards and career progression.

- **by agreement** – you return the goods and obtain a refund
- **by breach** – when the terms of the contract have not been met, e.g. failure to pay by the buyer or faulty goods supplied by the seller.

Consumer legislation

This gives buyers additional protection against faulty or unsafe products, shoddy services and unfair pricing. In addition to the laws that protect all consumers, sales staff need to know the specific regulations or codes of practice that relate to the product or services that they sell, for example:

- there are special Regulations to control distance selling, when the buyer and seller do not meet, such as the **Consumer Protection (Distance Selling) Regulations 2005** (see below)
- anyone who works in the catering trade should know about **Weights and Measures laws** and other legislation relating to food handling and food safety
- people who give financial advice and sell investment products must have special qualifications to do this and abide by several other Regulations to prevent mis-selling
- people who buy at home from doorstep sellers have additional rights, such as a seven day 'cooling off' period in which they can cancel the agreement.

The main legislation which affects personal selling is outlined in the table below.

Buyers sometimes have problems because they do not read the terms of written contracts of sale carefully. This is how mobile phone owners sometimes get locked into a contract with their network supplier for longer than they expected.

*The **Unfair Contract Terms Act 1977** prevents retailers from limiting or taking away a customer's legal rights.*

Sale of Goods Act 1979 as amended by the Sale of Goods (Amendment) Act 1994, Sale and Supply of Goods Act 1994 and Sale of Goods (Amendment) Act 1995 and Supply of Goods to Consumers Regulations 2002.

This states that all goods sold, whether new or second-hand, must be:

- **as described** – e.g. waterproof boots must not leak
- **of satisfactory quality** – in relation to the price paid, description and age of the item
- **fit for the purpose for which they are intended** – e.g. walking boots would be expected to be sturdy.

The goods must also be fit for any specific purpose the buyer has made clear (such as boots for hiking or climbing).

If these conditions are not met the seller must refund the buyer or, if reasonable, allow the buyer to opt instead for a repair or replacement. A free repair can be offered but if this is not satisfactory the buyer still has the right to a refund. Sale goods are also covered, unless the fault was clearly obvious or pointed out at the time of sale and the reason for the reduction.

Faulty goods can be returned by post if this is more convenient, or the customer can ask the shop to collect at its own expense. All goods posted by a supplier are at the seller's risk.

Supply of Goods and Services Act 1982

These cover buyers against services such as garage repairs and building work. The Act states that all services should be carried out:

- for a reasonable charge
- within a reasonable time
- with reasonable care and skill
- using satisfactory materials.

Consumer Protection Act 1987

This Act relates to price and safety. Under this Act it is an offence to:

- mislead customers as to the price of any item
- mislead consumers over sale prices and exaggerate price reductions
- supply goods which are not reasonably safe. In 1994, this aspect of the Act was strengthened by the General Product Safety Regulations.

Consumer Credit Act 1974

This Act controls consumer credit. Most businesses which offer loans to customers must be licensed. Retailers who arrange customer credit through a finance company need a different licence.

The Act also:

- requires lenders to state the true cost of the loan including the total charge for credit, the Annual Percentage Rate (APR) and the cash price for the goods

- protects borrowers against unfair deals and extortionate interest rates
- enables borrowers to claim compensation from a finance or credit card company as well as the supplier if the goods are faulty and cost over £100. This can be very useful if the seller has ceased trading or the goods were bought overseas
- gives a 'cooling-off' period of up to seven days to borrowers who sign a credit agreement in their own home
- prevents lenders demanding early repayment or trying to change the terms of an agreement without notice
- enables customers to find out the information held on them by a credit reference agency for a small fee and for retailers to provide details of the name of any CRA used to ascertain their credit rating.

Under the Act the wording of any advertisements promoting credit must be truthful and accurate with appropriate warnings, especially if the loan is to be secured on the borrower's property.

Trade Descriptions Act 1968

This Act makes it a criminal offence to give a false or misleading description of goods or services, for example:

- selling goods which are wrongly described by the manufacturer
- wrongly describing goods
- making false claims for services, accommodation and facilities.

Usually the spoken word of the seller overrides the written description of the goods, as the buyer can rely on the expertise of the salesperson. However, this can be difficult to prove if there is a dispute.

In this situation, the case should be reported to a Trading Standards Officers who could prosecute the firm concerned. Private individuals cannot do this.

Consumer Protection (Distance Selling) (Amendment) Regulations 2005

The Distance Selling Regulations were first passed in 2000 and amended in 2005. They protect customers who buy goods and services sold over the Internet, by mail order, by digital television, phone or fax. They include:

- providing clear information to consumers on all aspects of goods being sold and the transaction process
- sending written confirmation after the purchase has been made
- giving customers a cooling-off period of seven working days from the date goods are received or a service is requested
- giving a refund if the goods are not provided by the agreed date or within 30 days from the order.

Some goods and services are exempt and the Regulations do not apply to business-to-business transactions. The sale of financial services at a distance is covered by different Regulations.

*The **Consumer Credit Act** is being updated to allow for the various methods of obtaining credit today and more sophisticated advertising by lenders.*

All consumers have legal rights when they buy goods and services, either in a store, in their own home, over the phone or online as well as protection when they buy on credit.

Talking point

View 1: Paying salespeople bonuses or commission only encourages them to act unethically by pressurising customers into buying. They should be paid a fair basic wage instead.

View 2: Paying salespeople bonuses or commission is sensible because it rewards good performance. Otherwise everyone would earn the same.

With which viewpoint do you agree – and why?

Over to you

1 *Your friend Tom has applied for a sales job in a local computer store even though he has never worked in selling before. He tells you that the advert said he would receive full training and that he has been asked to go for an interview tomorrow.*

a) *What type of attributes do you think the interviewer will want Tom to possess?*

b) *What skills do you think the new sales staff will be taught during the training sessions? Discuss your ideas as a group.*

2 **a)** *Find out more about the rights of consumers at www.consumerdirect.gov.uk/. Do this by dividing into small groups with each one investigating one of the following topics and then give a brief verbal report to the whole group.*

- *Your rights when you buy goods.*
- *Your rights when you buy services.*
- *Your rights when you shop from home.*
- *Other things to watch out for, such as private sales and putting down a deposit on goods.*
- *Your rights to cancel an agreement.*

b) *Test your new found knowledge by saying how you would advise your friends and family if the following events occurred.*

i) *Your aunt bought an umbrella because it was labelled 'New, windproof design. Never blows inside out.' She tells you this is rubbish because last week, when it was very windy, that's exactly what it did.*

ii) *Your friend ordered a new leather sofa which was delivered last week. When he removed the protective packaging he noticed a scratch down the back. The firm says it is not liable because he signed the delivery note to say it was 'received OK'.*

iii) *Your sister received two identical CDs for her birthday and does not know what to do.*

iv) *Your mother's new toaster gets so hot around the sides that she burnt her hand. The shop that sold it says this is the fault of the manufacturer, not them.*

v) *Your brother left his watch to be repaired at a jeweller's. When he returned to collect it he was told it was stolen when the sales assistant left it on the counter. The notice behind the counter says that all goods for repair are left at the owner's risk.*

vi) *Your friend pays £250 by credit card to buy a mountain bike from a website supplier. The mountain bike never arrives and when he tries to contact the firm he gets no response.*

Case study Assessment practice

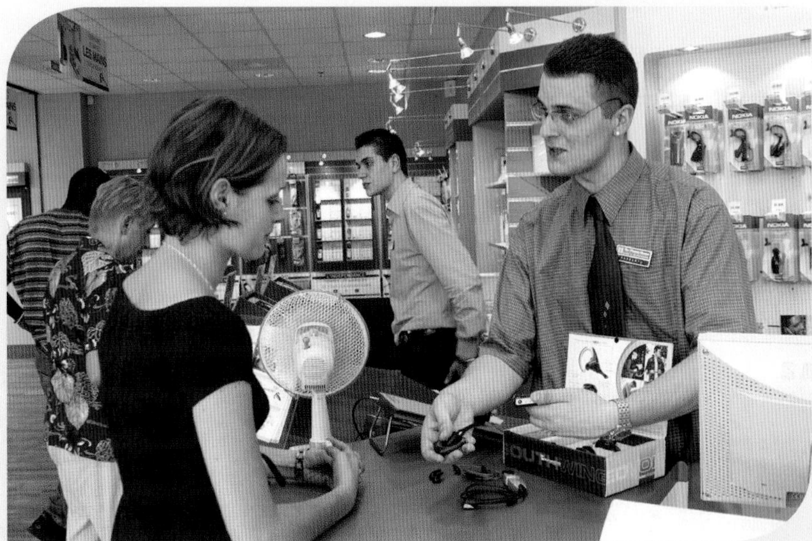

In 2006, Carphone Warehouse launched a combined call and Internet package to encourage more people to transfer to its home phone service TalkTalk. The company does not forecast making a profit on the service until 2008, by which time it intends to be BT's main competitor. Achieving its aim of 3.5 million customers by March 2009 will be a key objective for its sales staff.

Home phone companies work in a very competitive market, with many suppliers trying to persuade phone users to change their supplier to save money. They therefore need to offer excellent service and competitive prices to attract new customers. The problem is that some may be tempted to employ high-pressure sales techniques or give misleading information to get customers to switch. The two worst offences are mis-selling (lying about the prices or benefits or implying they work for another supplier, such as BT) and slamming – when a customer is switched from one company to another without giving consent. To prevent this type of behaviour, Ofcom, the regulator for the UK communications industry, has produced Codes of Practice guidelines which all providers must follow. Ofcom can investigate any allegations of mis-selling and impose substantial fines on suppliers which ignore the code.

The Code gives consumers greater protection than they have under consumer laws. It aims to avoid mis-selling and to ensure customers understand the services offered and the key terms of any contract that they enter into. It applies to all selling situations – whether by TV, radio, press, promotions in shops, by post, fax, telephone, email and in person. It determines how sales representatives must be recruited. It specifies that they must not be paid in a way that encourages misleading or exploitative sales practices and also stipulates how they must identify themselves and behave when they contact customers.

TalkTalk has been criticised in the press for the hard-sell tactics of some of its representatives. It has since published its own Code of Consumer Practice on its website, which details its own sales practices, customer services and the rights and obligations of customers – such as allowing customers longer to cancel a contract than the legal minimum if they change their mind.

Anyone who dislikes being contacted by unknown sales people – pushy or not – can follow Ofcom's advice and protect themselves from nuisance calls and mail by registering with the Telephone Preference Service and the Mailing Preference Service. As part of the Code of Practice, all telecoms suppliers must respect their wishes.

1(P) Describe the purpose of sales personnel who work for Carphone Warehouse. ***(P1 part)***

2(P) **a)** Identify the knowledge and skills someone selling mobile phones in a Carphone Warehouse store would need by checking out the job descriptions for the current Sales Consultant vacancies advertised in the careers section on www.carphonewarehouse.co.uk.

b) From the information on the website, describe how Carphone Warehouses uses career progression as a motivator for its retail sales staff. ***(P1 part)***

3(P) Describe the legislation which affects personal selling and which new staff at Carphone Warehouse would be told about. ***(P2)***

continued ▶

Case study *continued*

4 The extract from Oftel's guidelines below summarises some key points relating to the behaviour of sales representatives. You can also download TalkTalk's Code of Practice on its website at www.talktalk.co.uk (under 'About Us'). As a group, discuss how this will affect the behaviour of their sales staff in different selling situations.

5(M) Explain how legislation (including the code, where appropriate) might affect personal selling:

a) of TalkTalk services over the telephone

b) of mobile phones in a retail store. ***(M2)***

Summarised extract from Ofcom Guidelines for sales and marketing codes of practice for Fixed-line Telecommunications services

- Customers should not be contacted face to face outside the hours of 0900 to 2000 and by phone outside the hours of 0800 to 2100 except by customer request.
- All staff must be trained to provide information clearly and so that it is not misleading.
- Sales staff must explain:
  - how telecoms are supplied in the UK
  - the company's service they are offering and the price
  - the law on consumer protection
  - the cost of additional services
  - how to cancel the contract
  - the existence of the code of practice
  - how customer complaints are dealt with.
- All representatives must wear easy-to-read ID badges with a unique number, a photograph and expiry date and hand these back when they leave the company.
- They must immediately identify themselves, state the company they represent, the purpose of the call and its expected duration.
- They must be courteous, use appropriate language, offer clear and straightforward explanations and provide factual and accurate information.
- They must cease contact immediately if a person indicates it is inconvenient, unwelcome, inappropriate or too long. They must not contact anyone under the legal age to enter into a contract or visit people in sheltered housing, nursing homes or residential care without permission from someone in authority.
- A copy of the code, in plain English, should be available free to all customers.

Grading tip

Your explanation should make clear links between the requirements of the legislation and/or codes and what customers can do if they have a problem.

7.2 Know how to prepare for personal selling

Effective organisations have a sales strategy. In other words, they know who their customers are and how they intend to sell to them. They also train their sales staff on how to use this information to achieve sales targets. Although the selling method and sales situations will vary, one key factor for success is good preparation. The aspects to consider when preparing to sell are the focus of this section.

Identifying and finding potential customers

Large retail stores attract many customers by advertising. The job of their sales staff involves assisting visiting customers by providing information, answering queries, presenting or demonstrating a product and processing a successful sale.

This approach is not appropriate for all businesses. Some must be more pro-active in identifying sales opportunities to win new business – such as the telecoms companies described in the case study on page 287. In this type of situation different techniques are used to obtain new customers.

Cold calling

This means contacting an organisation or private individual to try to generate new business. It is a 'cold' call because there has been no previous contact and the recipient is not expecting the call. This may be made in person but is more usually by 'phone. An example would be regional newspaper staff ringing round local businesses on their database to try to persuade them to advertise.

Cold calling can be quite a scary thing to do unless you have been trained properly. You must be able to introduce yourself and quickly hold the attention of the person you are talking to. You also have to be able to cope with rejection. Success rates are not very high and it can take several calls to different people before you obtain one positive response.

Key term

The term ***prospect*** is often used for a prospective customer. This is someone who fits the profile for being a customer but has not yet bought anything.

Fact file

Businesses can actively identify and find potential customers by cold calling, following up leads, making drop-in visits, telemarketing or selling face to face.

Did you know?

The aim of many cold calls to businesses is not to make a sale but to arrange an appointment for a sales representative to visit.

Following up a lead

This is always easier and more successful than cold calling. In this case you have a name and a reason (or excuse) for making contact. 'Leads' can be obtained through recommendations from existing customers, from reps reports and from press reports about company developments. So a business which has been in the local news because of its expansion plans may receive calls from recruitment agencies offering to fill staff vacancies.

Face-to-face contact

This is used by all retail store staff as well as sales representatives who see their customers by appointment to promote new product lines, to obtain information on the customer's future plans and to obtain feedback on the current products they use. Face-to-face selling is also used at motorway service stations and in many shopping centres by people selling services such as membership to motoring organisations and 'no win, no fee' legal assistance.

Did you know?

Many firms offer their existing customers awards or discounts for providing the names of friends who may be interested in their products. This is done to obtain more leads and extend their database.

Did you know?

In the UK you rarely see shopkeepers outside their store telling passers-by about today's special offers, but this is quite common in some countries. In some tourist resorts, too, restaurant owners employ staff to tempt people walking past to come inside.

Drop-in visits

These are carried out by casual sellers who may call on small shopkeepers to sell their wares. It is also used by utility and telecoms companies whose reps call on people in an area to try to persuade them to switch supplier. They usually have a mixed reception as, without an appointment, they are simply 'cold calling'. Reputable sales representatives normally make an appointment first by telephone, even if they call on a regular basis, rather than just 'drop in'. They can then be certain the customer or prospect can talk to them and the visit is not a waste of time.

Telemarketing and telesales

This is used by many businesses to contact potential customers by phone, usually from a call centre. It can be inward or outward:

- **Inward** means staff are employed to respond to customer enquiries which may have been triggered by advertisements or special promotions.
- **Outward** means staff make calls to prospective customers to sell the product or service. The most successful are calls to previous customers who have not made a purchase for some time. Charities use this approach by contacting regular donors on their database to ask them to increase their contributions.

Did you know?

Most call centres use computer technology to distribute incoming calls amongst representatives and to dial and monitor outgoing calls.

Preparation for selling

Sales situations can vary enormously, but they all have one thing in common. The sales personnel involved in them will do far better if they have planned and prepared in advance. Normally, the more valuable the potential sale, the more work should go into the preparatory stage. For example:

- Nabil works for an estate agent. Before visiting a prospective customer who has a house for sale, he researches the prices of similar properties in that district to ensure he suggests a suitable selling price.
- Janine, Shahida, Zeb and Tom are directors of a Young Enterprise company. They are planning their stand at an Xmas Fayre and are deciding on their theme, which products should take pride of place and how many they need to take.
- Paul and Gerry have their own IT consultancy. They are finalising a presentation to a large firm when they hope to win a contract to revamp its IT system over the next three months.
- Jenny works for a charity. She is about to telephone regular donors to ask if they will give an additional contribution for a special campaign. She checks her facts about the campaign so that she can answer any questions. She also refers to each donor's profile on her computer screen as she makes the call.

Key terms

Cold calling is making an uninvited call to a customer.

Telemarketing is promoting the business and making sales by telephone.

Although the specific preparations are different each time, the key areas to consider are often the same. These are shown in the diagram below.

Did you know?

The length of time preparing to sell should reflect the value of the sale. It isn't sensible to think you can sell an expensive item or service without considerable effort.

Identifying the potential customer profile

Organisations carry out market research to find out about their customers. They need to find out how many people will want to buy the product or service, how much they would be prepared to pay and the best way to reach them. Anyone involved in selling needs to know how the following aspects apply to their own customers.

Buying habits This relates to the way individuals or organisations behave when they want to make a purchase.

The behaviour of individuals varies depending upon several factors including their age, gender and what they are buying. Tweens and teens, for example, between 7 and 17, want brands and products that are cool, highly fashionable and will impress their friends. These factors become less important as people get older. Women, generally, have different buying behaviour to men. One study classified them as 'hunter-gatherers' who look around and make comparisons before they decide, whereas men prefer to go for the quick kill. The product also affects buyer behaviour. Six in ten music buyers will browse around a music store and leave without buying. Clothes buyers do the same. But people only call in a superstore, chemist or petrol station when they want to make a purchase.

Did you know?

A study by Brunel University found that women feel harassed when they shop with a man and, as a result, spend 50 per cent less time shopping than when they are with another woman. This is why some women's shops have opened 'male crèches' with newspapers and TV to try to keep them occupied!

Businesses also have different buying habits. In a small company, there may be one person who makes all the decisions. In the public sector, businesses have specific procedures that must be followed and will buy at times that link to their budget cycle. Sales staff must know the buying habits of each firm they deal with.

Activity

You run a large retail store and have to position women's wear and men's wear. Which would you put on the ground floor and which on the first floor – and why?

Identifying the buying habits of customers helps businesses and their sales staff in several ways. Retail stores and supermarkets use this when they plan how to set out the store and where to position different items (see page 296). The store will also target incentives such as discounts, offers and vouchers to try to influence buyer behaviour. Tesco launched its 'Clubcard' scheme precisely so that it could obtain detailed information on the buying habits of its existing customers. It tracks every purchase made by members, analyses what was bought, how often and where from. It gives vouchers worth additional points to try to influence future buying behaviour.

Customer needs The aim of a business is to provide products or services that meet customer needs. Although customer needs may differ between individuals, based on their personal tastes and preferences, it is possible to identify common needs which apply to major groups of consumers. For example, gyms have been successful because they meet the needs of people in sedentary jobs who want to keep fit; cosmetic firms like L'Oreal are successful because they meet the need of women to stay looking young and attractive; easyJet and Ryanair meet people's needs for cheap air travel to Europe – and so on. Identifying customer needs and designing the product or service to meet these is the major ingredient in business success.

Business customers are more aware of their own needs and may draw up a product specification which identifies how it wants these to be met. For example, a clothes retailer may state the design and fabric it wants, as well as the type of fastenings and even the thread that must be used. The supplier must meet this specification at the agreed price. In some industries, the buyer and supplier work together to plan the design and features. This is usually the case with a specialist product or service, such as customised software or the format of an advertising campaign.

Reason for purchase Customers make a purchase for many different reasons. They may be buying for themselves or someone else. They may be making a routine purchase or treating themselves. Businesses who know the main reason(s) why their customers buy their products or service can use this to their advantage. This is why businesses promote flowers and other female presents just before Mother's Day, and travel firms and restaurants promote special packages for Valentine's Day. Knowing who buys the product is also important. More men's cologne and after-shave is bought by women than men – so the manufacturers target women as well as men with their adverts, and retailers do this through the placement of the product in stores.

Individual sales people also need to know why their customer is buying before they start to make any suggestions – as you will see on page 306.

Activity

Ask your tutor to explain the buying habits of your school or college, particularly for expensive items, how this is related to its budget year and when would/would not be a good time for a salesperson to call.

Activity

Take a poll and decide the top five customer needs of the students in your group when buying clothes. Then see if this is different from the top five customer needs of your tutor and identify the reason for any differences.

Did you know?

Victoria's Secret, a lingerie retailer, thought most of its customers were women in their 20s and 30s. Website monitoring showed that most site visitors were men aged 40–55. As a result the company redesigned its website to appeal more to this group.

Fact file

According to Business Link, ten things to know about your customers are: who they are; what they do; why, when and how they buy; how much money they have, what makes them feel good about buying, what they expect of you; what they think of you; what they think of your competitors.

Activity

Divide into groups to create a potential customer profile for four completely different makes and models of cars of your choice. In each case, consider buying habits, customer needs, reasons for buying and income. Then suggest how your findings would help a dealer to sell these vehicles. Compare your ideas with other groups.

Did you know?

Many travel agents send staff on selected holidays at regular intervals so that they can talk knowledgeably about different resorts and the facilities there.

The same applies if they are dealing with business customers. A business buyer may want some new chairs – but the exact requirements will vary depending upon whether the reason is to provide more seating in reception, for VDU operators or for the directors in the board room.

Income and revenue level The amount of money people have to spend, after paying all their routine bills such as rent and rates, is known as their **disposable income**. This affects the amount that a customer can afford to spend. Some retailers target affluent customers, such as Harvey Nichols and Selfridges – so do producers of luxury goods like Prada and Gucci. At the other end of the scale, stores like Aldi, Netto and IKEA target those on a tight budget.

Identifying the target market in terms of income influences many factors – the selling price(s), the type of packaging or extras that are appropriate, the magazines and newspapers to advertise in, where a retailer should locate, the layout and design of the store (see page 296). Usually a cluttered store will look downmarket and people will expect cheap prices.

Product knowledge

In addition to understanding the customer, the sales staff must also understand the product(s) they are selling. There is nothing more irritating for the customer than someone who does not seem to know what there is, where it is or how it works. To sell effectively, all sales staff must know:

- the range of products normally kept in stock
- the seasonal lines that are stocked – and over what period
- where particular goods can be found in the store
- the prices of individual items and the price ranges of different types of products
- the variations that are available, e.g. colour, sizes, models, additional options or extras
- the key selling features of each product
- the different uses of each product
- how to demonstrate a product (see page 308)
- the delivery time for products currently out-of-stock
- how to advise on use, care and maintenance
- the after-sales service available.

Activity

In groups, identify a product you all know – such as an Apple iPod, Sony PSP or Sky+ – and list its main selling features. Then outline these to the rest of your group to see if they agree.

Clarifying pricing issues

You have already seen that organisations have to decide the price of their goods or services bearing in mind the customer profile. In addition, they will also have strategies to maximise income from sales throughout the year, minimise unsold stock and encourage prompt payment. These include:

- **discounts** for trade and regular customers, to those who spend more than a certain amount and/or to business customers who pay promptly
- **special offers** or short-term **reduced prices** may be used to promote new products, sell-off unsold stock or increase sales at quiet times of the year.

Did you know?

Even if giving a discount to a customer is not company policy, staff may be allowed to throw in one or two 'extras' (such as a mouse mat or box of CDs in a computer store) to keep a customer happy.

Knowing the options available enables sales staff to suggest the best possible deal for the customer. For example, you may be able to offer a discount if a customer buys a more expensive model or agrees to purchase that day. However, it is important that you know the company's policies on price, and what you can and cannot do without specific permission.

Customer relationship management *(CRM) computer packages record details of all customer transactions and data on their individual buying habits, tastes and spending levels. This information is available to anyone who deals with a customer to help them to respond more appropriately.*

Methods of approaching potential customers

Potential customers need to know that the business, product or service exists before they will be tempted to buy anything. There are many different ways of approaching a potential customer. The business has to decide which is the most appropriate, bearing in mind the customer profile of the target group.

Direct methods include advertising – which may be in the press, on radio, TV, on public transport, by a poster campaign or online; sending out direct mail shots; using telemarketing; employing sales staff to make cold calls from a database or to contact previous customers; contacting and/or visiting potential business buyers.

Indirect methods include following up leads from other contacts, asking for recommendations, networking other industry contacts, obtaining press coverage of new products and services or awards that have been won (known as PR – public relations), speaking at trade events, taking a stand at a business exhibition.

Objectives to achieve during a sales call

Most sales staff have specific targets to achieve. These will relate to the sales of specific products or services and, often, optional extras as well. A common example is the sale of extended warranties for household appliances; another is special fabric protection for upholstery on furniture or car seats.

Experienced sales staff will aim to up-sell so that customers buy products which are the most profitable, and will promote these whenever they can. They will not do this, however, if there is any chance of losing a sale. In this situation they will have a number of 'fall-back' strategies, so that they can always make another offer to the customer.

In some industries, where business customers may be considering a very expensive purchase, negotiations may be carried out over several weeks or even months. In this case, each meeting or sales call will focus on moving the process forwards one step at a time.

You can therefore expect a list of objectives to include:

- making a sale/obtaining an order – preferably for more profitable lines/extras
- building up a relationship with a customer, such as by arranging an appointment or agreeing to send literature for further consideration
- identifying a future need/negotiating towards a future sale
- obtaining useful feedback and information.

Fact file

In addition to finding out about the target customer, sales staff also need to know their product, what discounts or offers they can make, how to approach potential customers and the objectives to achieve during a sales call.

Preparation of the physical environment

The physical sales environment is extremely important for a retail shop or store. An attractive, welcoming entrance which leads to a sales area with goods clearly displayed and easily accessible has many advantages. It encourages shoppers to enter, helps them to find what they want quickly and tempts shoppers to browse and look around – which encourages impulse buying.

The features which are considered are summarised below.

Accessibility Under the **Disability Discrimination Act** business premises must be accessible to disabled customers. If necessary, reasonable adjustments must be made to achieve this. For example, ideally all signs should be clear and easy to read, a ramp should be provided as an alternative to steps, access doors should be wide and easy to open, aisle widths should allow for wheelchairs and the height of counter areas and shelves as well as the design of changing rooms and toilets should take into account the needs of wheelchair users.

Did you know?

Superstores have capitalised on our desire for convenience by stocking more and more non-food items – from clothing to medicines, DVDs and insurance. This saves us time and boosts their profits.

Layout, furnishings and décor This will take into account the image of the business and the type of products sold.

- Self-service and convenience stores prefer a 'grid' layout, where customers enter at a fixed point and then walk around between display units. The store is clean and functional with fixed units. There is usually a tiled or wooden floor and bright lighting. Examples include Superdrug, PC World, Toys R Us.
- Clothes shops want customers to browse and handle the stock so use a different layout with goods grouped in displays. In some stores there will be carpeting, mirrors, chairs and soft or coloured lights. Examples include Miss Selfridge, River Island, Next.
- Other shops divide up the selling area into different types of products, such as bookshops (with areas for different subjects) large music stores and department stores. Examples include Virgin Megastores, Waterstones, John Lewis.

Key terms

Buyer behaviour is the way different customers act when they are buying.

Disposable income is the amount customers have to spend after paying essential bills.

Use of music Background music is used in many businesses to help customers relax, to avoid silence and to mask unacceptable background noises. Music is normally linked to the target buyer, so those targeting young people will play more upbeat music. Many stores play Christmas music from autumn onwards to get customers into the mood for Christmas shopping; music stores often play latest releases and Blockbuster stores play the latest films to promote them to people who are browsing.

Fast music makes customers shop more quickly (and buy less) whereas slow music encourages them to take their time. The University of Leicester proved that playing French or Italian classical music influences the type of food customers buy!

Health and safety This is a legal requirement for all businesses, including retail stores. All selling environments must be assessed for risks so that any hazards are minimised. Sales staff must also be trained to act correctly in an emergency, such as an evacuation when the fire alarm sounds. This is very important in large stores where dozens of customers will not know the emergency exit routes. Staff must also know what to do if an accident occurs. Many large stores have trained first-aiders who can be called to the scene.

The key areas of health and safety related to selling environments are summarised in the table below.

Aspect	Key points
The building	Building regulations require safety glass in doors, handrails on steps and non-slip flooring.
Delivery and storage of goods	Goods should be delivered to a special entrance which leads to the stockroom. Heavy goods must only be moved using trucks/trolleys and loads must be stacked safely. Perishable items (e.g. food) must be stored safely and appropriately as must hazardous items (e.g. glass).
Store fixtures and fittings	Shelves must be stable and preferably have raised front edges to prevent items falling forwards. Shelves must not be overloaded. Floor plinths should not protrude so customers could trip over them. There must be no sharp edges and wall hooks in changing rooms must be positioned safely.
Displays of merchandise	These should be created during quiet times and placed so that they cannot be knocked over. Heavy items must be stacked so that they are stable even if an item at the base is removed.
Equipment and appliances	Only specialists should maintain or repair equipment such as freezers and chilled cabinets. Staff must be trained to use any potentially hazardous equipment and observe safety precautions. Staff who undertake food handling must wear protective clothing, comply with hygiene regulations and know how to guard against hazards.
Cleanliness and tidiness	Shops or stores should be cleaned after customers have left or, in the case of 24/7 stores, at the quietest times. This should also include routine shelf cleaning and filling and the cleaning of chilled cabinets and freezers.
Working practices	Maintenance work should take place when the store is closed. Any areas under repair during opening hours should be cordoned off and merchandise re-sited. Stock repositioning should also take place at quiet times. Staff must be vigilant and act immediately if they spot a problem. Spillages and breakages must be cleaned up immediately and the area cordoned off until the floor is dry and/or safe to walk on.

■ *The sales floor and health and safety*

Did you know?

Tesco reviewed its restocking procedures after an 86-year-old grandmother fell and suffered a broken hip after she was hit by a 6-foot steel restocking cage. The cage had been left unattended in an aisle and was hit by a trolley being pushed by a toddler. The old lady later died two days later after failing to recover from surgery to repair the fracture.

Implications of market competition All stores want to make themselves different from their competitors. They can do this in several ways.

- Many chain stores have a distinctive image with a shop front, fascia, design and layout. This makes them instantly recognisable.
- They can offer special facilities to their customers, such as a coffee shop, car parking, cash machines, children's play area.
- They can offer additional services, e.g. help with packing, free delivery, a gift wrap service, free alterations for regular customers.
- They can open longer hours or more days a week than their competitors.
- They can operate an integrated online and high street operation – so that customers who want to exchange goods bought online can do so in store.
- They can have regular sales promotions or reduce their prices.
- They can constantly bring in new stock.

Buyer behaviour This was first mentioned on page 292. When any store is designed the merchandisers prepare a map, called a **planogram**, which identifies where every product should be situated – shelf by shelf and aisle by aisle. The aim is to maximise selling space – and therefore profits. **Power aisles** are identified. These are aisles which lead customers to all parts of the store and which will contain major displays of merchandise. At the end of power aisles are **power displays**, where goods sell very quickly indeed.

Did you know?

Retailers refurbishing their premises arrange for this to be carried out overnight – such as workmen laying a new floor or repainting an area.

Did you know?

Top Shop receives new types of stock every week. This has put pressure on its competitors to do the same because shoppers now expect to see something new every time they visit.

Store planograms are based on thousands of interviews with customers and hours of monitoring customer behaviour in stores. Researchers know, for example, that customers usually bear right as they enter a store. They know that they walk faster on wooden floors than on carpet and feel hungry if they smell newly baked bread or freshly brewed coffee. Experts claim that planograms have enabled them to predict almost 95 per cent of purchasing behaviour – which is why stores all over the world look the same.

Fact file

Preparing the selling environment includes checking accessibility, meeting health and safety requirements, ensuring the layout is appropriate, differentiating the store from competitors and taking account of buyers.

Over to you

1. *CACI Ltd provides information and marketing solutions to help businesses understand their customers better. Check out four case studies which appeal to you on www.caci.co.uk/msd.html to see how it has helped many household names to increase their sales.*
2. *John Whitley is a photographer. Until now he has specialised in doing portraits for family groups and weddings. He now wants to expand his operations by offering a commercial service to businesses too, such as producing photographs for brochures.*
   - **a)** *Suggest three ways in which John Whitley could identify and find potential private customers and give reasons for your choice.*
   - **b)** *John's target market has been for his wedding photographs. Describe a likely profile for these customers.*
   - **c)** *Suggest the preparations John now has to make before he starts to sell to business customers. For ideas, you might want to use Google to find websites of photographers in your area.*
3. *Members of your group have been asked to represent your school or college at a careers exhibition.*
   - **a)** *With your tutor, identify the methods used by educational institutions to approach potential customers and suggest reasons for these choices.*
   - **b)** *Suggest the objectives you would be expected to achieve at the exhibition.*
   - **c)** *Identify the preparations that would be required to get the most out of the event.*

Talking point

View 1: It is useful that many chain stores have a specific image and 'look' which sets them apart because this makes them distinctive and easily recognisable.

View 2: The common image of chain stores such as Next, Boots and Mothercare just means that every town in Britain looks the same – dull and boring.

With which viewpoint do you agree – and why?

Case study Assessment practice

Natalie owns a thriving hair and body workshop which has steadily expanded over the last few years. The hairdressers and manicurists she employs are all trained to recommend and sell a wide range of products to clients. This increases profits for the business, and also gives the staff benefits through commissions on sales and bonuses if they meet sales targets. Product suppliers also provide incentives. One hairdresser recently won a 5-day holiday as a prize for the sales she made.

Representatives from designer brands often phone for appointments and visit on a monthly basis. Natalie currently stocks Paul Mitchell, GHD and Matrix products, although the Redken rep has tried to persuade her to change her loyalties. Natalie knows her clients well and this influences her purchasing decisions. Most are young, female and fashion-conscious – which is why the GHD hair straighteners became an instant best seller. Although expensive, their performance made them a 'must have' product and GHD's customer service includes a no-quibble exchange policy if the irons develop a fault.

Natalie considers there are many benefits from talking to sales reps. A visit from Lloyds TSB resulted in savings of 20 per cent on the cost of card transactions when she changed to their Card Net swipe system. However, she will not see anyone without an appointment and gets cross if anyone turns up on a Friday and Saturday. She is also immediately put off if a rep looks scruffy, needs a hair cut or has dirty fingernails, which she feels is totally inappropriate for anyone working in the beauty business.

Similarly, she is very fussy about the way the sales area is set out and insists the shelves are kept fully stocked and scrupulously clean. She also personally oversees the training of all staff to ensure that their product knowledge is sound, that they can identify the most suitable products for their clients and recommend these without causing offence. Natalie's latest project has been to convert the first floor into a beauty salon and to employ two beauticians to carry out a range of specialist treatments.

1(P) Identify the purpose(s) of the face-to-face calls made by the reps. ***(P1 part)***

2(P) The professional hair care market is highly competitive. Describe the preparations that would be needed by an organisation or representative who wanted to sell successfully in this market. For additional information see www.paulmitchell.com, www.ghdhair.com, www.matrix.com and www.redken.com. ***(P3 part)***

3(P) **a)** Suggest ways in which Natalie and her staff can identify the profile of their customers.

b) Describe how this information will help Natalie when she is dealing with the representatives. ***(P3 part)***

4(P) Natalie wants the two beauticians to promote and sell related beauty products as well as carrying out treatments. They will do this from a special beauty shop area on the first floor, near the treatment rooms.

Describe the preparations that you think will be necessary for the beauty shop to be successful. ***(P3)***

Grading tip

Each of your descriptions should specifically focus on the preparations that you think are important in that particular situation.

7.3 Be able to demonstrate personal selling skills and processes

There are two important aspects to being an effective salesperson.

- **Personal selling skills** This relates to your ability to communicate and identify with the customer so that they enjoy talking to you. They should not feel pressurised, intimidated or exasperated.
- **Personal selling processes** This means understanding the sequence of events that take place to make a successful sale and knowing how to move smoothly from one stage to the next.

This section focuses on both these aspects.

Personal selling skills

The skills of the sales person dramatically influence the outcome of many sales situations. You know this yourself. In a store, if you are in a hurry and no one is taking any notice of you then you are likely to walk out. If you get prompt service but need help or advice, you can become irritated if an assistant is too pushy or cannot answer your questions. Usually, a sales person who is friendly, charming and knowledgeable will not only find it easier to sell to customers but will also enjoy the experience far more.

Activity

List your six top hates when you are dealing with a sales person. Then compare your list with other members of your group to see which traits everyone finds annoying.

Developing your own sales skills involves concentrating on your communication skills – both verbal and non-verbal – assessing your own style and appearance and learning a few tricks of the trade. If you enjoy dealing with people and trying to help them then you are already halfway there.

Communicating with customers

It is impossible to interact with a customer without good communication skills. This was first covered in Unit 2, when you learned about body language, listening skills and how to adapt the tone and pitch of your voice, as well as the pace of your speech and the language you use to the situation. You will also have learned more about oral communications if you have studied option unit 4.

Activity

Turn back to Unit 2, pages 65 to 68 now, and refresh your memory about communicating with customers. Then check out Unit 4, pages 145–150 for information about oral communications.

Types and purpose of communication

In a sales situation, you will communicate for many reasons and in several different ways. These are linked to the AIDA principle, where you focus on getting the customer's attention, developing interest, creating desire and then encouraging them to take action to buy.

You need to achieve . . .	By . . .
Attention	Greeting the customer positively and with a smile. Inspiring confidence. Pointing out relevant displays or products.
Interest	Talking in a friendly, approachable manner. Identifying the type of products or services in which the customer is interested.
Desire	Asking open questions to find out the customer's precise needs. Suggesting solutions that would meet these requirements. Pointing out the benefits to the customer of different options.
Action	Persuasively overcoming objections and closing the sale.

■ *The AIDA principle*

Greeting a customer must be done in a friendly, assured but non-threatening way so that you inspire confidence in the customer, who feels positive about meeting you.

Successful sales people are skilled at getting customers to talk about themselves. This makes the customer feel good (most people like to talk about themselves!) and enables the sales person to identify their needs easily.

Providing information needs good descriptive skills, which means you need a good vocabulary. You also need to speak clearly and at the right pace, so that the customer understands your explanations.

When you ask questions, you need to do this sensitively, so the customer does not feel as if it is an interrogation. Find out what your customer wants by asking 'open' questions – which cannot be answered with a 'yes' or a 'no'. Most start with 'who', 'what', 'why' 'where', 'when' and 'how', for example 'What type of computer were you thinking of?'. Check your understanding by asking closed questions, for example 'Is that right – you've never owned a laptop before?' You also need to be able to phrase questions tactfully so that you do not cause offence. For example, you should never ask 'How much can you afford?' The tactful version is 'What price range were you thinking of?'

You must listen to the answers or there is no point in asking the questions. Check back to page 68 to refresh your memory about active and reflective listening.

You are selling suitcases. Suggest two open questions you could ask a prospective customer. Compare your ideas.

Your body language should be appropriate and reflective so that the customer feels that you understand his or her needs and mean what you say (see page 60).

If you are giving a demonstration or presentation you need to do this in a logical order, explain clearly as you go and concentrate on the customer at the same time (see pages 306–308).

If you need to overcome customer objections you need to be able to do this persuasively (see page 312).

When you are closing a sale you need to be able to bring the discussion to a positive close, so that the customer leaves convinced that he or she has made the right decision (see page 314).

Activity

To quote an old saying: you don't get two chances to make a good first impression! Turn back to Unit 2, pages 59 and 60 and refresh your memory about personal presentation when you are dealing with customers.

Making a good impression

You make an impression on a customer in a few seconds. In a face-to-face encounter this is mainly through your appearance and your manner. Unless this impression is positive, you are fighting an uphill battle to convince the customer that you can do much to help them, if anything. The key points to note are given below.

Dressing appropriately Most organisations insist sales staff wear special uniforms and name badges so that they are smart and easily recognisable. It is the responsibility of each person to make sure that their clothes are clean and pressed and their shoes are polished. The style of your hair, the jewellery you wear and what you smell like will be noticed immediately. You may think you look great, but if you've slathered on too much perfume or aftershave or just returned from having a quick cigarette outside in your break, don't think your customer will not notice. Dirty hands and/or fingernails are another turn-off.

Positive attitude As you learned in Unit 2 (see page 63), your attitude affects your whole manner and appearance. People who are positive stand tall, smile and are always more pleasant to talk to than people who whinge and moan about everything. They are also 'can do' people, who will go the extra mile to try to help someone else – a major attribute for any sales person.

Good manners The days may be long gone when men automatically walked on the outside of pavements and stood up when a woman or older person entered the room, but in business these type of gestures will often get you a long way. Opening a door for a customer should be second nature, so should offering to carry anything heavy or finding a chair for someone who has to wait. Basically, good manners are simply a demonstration of courtesy and consideration, and putting someone else's needs ahead of your own, which is always impressive.

Professional, courteous and considerate behaviour Professional behaviour basically means never doing or saying anything that would make you look out of place in a business – running, shouting and giggling are all signs of immaturity; lying, exaggerating or misleading a customer is unethical; arriving late, hung-over or looking such a mess it takes you half an hour before you can face a customer is unacceptable. Be aware that many of these sins do not just inconvenience your employer and your colleagues, they are also likely to result in a formal warning and possible dismissal. In addition to acting professionally in front of customers, you also need to display the same respect for your colleagues, too.

Did you know?

Major communication errors include interrupting, talking too much, using jargon the customer does not understand and finishing your customers' sentences for them.

Did you know?

If you are having a bad day and feel really out of sorts, you are better offering to tidy the stock room rather than losing potential customers.

Activity

Practise demonstrating your good manners. Open the car door for your mother before getting in yourself, give someone elderly your seat on a crowded bus or train, open the door for a tutor carrying a pile of books. Unless this is your normal behaviour, expect a positive, if slightly stunned, reaction!

Did you know?

A golden rule with professional sales people is not to 'knock the competition'. This often annoys and alienates a potential customer.

Fact file

Good communication skills are essential for anyone involved in personal selling. Also important is their ability to make a good impression, which requires appropriate dress, attitude and manners and a professional approach.

Activity

*In small groups, list the behaviour that you consider is disrespectful or discourteous when you are a customer. Then compare your ideas with other groups. In each case identify what the sales person **should** do, instead.*

Personal space Respecting customers' personal space means not standing too near customers when you are talking to them, or eavesdropping on conversations between two or more people. If you are dealing with a couple it is often good strategy to say that you will leave them to talk about their options for a few minutes, and then return when their body language shows that they have reached agreement or have further questions.

Maintaining eye contact This does not mean staring at the customer, it does mean looking at them when you are talking to them. If you are dealing with a couple or a group, try to look at each person in turn. Otherwise, you could inadvertently ignore the one who is the key decision maker in the group, which could lose the sale. It is also important that you remember to make eye contact during a presentation or demonstration and do not stare at a screen or product instead!

Treating customers with respect and consideration This is shown by your attitude, your manners and the vocabulary you use. For example, no matter how old they are, customers will always respond positively to being called 'Sir' or 'Madam'. Today, many organisations have policies which state their commitment to ensuring that all customers are treated fairly and equally to prevent any discrimination.

Personal selling processes

There are a number of steps to making a sale, which were shown on page 281. The first is preparation, which you learned about in the previous section. In this section you learn about the next four stages in the process.

Greeting and introduction

The first step is to meet and greet a customer and introduce yourself. The best way to do this obviously depends upon whether you are speaking to someone on the telephone or meeting them face to face. Equally, business buyers will have different expectations than private customers.

In a store, there is always danger you will scare away customers if you pounce on them too eagerly the moment they arrive. But if you leave them alone too long, the next time you look they may have gone! Getting the balance right is often a question of experience. Useful tactics include:

- **smiling and making eye contact** when customers walk in, so that they know you have seen them. You can do this even if you are dealing with someone else.
- **saying 'Hello' or 'Good morning (or afternoon)'**. Then add: 'I'm (*give your name*) Do look around and let me know if you need anything, won't you?' This does not put the customer under pressure. It is also better than 'Can I help you' to which the customer can easily just say 'No, thanks.'

Meeting by appointment. If you are meeting business customers who are visiting by appointment, it is usual to greet people by name and shake hands. The same applies if you were visiting business buyers by appointment, when you need to introduce yourself and give the name of your company.

Telephone sales call If you are making a telephone sales call, introduce yourself and your organisation. Then explain why you are ringing. Use the customer's name during the conversation. You can find out more about making business telephone calls in Unit 6, pages 244 and 245. Many sales calls are scripted, particularly in call centres.

Sales events If you are representing a business at a sales event, such as an exhibition, greet customers promptly as they approach and ask how you can help them. Introduce yourself, say what your role is and what your organisation does. If you are dealing with one person when someone else approaches, a useful tactic is to include the newcomer in the conversation if you are talking generally about the products or services you offer.

There are certain rules of behaviour at an exhibition. These include: staying on your own stand, not drifting about in the aisle or onto other stands, not sitting down or standing in a group with your colleagues.

Attracting customers' attention and interest

In a store, product displays (see below), brochures, posters, sales and special offers are all designed to attract the attention and interest of customers. You cannot necessarily rely on customers to spot these on their own. If a customer asks you for help in finding a specific product at the outset then this makes life easier because you immediately know what they are interested in. If a customer prefers to be left alone to look around, then you have to use your initiative and judge the best time to start a conversation.

If you are making a telephone sales call then you have to obtain the customer's interest very quickly. The call will therefore often start with a special offer to tempt a previous customer to place a further order.

Watching body language is the best guide. People pause when they see something that interests them. At first they will just turn their head. If they then turn their body as well, this denotes greater interest. The next stage is usually to touch the product – feeling the texture of material, opening doors on an appliance or picking up a pack and reading the instructions. At this point, many customers look up and try to attract the attention of a sales person to find out more.

The ability to develop a rapport with your customers is invaluable.

Even if this does not happen, now is still a suitable time to approach the customer. Walk up from the front or side with a friendly comment rather than sneak up behind them and make them jump! A useful opening remark is to comment positively about the item they are looking at, such as, for example, 'Those only came back in stock yesterday, they are a very popular line.' The customer's response will enable you to gauge the level of interest in that item. You can then either build on this or indicate alternatives which may be more suitable.

Identifying, meeting/exceeding customers' needs

The only way you can identify your customers' needs is to ask questions. Never assume you know what a customer wants. All customers are different and what suits one person rarely suits another. You need to find out:

- how much the customer is expecting to spend
- their specific preferences, such as a particular brand or features they need
- any personal requirements, from a favourite colour to a specific size
- any problems or concerns, from lack of space if you are involved with domestic appliances or furniture, to worries about technical support if you are selling computers.

This is when your skill at asking open questions comes into play. Remember that you should aim to do more than just meet your customers' needs. Ideally, you should exceed them by offering more than the customer expected.

Presenting products, giving product information

The next task is to identify the products that match the customer's requirements. Remember that you will only be able to do this if you have been listening to the answers to your questions.

Try to offer a customer a few options, not just one, but not so many that it's confusing. Explain the benefits and/or drawbacks of each one and use this to find out which one would most meet his or her need.

Customers vary in their product knowledge. Some may only have a very vague idea of the range available and expect to be given all the information they need. Ideally, for complex items or services this will be available in printed form so that anyone who is 'just looking' can take it home to read. Examples include your college prospectus and holiday brochures available from travel agents.

Other customers may have spent some time researching online and know more than you! You need to adapt your approach to allow for this and not feel threatened or overpowered. Often this sale may be easy to make if the item is in stock, although you need to check that it will meet the customer's expectations. Sometimes there may be alternatives that would be better and these can be discussed, together with their comparative benefits.

Customers who are indecisive can be the hardest to deal with. Avoid confusing everyone – including yourself – by giving too many options at once and take time to discover what the customer really wants.

Product display

Retail stores are well aware that goods in the stockroom or those out of sight do not sell. They therefore promote their goods by displaying them effectively, to make them more desirable and encourage impulse buying.

The type of displays you find in a store will usually depend upon the items being sold and the time of year.

Seasonal displays are most obvious at Christmas, but DIY stores will focus on Easter and other special days like Mother's Day and Hallowe'en also present sales opportunities for some products.

Manufacturers' displays are often seen on special rotating stands, usually with the name predominantly shown.

Impulse and themed displays are often related to cross-selling – such as paper near computer printers, luggage locks, sunglasses and suncream near suitcases.

Mass displays are dozens of items of the same product – from computer software to books by a particular author.

Describing the product

The way you approach this part of the process depends upon what you are selling. Providing product information effectively means knowing its specification, options, features and advantages and then converting these into benefits for that particular customer. This is obviously easier for a DVD than a car. As an example, if the customer buying the suitcase is a frequent flyer, you could point out that the benefit of a hard case is that it would be more resistant to damage, given the rough handling it would receive. Similarly, you should not stress what each button does on a TV remote control but the fact that the customer can do these operations without moving.

Presenting to business buyers can sometimes involve a formal PowerPoint presentation which has taken several weeks of preparation by a team of people. This is well worthwhile for a large contract worth thousands of pounds.

Identifying specific customer benefits enables you to focus on key selling points. Some examples are listed in the table below.

Potential customer benefits

- **A brand name** that is known and trusted, e.g. Nokia or Apple
- **Value for money** by obtaining great quality at a reasonable price
- **Convenience and accessibility** because it is available locally or online
- **Reliability** because the product has a good reputation and service is excellent
- **Complementary products** to extend the range such as iPod accessories
- **Additional features** such as superb packaging for a gift or kudos with friends because it is a 'must have' item.

Some products require a demonstration because you can only talk about performance; you cannot prove it in words. Describing a plasma screen or HD television is not the same as seeing one switched on; explaining that a vacuum cleaner is powerful is not as effective as switching it on and showing how it works. Then let the customer handle it – that helps to convince the buyer of its quality.

Remember that you should be able to describe the products you are selling simply, clearly and in language the customer will understand *and* know enough to be able to answer any questions that you are asked!

The selling process involves greeting customers, introducing yourself, attracting the customers' attention and interest, identifying and meeting (or better still, exceeding) their needs as well as presenting and describing the product and related aspects such as options, availability and associated services.

Product options and availability

Many products are available in different sizes or versions. Knowing the range you have in stock and those you can obtain – and by when – is important. If the customer is unhappy with those you have shown so far, you may be able to offer an appropriate substitute. If you are lucky – or very skilled at selling – you may find that this suits the customer better than his or her original choice.

If you genuinely have nothing that remotely matches the customer's needs then be honest and recommend a likely source. If you are helpful, even if you cannot make a sale, most customers remember this and may happily return at a later date to see you again.

Associated service

Many organisations offer associated services to help to boost their sales. Clothes shops may carry out alterations, free of charge to regular customers. Computer shops may offer after-sales support services. Travel agents may offer free transport to the airport – and so on.

It is important that you are aware of all the associated services that you can offer a customer, as these can often be the deciding factor to clinch the sale.

Activity

Identify the members of the group who have experience of selling at work. Arrange for each person to describe the skills that they need and the selling processes they have been trained to carry out.

Talking point

View 1: Most people have made up their minds at the outset and the sales person can do little to influence this.

View 2: A knowledgeable, skilful sales person is a huge influence on the purchasing decisions made by customers.

With which viewpoint do you agree – and why?

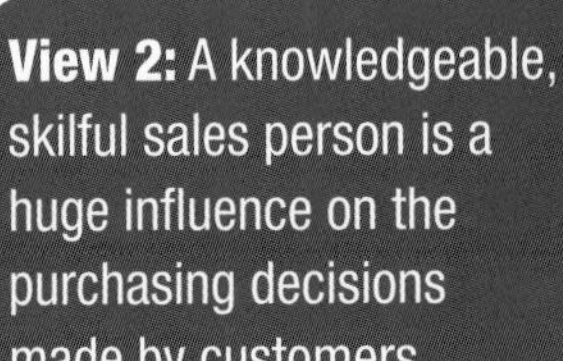

Over to you

1 *Select any product of your choice and gather information about it by visiting a variety of stores and obtaining literature and asking questions yourself. Try to note the sales person's attitude and responses and identify which approaches you find helpful and which you do not. You can also check how many ticks they would get against the list of good sales habits on pages 281 and 282.*

2 *Select any everyday item in the room – the whiteboard, chair, table and spend five minutes listing the benefits (rather than the features) for a buyer. Compare your lists.*

3 *Divide into pairs. One of you will be the customer and the other the sales person – then you will reverse roles. Select one of the following products to buy/sell, research it properly and if you own one, bring it to class to demonstrate. Both your fellow student and your tutor should evaluate your performance.*

- **a)** *An Apple iPod*
- **b)** *Your mobile phone*
- **c)** *A hairdryer*
- **d)** *An electric shaver*
- **e)** *A similar product of your own choice.*

Case study Assessment practice

Ancient and Modern is a thriving family jewellery business, which people travel to visit from miles around. Dom, Emily and Jane took over its running four years ago, when their parents retired. Each has a different approach to selling and different preferences for working in the business.

Emily is a traditionalist. Her product knowledge is superb. She is passionate about antique jewellery – brooches, rings, bracelets, necklaces and pendants of every description and every age. She loves explaining to customers which items are Georgian, Victorian and Edwardian and the stories behind some of the pieces they sell. She is happy pottering around in the shop, re-arranging the displays and will always suggest to customers how pieces can be personalised for them – by adding an inscription or by resizing, for example. She also offers a free valuation certificate with every antique item she sells.

Dom is more interested in clocks and watches. He has researched the market and knows that, in the area, there are few jewellers that stock expensive designer brands such as Patek Phillipe, Rolex and Tag Heuer. He also likes to stock unusual vintage watches and period clocks. He is a firm believer that the business needs to do more than rely on its reputation and passing trade. He is therefore building up a database of trade contacts and collectors whom he contacts by phone if he buys a watch or clock that would interest them.

Jane prefers selling modern jewellery and supervising the staff. She believes that all the staff they employ must be trained thoroughly so that every customer gets a superb experience, no matter which assistant helps them. She is therefore insistent that all the staff develop excellent selling skills and dress appropriately. She encourages them to study for gemmology so that they will learn more about the gemstones with which they work.

In addition to the shop, the business also takes a stand at some of the leading antique fairs in different areas of the country. Emily selects a mixture of pieces to take and enjoys the hurly burly of dealing with both trade clients – who always want a good discount – and private customers who are apt to think they will get better value at a fair than in a shop. She prefers it when Dom joins her to display his vintage watches, because it is easier to cope when they are very busy.

1(P) Describe the personal selling skills and processes that Dom will have to demonstrate in each of the following situations:

- **a)** when he deals with customers in the jewellery shop
- **b)** when he contacts collectors over the telephone. ***(P1 part)***

2(M) Compare and contrast the skills and processes you noted in question (1) above to identify any differences. ***(M3)***

3(P) Select a watch, item of jewellery or other possession you own which you feel passionate about. Your tutor and then a fellow colleague will take the part of the customer and then a collector.

Demonstrate your personal skills and the selling processes required in both situations. ***(P4 & P5 part)***

4(D) As a group, plan your own stall to sell items for the charity of your choice. It may be useful to hold this when you have completed the final section of this unit and can demonstrate all the stages of the selling process, so talk to your tutor about the best date.

Suggested ways to do this include:

- making items to sell. This will be the case if you are part of a Young Enterprise group, for example
- contacting local and national charities, some of whom will supply a supporter group with items to sell – such as pencils or cuddly toys. Your tutor, though, will probably have to take responsibility for ensuring that all unsold stock is returned, undamaged, to the charity together with all income earned
- selling ethical items, such as adopting an animal or sponsoring a child in the third world. This saves having to obtain any stock.

Research your preferred option and undertake all the preparations required to make your stall successful. Decide the best times and duration and agree a rota so that everyone will be involved.

continued ▸

Case study *continued*

Next decide how to promote the event(s). In addition to advertising, this should also include some element of persuasion – such as individually visiting classes (by appointment) or contacting tutors (perhaps by telephone) to explain what is happening and answering questions.

Then demonstrate your personal selling skills at the event. Afterwards write a report which includes:

a)(M) An account in which you compare and contrast the personal selling skills and processes used when you visited other classes or tutors *and* dealt with customers at the stall. ***(M3)***

b)(D) An evaluation of the preparation the team undertook for *both* promoting the event and preparing the stall which identifies what went well and what could have been done better. ***(D2 part)***

c)(D) An evaluation of your own role and ability to sell effectively in both situations. ***(D2)***

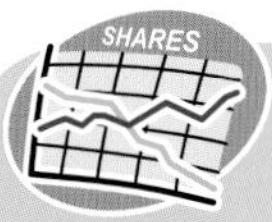

Grading tip

Compare and contrast means identifying the similarities and differences between two situations.

Your evaluation should show that you can identify the strengths and weaknesses of your own and your team's performance and show how you would learn from the experience.

7.4 Understand how to identify customers' objections and closing sales techniques

The final stage of the sales process concentrates on obtaining the customer's commitment to make the purchase. In some cases, this is very easy and straightforward. You will have identified the best option to meet your customer's needs, the customer agrees and the sale is made. In other cases, you may have to work a little harder to get to this stage.

Did you know?

The presence of friends or partners often complicates the sales process. For example, a friend may point out objections that the purchaser might not have thought about.

How to do this and how to follow up the sale and record the customer information are important techniques in the armoury of all successful sales people.

Responding to objections

Kerry works in a computer store. She has just spent half an hour with a man who wants a new printer for his home computer. Kerry asked questions to find out about usage, the features he wanted and how much he wanted to spend. They have now discussed six different models in detail but he seems no nearer to making a decision. Kerry recognises that whilst many customers make up their mind very quickly, this customer is not one of them.

Key term

Customer objections are reasons why a customer hesitates to commit to a purchase.

Customers hesitate to commit themselves for a reason. Sometimes, they will voice these objections. On other occasions, the sales person has to find out the reason(s). Good sales staff will know the main reasons why their customers may hesitate. They also know that unless they overcome these objections then the sale will be lost.

Types of objections

The main reasons customers hesitate to purchase include:

- **price** – the items may cost more than the customer planned to spend
- **timing** – the customer may be in no rush to make a commitment or not able to take delivery for some time – such as a couple buying flooring for an extension that has not yet been completed
- **competition** – the customer may consider it is worth shopping around to see if there is a better deal available
- **the item itself** – the size, colour, type of material, design or other feature may not appeal to the customer
- **the brand or manufacturer** – particularly if the customer has had a bad experience with a similar item or something from the same manufacturer.

The sales person needs to find out which objection(s) apply to find the reason for the hesitation.

Overcoming objections

The cleverest way to overcome objections is to build positive reasons to purchase into the discussion at the start. For example: 'This item is slightly more expensive but the print quality is superb, so it's excellent value for money. There's also a two-year guarantee so you wouldn't have to worry if a fault developed because we would repair it without charge.' 'This is a very popular line and we have it in red, blue and yellow – whichever you prefer.'

If the hesitation concerns the product or manufacturer then there may be other options to offer. You may be able to order a different model or show a range from other makers. A more senior member of staff may be able to make some useful suggestions if you run out of ideas or cannot think how to meet the customer's particular needs.

Remember, too, that you can overcome several problems at the start, by offering one product at once and 'fine-tuning' your suggestions to the customer's needs by discussing each option in turn. Remove rejected items so that the selling area stays free from clutter. If the customer still cannot decide and wants to think about it – do not object. If you stay positive and helpful, the customer may well return to buy the item later.

Activity

Work in pairs to take the part of Kerry and her customer. Start by researching popular models of computer printers online. As the customer, decide on your main requirements and raise objections to the models you are shown. As Kerry, suggest appropriate options and overcome the objections that are raised.

Did you know?

Customer objections are sometimes called 'barriers to a sale'. Attempts to find out if a customer has any reservations which may prevent a sale should be made throughout the whole sales process, not just at the end.

Fact file

Customers often hesitate before they buy because they are concerned about an aspect of the purchase. It is important to know the objections you are likely to meet and identify ways to overcome them.

Did you know?

It is never wise to talk too much to justify the price of a product – and never argue with the customer. Keep your responses to objections brief and to the point.

Some sales people use overcoming an objection as their closing technique, for example, 'If I can arrange for it to be delivered tomorrow, do you want me to do that?'

Traditional sales training often included the ABC – Always Be Closing technique. Not everyone agrees. Some people think it can annoy too many customers – particularly business buyers.

Closing sales

This means getting the customer to commit to buying the product or service. Sometimes the customer will close the sale. Saying 'That's fine, I'll have it' achieves this purpose. Some customers are less decisive, and even after you have overcome their objections they may still hesitate. At this point it is helpful to have a few closing techniques up your sleeve!

Persuading customers to buy the product

Experienced staff are persuasive throughout the selling process. They have worked hard to meet the customer's needs and identified the benefits of the purchase from the customer's point of view. They have overcome any objections. They now have to influence the customer to make the final decision to buy.

There are several signals that customers may give that show they are ready to make a decision. One sign is when questions are asked about delivery, guarantees, after-sales service or credit facilities. This indicates the customer has stopped thinking about the product and is now assessing other aspects of the purchase. Another sign is when the customer starts visualising ownership: 'It would fit in the small alcove in the dining room' or 'Imagine Jon's face when we arrive in it!'

It's at this point that the sales person will try to close the sale.

Trial close

Sales people use a trial close to check whether the customer is ready to make a decision. This usually involves asking questions that assume the customer owns the item. 'Wouldn't it be useful to be able to print, scan and photocopy documents from just one machine? Just think of the space you'd save.'

The reaction of the customer is very important. If the customer has further unstated objections, you are likely to find out what these are. If the customer agrees with the first question, the normal procedure is to ask another question. 'Would you want us to deliver it? What day is best for you?' By now the customer is being moved a step further towards closure. If the customer continues to say 'yes' to the trial close questions, then the sale will be concluded.

Closing techniques

Experts have mixed views about closing techniques. Some are equated with 'hard sell' or even unethical methods of pressuring people to buy. This can be counter-productive if the customer rethinks the purchase and returns the goods after he or she has had time to think about it.

On the other hand, you cannot carry on discussing a purchase with an indecisive customer forever. One of the most honest closes is simply to say: 'Have I covered everything properly? Is there anything else you would like to know about or are you happy to go ahead?'

Other options include:

- **the direct close** – this can be quite high-risk if you get the timing wrong. It means asking a straight-forward question, for example,

'Shall I wrap it?' 'Are you happy to place an order now?' 'Are you ready to buy now?'

- **the indirect close** – is a more round-about method, such as 'What do you think?' 'Are you happy with this colour?' This is gentler than the direct close.
- **the silent close** – this involves asking a closing question and then keeping quiet. It is helpful because it means you give your customer thinking time and do not interrupt. It isn't much use if your customer also goes quiet so you just stare at each other.
- **the alternative close** – is when you offer your customer two options as your closing question: 'Would you prefer yellow or red?' 'Would you prefer delivery on Friday or Saturday?'
- **the presumptive close** – is when you assume the buyer already owns the item: 'And you do know that when you bring it in for its first service we will lend you a courtesy car?' or 'You do know how to connect it, don't you?'

The main point to remember is that all customers and all sales situations are different. Therefore the close that is appropriate in one situation will not work in another. In particular, regular customers usually require a different approach. If you cannot find what they want, for example, you could offer to 'phone them when you receive more stock. This is one way of following up sales – as you will see below.

Knowing when and how to close a sale is crucial. There are a variety of techniques that can be used, depending upon the situation.

Find out more about closing techniques online at http://changingminds.org/disciplines/sales/closing/closing_techniques.htm Then, as a group, decide which ones are ethical and which are less so!

Following up sales

Most businesses rely upon prompt payment, repeat sales and recommendations from existing customers to be successful. For these reasons, they need to follow up their sales to check customer satisfaction and to ensure that any problems are resolved promptly. The last thing a business needs is a dissatisfied customer notifying the press or setting up a critical website – like Matthew Peterson did when his iPod Nano screen was cracked (see page 82).

The best way(s) to follow up sales will depend upon the produce or service you are selling, but the most usual activities include the following.

Product delivery

Many organisations offer a delivery service at timeslots to suit the buyer. For private sales this may be to the customer's home or workplace. If you make a sale it will normally be your responsibility to complete the paperwork that enables the order to be processed promptly and accurately. The paperwork should also include your name, so that if any problems or delays occur, you can contact the customer immediately. If you can, it is also useful to track the delivery to ensure it takes place as agreed, or check this during a follow-up call (see below).

Customer satisfaction and feedback

Customers are only likely to make repeat purchases or to recommend your firm if they are satisfied with their buying experience – and the only way you can establish this is to ask them. It is important to make contact to confirm the customer is happy with the way the order is being progressed, to check the item was delivered intact and on time and that the customer is satisfied with the purchase.

Fact file

You can follow up a sale in several ways, such as by making a follow-up call. Checking the customer is satisfied provides useful feedback and encourages repeat sales.

Follow-up call

This is a popular method of assessing customer satisfaction. Richer Sounds, the high street electrical retailer, calls these 'Customer Happy Calls' and staff make them two or three days after a customer has made a purchase in a store. They check that the customer has had no problems setting up the equipment and that it is working satisfactorily.

Handling complaints

Obviously it is ideal if every customer you contact says the service was wonderful, the goods arrived on time and everything functions perfectly. Unfortunately, the law of averages means that if you make 100 follow-up calls, a few people will have a complaint. Some may be minor issues that you can sort out immediately – others will be more serious. It is important to know:

- the procedures you must follow to record and/or report a complaint
- the type of problems you can deal with yourself – and what you can and cannot do
- the type of problems you must refer to a supervisor.

Did you know?

Never ignore or gloss over problems a customer mentions during a follow-up call. Do not delay doing something, either. Otherwise, you will disappoint the customer twice. Always follow up the solution to a complaint, too – to ensure that the problem has been resolved to the customer's satisfaction.

If you are really enterprising then you will use problems as opportunities to show how effective your customer care is. Quickly replacing a faulty product, promptly cancelling a missing delivery and sending a replacement or sending a voucher to compensate your customer for inconvenience can easily earn your firm additional brownie points!

Customer care

During the follow-up call, it is useful to check that your customer knows about all the other aspects of customer care you can provide – such as your free customer helpline, FAQs pages on your website, how to order new parts or spares and the fact that you will send a reminder when a service is needed.

Repeat sales

Happy customers are far more likely to place another order. It is sensible to maintain contact by email, phone, mail shots (and meetings for a business customer) so that you can point out new products or special offers that may be of interest.

Activity

In small groups, identify six products that are frequently upgraded or enhanced to encourage repeat business. Then compare your ideas.

Up-selling, cross-selling and further sales

As you saw on page 278, up-selling and cross-selling are ways of increasing either the value or the range of goods sold. This can be achieved by telling customers about upgrades or new versions of a product, by finding out about their future plans and identifying products that would meet those needs and by discussing items that would complement the products they already own.

Recording customer information

Collecting and recording customer information is essential for accurate marketing. It enables accurate customer profiles to be created; customers can be sent mail shots about interesting events and new products, and vouchers or discount offers can be sent, linked to key areas of interest. This increases the opportunities for making repeat sales.

Customer information

Basic information on private customers includes their name, title, address, telephone/mobile number and email address. For business organisations other details are required, including the name of the buyer/decision maker in the firm, his or her title, size of firm and type of business.

Customer history

At the very least, this should include information on all the orders the customer has placed, both in terms of items placed and value of order. It may also include other types of contact, such as meetings or phone calls between the customer and the business. For business contacts, it may also note whether the customer is a prompt payer.

Fact file

Recording customer information assists marketing and future sales because the company can target its future selling initiatives more accurately.

Customer needs and motivation

Customers' current and future needs may be gleaned from questionnaires or from talking to them. Analysing orders can also identify changes to order patterns. Sales consultants and reps who visit business organisations chat about what they buy and don't buy, who from, what they might want in the future and what their priorities will be. This information is added to the customer record to help to identify future customer needs.

Methods of recording

Today, most organisations record this information in a customer database. This means that:

- key information is recorded in a systematic, organised and concise way and easily searchable under a range of criteria
- specific fields can be compared to give rankings, such as in the value or number of orders to find the most valuable customers on whom the most time and energy should be spent.

Activity

Customer relationship management (CRM) software (which you read about on page 295) enhances the traditional type of customer database to enable the business to respond more precisely to customer needs.

Find out more about this at www.businesslink.gov.uk – then search under CRM.

Talking point

View 1: Asking people if they have a problem is a recipe for disaster. Most customers love an excuse to moan.

View 2: Asking people if they have a problem gives useful information for business improvements. Most customers won't say anything otherwise.

With which viewpoint do you agree – and why?

Over to you

1 *Work in pairs to develop your skills at overcoming objections and closing a sale.*
   a) *Identify a product to sell, such as a particular type of mobile phone.*
   b) *Each of you list the benefits and the possible objections to the purchase.*
   c) *Try to sell to each other.*

   The buyer can choose to be reticent or talkative and can raise objections. The seller should practice using 'open questioning' to find out customer needs if the customer is reticent and listening skills if the customer is talkative. In addition, the seller must try to overcome objections and, at a suitable point, close the sale.

   Then reverse roles and choose a different product to sell.

2 *Work in small groups to suggest the type of information each of the following organisations would record on customers and the best ways to follow up sales. Then compare your ideas.*
   a) *A designer clothes store.*
   b) *A business stationery supplier.*
   c) *A painting and decorating business.*
   d) *A firm of house builders.*

Case study Assessment practice

Carl Jackson sells cars at A1 Autotraders. The business is an authorised agent for a major international car manufacturer, Yoshiko, whose headquarters are in Japan. The premises consist of a showroom (where Carl is based) and a workshop where pre-delivery inspections are carried out as well as routine servicing, repairs (some under warranty) and MOTs.

continued ▶

Case study *continued*

Yoshiko produces several models, ranging from a small economy saloon, through a middle-size car to a large family saloon. They also make a people carrier and a sports car. The company has a reputation for producing vehicles which are very reliable with many 'extras' fitted as standard, including air conditioning, heated mirrors and CD players. Prices are competitive and all new cars carry a three-year warranty.

A1 has a computerised database which records information on all enquiries as well as sales. Depending on circumstances, the information can include names, addresses, vehicle(s) purchased, servicing undertaken, repairs (with or without warranty) and any complaints made. The data is used to produce an analysis of customer profiles, as well as automatically reminding them when servicing and MOTs are due. A1 always 'phones customers a few days after a sale or service to see if they are satisfied. The national Yashiko organisation also checks customer satisfaction by sending out questionnaires, asking people what they think about their cars and the service they received from the local dealer. It also sends out a magazine every quarter, which describes new models.

Today Carl has two appointments with people who may be interested in buying a new car. The first is a young woman, Louise Barker. She will be accompanied by her father, who is buying her the car as an 18th birthday present. The second is Jon Turner, a family man with three children in his mid-30s. He works for a local bank.

1(P) Suggest the preparations for selling that Carl can make before he meets each of the customers with whom he has an appointment. ***(P3 part)***

2(P) Describe the reasons why A1 Autotraders follows up its sales and records customer information. ***(P7)***

3(P) Work in groups of four to take the part of Carl and his customers.

a) Louise and her father should decide on their requirements before they meet Carl, and think about the type of objections they may raise.

b) Jon Turner should do the same.

c) Carl should prepare by carrying out the activities identified in question 1.

In each situation, 'Carl' should identify his customer's needs and demonstrate how to respond to his customer's objections and how to close the sale.

The groups should then change roles. ***(P5 & P6)***

Grading tip

Remember that your demonstration must show how you would deal with a specific situation.

8 Doing business online

Today few firms can ignore the potential benefits of doing business online, but this does not mean that there are never any problems with setting up an online operation. Learning how organisations overcome these and identify the most appropriate type of online presence for their business are the main focuses of this unit.

What you need to learn

- Different types of online business activities
- The business feasibility of going online
- The operation of an online business
- The benefits of an online business presence

8.1 Understand different online business activities

Did you know?

A government survey in October 2005 identified that 64 per cent of adults in Britain (29 million) had accessed the Internet in the previous three months, most to buy goods, tickets or services. In January 2006, another survey found that web sales accounted for 10 per cent of all retail transactions.

If you use the Internet regularly, then you may have some idea of the vast number of organisations and individuals who have an online presence. In 2006, there were over 76 million websites worldwide, with over six billion pages of information. Some are run by private businesses, others by governments, pressure groups, charities and individuals. They range from the very basic to the extremely sophisticated.

In January 2006, the Interactive Media in Retail Group (IMRG) announced that in the UK, £19.2 billion of goods were sold over the Internet during 2005 – a 34 per cent increase from 2004. It predicted that this would increase to £26 billion in 2006. This is 3,250 per cent more than the £800 million worth of goods sold online in 2000!

There are many reasons for this huge increase – the increasing number of broadband connections, which give users much faster download speeds; better security for online payments; increased Internet accessibility through laptops, PDAs, mobiles and WiFi zones and greater customer confidence. This has resulted in huge benefits for many businesses. Today, few firms can afford to ignore the Internet if they want to be successful.

Activity

Find out the latest information on Internet use by going to wwwstatistics.gov.uk and entering 'Internet' in the search window.

Range of online business materials

Businesses undertake different activities online. Broadly these can be divided into the following categories.

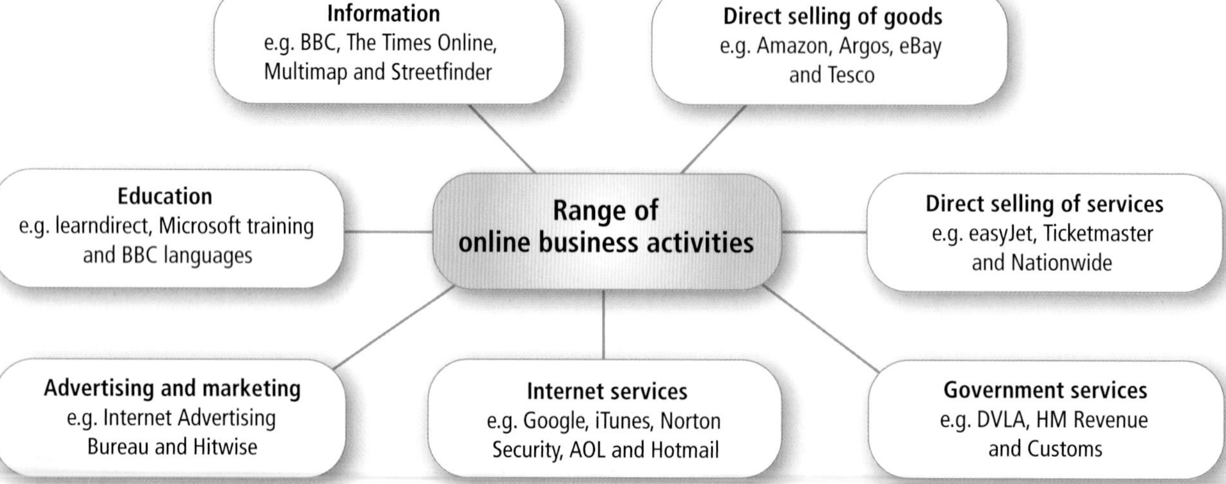

Direct online selling of goods

These are the 'shopping websites' which are so popular with Internet users. With the exception of Amazon and eBay, which operate only online, the most successful are traditional retailers whose online stores complement their high street operations. This is because they are recognised and trusted by consumers. Because they buy cheaply in bulk they can also sell goods more cheaply than small firms. They are also used to giving excellent customer service, promoting their goods effectively and delivering promptly – and all these attributes are just as important online as offline.

Key terms

Bricks and mortar is a business which sells only from a traditional retail store, e.g. your corner shop.

Clicks and mortar is a business which sells from a traditional store *plus* a website, e.g. Tesco or Argos.

Dot.com company or virtual business are businesses which only operate online, e.g. Amazon or eBay.

Activity

Find out what IMRG does and its role in relation to e-retailers by going to www.imrg.org and then check out Hitwise at www.hitwise.com.

Direct online selling of services

The range of online services available is tremendous – from changing your job to searching for a new house, paying a bill or booking your holiday. Today, you can do almost anything online.

The airline industry was one of the first service providers to spot the potential of the Internet because selling tickets online reduces costs. 'No frills' airlines only sell tickets this way. Other travel businesses which benefit from an online presence include train and coach companies, travel agents, tour operators and hotels. Online firms like Lastminute.com and Expedia offer more specialist services – such as last minute cut-price bookings or comprehensive travel packages to be custom built online.

Online banking has been another area of rapid growth. Now virtually all banks offer customers the facility to manage their accounts online.

Did you know?

According to Hitwise, the top 10 UK shopping websites at the end of 2005 were ebay UK, Amazon UK, Argos, Play.com, Tesco.com, Dell Europe, Comet UK, Currys, Next, Marks and Spencer.

Activity

If you do not use online banking yourself, find out if anyone in your group does (including your tutor). Ask them to describe how it works and what they like best, and least, about it.

Did you know?

A Directgov survey found that 60 per cent of UK web users visit just a handful of trusted websites and bookmark these to save time searching. Popular 'supersites' included Amazon, BBC, eBay, Google, Lastminute.com and Streetmap.

Government services

The main UK Government website is the Directgov portal at www.direct.gov.uk which directs users to dozens of public service websites, such as Business Link, local councils, central government departments and related areas, such as the Met Office. It also lists all the things you can now do online – from getting a passport to booking your driving test.

Activity

A portal *is a site, often featuring a variety of services, which is often used as a hub or gateway, either to the Internet, or to a specialist topic. One large UK portal is Lycos at www.lycos.co.uk. This site is aimed at UK net users aged about 18–30. Check it out to see how its content reflects this.*

Did you know?

Asking users to register on a site is a marketing device to obtain information about potential customers (see page 355). The firm also hopes that the user will agree to receive regular email updates or newsletters.

Did you know?

Even if you cannot get into subscriber areas of a website to find out about the organisation, you can often find what you need if you read the 'About Us' section and/or look through past press cuttings.

Information

Some people argue that the amount of information on the Internet can be more of a curse than a blessing because they struggle to find what they want. Whether you want to check the latest news or weather, find out how to get from A to B, learn the meaning of a word or phrase, discover the answers to a quiz – the answers are all there, if you know where and how to look. And this is why search engines such as Google are so popular.

A vast amount of information is still free of charge on the Internet, such as at sites like www.wikipedia.com, although specialist sites do charge for research reports – such as Jupiter Research at www.jupitermedia.com/ and www.euromonitor.com. Businesses usually subscribe to obtain the information they need.

Internet services

These sites relate to those businesses that provide information and services specifically related to Internet activities. They include:

- search engines, such as Google and Yahoo
- shopping comparison sites, such as Shopping.com and Kelkoo
- Internet service providers, such as AOL and MSN
- music download sites, such as iTunes and Napster
- suppliers of security software, such as Norton AntiVirus and Spysweeper
- email providers, e.g. Hotmail and Gmail.

Advertising and marketing

A major purpose of having a website is to promote the business, as you will see on page 354. Equally, it is pointless having a website if no one knows about it. Businesses promote their websites using both e-marketing and print advertising – so you will see the website quoted on letter headed paper, compliment slips, adverts in the press and even on lorries or vans.

Many businesses specialise in providing advertising and marketing services – such as specialist agencies. Examples include www.AKQA.com and www.gluelondon.com. Others assess the relative success of different websites and offer a competitive marketing intelligence service such as www.hitwise.com and Nielsen Net Ratings at www.nielsen-netratings.com.

Fact file

Online business activities include the direct selling of goods and services – including government and Internet services – as well as providing information, advertising and marketing and education.

Activity

E-marketing no longer means annoying pop-up ads when you are searching for something else – marketing online is far more sophisticated today. Check out www.akqa.com and the type of campaigns it has done (under Work/Clients) to find out more!

Education

Education-based sites include:

- **training online** websites (such as learndirect, Microsoft, the BBC and many others)
- **information on courses of study** – such as at UCAS and on college and university websites
- **support for students.** Academic support is provided at sites such as BizEd and Times 100, information and social/financial support is provided at the website of the National Union of Students
- **information to tutors and learners** – such as that provided by awarding bodies such as Edexcel at www.edexcel.org.uk.

Key terms

B2B = business to business trading, e.g. Heinz to Tesco.

B2C = business to consumer trading, e.g. Tesco to you.

C2C = consumer to consumers, i.e. one individual dealing with another such as a private buyer and seller on eBay.

Activity

Did you know that the NUS welcomes both school sixth-form and college students? Check out the benefits you would gain at www.nusonline.co.uk.

Did you know?

You can identify a UK Government website because it ends .gov.uk. At the last count there were over 3,400 with this suffix.

Sectors online

You should remember from Unit 1 that there are three main sectors – the public sector, the private sector and the voluntary/not-for-profit sector.

The public sector

This sector includes the government, its departments and associated agencies (such as the JobCentre or Benefits Agency); local authorities and public corporations such as the BBC, the Bank of England and British Nuclear Fuels plc.

The portal for accessing most UK public sector sites is www.direct.gov.uk. This site does not contain links to public corporations as these operate as separate and independent organisations at www.bbc.co.uk, www.bankofengland.co.uk and www.bnfl.com.

The private sector

Most websites on the Internet belong to private organisations – from small hotels and retailers to large multinational enterprises. The main suffixes for British companies are .co.uk and .com.

Because private sector companies are in business to make a profit they will only want an Internet presence if this will help them to achieve this objective.

Activity

Check out www.fundraising.co.uk and identify how it could help you if you were involved in a local charity.

The voluntary/not-for-profit sector

This sector includes a wide variety of organisations – from Network Rail at www.networkrail.co.uk (which reinvests all its profits into making train travel safer), to several agencies which provide services to the public such as the Prince's Trust and Citizens Advice Bureaux and all the voluntary and charitable organisations in the UK. Most of these are identifiable online by the suffix .org.uk.

Charities benefit because they can promote their cause online. You can find any registered British charity via the Charity Commission at www.charity-commission.gov.uk/registeredcharities/first.asp. At Charity Net (www.charitynet.org) you will also find links to a wide range of not-for-profit organisations.

Fact file

Private sector businesses sell goods and services online; the public sector uses the Internet to provide information and access to government services; and the voluntary sector benefits through promoting its cause online to recruit new supporters.

Levels/types of online presence

The type of online presence will depend mainly on the main business activity of the organisation and the main purpose of the website. Whichever option a business chooses, the website may be simple or sophisticated, depending upon the size, scale, image and objectives of the organisation.

Passive brochure ware

This type of site is used to promote the business online and to provide information which helps to build the business or brand name either locally, nationally or internationally.

The name derives from the original, minimalist website which was just the firm's brochure replicated on the site. Drawbacks are that the functionality of the site is very limited, the layout of a printed brochure and its style is rarely suitable for a web page and most users are used to more complex sites. They do not want to have to pick up the telephone to place an order or make a booking. In most cases it is better if the customer can interact electronically, such as by email, even if this is just to request further information.

Did you know?

*The term **functionality** is often used to describe the range of functions or operations that are possible on a website.*

However, if the site is well designed so that the information is clear and easy to read and graphics are used effectively then brochure ware can be useful for a small enterprise. The main aim of the site is to tell customers the name of the business, what it does, where it is and how to make contact.

Complementing offline services

Many businesses use their website to extend the range of services and methods of contact with the customer.

A service organisation can offer online facilities, such as banks offering online banking, the Royal Mail site featuring online parcel tracking and postcode searches; the Passport Agency includes online applications for new or renewed passports. WeightWatchers encourages people to join its programme online and Samaritans now encourages email as well as telephone contact.

Manufacturers can provide online technical information and support to customers as well as FAQs (frequently asked questions) pages. Software downloads are available for computer devices such as printers and wireless routers and from computer security suppliers such as Norton. Microsoft provides online tutorials as well as regular free downloads to improve its software.

Retailers who do not sell online can provide additional information about the business, such as product information and customer support. Two good examples are Habitat at www.habitat.net and Ikea at www.ikea.co.uk. Neither sell over the Internet – but both still find it useful to have a comprehensive website with a number of useful features.

The media can provide news online as well as offline; for example, the BBC website complements television broadcasts and newspaper websites complement daily papers.

Event organisers, such as www.glastonburyfestivals.co.uk and www.wimbledon.org provide information on tickets as well as operating souvenir shops and may broadcast webcasts when the event is in progress.

Activity

Check out the website of your local football team (or another sporting team you follow) and identify its main features to see how these complement its offline operations.

Inviting online transactions

Many mail order companies have extended their operations to include a web-based catalogue, such as Lands End clothing and Lakeland Ltd at www.landsend.co.uk and www.lakeland.co.uk. In other cases, traditional bricks and mortar companies have started an online operation with a web storefront, for example, Thornton's Chocolates at www.thorntons.co.uk and Betty's and Taylor's of Harrogate at www.bettysandtaylors.co.uk. The key features of the website must include an ordering system and the facility for receiving and processing payments securely.

Activity

www.smoothHound.co.uk is an online directory of small accommodation. It passes on emails rather than taking bookings online. Clicking on many of the entries on the site (and related websites) will give you good examples of passive brochure ware.

Did you know?

Most mail order companies today also take orders online. You can check out the full list at www.britishcatalogues.co.uk/index.htm.

Key terms

Passive brochure ware is a basic site, with limited functionality, which resembles a leaflet online.

Interactive customisation means a site which changes in response to user input and feedback.

A ***dynamic website*** is a site, linked to a database, which is constantly being updated.

Did you know?

Dynamic websites *are driven by databases programmed to manage and display information. The BBC website is automatically updated through reports logged into the news database. The Amazon site is linked to its product and customer databases. New books are added to the product database and promoted to customers with related interests when they access the site.*

Did you know?

Wikipedia has been criticised because some articles have been wrongly updated. If information is vital you may be wise to check it against another source.

Activity

An e-catalogue is the latest way for a mail order company to publish its catalogue online. It enables searching, zooming and flick through using new technology. Check out those available at www.northsafety.com/euo/en/bs_home.html and search on Google for other examples.

Interactive customisation

Interactive customisation – or site personalisation – relates to sites that respond to user use. This is because they are programmed this way or because they provide a framework for users to adapt.

Sites that are intelligent, and adapt when users register their personal preferences or purchase certain items include Yahoo, which creates 'My Profile' pages for each user which are displayed at www.my.yahoo.com and Amazon, which 'up-sells' to registered customers by offering suggestions for their new purchases based on their interests, previous purchases and purchases of people with similar buying habits. It also compiles a list of 'recently viewed' items so that visitors will not forget items they have browsed. The main areas of interest and buying habits create the customer's 'own store' area, which is displayed when a returning customer re-enters the site from his or her usual computer. The site then uses this information to 'push' similar content of interest to that particular user.

Sites that users can adapt include:

- www.flickr.com – a site where users can upload, organise and share digital photos online as well as add captions and tags
- http://del.icio.us/ where you can save, search and share information and bookmarks
- www.myspace.com where users create their own website within the website, e.g. www.myspace.com/chrismoyles
- Wikipedia, the free online encyclopaedia at http://en.wikipedia.org/ where anyone can edit the entries. You can find out more by clicking on the History tab at the top of a page.

Activity

If you take digital photos, check out www.flickr.com or http://moblog.co.uk/ to see the features – or check out any of the digital image processing sites by searching on Google.

Providing information only

Many websites simply provide information – some of it serious, other types useful and some humorous. Examples include http://www.imdb.com/ – for all the information you ever needed about films; www.upmystreet.com – for information about your area; www.hoovers.com/freeuk/ – for information on UK companies; www.sportinglife.com – for everything about sport in the UK; www.worksmart.org.uk – for everything you need to know about your rights at work, taxes and unions; www.bbc.co.uk – for lots of useful everyday information and www.studentfreestuff.com/ – for information about give-aways to students.

Your college or school will have an informational website, targeted at future students and/or their parents.

Activity

Check out www.web100.com where you can find the top 100 websites on the Internet under different categories, such as Arts and Entertainment and information topics. These are mainly American sites. At www.alexa.com you can find out information about the top 500 sites – and lots of other things besides.

Over to you

1 *From the following options, suggest the most appropriate type of online presence for each of the businesses listed below. In each case give a reason for your choice.*

Businesses:

a) *Local estate agent*
b) *Private language college specialising in intensive business courses*
c) *Virtual company specialising in tailor-made holidays*
d) *Central London hotel*
e) *National toy retailer*
f) *Small retail company selling specialist food products.*

Options:

i) *Passive brochure ware with contact number*
ii) *Basic online transaction (e.g. booking or reservation)*
iii) *Catalogue online and online shopping facility*
iv) *Interactive customisation.*

2 *Divide into groups and investigate the following sites. In each case decide:*

a) *the sector in which the business operates*
b) *the level or type of online presence.*

Site 1: NHS Direct at www.nhsdirect.nhs.uk
Site 2: The Heinemann website at www.heinemann.co.uk
Site 3: Your own college website
Site 4: Guide Dogs for the Blind at www.gdba.org.uk
Site 5: Thornton's Chocolates at www.thorntons.co.uk
Site 6: The Samaritans at www.samaritans.org.uk

Fact file

Levels or types of online presence range from passive brochure ware, and sites that offer only information to those which invite online transactions or offer interactive customisation.

Activity

For a topic in which you are interested, find three sites that will give you useful information. Then describe your findings to the rest of your group.

Talking point

View 1: By 2020 most high street shops will have ceased to exist – most people will shop online.

View 2: There will always be high street shops because some people don't like buying online and some products aren't suitable for selling online.

With which viewpoint do you agree – and why?

Case study Assessment practice

According to Nielsen//NetRatings, the popularity of different website brands varies according to people's ages, and reflects their major interests, as you can see below.

Kids and teens	20s	30s	40s	50s
Friends and Fun	**Web Giants**	**Money**	**Variety**	**Information**
Bebo Piczo Nickelodeon MiniClip RuneScape Tickle MySpace IGN/GameSpy UGO Disney Online	BSkyB PayPal Amazon Wanadoo MSN eBay Google AOL Yahoo! Microsoft	Barclays Argos Halifax Play.com PayPal The National Lottery Tesco eBay Channel 4 Amazon	Premium TV Abbey National Genes Reunited Demon Ryannair Aliance Leicester NHS Marks and Spencer Ebuyer Yell	IncrediMail uSwitch OneTel Ebookers Information Britain ViaMitchelin Telegraph Symantec Epson Weather Channel

■ *Top 10 website brands by age group, 2006*

Source: Nielsen//NetRatings

1 Identify the online activities of two different website brands popular with 'kids and teenagers'. Explain why these are likely to be popular with this age group.

2 Few students of your age will be interested in Disney Online. Identify the top five sites that you think are popular with your own age group and give a reason for your choice.

3(P) Select any two different 'Web Giants' that are popular with people in their 20s. Investigate them and then describe each organisation and its online activities. ***(P1 part)***

4(P) Select one website that is popular with any of the other age groups. In each case describe the organisation and its online activities and explain why it is popular with that particular age group. ***(P1 part)***

Grading tip

When you are describing an online activity, remember to include details about the level or type of online presence that it has.

8.2 Understand the business feasibility of going online

Most organisations can obtain several benefits through an online presence. They may be able to increase their sales, reduce costs or provide information to customers more effectively. They may be able to achieve other business aims and objectives more efficiently. However, they must also think about the potential difficulties and plan carefully to ensure they are prepared for these and to overcome them.

Planning issues

Suitability of the business for an online operation

The first question to ask is whether the business should have an online operation at all. Many local independent traders, such as hairdressers, child-minders, taxi firms and plumbers do not have one. They reason that their customers find them by a combination of personal recommendation and traditional advertising, such as in *Yellow Pages* or a local newspaper, not by looking on the Internet.

If there would be obvious benefits to be gained, the next step is to decide *how* to go about going online.

Activity

Many people think that even small businesses should have a listing since the launch of Google local. Use it to find a taxi or hairdressers near you at http://local.google.co.uk/!

Did you know?

Just typing a domain name into your browser will not tell you if it is still available, only whether it is currently active or not. To find out if a name has been taken you must use the WHOIS query at www.nominet.org.uk/ (for UK names) and at www.internic.net/whois.html (for suffixes such as .com and .net).

Choice of domain name

All websites have a domain name – which is normally the same as the organisational name, such as www.boots.co.uk. Ideally, the name should be easy for customers to remember, say and spell and as near to the operational name as possible.

Many UK businesses own the domain name ending with .com *and* .co.uk (and possibly .net as well) – and may even register common mis-spellings of their name so that anyone entering these will be automatically redirected to the main site. British Gas have gone one further and registered www.house.co.uk as well as their own name.

A name must be officially registered before it can be used. It is then leased to the owner for a specified period, after which time the owner can choose to renew it or not.

Activity

The domain name for B & Q is www.diy.com. It has since obtained www.bandq.co.uk and advertises on Google to pick up other prospective customers. Find out what happens by typing variations into Google. Then suggest why B & Q have done this.

Activity

Find out more about choosing a domain name at www.thesitewizard.com/archive/domainname.shtml, about registering domain names at www.netnames.co.uk and about services offered by registration companies at www.internetters.co.uk and www.easyspace.com/index.html.

Key terms

A ***browser*** is a program which enables you to view the Internet, such as Microsoft's Internet Explorer.

A ***domain name*** is the unique name that identifies a website.

An ***Internet Service Provider (ISP)*** is a company that provides its customers with Internet access for a fee.

Outsourcing involves paying another business to provide specialist services.

Set-up issues

Businesses have to choose whether to create the website 'in-house' or whether to ask a specialist company to do it.

In-house A basic website can be created quite easily from 'off-the-shelf' web authoring software such as Microsoft FrontPage. This has wizards to help non-experts to create a simple website. A small business can also obtain help and advice through many free services and local agencies, such as the Chamber of Commerce. More skills are needed to use specialist packages like Macromedia's Dreamweaver, Fireworks and Flash technology which enable professional developers to produce many different effects and designs.

Outsource Many businesses prefer to obtain the assistance of a professional web-design agency which will give advice on all aspects of the site, including security. This is particularly important if the business will be receiving payments online. The cost of employing a professional agency can run from £3,000 to over £100,000 but a business may decide this is worthwhile to ensure that the site positively promotes the company's image.

Did you know?

The main benefit of out-sourcing is that common pitfalls are avoided because the business is paying for an expert to do the work.

Activity

Find out more about the dos and don'ts of building a website yourself at www.webwizguide.info/web_design/default.asp.

Availability of resources to cope with potentially global demand

Even the most basic website should include a contact email address. This means that someone needs to regularly check for emails and reply to them. The same person may also be employed to keep the site up to date and to suggest future developments based on customer feedback.

This is a basic minimum. A business that intends to sell online will have other demands to take into account. It will need to produce and/or keep enough stock to be able to meet orders promptly. This is likely to involve greater monetary outlay and require extra storage space. Extra staff may be needed to process orders or pack and despatch items. There must be checks to ensure that payments have been received before goods are sent. If demand increases rapidly the business could struggle to cope, especially if it also handles face-to-face customer enquiries.

Availability of skills available to run an online business

These will depend upon the scope of the online business, the type of site and whether it is hosted in-house or by an ISP. They may include:

- **technical skills** – to ensure the website stays operational and is fully secure
- **website design and maintenance skills** – to develop or update the site on a regular basis
- **e-marketing skills** – to ensure that the site is ranked highly by Internet search engines and is easy for customers to find
- **admin and customer service skills** – to respond to customer enquiries, orders and feedback promptly and appropriately
- **management skills** – to take account of the legal responsibilities related to operating online (see pages 340 and 341), to identify opportunities for improvements and future developments, to ensure staff are well-trained and resourced and capable of coping with the additional and different demands received.

Did you know?

More resources are required if the website is hosted in-house, in terms of hardware, software and technical skills, than if it is hosted by an Internet Service Provider (ISP) who will take responsibility for keeping it operational and secure.

Did you know?

Normally, hosting a website in-house is only appropriate for large companies that can afford to employ specialist IT staff to maintain it.

Fact file

Even if a business would benefit from an online operation it needs to plan carefully, choose a suitable domain name, decide the best way to set up the website and identify the resources and skills that are required.

Implementation issues

Even with good planning, going online can mean making quite substantial changes to the way a business operates. This can create problems for staff inside the company and with customers. There may also be additional difficulties if people are so involved in implementing the online operation that they neglect their current jobs.

Potential difficulties of online implementation

The biggest potential problem of going online is that the information will be badly organised. Websites should be planned so that users can easily find what they are most likely to need. Customers can decide whether they like a website within two clicks – if they see a badly designed site with too much text or cannot find what they want they are likely to leave it very quickly. Important checks that should be made are shown in the table below.

Website checks	
Appears properly on all browsers and operating systems (e.g. Apple Mac, FireFox, Opera, Internet Explorer)	✔
Loads quickly	✔
Any elaborate opening graphics can be skipped if required	✔
Text is structured in easily-digestible small chunks	✔
Does not request personal information before people can access the site	✔
All links work properly	✔
There are no factual errors or mistakes with grammar, spelling or punctuation	✔
All information is up to date	✔
Navigation is consistent – it is easy to find the way around the site and return to the home page	✔
Instructions are clear and easy to understand	✔
Advertising is not intrusive	✔
There is clear contact information	✔
There is an easy-to-use search facility which brings up accurate results	✔
There is a print option which omits graphics and other unnecessary text and ensures all text is printed clearly.	✔

Did you know?

Key aspects of a website are design, usability and navigation (how easy it is to move around the site). 'Sticky' websites are those that keep a customer's interest for some time as they go from page to page.

Availability of technical and design skills

Whilst a basic site may be all that is required, it is dangerous to assume that anyone with a basic knowledge of IT can create a suitable business website. Commercial sites are often both large and complex with thousands of pages, links to a product database and with security encrypted pages for receiving payments. In this case, expert programming and design skills are required, as well as a good knowledge of database technology and familiarity with different types of web servers to:

- plan the structure and design the site to reflect the business image and to allow for future development needs
- design the pages so that they provide a consistent image to users
- add text, graphics, links and any effects required
- ensure that the site is accessible to disabled users (see page 356)
- include security features such as encrypted pages and protection against hackers.

Unless the organisation is very large, and website development will continue, it is usually more cost-effective to outsource this task to experts.

Requirement for customisation

A customised site is one that has been specially created to meet the specific needs of the business and its customers. The greater the need for customisation, the more expert skills are needed. This also means that the design costs are likely to be higher.

Desired extent of online operations

As you have seen, websites can range from passive brochure ware, to limited interactivity by customers (who can communicate or order online) to those which are fully interactive, e.g. Amazon or MyPlaces. The more functionality that is required the more specialist skills are needed and the greater the cost of developing the website.

If the business intends to sell online then considerations must include which stock to feature, whether additional stock will be required, where it will be stored, how payments will be accepted, how the goods will be distributed and the legal issues of selling online (see pages 340 and 341).

The website must also be able to cope with the projected number of visitors, otherwise it will crash or perform so slowly that it is useless. This means carefully considering site capacity and the projected amount of 'traffic' to the site. Famous examples of website crashes include the BBC site on 9/11 and the Government's Census site on its launch date.

Changing user specifications for desired service levels

All websites must be kept up to date, accurate and relevant to the customer. In some cases, the needs and demands of the customer may change over time, so that the website has to be revised to incorporate increased service levels, such as automated confirmation of orders, online order tracking and online communication with staff.

For this reason, from the outset, the updating and review of the website content must be planned to take place routinely to ensure that it always meets the needs of its users. Changing the design at regular intervals also has benefits, because it enables the website to be improved and modernised as well as being made more appealing to customers.

An important aspect of a commercial website is that it is optimised for the type of searches customers will make. This is known as ***search engine optimisation*** *(SEO) and is also a job for experts.*

A ***scalable*** *website is one that has been designed to grow or change to continually meet business needs.*

If you think websites rarely change, try this. Go to www.archive.org and enter the name of a famous website, e.g. www.cadbury.com or news.bbc.co.uk then click 'Take me Back'. Then choose any date listed to see what the website looked like then and compare it with how it looks today.

Key terms

Customisation is adjusting a design to meet the specific needs of a business and its customers.

An ***extranet*** is a website where access is restricted, either by password or by encryption. It is made available to key partners, such as suppliers or distributors, who respond to information they receive on stock levels and/or sales orders.

SEO (search engine optimisation) optimises the website content so that major search engines include the site high in their listings.

Did you know?

Many companies outsource both the warehousing and distribution of their stock to a specialist organisation which is responsible for fulfilling all the orders they receive online, such as Amtrak Express Parcels at www.amtrak.co.uk

Relationships with partners

Setting up an online operation is likely to involve collaboration with several partners.

Additional finance may be required to pay for site development costs, additional stocks or raw materials that are required and any expert staff that need to be hired.

Financial services will be required if the business will receive payments online. This can be done in one of two ways:

- The business can pay a Merchant Service or Payment Service Provider to collect and process payments on its behalf. This is useful for small firms because payment is captured on the PSP's secure site – not that belonging to the business. PSP charge a fee for this service. They also hold on to the money for between 30 and 60 days as a precaution against fraud. Examples include WorldPay at www.worldpay.co.uk. and NetBanx at www.netbanx.com.
- The business can arrange with its bank to operate its own Merchant Service and process its own payments on a secure website. Banks only agree to this if they are convinced of the financial status of the business, the security arrangements in place and are satisfied with the terms and conditions of online trading.

Increased supplies may be required if the business is selling online to avoid disappointing customers because items are out of stock. However, the company will also want to keep stock levels to a minimum level to avoid too much money being tied up in slow-moving stock. Ideally, the business will liaise with its suppliers through its **Extranet** or via an online marketplace where buyers, sellers and agents offer goods to each other – rather like eBay for businesses.

■ *When Tesco started selling online it quadrupled its sales*

Distribution and delivery must be excellent for businesses that sell goods online. Today, customers expect goods they have ordered online to be delivered promptly, to an address of their choosing. They also like to track deliveries online and expect any problems or returns to be dealt with promptly by the seller. In addition, many orders may be received from overseas and require specialist packing or the completion of specific customs forms. For these reasons, many online sellers appoint a specialist distribution partner to do all these tasks for them. In some cases, this partner will also control stock levels and warehousing as well.

Fact file

Difficulties relating to online implementation can include the availability of technical and design skills to ensure the website is up to date, easy to use, appropriate to the online operation and can be developed as the business expands or changes. Good relationships with financial service partners, suppliers and distributors are also crucial.

Over to you

1 *Technology Means Business provides advice to small- and medium-sized businesses both online and through a national network of advisers. Another source of help to small businesses are eBusinessClubs, set up by The British Chamber of Commerce. Both websites contain case studies which describe how small businesses have been encouraged and helped to go online.*

Working in small groups, go to either www.tmb.org.uk or www.ebusinessclubs.co.uk/ and find a case study that interests you. Summarise the main issues that were considered at the planning and implementation stages and compare your findings with other groups.

2 *Jane Foster and Joe Porter both specialise in making unusual silver jewellery which sells well at craft fairs in their area. They would now like to expand their business and are thinking of having an online presence. Joe is particularly keen on this since he heard about several small-scale jewellery entrepreneurs who were doing well online.*

Jane is more cautious. She knows that neither of them have the IT skills to create a good site and is worried that they could lose money, rather than earn it, by operating online.

a) *Research some online jewellery sites, which advertise unusual handmade pieces, such as at www.pennyserenade.com and www.justind.co.uk . Suggest the type of site that you think would be appropriate if Janine and Joe went online, with reasons, and the information it should include.*

b) *Identify the main planning issues they would need to consider.*

c) *Explain how Janine and Joe could minimise typical problems related to the site's implementation.*

Talking point

View 1: Businesses must go online quickly if their competitors are online. If their website or service is mediocre it can be improved later.

View 2: Businesses must take their time and plan carefully before they go online. It is better to have no website than an awful one.

With which viewpoint do you agree – and why?

Case study Assessment practice

Toys may seem an obvious product to sell online. Mothers may be housebound with small children, present-givers find it useful to look online to compare prices and appreciate guidance on the best toys for different age groups. Yet the success of online toyshops has been very varied – for several reasons.

Large companies, such as Hamleys at www.hamleys.com outsource the planning and implementing of their website to experts who obtain the domain name(s), design and host the site and ensure it is user-friendly and secure. Customers can register to receive email newsletters and can buy online in confidence. Packaging and distribution is often outsourced to specialists.

Smaller companies find this more difficult. In 2005, the Sunday Express featured The Farmyard, a small specialist toyshop selling children's gifts in Richmond and Barnes, south-west London. The two owners, Julia and Emma, had run a profitable business for five years before setting up their website, which cost more than expected and failed to generate many sales. They were advised to keep costs low by continuing with a passive site and to rethink their domain name – www.thefarmyard.co.uk – as searches kept leading to sites relating to animals. Another problem is that some items on the site, like the toy boxes at £275, are expensive to buy and despatch. Many people prefer to see these types of goods before they decide to purchase.

These issues have not been a problem for Fun to Learn – a small enterprise in Newry (Ireland) run by Clodagh Welsh. Her educational fun books and other items are small, light and cheap to despatch. A demonstration area on the site at www.fun-2-learn.com enables potential buyers to find out more before they place an order. The only problem is that custom could be lost (or gained) because of its similarity to www.fun-2-learn.co.uk – an entirely different business.

1 Access each of the sites listed above and compare the features and the extent of each online operation.

2(P) Describe the main planning and implementation issues a business has to consider before it sets up an online operation. ***(P2)***

3 Do you think toys are suitable for selling online? Give a reason for your answer.

4 To what extent do you think the choice of a domain name is appropriate in each of the examples above – and why?

5(M) Explain the online planning and implementation issues which have affected The Farmyard. ***(M1 part)***

Grading tip

When you give an explanation it needs to include details about the specific business you are discussing.

8.3 Understand the operation of an online business

Even if there is an excellent case to be made for a business to go online and a website specification has been carefully drawn up, this does not mean that the whole process will then operate smoothly. Once the site is operational it must be maintained by staff who understand how an online business operates and the problems it might face.

Operation issues

Payment security

Most online customers expect to be able to pay for goods they buy by debit or credit card. However, they also have to be certain that their personal details will be kept confidential. Newspaper headlines about fraud, hackers and identity theft obviously put people off. To be secure, all online payments need to be:

- **private and confidential** between the buyer and the seller
- **authentic** because both people are who they claim to be
- **conveyed intact** and without any changes or alterations during transmission
- **erased** from the system after the process has been completed.

This is achieved by specific security standards. The most commonly used – **SSL (Secure Sockets Layer)** – allows a standard browser, such as Microsoft Explorer, to transmit and receive information securely. This is because the data is encrypted – or scrambled – using encryption keys that change every time the browser is used. Customers are warned that they are 'about to view information over a secure connection' and then see the locked padlock symbol and 'https' on the address line. They can then double-click the symbol to read the security certificate that confirms the site is legitimate and the 'seller' is who he claims to be.

SET (Secure Electronic Transfer) is a more sophisticated system for credit card transactions. When the card holder buys online the credit card company authenticates the card via a digital signature. This proves the card holder is genuine. It will only pay the seller when it has checked the seller's identity – against a digital certificate. Critical information such as the card number is encrypted and decrypted but never made known to the seller – only to the card's issuing bank.

Unfamiliar trading conditions

These can affect both the business and its customers. The main reason online trading was relatively slow to take off was because customers were

SSL protects the buyer but not the seller. This is because there is no check that the buyer is genuine and is the true owner of the credit card being used to purchase goods. SET protects both parties.

CNP stands for 'Card not present'. This is the situation when an online buyer types in his or her card number. The supplier is vulnerable to fraud because the buyer could be using a stolen card. Find out the steps that online businesses can take to protect themselves against CNP fraud at www.cardwatch.org.uk.

Did you know?

The ***E-commerce (EC Directive) Regulations 2002*** *require online business to have specific information on their website, such as the business name, email address and VAT registration number as well as giving clear prices which say whether tax and/or delivery is included.*

Did you know?

All organisations that sell products online must comply with the ***Distance Selling Regulations 2005****. This gives online buyers the same rights as people who buy from a retailer or mail order firm and the right to cancel goods or services up to seven days after the goods were received or the service was ordered.*

Did you know?

When customers buy goods online they ***must*** *receive written confirmation by post, fax or email. This confirmation should also include information on their cancellation rights.*

worried about buying online. Normally, once new customers have successfully bought goods online they become immediate converts to online shopping.

However, businesses that are used to operating on a small scale or dealing with customers face to face can struggle to adapt. They may misjudge the popularity (or otherwise) of their website, the type or quantity of orders they receive, the costs of packaging and distribution and the time taken for staff to fulfil online requests.

A business which is less successful than anticipated may have unsold stock and struggle to repay any money borrowed to pay for the website development. If it cannot answer enquiries quickly, or fulfil orders promptly because of insufficient stock, or too few staff then it will not only fail to take advantage of new business but may have done itself a disservice as dissatisfied customers are unlikely to contact it again in the future.

There may also be problems coping with the legal requirements of trading online or with dealing with cultural expectations or other restrictions relating to foreign buyers. Unless the business can obtain specialist help and advice it may take some time before it can respond to all the pressures and challenges it may meet.

Errors in ordering

Order forms should be designed to be as foolproof as possible to minimise customer errors. The site should also be designed to prevent customers making other obvious mistakes, such as duplicating an order by submitting the same order form twice. There should also be a comprehensive returns policy that takes into account the legal rights of consumers (see opposite).

Key information is entered before order is accepted Most forms are designed so that all key information has to be entered before they will be accepted. It is also useful if excessively large quantities or other seemingly obvious errors are queried before the order is processed. This may be an automated process. Otherwise very large (or possibly duplicate) orders may be singled out for the customer to be contacted by telephone before they are processed.

Online customers are protected by the **Sale of Goods Act** and the **Supply of Goods and Services Act 1982** in just the same way as other consumers. (See Unit 7, page 284). **The Sale and Supply of Goods to Consumers Regulations 2002** also gives consumers the right to return goods that are faulty – whether they are bought in a shop or online. Many sellers are also prepared to exchange goods that are not faulty but are unsuitable for another reason, such as clothes that do not fit properly or duplicate gifts. The terms which apply to the return of goods and queries about faulty goods should be easy to find on the website.

Potential use of personal information

All organisations that store and process information about individuals, whether on a computer system or in written records, must register with the Information Commissioner and comply with the terms of the **Data Protection Act 1998**. This means that the data must be accurate, secure and not kept for longer than is necessary. It also means that an online business cannot put private information on its website or disclose customer details to other people. For these reasons, websites usually include a privacy policy which states how information is used by the business. This includes visitor details collected by cookies (see opposite) or during a registration or ordering process.

The **Privacy and Electronic Communications Regulations** also allow businesses to send emails only to people who have 'opted in' by giving their active consent to receive these. This means they cannot send promotional emails without the recipient's permission. This is why such emails also include an option for the recipient to unsubscribe at any time.

Activity

Find out about your personal rights under the Data Protection Act at the website of the Information Commissioner at www.ico.gov.uk – then check out the privacy policy on your favourite shopping website to see what it says.

Key terms

A ***cookie*** is a small data file, placed on the user's computer when they first visit a site. It identifies repeat visitors and registered users and also provides information about the user's habits on the site.

A ***denial of service (DOS) attack*** bombards a website with data until it crashes.

Phishing occurs when users are directed to a spoof website (e.g. a retail store or bank) and told to enter personal details of credit card information.

Pharming is a spoof website set up by hackers. When users type in the URL they are directed to this website instead of the authentic one.

Vulnerability to hostile attack

According to the National Hi-Tech Crime Unit (NHTCU), cybercrime costs British businesses billions of pounds a year. It is not just large businesses that are threatened by hackers, spoof websites or denial of service attacks. When Alex Tew set up his highly successful Million Dollar Website he was threatened with a denial of service (DOS) attack unless he gave in to blackmail demands (see Unit 9, page 392).

A DOS attack occurs when a website is overwhelmed with data, such as email messages, in a very short time so that the site is brought down. Hackmailers – as they have been called – target sites at their most vulnerable times, such as at Christmas when a DOS attack would lose an online retailer millions of pounds.

Hijacking a website is when the site is duplicated so that there is a 'spoof' version on the Internet which customers use, thinking they are dealing with the original organisation. Sometimes the pages are badly copied and genuine links are replaced with those that lead to pornographic sites to destroy the company's image and reputation. On others, customers are asked to enter bank account or credit card details which can then used by the hackers to obtain money.

Fact file

There are many operation issues that can affect an online business. These include ensuring payments are secure, coping with unfamiliar trading conditions and errors made by customers when ordering, protecting personal information, guarding against hostile attacks and financial fraud.

Did you know?

Because of security attacks on bank customers, many financial institutions are introducing additional authentication procedures in the future. Many believe that just asking customers to enter a username and password is no longer sufficient.

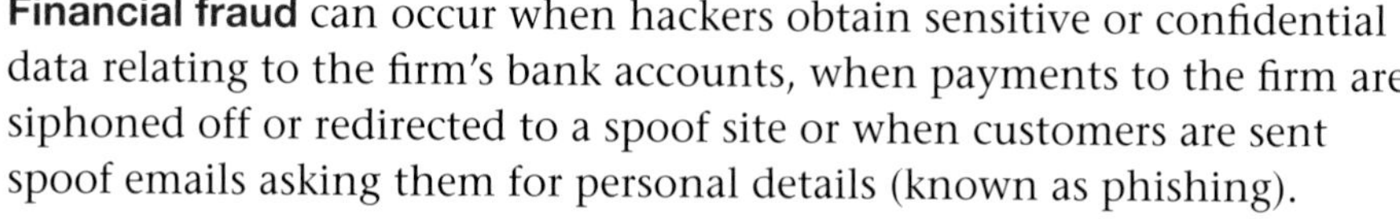

Financial fraud can occur when hackers obtain sensitive or confidential data relating to the firm's bank accounts, when payments to the firm are siphoned off or redirected to a spoof site or when customers are sent spoof emails asking them for personal details (known as phishing).

Activity

Find out how to make your own PC secure, as well as what small businesses should do at http://www.getsafeonline.org/.

Operational risks

Website updating

Websites need updating regularly so that the information provided is current and product descriptions and lists are accurate. There is nothing worse than for a customer to see pages that have not been amended for a year or more. In some cases incorrect or out-of-date information can create serious problems.

Did you know?

In 2005 Argos advertised a television on its website for 49p instead of the £350 it should have cost. It was inundated with orders and had to apologise to 10,000 customers but there is no law that forced it to sell the goods at that price.

Liability for wrong or out-of-date information

Under the **Trades Descriptions Act** and the **E-commerce (EC Directive) Regulations 2002** information given on the website must be clear and descriptions must be accurate. A business that deliberately misled customers could be liable under the terms of these Acts. Equally, if a customer took action based on outdated or inaccurate information there may be a case to answer – although most websites have a 'disclaimer' clause to cover this type of problem. However, much depends upon the type of website. For example, the NHS has to be more careful about the accuracy of the information it provides than Tesco.

Did you know?

Uniliver makes Flora, Hellmanns, Knorr and many other famous brands. Its website at www.unilever.com enables you to choose between 56 different country websites from Argentina to the Yemen, each specifically written and designed for customers in that country.

Activity

Terms and conditions on a website cover the responsibilities of a business in case of an error and other issues such as buying goods from abroad. See an example at the Marks and Spencer website at www2.marksandspencer.com/help/policies/terms.shtml.

Language problems with global customer base

Multinational businesses with overseas customers normally have a facility to enable users to choose the website version they want, sometimes by identifying their national flag as at www.vittel.com. This automatically displays a specific language version.

Smaller organisations will not have this facility and there is therefore more scope for confusion when foreign buyers want to purchase goods. This is why many firms include disclaimer clauses, such as those at the Marks and Spencer website, where orders are only accepted if the description accurately matches that on the site and the company takes no responsibility for the suitability of goods to be used abroad or any local laws that would affect the purchase.

Small firms that want to sell to foreign business customers have two choices. They may try to work through a local agent or have enquiries for their services translated. This should be done by an expert. Online translation services such as Google's may be useful for phrases to a pen friend but are not recommended for important business documents!

Activity

Check how a multinational b2b website offers choices for its global customers at www.ibm.com/planetwide/select/selector.html.

Hardware and software failures

All computer users are dependent upon their Internet Service Provider to stay online. If the system develops a technical fault, then Internet access is lost until the fault is repaired. This can create serious problems for an online business, particularly if the website is 'down' for any length of time.

Did you know?

A UPS (Uninterruptible Power Supply) stops power surges that can damage computer hardware during a lightning storm.

Even if there are no problems with an ISP, the system itself might develop a fault. The hardware might malfunction or software may be corrupted. For this reason, most businesses have back-up servers, so that they can simply switch to another if a server goes down. Software problems may be caused by programming errors or through a virus. Appropriate anti-virus software and appropriate network security are crucial.

None of these measures will help, though, if there is a major disaster. For that reason, some businesses have their website hosted offsite, in a secure location, where there are specialist staff available to repair and restore the system quickly (see page 346).

Did you know?

Data recovery firms specialise in trying to restore data that has been damaged or accidentally deleted. See www.diskdoctorsdatarecovery.co.uk/ for one example.

Data loss

Data can be lost for many reasons. A report about data loss in Europe identified a total of 1.7 million incidents every year, as a result of the following problems.

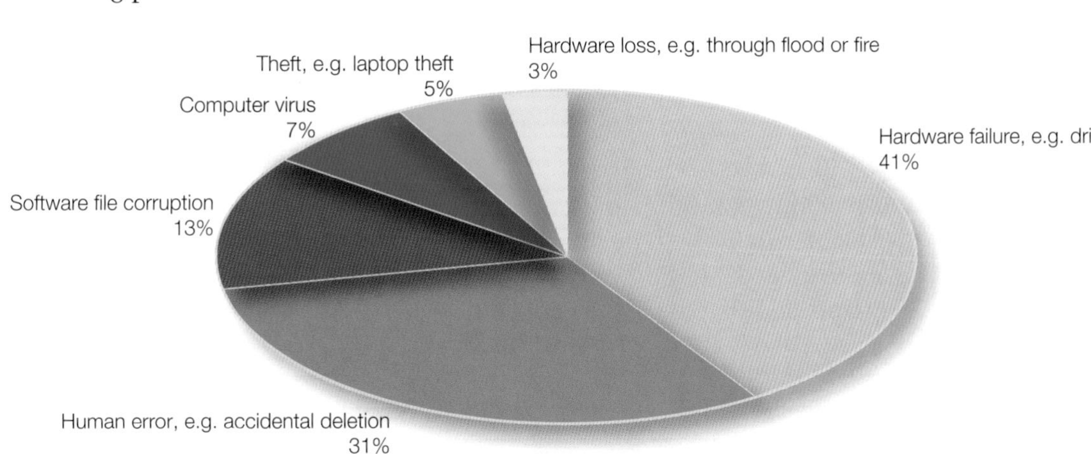

■ *Main reasons for data loss*

Did you know?

Even big businesses have to adapt to foreign sensitivities to do business overseas – as Google found when it had to agree to Chinese censorship to operate in that country. This meant it had to remove any references relating to the 1989 student massacre for searches under Tiananmen Square on its Chinese website.

Fact file

Online businesses face several operational risks. They need to keep their website up to date and may be liable for inaccurate information; they need to ensure global customers can understand the website, deal with equipment and software failures including loss of data and comply with global business regulations.

Did you know?

BSI stands for the British Standards Institute. It advises British exporters on legislation, regulations and standards that may affect their products and services and can also help by translating technical specifications.

Daily back-ups of the whole system mean that a business can always reinstall its systems to within 24 hours of a problem occurring. It is also common practice to back-up a system before making major changes, again so that the earlier version can easily be restored if there are any problems. Individual users should also be trained in the importance of keeping data secure and backing up their own work regularly.

Global business regulations

Most people are aware that there are many differences between products they see abroad and in Britain. A box of cornflakes or a packet of biscuits you buy on holiday, even if made in the UK, will be labelled and packaged differently – usually to conform to the culture and the language of the country where it is being sold. Cars are made with left- or right-hand drive, record distances travelled in miles or kilometres, and are designed to comply with specific regulations on emissions and noise levels – which again vary from one country to another.

Any business intending to sell on a global basis has to ensure that its products comply with the relevant laws and technical regulations that apply in the country of sale – and just because a country is English-speaking this does not mean that the regulations will be the same. Australia, for example, has different standards than the UK so many products need to be modified or 'Australianised' before they can be sold there. In many countries, such as the USA, health and safety requirements are also different than they are in the UK or Europe.

If a product fails to comply with the regulations that apply, it is likely that they will be stopped on entry by the customs authorities.

Activity

Divide into small groups to find out what you would have to do to sell goods abroad. Go to www.uktradeinvest.gov.uk/ and click on the 'countries' tab at the top. Decide on a country, click to read the report and find out about customs and regulations. Then compare results to see the differences.

Staffing issues

Developing an online presence may cause concerns for staff. Much depends upon the type of operation, its size and the way any changes are managed. Staff may be concerned that their jobs will change or disappear altogether.

Potential outsourcing of key functions

This means paying specialists to provide certain services rather than do them in-house. Examples include:

- **hiring an agency** to create and/or develop the site

- **paying a specialist hosting company** – such as The Bunker (see page 346) – to keep the site secure and to undertake routine maintenance
- **using e-marketing experts** to promote the site and to devise associated marketing campaigns.

Only in a large organisation would it be cost effective to employ a specialist web team in-house.

Use of call centres

Many large businesses with a popular website, such as John Lewis, Marks and Spencer and Tesco, use a call centre to answer customer queries. This is an external operation where customer service staff are employed to respond to customer calls. They have access to the customer and product databases so that they can see relevant information on screen during the call.

Did you know?

According to one survey by Evalueserve/ NASSCOM, by 2010 about 272,000 British IT jobs will have been outsourced offshore, from help desks to software development. One reason is to save money. Average call centre salaries in India are about £1,200 a year compared to £12,500 a year in Britain.

Many organisations that provide computer supplies and ISP services online – such as Dell and BT – operate a 'help' facility through a call centre, where trained staff can talk customers through procedures to resolve faults or connection problems they are experiencing.

Lack of personal contact with customers

Many staff may find that, as a result of the website, they have less personal contact with customers who can now place orders online, email if they want information or contact a call centre if they have a query. This may dishearten some staff and delight others!

Unfamiliarity with technology

Many staff need special training so that they feel comfortable working with the new technology. This is important because staff will not work efficiently or effectively if they are unsure what to do or are struggling to understand the new system.

Fact file

Staff may be concerned about online business operations because of the outsourcing of key functions, the use of call centres, the lack of personal contact with customers, because they are not confident using the technology or are worried about service breakdowns.

Today, most job descriptions specify that staff must be reasonably flexible so that the business can take advantage of new technology. However, it is still better if staff are consulted at the outset and involved in plans that will affect them.

Breakdowns in service

Problems relating to hardware and software failures, and loss of data, were dealt with on page 343. Any breakdowns obviously put more pressure on the staff, who are unlikely to be able to do their own jobs if there is a major system problem and may have to deal with calls from angry customers too.

Did you know?

In 2005 a fire at the Hertfordshire Oil Storage Terminal caused many business websites to crash because it caused serious damage at a major web hosting company – Northgate Information Solutions.

Having a contingency plan to cover possible breakdowns helps staff to identify their own role and know what to do if a serious problem occurs.

Financial issues

Although setting up a small informational website may be done quite cheaply, there are more costs involved for firms who want to carry out a substantial amount of business online or use their website as a major way of promoting the organisation. In addition, calculating the potential financial benefits is not easy. The last thing a business can afford is an expensive online presence which brings few, if any, financial benefits and actually incurs costs to keep operational.

Activity

Find out about the services offered by firms such as Northgate Information Solutions at www.northgate-is.com or www.thebunker.net/ to keep business systems secure.

Initial investment costs of hardware, software and program adaptation

The specific costs will depend upon whether the developments are being managed by a specialist agency or being done in-house and the scale of the operation. Generally, the most typical categories of expenditure are likely to include the following:

- **additional hardware requirements**, e.g.computers, servers, printers, scanners etc.

- **software requirements** – including the operating system, applications programs (e.g. Microsoft Office), web authoring software, graphics packages
- **program adaptation** – such as adapting the customer or product database to link with a web store.

Other set-up expenses will include registering the domain name, arranging for an ISP to host the site if this is not being done in-house, paying agency specialists to design the site, marketing and promotional costs (so potential customers know the site exists) and any staff training requirements.

Key terms

Hardware is IT equipment and components, e.g. the VDU, keyboard and printer.

Software is IT programs that tell the computer what to do.

Set-up expenses offset against uncertain future revenue streams

Regardless of the type of site being planned, it is important that a realistic budget is agreed at the start which takes into account the main aims and projected benefits of doing business online.

It is less easy to forecast future running and development costs once the site is operational, and even harder to forecast potential income. This will depend upon whether the site successfully achieves its objectives and how quickly this happens.

Did you know?

Many companies set targets they want to achieve by a certain date, called performance indicators.

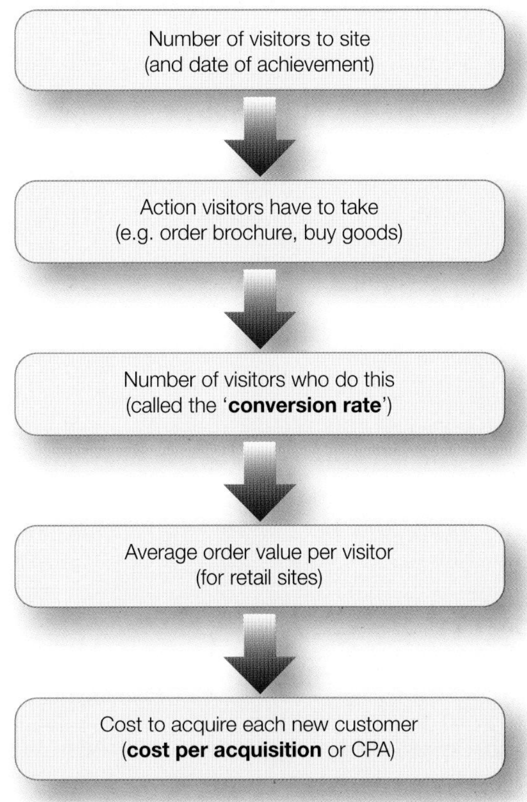

■ *Key performance indicators*

Activity

Check out the set-up expenses and performance of the Million Dollar Homepage by reading the case study in Unit 9, page 392.

Ability to cope with massively increased market interest

All businesses go online in the hope of generating additional business. A problem occurs if there is a huge surge of interest which the company cannot handle. This can result in the site crashing, because too many

Did you know?

Buying an item from an overseas website means you have to pay postage and insurance costs, then import duty and then VAT. In the case of a cheap trumpet from China, one buyer found that this increased the price from £24.99 to nearly £130!

people are trying to use it simultaneously. It may mean that enquiries cannot be answered quickly or orders cannot be filled because there is insufficient stock or too few staff to process them. Buying more stock or employing more staff both cost money and may result in cash flow problems. If the company gets a bad reputation because it cannot cope, the site may lose customers rather than help to gain them.

Activity

Word quickly spreads online if businesses get a poor reputation. Some websites are even set up in protest such as www.btsucks.com and www.tescopoly.org.uk .

Go to www.grumbletext.co.uk to see how customer dissatisfaction can quickly spread online or go to www.blogger.com and search by brand or company to see what people are saying about it.

Key terms

Import duty is tax paid on imports from non-EU countries.

VAT stands for Value Added Tax which is also charged on imported goods.

Tax liabilities for international transactions

International transactions are often subject to both customs duties and Value Added Tax. This can substantially increase the price of goods bought from overseas that, at first glance, seem to be a bargain.

Goods bought from within the EU are not subject to import duty, but those from other parts of the world are. The duty to be paid depends upon the type of goods, their value and country of origin.

VAT is also levied on imports, normally at the same rate it would be charged if the goods were bought in the UK. It may be reclaimed for goods that a firm buys to use itself in the business (such as a computer) but not for goods it will resell in the UK (such as towels imported from Egypt by a retailer).

Concerns about finance can include the costs of IT hardware and software, set-up expenses and tax liabilities for international transactions. In addition, future revenue is uncertain and there may be problems coping if the business grows too rapidly because of a surge in interest or orders.

Did you know?

The term 'shipping' goods means sending them from one country to another. It does not have to be on a ship. It can be by air, rail or road. Find out more about this – and the type of charges made – by clicking on 'shipping' at the website www.charliecrow.co.uk.

Distribution users

It is one thing setting up a website, promoting goods for sale and receiving orders. It is quite another fulfilling these orders, particularly if some are from remote or far-flung places overseas. The situation is even trickier if the business sells very fragile items – or even very heavy ones, such as cars or pianos.

Scale of the business

'Scale' was first mentioned in Unit 1. It relates to the distance over which the business trades with its customers. One that operates only within the UK has few problems with distribution. It simply needs to ensure that the goods are packed securely, correctly addressed and then despatched by the most appropriate method.

Businesses that distribute goods on a global basis have other concerns including:

- **special documents** which must be completed to comply with customs and other shipping regulations
- **special labelling or packaging** which is needed for some items, such as perishable or hazardous goods
- **the best method of transport** which will depend upon the type of goods and destination, as well as the cost
- **insurance** to protect the sender in case the goods are damaged or lost en route.

Did you know?

Most suppliers charge customers more for fast delivery to cover the additional costs incurred.

Activity

Amazon has separate operations in different countries. This reduces distribution problems and enables its depots to stock the correct DVD format and most popular books for each country.

Check out their different websites around the world at the bottom of the Amazon UK page and find out more about international shipping rates and restrictions either at the US site or at www.thebigproject.co.uk/amazon/.

Cost of distribution of physical goods

The cost of distribution depends upon the method used. It is cheaper to send goods by sea – and slower – than it is to send them by air. But these are not the only choices and a combination of transport services may be used.

The two most important factors to consider are the type of goods and the speed at which they must be transported. Heavy goods are more expensive to transport than those which weigh very little; bulky goods are dearer than small ones. It always costs more for express deliveries.

Did you know?

For some types of goods to be exported, the seller must have an export licence. These include drugs, cars and flower seeds.

Special requirements

Several types of goods need special attention.

Fragile goods will need to be packed very carefully with bubble wrap or other protective material. They will also be labelled 'fragile' and other handling instructions may be attached (for example 'This way up').

Perishable goods must be delivered promptly. They will be labelled accordingly and may be transported in special vehicles, such as refrigerated lorries.

Hazardous goods may need to be accompanied by special paperwork such as a Dangerous Goods Note.

BIFA stands for the British International Freight Association. Find out the type of training it offers to businesses just starting to distribute goods globally at its website: www.bifa.org.

Did you know?

Many Internet retailers are compiling a database of problem UK postcodes for which goods sent by mail frequently go missing. In the future they may refuse to dispatch to addresses on this list.

Did you know?

Many b2b firms outsource the global distribution of their goods to specialist freight forwarding agents who are experts at completing and checking the paperwork and understanding customs regulations.

Fact file

Distribution problems will depend upon the scale of the business and the type of goods. Global businesses are most likely to be affected. In addition to the costs of distribution, many goods need special handling. Services are far easier – and cheaper – to distribute.

Ease of distribution of services

Providing services on a global basis is usually easier than providing products, simply because there is no need to physically move anything. There may still be charges such as VAT to take into account, but other costs will relate purely to the costs of managing and administering the service. Examples include:

- online insurance quotes for cars, houses, travel and even pets
- booking flights online with airlines all around the world
- booking hotel rooms
- downloading music and ringtones
- downloading software
- applying for a job through an online recruitment site
- finding a house for sale at house builders' sites or estate agencies.

Activity

Check out how firms such as UPS and DHL can help businesses to distribute goods globally at www.ups.com and www.dhl.com.

Over to you

1 *In a survey carried out by Forrester Research, the following were listed as the main issues relating to operating an online retail website.*

Challenges of operating a retail website
Keeping promises to customer
Offering superb customer service
Operating an effective and reliable IT system
Converting 'browsers' into 'buyers'
Attracting new customers
Seeing competitors copy our ideas and strategies
Keeping stocks at the right level
Promoting the site but within budgeted levels

a) *Add five further problems some other businesses may face, as a result of the issues you have read about in this section.*
b) *As a group, suggest any other reasons that you can think of, which you did not list under a) above.*
c) *As a group, suggest ways in which all the issues you have listed may be minimised or overcome.*

2 *The Business Link website at www.businesslink.gov.uk gives advice on IT and e-commence. Divide into small groups and each investigate one of the following aspects of the topic on the website. Then give a short presentation on your findings to the other groups.*
a) *Best practice in web design.*
b) *Create an online shop.*
c) *Fulfilling customer orders.*
d) *Accepting online payments.*
e) *e-commerce and the law.*
f) *Maintaining your web content and technology.*
g) *Securing your e-commerce systems.*

Talking point

View 1: There are so many complications buying and selling abroad, it simply isn't worth it for most small businesses.

View 2: There are few problems in taking advantage of overseas opportunities providing businesses plan carefully.

With which viewpoint do you agree – and why?

Case study Assessment practice

When 21-year-old James Murray Wells was quoted £150 for a new pair of glasses this started a chain reaction that led not just to a new website, but a challenge to some of the biggest names in an established business, including Boots, Specsavers, Vision Express and Dolland and Aitchison!

James was still at university when he discovered a new pair of glasses would cost him as much as half his month's rent. When he found out that frames priced at £140 actually cost about £7 to produce this spurred him into action. He carried out market research, found a lab to make a pair of prototype glasses for him, then hired an optician. His next step was to find a reliable supplier. His first supplier abruptly pulled out, without giving a reason. James suspected this was because it came under pressure from his competitors. Undeterred, he recruited another.

James launched his site in summer 2004, working from his parents' house. He enjoyed planning the design, but used an expert computer programmer to build it. He spent very little on advertising – just handed out flyers in Bristol and placed an ad in a local business directory, preferring to rely on word of mouth to spread the message. And spread it did. By spring 2005 he was reporting sales of 21,500 pairs of glasses at an average price of 50 per cent less than those sold on the high street.

In response, his major competitors launched an onslaught in the trade press, criticising his business and alleging making glasses from prescription data sent in online could be potentially damaging. They argued, too, that high street opticians have additional overheads which accounts for the prices customers pay. They also claimed an online service cannot provide personal service by an optician.

James insisted that allegations about unsafe glasses were withdrawn and hired additional opticians so that customers could access an expert by email or telephone. He then started selling contact lenses. He now employs several staff and operates in business premises near Malmesbury in Wiltshire. He now wants to develop the website so that customers can see how they would look wearing different types of glasses. To find out more go to www.glassesdirect.co.uk/.

1(P) Identify the operational issues and risks that James would have had to consider before he could go online. ***(P3)***

2(P) Describe the staffing, financial and distribution issues that James would have had to consider. ***(P4)***

3(M) Analyse the advantages and disadvantages for James of launching and running his business online, bearing in mind the operational issues and risks that he has taken. ***(M2)***

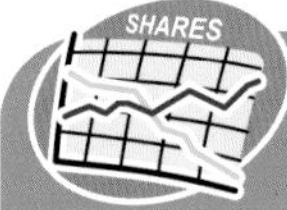

Grading tip

Analyse by identifying all the separate factors that apply, then explain the effect of each one on James' business.

8.4 Know the benefits of an online business presence

The benefits businesses gain by going online depend upon the size and type of business activity carried out. A small manufacturing company, for example, may want to reduce its costs by buying its supplies online and reducing its storage space, whereas an online store will want to attract new customers and increase sales. Many service industries and public and voluntary sector organisations go online mainly for promotional reasons, to give themselves a higher profile and provide more information about their work to the public.

Market presence

The general benefits of online trading are quite straightforward.

Global presence

The website is available to customers from any location in the world. This can vastly increase promotional and trading opportunities, especially for small businesses.

24 hour visibility

Websites never close and are available to customers 24 hours a day, seven days a week so information can be provided or orders received at any hour of the day of night – and automatically acknowledged.

Equality of presence regardless of size of business

The customer judges the business on the appearance and usability of its website, not on the size of the business. Therefore, a small business with a well-designed site and excellent service can compete, in theory, with much larger businesses.

Activity

A useful marketing strategy is to buy a domain name that links to a product benefit and advertise this – with a link to the main site. Check out www.runonflat.com, which takes you to the main Goodyear tyres site.

Rapidity of response to customer interest

A web presence provides the opportunity to respond quickly to customers – but not all firms take advantage of this. A website can provide several opportunities for customer contact, such as 'call me' buttons and email messages, but speed of response is vital. Research has shown that Internet users expect a faster response than customers who enquire by telephone or letter. If the company responds very late or, even worse, fails to respond altogether, then not only is a potential sale

Did you know?

Businesses aim for a listing on the first page of a relevant Google search by tailoring site content so that it is recognised by the 'webcrawlers'. But they must play by the rules. When BMW didn't, Google banned it for two days until it made the required changes.

Did you know?

On Google's search results, the shaded entries at the top and the blocked ones down the right are placements paid for by Advertisers on a 'pay-per-click' basis. The fee is based on how many people click through to the site.

Did you know?

Most websites provide ***links*** *to other useful, related sites. Getting on a 'links' list is an obvious benefit for firms because it encourages more people to visit their site.*

Did you know?

*A **microsite** is a miniature version of a website – which may be completely separate from the main site – which is created for a specific purpose, often linked to promoting a brand. A good example is www.runlondon.com – which is a Nike microsite.*

lost, but the image of the business is tarnished. To prevent this, nominated staff must be given the task of responding to website enquiries promptly. Alternatively, this can be handled through an automated system.

Opportunities to analyse online competition

It is quicker and easier to understand and compare competitor activities online than by visiting their stores or obtaining information on their products and services offline. Even before a business goes online it should analyse the web presence of each of its main competitors. This shows the size of the electronic marketplace and the style and content of competitor's websites. The aim should be to be at least as good – and preferably better. Businesses should also realise, though, that once they are online then their competitors can also keep an eagle eye on their operations.

Activity

Comparison websites such as www.pricerunner.co.uk, www.travelsupermarket.com and www.moneysupermarket.com have put greater pressure on online retailers to be competitive. Check these out yourself to see how they work.

Fact file

Online businesses have a higher profile through a global, 24/7 market presence. Small businesses can compete effectively with larger competitors providing they respond promptly and constantly review their products or services.

Opportunity to keep up with competitors

The aim here is to prevent competitors getting the online 'edge'. This may be by improving on the products or services offered, the speed of delivery, the cost of delivery and/or constantly reviewing the style and design of the website itself to utilise new technological developments.

Marketing benefits

Marketing benefits relate to those gains a business makes in relation to knowing more about its customers, being able to contact them easily and being able to target its products, services and the website itself to meet their needs.

Collecting market research information from online enquiries

There are several ways in which organisations can obtain information from users of its website:

Through log files and cookies Both log files and cookies (see page 341) collect information on site usage and provide valuable marketing information. Users can set their browsers not to accept cookies and not all sites use these. Every site, though, produces **log files**. These are the records created by the web server that hosts the site. They provide data such as the number of visitors to a site, the number of hits (requests for a web page or graphic) they made and how long they stayed in the site. Some ISPs will analyse their log file data for their customers, others provide the software and expect the business to produce its own reports.

Website activity software provides more detailed analysis of the log files than an ISP would provide. Subscribers can find out which search engines 'drive' traffic to the site, which pages are the most popular and which 'turn off' customers. If lots of people leave after viewing one particular page, that might be significant. Examples include www.webtrends.com and www.clicktracks.com.

Registration and order forms Many sites ask users to register, free of charge, even if they only want to access information. They may also offer customers an incentive if they will agree to receive regular email newsletters or place an order, such as a product code they can enter in the order form to receive a discount. This enables them to obtain information about the type of people who are using the site, where they live and their wants and needs.

Online market research This can range from a small pop-up questionnaire that asks a user to assess their online experience to a comprehensive customer survey sent by email to registered users of the site or to volunteers who have agreed to form an online focus group. Customers respond by clicking a link which takes them to the survey. As they answer, their replies are automatically entered into the database so that feedback is immediately analysed, even if several customers fail to respond.

Activity

Customers should be told what type of data is being collected about them. As an example check out http://www.coi.gov.uk/privacy.php which tells you what information is collected on you at one government site.

Access to new markets

Going online enables even the smallest business to make contact with a wider range of customers.

Remote locations The Internet is a boon to anyone who lives miles away from a main shopping centre because they can simply select the items they want and order them online. This vastly increases the choice of goods and services available to someone who lives in the Highlands and Islands of Scotland for example.

Customers with travel difficulties Even people who live in urban areas may not be able to get around as easily as they would wish – from mothers with young babies to the elderly. In this case, it is far more convenient to buy online – particularly when the weather is bad.

Poor transport links In many rural areas bus services are very limited and train services may be non-existent or mainly available during the rush hour. Whilst it may be worthwhile taking a long or tedious journey on a special occasion, most people would prefer to make routine purchases quickly and easily online.

Did you know?

It is the number of ***unique visitors*** *that indicates the popularity of a site, not the number of hits. This is because unique visitors are the individuals who access the site and each one may account for several hits.*

Fact file

Marketing benefits of an online presence include being able to collect market research information from online enquiries as well as being able to access new markets and provide information for customers on their mobiles or PDAs.

Did you know?

Target customers for many online businesses are busy young professionals, who simply do not have the time to search the shops for what they want or make dozens of telephone calls to find out information.

Did you know?

A 2004 report by the Disability Rights Commission (DRC) identified that 81 per cent of British websites are still not fully accessible to disabled users, despite the requirements of the DDA. To help, the British Standards Institute (BSI) has published guidance for businesses.

Customers with disabilities The Internet is a godsend to anyone who has a disability, particularly those with mobility problems, because it provides easy access to a wide range of information and competitively priced products from home. Under the Disability Discrimination Act website owners have a legal duty to ensure that services they provide on the Internet are available to disabled people.

Access from a wide range of devices

Today, websites may be viewed in a number of ways, from interactive TV in the home to a variety of mobile devices, such as WAP and 3G mobile phones, pocket PCs and PDAs (personal digital assistants). Information stored on a PDA can be downloaded to a PC quickly and easily. A Blackberry is a version of a PDA which also receives email. As WiFi zones increase in number and size in the UK, Internet use 'on the move' will increase dramatically.

Key terms

PDA stands for Personal Digital Assistant. These are small, mobile computers which operate as a planner, calendar, notebook and communications device all in one.

WiFi stands for Wireless Fidelity.

Hotzones are local area networks where users can connect wirelessly to the Internet.

Activity

Find out more about PDAs at http://www.discoverblackberry.com/discover/ and http://euro.palm.com/uk/.

Did you know?

There are now over 10,000 WiFi 'hotzones' in the UK, the largest in Canary Wharf. Nine urban centres, including Manchester, Birmingham and Leeds are also permanently online. At www.thecloud.net you can find out about those near you!

Level of response

The degree to which an organisation responds to the needs of all its potential customers will depend upon its business activity, the scale of the business and the degree to which it intends to do business online. Factors it will need to consider are given below.

Sales features

These can include delivery to door, delivery to an alternative address or the ability to select a specific delivery slot. Other options can include a gift-wrapping service, a returns service to a nearby 'bricks and mortar' store and notification by email when new goods arrive in stock.

Access from a wide range of devices

For access to a website to be possible from mobile phones and PDAs, key content on the site must be viewable on a small screen. This is done by creating a cut-down, text version of the site in Wireless Markup Language (WML) to reduce the size of the Internet page to key text only. Users can nominate specific keys to access information they need regularly, similar to storing frequently used telephone numbers, and switch easily between making calls and obtaining Internet information. This has mainly been used by sites that publish time-sensitive information, such as news and weather reports, sporting results, train and airline schedules and stock exchange quotations.

Access out of business hours

Providing online support and information through FAQs (frequently asked question) pages means that customers can obtain assistance from the website 24 hours a day, 7 days a week, regardless of whether the sales or customer service team is physically present outside normal working days. Additional information can be made available to employees who may be working from home or travelling abroad and continually need access to information at all times of day or night.

Access from around the world

This is a key benefit for many organisations that provide products or services with global appeal. Football teams such as Manchester United, FC Barcelona and Real Madrid can sell merchandise and open up their fan clubs to supporters all over the world. Businesses involved in the travel and tourist trade also benefit, such as hotels and tourist attractions, as potential customers can obtain the information they need, and make bookings, quickly and easily online.

Did you know?

Online sales features *vary depending upon the type of business. House builders and interior designers provide virtual tours of properties. Equipment manufacturers provide technical support, such as online manuals, tutorials and/or software downloads.*

Did you know?

According to a Google survey, fewer than 1 per cent of websites are published in WML. This means lost opportunities for firms who could provide their customers with key data, such as price lists and contact information, on their mobiles.

Rapid response to orders and enquiries

Businesses can respond to customers far more rapidly electronically than they can by 'snail mail'. Even if information, samples or orders have to be fulfilled using traditional systems, then the fact that customers have been able to register on the website means that the business can benefit from impulse responses and orders from customers. The addition of an email link on the website enables any customer with an enquiry or complaint to contact the company immediately. Customer service or sales staff can respond promptly with a friendly and informal email reply which helps to build good customer relations and ensure repeat business.

Did you know?

It is good practice to send customers an automatic email when their goods have been despatched. This is better than expecting them to continually check their order status online.

Online order tracking

Many websites enable customers to track their orders online to identify when it will be delivered. On the Dell website, customers can check when their computer is assembled, when it is shipped to the UK, when it is at a local warehouse and when it is due to arrive at its destination. The Royal Mail allows you to track any package sent by recorded delivery or special delivery. All you do is enter the receipt number. At Amazon you do not even need to do this – clicking in to your account will automatically show you which products have been despatched and which have not.

Fact file

The level of response online by a business will depend upon its activity and scale of operations. It may offer special sales features, access from many devices, out of hours or from around the world. It may provide a rapid response and online order tracking and benefit from being able to hold lower levels of stocks.

Reduced stockholding

Flexible and responsive electronic ordering systems means that the quantity of stock which must be held at any one time is reduced. This creates savings in terms of the amount of money tied up in stock, the space required, the number of staff needed to handle or maintain the stock as well as the security precautions and insurance that is required.

Activity

Many businesses are now setting up business blogs, to give customers continual information about new products and services. They can also check blogs online to see what customers think of them!

Use Google Blog search to find blogs on a large company that interests you. Then compare your findings.

Financial advantages

Improved cash flow through fewer bad debts

Cash flow improves if customers pay as they make a purchase. This is the case with b2c transactions online because all customers pay by credit or debit card. The card payment is always checked and authorised before the goods are dispatched, so there is less chance of sending goods which are never paid for. In b2b transactions, electronic ordering and payment systems speed up the whole process and reduce the need for lengthy credit terms. Buyers cannot make the excuse that 'the cheque is in the post'. This means fewer bad debts overall for the business (see Unit 3, page 110).

Did you know?

If a business can increase its sales without its overheads increasing to the same extent it will make higher profits.

Freedom of low-cost location

A virtual business which trades purely over the Internet has far more freedom in choosing its location than other types of businesses. If it sells goods over the Internet then it must ensure that it can obtain and despatch these without problem, so a distribution channel is still important. If the business provides a service, such as website design or writing technical manuals, then it can locate absolutely anywhere, as it can deal with all its customers or clients online.

Online businesses can sometimes save tax and therefore sell products more cheaply by moving their businesses offshore. Both Tesco and HMV now operate online stores from Jersey, where taxes are much less than in the UK.

Did you know?

An online business should not process payments for goods before they can be despatched or delivered to stay within the law.

Low overheads

The overheads incurred by an online business are likely to be fewer than those of a 'bricks and mortar' organisation. Apart from saving on rents and rates, it is likely that fewer specialist staff will be needed to give sales advice or handle orders or enquiries. Instead, the firm is more likely to employ call centre staff and/or packers and despatchers. The running costs of the website are low and online marketing campaigns are likely to be much cheaper than equivalent campaigns in the press or on television.

Key terms

Cash flow is the balance of money flowing into and out of the business as sales are made and bills are paid.

Bad debts are money that is owed but never paid and has to be written off.

Rapid payment

You cannot buy goods online unless you pay immediately. This enables a business to control its cash flow far more easily and means that there should be less need for emergency loans or overdrafts to be required to keep the business afloat during a lean period (see Unit 3, page 114).

No expensive cash handling

When you pay online your money is transferred direct to the seller's bank account. This saves the seller the costs involved with handling cash, for example:

- costs involved in recording and storing the cash, such as buying computerised cash registers and safes
- costs of collecting and transporting the cash to the bank which may require the services of a specialist security company
- costs of vetting and protecting staff who handle or carry large amounts of cash
- the cost of insurance to protect the organisation in case of theft or fraud
- the cost of security precautions to protect against fraud (see Unit 3, page 134).

Did you know?

Because it is cheaper to operate online many businesses pass on some of their savings to customers – such as insurance companies who sell policies cheaper online.

Fact file

There are many potential financial advantages to operating online including improved cash flow, a low-cost location, low-cost labour, low overheads, rapid payments, no expenses or risks involved in handling cash. In addition, a basic presence is possible with little outlay.

Talking point

View 1: A bricks and mortar retailer who sells online can never compete with an online business like Amazon because it has more overheads. It will just be undercut every time.

View 2: Retailers who cannot compete online are behind the times and need to change the way they operate. All businesses gain benefits by going online.

With which viewpoint do you agree – and why?

Ease of entry

Entering a new market, or increasing the scale of business operations, has long been difficult for many small businesses. The Internet has changed that. A simple, clear website can enable a small firm to have a global presence quite cheaply. Providing distribution costs are low and the goods are easy to send by post, the opportunities are excellent.

Over to you

1 *The benefits of an online presence should link to the aims of the business. For each of the following examples, suggest two likely aims of the business and three related benefits that are likely to be gained from an online presence.*

- **a)** *A holiday complex, e.g. www.centerparc.com*
- **b)** *A school uniform manufacturer, e.g. www.trutex.com*
- **c)** *A supplier of office products, e.g. www.viking-direct.co.uk*
- **d)** *A mobile phone retailer, e.g. www.carphonewarehouse.com*
- **e)** *A small business supplying wedding cars, e.g. www.whittoncars.co.uk*
- **f)** *A charity such as Help the Aged at www.helptheaged.org.uk.*

2 *Today many organisations in your own area will operate both offline and online. These are likely to include your local council, your school or college, local estate agents, many local companies and even your local football club.*

- **a)** *For two of the organisations named above, suggest three benefits of operating both offline and online.*
- **b)** *A friend argues that whilst a Premiership team like Manchester United should have a website, it is pointless for smaller clubs, particularly in the lower divisions. Do you agree or disagree? Give a reason for your answer and compare your views with other members of your group.*
- **c)** *Suggest three other examples of businesses (preferably local) that now operate both online and offline and, in each case, identify the benefits the organisation has gained by going online. Then compare your ideas and suggestions with other members of your class.*

Case study Assessment practice

Three Owls is one of several bird sanctuaries in the UK, dedicated to the care and rehabilitation of any wild bird that is in distress. If possible the bird is then released back into the wild. The sanctuary has many local helpers near its centre in Rochdale, as well as supporters from all over the world. Many of them keep in contact with the sanctuary through its website at www.threeowls.co.uk. Without the work of volunteers and the donations of supporters and members, the sanctuary could not carry out its work.

Three Owls is one of dozens of sanctuaries in Britain which help rescued birds and animals and which has an online presence. You can find a list of those in your area, and links to their websites at www.animalrescuers.co.uk. Just click on your area in the menu under 'Centre in the UK'. You can also find animal centres abroad under 'Non-UK sites'. These are invaluable for anyone who finds a stray or homeless animal when they are on holiday – when asking for assistance or checking the local Yellow Pages may not be very easy. All you need in that situation is Internet access and a good search engine. You can then keep in touch with the centre, and stay a supporter if you want, through its website.

The site also gives links to dozens of sites related to caring for animals as well as a jobs board if you are interested in becoming a volunteer.

1(P) Describe the benefits to a charitable organisation that decides to market its product or services online. ***(P5)***

2(M) You are a volunteer at your local animal rescue home and are involved in plans for it to go online.

a) Using the Three Owls website or the website for a sanctuary in your own area as an example, explain the potential benefits for the rescue home to go online. ***(M3)***

b) Explain the planning and implementation issues that would be involved. ***(M1)***

3(M) At the next meeting of the planning group, the members cannot decide whether to have a simple informational site or whether to ask for donations

continued ▶

Case study *continued*

online. Some also want to set up an online shop to raise funds.

Analyse the operational issues involved with these different ideas and identify the possible advantages and disadvantages and/or risks in each case. ***(M2)***

4(D) Research different animal sites online to find those you think are the most effective. Then make and justify your recommendations for your animal centre to go online. Include a suggested plan which states how the centre could prepare for, and overcome, the main operational risks involved. ***(D1 & D2)***

Grading tip

Analyse the operational issues by identifying which apply to each type of site. Then identify the possible effects on the business.

Justify your recommendations by giving reasons or evidence to support your opinion and show how you arrived at this conclusion.

9 Exploring business enterprise

About 400,000 new businesses are started in the UK each year but many fail to survive. This unit looks at the factors that help new businesses to succeed and enables you to apply these to a practical situation.

Note: If you are part of a Young Enterprise team, talk to your tutor about ways in which your activities may link to the assessment criteria for this unit.

What you need to learn

- How to prepare for running a business
- The different aspects that affect preparation for a business
- How to start and run a business

9.1 Understand how to prepare for business

Key term

An ***entrepreneur*** risks his or her own money to start a business enterprise with the intention of making a profit.

Did you know?

Many local newsagents are run by their owners who often have to get up at 5 am to sort newspapers ready for delivery.

Fact file

Not everyone has the ability to start and run a small business. And although most people start one hoping to make lots of money, for some the reality is different. They work long hours and only make just enough to survive.

Your own strengths and weaknesses

When you discuss your future career with an adviser you probably talk about subjects you like and how these link to different jobs. If you enjoy working with figures, for example, then you may look at accountancy as an option. What you may not discuss is the size and type of organisation you would prefer, whether you prefer to have a job with fairly predictable tasks to do, to travel and/or to work mainly on your own. These are just a few of the many types of business-related jobs. The point is that different people are suited to different types of employment. The aim of this section is to look at the personal skills and attitude needed to start and run a small business. This will give you an opportunity to think about your own talents and how suited you may be to this type of work.

Personal circumstances

The two main factors that affect the personal lives of small business owners are long working hours and financial insecurity. In most other types of employment these are fixed. By law, employees must have a contract of employment which states their salary and working hours. Even if the starting and finishing times are flexible, in most occupations the total hours of work are limited by the Working Time Regulations to a maximum of 48 hours a week. If you are self-employed, these regulations no longer apply. You decide your own working hours and in many cases these are far longer. This is because of the additional work required such as keeping financial and customer records, ordering stock, sending out bills and checking cash flow.

Working long hours means that there is less time to spend with family and friends. This may not matter too much if an entrepreneur is young and unattached but this situation often changes. Partners of business owners need to be very understanding, especially when there are children involved, too.

Another factor which affects the owner's family is uncertainty about money. Starting a business involves risk and, particularly in the early days, income could be low. This means that, at least temporarily, there may be little money spare for new clothes or holidays, as any profit is immediately ploughed back into the business.

Activity

Monitor the opening hours of small shops in your neighbourhood. Then think about the jobs that need doing outside those hours. If you know the owner, find out how many hours he or she works each week. Compare your findings as a group.

Experience

It is obviously helpful if a person starting a business has already had some relevant experience. This could be:

- experience of working in a similar type of business
- some involvement in running a small business.

Some businesses are started by people with little direct experience but they have found out as much as they can first and are prepared to learn from their mistakes.

Did you know?

Being involved in a Young Enterprise business can give you useful experience for running a business.

Skills, knowledge and abilities

Skills and abilities are personal attributes which enable people to carry out tasks. Knowledge is information which could be obtained from other people, trade associations, books, journals, and so on.

Activity

What skills do you think Paul Stanyer (see opposite) learned in the travel company that proved useful for running his own business? Discuss your ideas as a group.

Did you know?

Paul Stanyer set up a successful business providing taxis for independent travellers going to and from airports. He already had several years' experience as a manager in a large travel company before he started out on his own.

Some people learn a trade such as plumbing by serving an apprenticeship while working for an employer. When they are fully skilled, they start their own business by becoming self-employed. They can do this because they possess all the technical skills required.

However, there are other skills which new business owners need. Although some vary depending on the type of business, others do not and these include:

- being able to market and sell the product or service effectively
- good organisational abilities so that work is scheduled efficiently
- understanding how to record and analyse financial information
- good personal skills for building customer relations.

Key term

Aptitude is the ability to learn a skill quickly.

One way of assessing the skills needed for a particular business is to write down all the tasks that must be done. For each one, the owner should carry out the following assessment.

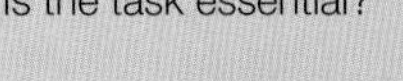

Is the task essential?

If YES → Can the owner perform it competently already?

If NO → Could the owner quickly learn how to do it?

If NO → Can the owner afford to employ someone with these skills?

If NO → The business idea must be rethought

Later in this section you will complete a checklist to help you to assess your own aptitude to start and run a small business.

Areas for development or improvement

Most successful business owners will admit that, usually in the early years, they made mistakes and learned from them mainly because there was a lot they did not know at the beginning. The important message is that successful business people *develop and improve*. The skills required for this to happen are as follows.

Did you know?

Successful entrepreneurs do not delude themselves that things are going well when they are not, or that they are good at something when the evidence says the opposite.

Observation skills This means being alert to what is happening – for example, by observing patterns or trends in sales.

Identifying causes or reasons This involves considering the factors that contribute to causing events or situations – for example 'Why aren't I attracting more younger customers?'

Willingness to adapt The owner must be prepared to change, even if this means changing personal behaviour or being self-critical – for example 'I must remain calm when customers criticise' or 'That idea of mine didn't work'.

Suitability for self-employment or a small business

Ultimately, individuals can never be sure that they can successfully start up and run a business until they try, although it is possible to look at some broad attributes. On page 371 you can assess your own aptitude for running a business.

Fact file

Everyone has to learn and develop as their careers progress. However, people running small businesses have to be particularly adaptable.

Contributing to a business

Own contribution

If you work for an employer, your contract of employment states what is expected of you. Broadly, you will be expected to contribute in the following areas:

- skills, knowledge and expertise relevant to your job
- your time during working hours
- enough effort and commitment to get the job done to a certain standard by a stated deadline.

Activity

Think about a small business you know well. Write a list of skills which you think the owner would need at the start. Then think of additional skills the owner may have learned through experience. Compare your list with those made by other members of your group.

If you run your own business the contribution you make will be over a much broader range. This includes the following.

Personal time When people work for an employer their work time is clearly defined. Self-employed people often say that they are hardly ever 'off duty'; that the business is their life.

Money In the early days, a business needs money to get it started. Often owners provide this from their personal savings.

Space For some types of business, separate premises are not needed and the owners use space at home – perhaps a spare bedroom.

Ability Running a small business requires a broader range of skills than are needed in conventional employment.

Personal savings

All businesses need money to get started – known as **start-up capital**. This is needed before the business starts earning income, which can be used to pay the running costs (see Unit 3, page 91). On page 386 you will learn about the various possible sources of start-up capital but an obvious one is the owner's own money. Many entrepreneurs use their own savings and may even remortgage their home to raise money to start a business. If the business fails then some, if not all of the money could be lost (see also page 390).

The other financial 'contribution' which may be necessary is a drop in earnings. If someone leaves employment to work for themselves, they may earn less money – particularly in the early stages. They may even have to use personal savings as living expenses for a time.

Key terms

Start-up costs This is the money spent before a business begins trading.

Running costs This is the money spent by a business on a day-to-day basis when it is up and running.

Availability of time

People who run small businesses often say that one advantage is that they have no boss to tell them what to do and when. The disadvantage is that they often have to work longer and more irregular hours. Even a shopkeeper who only opens from 9 am to 5 pm may have to spend some time in an evening compiling financial records or re-ordering stock.

Many people who run their own business have to be prepared to sacrifice their leisure time and work at times when their friends may be watching television or going out. They must also remember to schedule time to relax. No one can work for 16 hours a day over a long period without any ill-effects.

Did you know?

Rudi Budhdo won a national award for being the hardest working business person. He runs a fashion business and is reckoned to work 115 hours a week.

Impact on working and personal life

Many people start off their business whilst they are still employed by an organisation. The advantage is that they still have a steady income and do not depend on the unpredictable income from the new business. The disadvantage is that time for their new enterprise has to be found outside their normal working hours, such as in the evenings and at weekends. This will mean there is even less free time. This is why anyone considering starting a business needs to talk it through with close family members who would be affected by the decision.

Did you know?

Many contracts of employment have clauses that try to restrict employees from setting up a competitive business or having another job at all.

Barriers to starting/running a successful business

The mental approach to starting and running a successful business needs to be a curious mixture of both optimism and pessimism. Problems and obstacles cannot be avoided and must be met head on. The business owner must consider what could go wrong and make plans to overcome any perceived difficulties.

Typical potential barriers to starting and running a business are:

- not enough time
- lack of technical and business skills
- insufficient start-up money
- too few customers.

Did you know?

Reasons given for small businesses failing include:

- *customers going bankrupt*
- *overtrading – trying to expand too quickly so that there is not enough money to pay for goods*
- *high interest rates charged on money loaned to the business.*

Activity

Do you know of any small businesses that have closed in your area? What factors do you think contributed to this? Compare your ideas as a group.

Professional help

One way to overcome many barriers is to seek professional help. There are many sources of help available to people planning to start a business (see page 400). Two important sources are:

- **the Business Link network**, financed by the government. The government is keen to support new enterprises because they boost the economy by providing employment and, hopefully, making profits
- **high street banks**, which employ professional advisers to work with new entrepreneurs if they are asked to loan money for a business start-up. This is sensible because they do not want the business to go bankrupt whilst it owes them money.

Did you know?

It is in the Government's interest to support new businesses because business owners pay tax on their profits.

The most important point is that the prospective entrepreneur should seek as much advice as possible – from several sources – and then *act on it*. Unfortunately, people do not seek advice because they think it is unnecessary or because they are too proud or nervous to ask.

Activity

Access Business Link online at www.businesslink.gov.uk to see what it offers. You can find the address of your local Business Link by entering in your postcode.

Benefits of running a business

Personal objectives

There are several reasons why people go into business for themselves. These include the following:

- To make money. Some people aim to get rich, other want to make more than they could if they worked for someone else. Others just want to make enough to live on comfortably.

- They spot a business opportunity, for example they see a small business is up for sale.
- They have a good business idea. This may be a new type of product or service or a gap in the market which could be filled, such as opening a newsagent's shop on a new estate.
- A change in circumstances, such as being made redundant or inheriting some money.
- Personal satisfaction of seeing the successful end results of their own work.
- To have more control of their lifestyle. Some small business owners can make enough to live on and only work two or three days a week.
- To turn a hobby, which they would do anyway, into a business.
- To provide work for family members.

For most people, more than one of these would apply.

Activity

Bill Gates co-founded Microsoft. It probably helped that he was born with a million dollar trust fund set up by his grandfather and used computers from being a small child. Read more about his background, skills and aptitudes at http://en.wikipedia.org/wiki/Bill_Gates.

Business objectives

Objectives are targets which people set to help achieve their aims – as you saw in Unit 1 (see page 22). For example, one of your objectives should be to achieve a good grade in this unit of your BTEC First in Business. Setting objectives in business helps to focus people's minds on what needs to be done to make the business a success. Business objectives will link with the main aims of the businesses and will specify short-term targets which must be met to achieve these, such as for example:

Fact file

People who offer professional advice have often run businesses themselves.

Activity

Good objectives are SMART (see Unit 1, page 22). Identify the objectives opposite that are SMART and any that are not and justify your choice.

- to make a profit of £20,000 next month
- to have a sales turnover of £150,000 over the next two months
- to move to larger premises in six months
- to provide the highest possible quality service
- to keep consumable stock levels down to two weeks' usage.

Activity

As a group, suggest reasons why a small business should be careful not to invest too much money in stock – either for resale or for using in the business, such as office stationery.

Profitability of the business

The subject of profitability is covered in Unit 3, page 93. The same basic principles for small businesses are similar to those for large organisations. The main points are as follows:

- the profit figure is found by subtracting the total expenditure from the total income figures
- profit can be used to pay an income to the owners and for re-investment to improve and expand the business
- business owners, particularly those of small businesses, have to strike a balance between the income they take and the amount they re-invest. In the early years some try to take as little income as possible so that the business can grow faster
- tax is levied on the profit in different ways depending on the legal status of the business (see page 373)
- the profit figure is one of the best ways of measuring the success (or otherwise) of the business
- if profits are low, or worse still the business makes a loss, it could be forced to close down.

Other considerations

Other potential benefits of setting up and running a small business are often personal to an individual. There may be a positive impact on the personal and working life, particularly if employment has been poorly paid or the hours worked have been very unsociable. For some types of business, the flexibility of working hours can be very useful for organising childminding, holidays and leisure activities. Many people also feel more in control and less stressed if they are their own boss. They also achieve far more job satisfaction working at something they love doing.

Over to you

1 *Assess your own aptitude to run your own business by deciding whether, for you, each statement is True or False.*

- *A I am prepared to take a reasonable risk even if it could lose me money.*
- *B I am good at finding people who can help or advise me.*
- *C I can take criticism and learn from it.*
- *D I generally feel confident and able to overcome problems.*
- *E Having a variable income would not bother me.*
- *F I can work long hours (evenings and weekends) if necessary.*
- *G My family and close friends would support me if I needed them.*
- *H I can handle money and always have enough for essentials.*
- *I I can usually persuade people round to my way of thinking, so I should be able to sell my product or service.*
- *J I am well organised and rarely or never lose things.*

Check the number of 'True' answers with the analysis on page 404.

Final point. If you are feeling brave, you could ask a close friend or a family member to see if they agree with your answers – but be prepared to hear a few home truths you may not like.

2 *Emma has started doing a self-evaluation which might give her ideas about the types of businesses for which she would be suited – and the possible disadvantages, too!*

My skills, talent, aptitudes, interests/hobbies, work experience, etc.
Quite artistic/creative
Can drive
Like caring for animals
Work experience (school) at a vets – enjoyed it
Enjoy IT but only basic qualifications

Likes
Exercise and keeping fit
Going out
Listening to music

Dislikes
Working with figures
Getting up early

Ideas
Dog walking (rainy days?)
DJ-ing (need equipment – cost?)
Cattery or kennels
(cost of setting up/no holidays?)

Either by copying Emma's format, or by adapting this to suit yourself, identify your own strengths and weaknesses and see what ideas this generates. Then think about possible disadvantages for each one.

When you have completed it, talk it through with a colleague or with your tutor. Answer any questions they may ask and be prepared to defend any decisions you might have made with appropriate evidence.

Talking point

View 1: Owners of businesses should live frugally and put most of the profit back into the business so that it can expand.

View 2: Owners of businesses should have most of the profit for themselves. They work hard and deserve it.

With which viewpoint do you agree – and why?

Case study Assessment practice

At school, Alastair Lee did not have a clue what he wanted to do. His parents owned a bakery and he had always felt that he would run his own business, too. Despite that, when he left school he felt under pressure to find a 'career' rather than just work for his parents. He was very fit, mainly through his love of sports and climbing, so decided to try for the fire service. He was quite devastated when he just missed being selected – and then had to think of something else to do.

He could not imagine working indoors or in a routine job – or even for an employer. So he indulged his passion by travelling to Australia to go climbing, taking unusual photographs of the cliffs and mountains he tackled with his trusty Instamatic camera. On his return, he researched possible publishers who would be interested in his idea of writing a climbing guide to Oz. Cicerone Press, which publishes guide books, was duly convinced and produced *Oz Rock*, Alastair's first book in 1997. Alastair's next climbing adventure was in New Zealand. Before he left he emptied his bank account to buy an SLR camera with the aim of taking photographs that would 'blow everyone away'. Despite returning with stunning photographs, this time finding a publisher proved more difficult. Undaunted, he wrote his book anyway, commissioned a printer and published it himself. He supplemented his writing by giving talks about his trips to schools, colleges and universities – to help finance further trips to Canada, Turkey, China, Morocco and, most recently, Bolivia.

Today Alastair has climbed in six continents and is established as one of the UK's top mountain film makers and his local area's foremost landscape photographer. He produces calendars, fine art prints, books and films. In 2004 he teamed up with fellow film maker Dave Halsted to produce *Twice Upon a Time in Bolivia*, which has been a finalist at several international mountain film festivals and has won three top awards. Their film *Storms* won two awards at the Kendal Mountain Film Festival 2005.

Alastair is convinced that self-belief, persistence and the ability to learn from experience are key factors in his success. He never worried that he had no formal training or qualifications in photography or film making. He read books and magazines, talked to experts and continually worked at improving his skills. Alastair also admits that his first colour photo book was a commercial disaster. He ended up £12,000 in debt but learned a lot from it and immediately started working on *Forgotten Landscape*, which has sold over 2,500 copies.

Alastair enjoys giving talks to students about his exploits. You can read more at his website www.posingproductions.com or, better still, ask your school or college to book him – not just to talk about climbing but to tell you more about his very different but extremely successful business!

1(P) Describe how knowing his personal strengths and weaknesses has helped Alastair by answering the following questions:

- **a)** Why did Alastair decide to work for himself instead of choosing to be employed?
- **b)** Identify the strengths and/or skills Alastair has that have helped him in his chosen business.
- **c)** For *four* of these skills, explain how they have directly contributed to his business success. ***(P1)***

2(M) Find out more by going to www.posingproductions.com and then explain, using examples, four benefits you think Alastair gains from running his own business. ***(M1)***

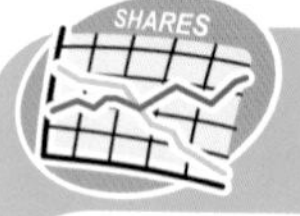

Grading tip

A good explanation provides details and examples to support the arguments you are making.

9.2 Know how different aspects affect preparation for a business

Regulations and laws for small businesses

All businesses have to abide by the laws of the land as well as specific regulations that apply to their type of business. Although there are too many different laws and regulations to list here, it is possible to assess those most likely to apply to any business. Do this by identifying its legal status, the statutory regulations that apply to any business and those regulations which relate to specific types of businesses.

Legal status

In Unit 1 (page 4) you saw that there are several different types of business ownership. The most appropriate options for an entrepreneur are usually sole trader, partnership, private limited company (Ltd) or franchisee. Each of these has different advantages and disadvantages, which are shown in the table below. In each case the choice affects the legal status of the business and the owner – which has other implications for the way the business must be run.

As a sole trader or a partner you will be self-employed. You will not pay income tax on a PAYE (pay as you earn) basis like employees. Instead you must complete a tax return and then pay the income tax you owe twice a year.

Legal status	Advantages	Disadvantages
Sole trader	Freedom to do things the way you want to Minimal reporting to government bodies	Unlimited liability Lonely existence Need to have a wide range of skills – marketing, finance etc.
Partnership	(As for sole trader) + Shared problem-solving More money to invest	(As for sole trader) + Risk of disagreeing on key issues One partner may not work as hard as the other but still take 50% of profit
Private limited company (Ltd)	Liability for debts limited to the amount of money invested Opportunity to attract more money from additional private shareholders Seen as a more solid enterprise by banks and customers	Additional regulations and paperwork. In some cases accounts may have to be independently audited Accounts have to be sent to Companies House as well as HM Revenue and Customs
Franchise	Product/service already designed/known Training, support and advertising provided Could be halfway stage for someone who wants to own their own business	Franchisor charges a fee and takes a share of the profit There is a limit to how much freedom the franchisee has to make own decisions

■ *Advantages and disadvantages of types of legal status*

Key terms

Unlimited liability The business owners can lose their personal assets, such as their house, to pay off the business debts if the business fails.

Limited liability If a business gets into debt the liability of the owner(s) is limited to the amount they have invested. Personal property is safe.

Did you know?

A small private limited company pays corporation tax not income tax.

Did you know?

In a partnership, all the active partners are 'jointly and severally liable' for the debts. This means that if one partner disappears, the other is responsible for all the debts incurred, not just half of them.

The process for starting a business legally

All businesses have to inform one or more government bodies about their business at the time it is being formed, or shortly afterwards. HM Revenue and Customs (HMRC) must *always* be informed because tax is due from profits.

Sole traders must inform HMRC within three months of starting the business. After this they have to complete an annual self-assessment tax return and pay income tax on their profit. In addition they pay a fixed rate National Insurance contribution, called class 2 and another contribution based on their profit – called class 4. Owners who use their own name do not need to register this, but if the owner uses a different business name to his or her own, then the stationery and premises must also include the name of the owner. A sole trader is personally liable for all debts incurred by the business.

A partnership must also follow the same procedure and the partners must notify HMRC of their existence. Although not compulsory, it is advisable for a Partnership Agreement to be drawn up by a solicitor. This will state the share of the profit each receives (important for tax purposes) and also what decisions both partners have to agree on. One form of partnership is where one (or more) partners, called **sleeping partners**, invest money in the business but play no active role in day-to-day decision making.

Limited companies must be registered with Companies House. The documents required are a Memorandum of Association, which sets out the structure of the company, and the Articles of Association which explains how it will operate. At least two people must set up the company by investing money in it. They are called shareholders because they each own a 'share' of the business. They are also directors and one is the company secretary. They will receive a dividend payment based on the number of shares that they hold. They will probably also work for the company as employees and receive a salary. Limited companies with an annual turnover of over £5.6 million must have their statutory annual accounts audited and send a copy to Companies House. Returns detailing directorships and shareholdings have also to be submitted each year.

Franchising Franchisees can choose which legal form of business they wish to set up – some are sole traders, others form private limited companies. They then have to follow the appropriate registration and reporting procedures. The franchisee also has to comply with any rules and administrative tasks imposed by the franchisor (see Unit 1, page 4).

Did you know?

A limited company has a separate legal entity, distinct from the shareholders and directors.

Fact file

People who start businesses have to decide what type of ownership they want to have. This affects the legal status. The type of ownership can be changed later, if this would be appropriate.

Activity

Company formation agents specialise in setting up limited companies. Find out how to form a company by searching for these agents on Google and seeing what they do and how much they charge.

Statutory regulations and laws

All businesses are affected by some forms of legislation. These can be divided into six broad categories as shown in the table below.

Category	Examples
Business formations and operations and the payment of tax	Partnership Act, Companies Acts
Health and safety in the workplace	Health and Safety at Work Act, Workplace (Health, Safety and Welfare) Regulations, Health and Safety (Display Screen Equipment) Regulations
Employing staff and discrimination	Employment Act, Employment Relations Act, Working Time Regulations, Race Relations Act, Disability Discrimination Act, Sunday Trading Act
Paying staff	National Minimum Wage Act, Equal Pay Act
Information and data handling	Copyright Act, Data Protection Act
Selling goods and giving credit	Sale of Goods Act, Consumer Protection Act, Trade Descriptions Act, Consumer Credit Act, Distance Selling Regulations

■ *Laws and regulations applying to all businesses*

Activity

Companies House regulates all limited companies in two ways. It requires the business to be registered when it starts, then it requires annual company accounts to be submitted. Find out about the information it provides on UK companies at www.companieshouse.gov.uk/.

However, there are many more specific laws and regulations that might apply depending upon the type of activities being carried out by the business. A few examples are given below.

- Establishments which deal with food handling have to comply with food safety laws and those that apply to food labelling, weights and measures and food handling.
- Road haulage and distribution companies have to monitor and regulate the hours their drivers spend driving and comply with laws relating to safe loads.
- Organisations that deal with large amounts of money, such as travel agents and solicitors have to comply with money laundering legislation.
- Businesses that operate a website to sell or market their products must comply with regulations such as the E-commerce (EC Directive) Regulations and the Distance Selling Regulations.
- Many businesses have to comply with environmental legislation relating to air, water and noise pollution, the disposal of waste materials and the use of packaging (see page 386).

Did you know?

Most firms that employ staff must have Employers' Liability Insurance to protect themselves against claims for injuries or accidents that might occur at work.

Activity

Find out about environmental legislation that relates to small businesses at the Net Regs website at www.netregs.gov.uk

Activity

Many business owners complain about the amount of legislation or 'red tape' they have to comply with. The organisation that lobbies the government about this cause and others is the Federation of Small Businesses. Find out more about this organisation at www.fsb.org.uk/.

Licences

Licences give businesses permission to carry out various types of activity. They are issued by several local and national government bodies. For example, a take-away food shop may need to contact the following authorities when it starts up:

- the local authority if the business is located in a restricted parking zone – to have permission to park a trade vehicle
- the local fire authority for a fire certificate
- the Information Commissioner if customer details are kept or a CCTV is used
- the local authority if chairs and tables are to be placed on the street outside the shop.

Did you know?

The Licensing Act 2003 has meant that licences are required for premises that sell alcohol or provide entertainment. Personal licences are required for those who run these establishments.

Activity

Go to the website for your own local authority and search under 'licences' to find six types of organisations in your area which need a licence. Then check the restrictions on obtaining a personal licence, if you wanted to run your own catering business.

Formal records

All businesses have to keep records. Large organisations probably record millions of facts every day, ranging from customer purchases to staff accidents. All records fall into two main categories: those required by law and those which help to run the business. Some of the more important records which need to be kept are given below.

Leasing arrangements Rather than buy large items of office equipment (such as a photocopier), premises or vehicles, businesses sometimes lease them. This means that the business does not have to find the money to buy the item outright. Instead a fixed amount is paid monthly. Sometimes maintenance is included in the leasing arrangement and this will be stated in the formal contract.

Tax returns Self-employed people (e.g. sole traders and partners) complete a self-assessment tax return and send it to HMRC once a year. The form has space for allowable expenses, which are deducted from the income to calculate the amount of tax due. HMRC has the right to investigate people's finances if it is unhappy with the information supplied. For this reason, many businesses employ professional accountants to complete their tax return. It is also essential that businesses keep complete, detailed and accurate records of *all* sales and purchasing transactions including salaries paid.

Limited companies have to send financial summaries (profit and loss accounts and balance sheets) to HMRC and Companies House every year.

VAT returns Value Added Tax (VAT) is a tax charged on most sales transactions. VAT-registered businesses can reclaim the VAT they pay on most purchase transactions. Businesses with a turnover of (currently) more than £60,000 must be VAT registered and send a VAT return to HMRC, normally every quarter. The business can be visited at random by a VAT inspector to check the financial records and VAT account.

Did you know?

All documents relating to a tax return must be kept for at least six years in case of investigations by HMRC.

Did you know?

Many standard computer packages allow businesses to store and process customer, supplier and financial information. Find out more at www.sage.co.uk.

Activity

According to the HSE, about 600,000 people are injured or become ill because of work each year and small businesses suffer more than large ones when employees are absent. The HSE argues that preventative safety measures are cost effective. Find out more at www.betterbusiness.hse.gov.uk.

Then visit www.riddor.gov.uk to find out more about RIDDOR, the type of incidents that must be reported and the information that must be provided.

Key term

PAYE stands for Pay As You Earn. It applies to all employed people who receive a pay slip showing how much tax the employer has deducted from their pay.

Health and safety All businesses with premises have to inform either the local authority or the Health and Safety Executive (HSE) area office that they exist and give the name and address of the business. If the business employs five or more people then a formal risk assessment has to be carried out and the results recorded. Businesses of this size have also to produce a written safety policy. All businesses have to report serious accidents and incidents under the RIDDOR regulations (see below). An HSE inspector can visit any industrial premises to investigate an accident or complaint or inspect the premises. Offices and shops are visited by an environmental health officer employed by the local authority.

Activity

Find out more about the work carried out by environmental health officers by searching under 'environmental health and careers' on Google.

Keeping and submitting business records

Because businesses have to collect and store several types of records the first step is to ensure that the information is stored systematically so that it is easy to retrieve – which normally means a manual or electronic filing system. Many types of records can now be submitted online, such as tax returns, VAT returns and accident reports.

Regulations and laws relating to records

There are two main Acts related to income tax, one relates to the deduction of tax from employees pay under the PAYE system, the other is concerned with other forms of income, particularly self-employment income. The requirement to file company reports and financial summaries for limited companies is written into the Companies Act. VAT is collected under the Value Added Tax Act.

Safety records and incident reporting are required under the Health and Safety at Work Act.

Activity

Visit the HMRC website at www.hmrc.gov.uk and find out what items are exempt from VAT and what items are zero-rated. Also check if the current minimum turnover limit for VAT registration is still £60,000.

The importance of completing and keeping correct records

It is important to complete and keep correct records for legal reasons, but there are other reasons, too, including:

- to monitor financial performance such as profitability and cash flow on a regular basis
- to monitor sales trends – for example are some products selling better than others?
- to check that customers are paying their bills on time
- to make sure that the business's own bills are paid on time.

Marketing and sales

Commercial businesses cannot exist without customers. Marketing is involved with attracting new customers and then keeping them. In small businesses, the owner often meets customers face to face which means that good interpersonal skills are essential.

Reaching and retaining customers

When businesses provide a personal service, such as plumbing or hairdressing, the owner is in direct contact with the customer. The main issues in these cases are how customers find out about the business and how they decide which business to choose.

When a business supplies a product, there are more ways of getting the product to the customer. This is sometimes referred to as **sales channels**. The main options are:

- **Direct selling** either by having a shop or visiting customers. Normally, for a shop to be successful, it has to be in a good location with plenty of passing trade. Visiting customers have the advantage of face-to-face contact but this is expensive and time-consuming.
- **Selling to wholesalers.** This reduces distribution costs but there is no direct contact with customers.
- **Distance selling** using the telephone, direct mail and/or the Internet. This has the advantage of being inexpensive but there is less opportunity to interact with customers and there are several regulations about this type of selling.

Businesses could use a combination of these channels. Once a customer has made a purchase, it is important to encourage them to buy from the business again. This is where using different sales channels is useful. For example, a customer could make an initial purchase via the Internet and then be informed about new products by direct mail as well as by email newsletters.

Talking point

View 1: The government should increase legislation to improve health and safety and the environment and to ensure that businesses treat employees fairly.

View 2: Too much legislation takes up valuable time for businesses and stops them making more money. Legislation should be kept to a minimum.

With which viewpoint do you agree – and why?

Fact file

All business owners must find out and obey the laws and regulations that apply to their particular business. Even the smallest business may need one or two licences allowing it to trade. All businesses must keep accurate and correct records and submit these as required.

Did you know?

Customer relations is covered in depth in Unit 2 and Personal selling is covered in Unit 7.

Customer care

Customer care means looking at every aspect of the business which can affect the customer and trying to make them as good as possible. For example:

- the product or service exactly matches customers' needs
- customers get value for money
- orders/services are delivered promptly and efficiently
- people in direct contact with customers are professional and friendly
- customers are kept up to date with developments
- an excellent after-sales service is provided which includes advice when needed
- complaints are dealt with promptly, courteously and thoroughly.

Did you know?

***E-marketing** relates to electronic methods of promoting the business, such as by text messaging, email or online. The next application is predicted to be business blogs in which the firm keep customers up to date about new developments.*

Activity

Working in groups, each choose a different type of business and write down all the factors you think contribute to good customer care. Then compare notes to find similarities and differences. Aim to choose a range of different small businesses such as a driving school, a clothes shop, a takeaway, a newsagent, to see how they compare.

Did you know?

Many businesses use this information to carry out a SWOT analysis, in which they analyse strengths, weaknesses, opportunities and threats relating to the business. You can find out more about this, as well as how businesses assess their competitors and customers by selecting the Competition, business success and failure options at www.bized.ac.uk/educators/level2/index.htm.

Marketing information

Marketing relates to everything which a business does to identify and satisfy potential customers. Whereas market research (see below) mainly relates to finding out about potential customers, marketing information applies to all information relating to the market as a whole. This can include:

- the actions of competitors in the market
- the views, thoughts and actions of existing customers. This is the main reason why Tesco runs its loyalty scheme – so it can analyse customer spending habits and target specific goods and special offers to each member
- external research about trends in the market, such as that undertaken by Mintel or Euromonitor.

Market research

Market research is concerned with finding information about existing and potential customers. This is particularly useful when someone is planning to start a new business. The aim is to build up a profile of the **key customer**. The information required will depend on the product or service being offered and may include the following:

- personal factors, such as age, gender, culture, occupation, income, family size, lifestyle and leisure activities
- location
- attitude to price
- the products/services they currently use
- the potential size of the market.

There are two main ways to carry out market research.

- **Primary research** is where information is obtained directly from customers. Methods include interviews, questionnaires, analysing purchase records and focus and feedback groups.
- **Secondary research** uses published information such as electoral rolls, Yellow Pages, newspaper reports, articles in trade journals etc.

Activity

Turn back to Unit 1, page 36 and refresh your memory about the ***marketing mix*** *– in particular the four Ps.*

Activities

1 *Find out about the type of market research reports published by large organisations online at www.mintel.co.uk and www.euromonitor.com and www.keynote.co.uk.*

2 *In small groups, design a short questionnaire to discover what people think about a local cinema. Then exchange it with another group. Complete and assess the other group's questionnaire and decide its effectiveness by evaluating how useful the information would be to the manager. Give feedback to each other and see if this can help you to improve the questionnaire you first designed.*

Did you know?

Today many organisations recruit customer feedback groups online to answer questionnaires sent by email.

Key terms

Marketing mix is the combination of decisions which a business makes about key areas which influence sales – product, price, place and promotion.

Primary market research is information directly from staff and existing customers.

Secondary market research is published information relevant to a particular market.

Key customer is a profile of the customer(s) accounting for most of the business profits.

A ***Focus group*** is a small group comprising a sample of customers who give their opinions on various issues.

Fact file

The more a business knows about its customer the better its chances of improving profitability.

Analysing and meeting customer needs

Businesses need to analyse the results of their market research to identify the needs of their key customers. This helps them to decide the best composition of the marketing mix for their particular business by asking questions focused on the four Ps, such as:

- Is the **product** or service what customers want? Could it be improved or should additional facilities or enhancements be introduced?
- Is the **price** right, bearing in mind our customers' expectations and our competitors? You may think that customers always want prices to be low but this is not always true. It may be possible to increase the price and attract as many customers.
- What is the best **place** (or places) to reach our customers? Is it best to open a shop, sell online, by mail order – or all three?
- How do we **promote** our product or service? Is it best to use posters, local or national papers, specialist magazines, Yellow Pages or advertise online? Many small businesses rely mainly on word of mouth to attract customers.

Did you know?

In 1908 Henry Ford invented his 'Model T' – the first car ordinary people could afford. He sold millions. The car was very basic with little weather protection and Ford boasted 'You can have any colour you want so long as it is black'! He refused to develop it and almost went bankrupt when competitors produced more sophisticated models. Although he was tuned into customers' needs at the start he never thought these would change over time.

Competition

Very few businesses operate without some form of competition. If any competitor is more successful at satisfying customers then the business could be in trouble. For that reason, businesses need to know as much as they can about their competitors and their operations, including the following.

- How many competitors are there and where are they located?

- What are their products/services and how do they compare?
- What prices do they charge?
- What is their customer service package?
- What is their customer profile?
- What is their sales turnover?
- What is their Unique Selling Point? (See page 385)

Some of this information is easier to find for large organisations which are the subject of market research reports (see page 381). Entrepreneurs competing against smaller firms may find it better to use the following methods:

- reading competitor's adverts or leaflets
- checking press reports
- issuing questionnaires
- noting comments made by a business's own customers or sales staff
- checking out their website
- visiting the competitor as a 'customer', if possible.

Building customer relationships

All businesses aim to convert casual customers into 'regulars' who buy frequently and, hopefully, are high spenders as well. For these customers, it is particularly important that they feel that they have a special relationship with the business – normally a personal one with the owner.

This does not mean that all customers should not be treated well. What it does mean is giving extra special attention to loyal customers who are also high spenders – particularly those who also pay their bills promptly. This could include:

- keeping valuable customers informed of new developments
- taking them to lunch periodically
- getting to know them personally, such as finding out about their family, holidays, and so on
- giving them slightly better discounts
- dealing with any complaints personally.

Cost and price of product or service

Financially, the two important features about a product or service in which a business is interested are the cost and the price.

For retailers, the cost is the amount they pay their supplier for the product plus the costs incurred in running the store. Similarly manufacturers must allow for direct and indirect costs (see Unit 3, page 90).

The main considerations when the price is set are as follows.

Did you know?

Businesses which do not have any competitors are called monopolies. The government believes that this is unhealthy – that competition is better. Find out more at www.competition-commission.org.uk

Activity

Working in small groups, chose two competing businesses you know well, for example two mobile phone companies or two sandwich shops. Use the marketing mix four Ps to decide in which areas they compete. Then decide which is the better of the two in each area. Be prepared to justify your decision.

Fact file

In most businesses 80 per cent of the income comes from 20 per cent of the customers. It is particularly important for the business to fully understand these customers' needs.

- The price charged must be more than the total cost, i.e. the direct plus the indirect costs. The difference between the selling price and the total cost is profit.
- Some businesses, such as retailers, may just add a percentage to their purchase price to arrive at the selling price. This is known as **mark up**.
- Sometimes the selling price is based on value to the customer. This is the case when customers are prepared to pay a high price because of special circumstances (e.g. a shortage of supply) or because the item is a luxury good, such as designer clothes.
- Competition reduces prices because fierce rivals have to make sure that their prices are competitive.
- Sometimes pricing is tactical – to get customers to spend more overall. Most computer printers are sold below cost price to obtain customers who will buy the firm's cartridges, which make a very healthy profit.

Did you know?

Drinks and food at festivals and music events are often far more expensive than they are in ordinary shops. This is because customers cannot buy anywhere else, so the value of these items is higher than it is outside.

Fact file

A major consideration in setting prices is that the business in the long term must make a profit.

Key terms

Promotions are methods of bringing the product or service to the attention of customers and persuading them to buy.

Selling means providing a product or goods in exchange for money. The term is also used for the process of encouraging or persuading a customer to make a purchase.

Promoting products or service

Whilst promotion is one component of the marketing mix, many firms talk about their **promotional mix**. The best mix will depend upon the type of product, the target market, the actions of competitors and the budget available. The main reasons for promoting the business include:

- telling people where the business is located or how it can be contacted
- giving information on products and services
- stating their attributes and the benefits associated with buying them
- telling people about changes and improvements that have been made
- publicising special offers or events, including competitions or sales
- building up a positive image of the business.

The chart below shows some of the most common promotional methods used by small businesses selling locally.

Advertising and brand marketing	Direct and promotional marketing
Adverts in the local press and trade/professional journals Commercial radio Billboards and posters Bus and tube advertising New media, e.g. Internet adverts, by email or text message Cinema adverts	Sales literature, e.g. leaflets, brochures, catalogues, Point of sale materials, e.g. posters, display stands, LED displays, free samples Calendars Carrier bags CDs and DVDs Clothing and bags Give-aways, e.g. pens, key fobs, badges and stickers

Unique selling point (USP)

One way of assessing the potential of a business is to ask 'What is its USP?' The idea is that every business must have *something* which makes customers choose it rather than its competitors. The USP could be many things, such as:

- high quality
- lowest prices
- the only shop of its type in the area
- very friendly staff
- ample free parking.

The list is endless. The key aspect is for anyone starting or running a small business is 'What makes me special?'

Did you know?

Linked promotions *benefit more than one business, such as your student ID card giving you discounts in local shops which advertise in your college diary.*

Selling techniques

Selling means agreeing to provide goods or services in exchange for money. The most obvious selling technique is where customer and supplier meet face to face to negotiate the deal. However, sales transactions can also take place over the telephone, on the Internet, by mail order or by the customer completing a newspaper or magazine coupon. Business-to-business sales are often carried out by a formal presentation, followed by individual contact by a sales person when prices and other terms are discussed. Selling techniques are covered in more details in Unit 7, Personal selling.

Fact file

*Most businesses carry out some type of promotional activity, even if it is only placing an entry in Yellow Pages. Every business needs a **U**nique **S**elling **P**oint which makes customers prefer it to its competitors.*

Activity

Write down the names of three businesses which you know. They could be local, national or multinational. Now against each one write down what you think their USP is. Discuss your ideas as a group to see if you agree.

Personal selling

This occurs when customer and supplier meet face to face to complete the transaction. Sometimes salesmen can adopt an aggressive approach but there are sound principles which apply to good face-to-face selling:

- if the person you are dealing with represents a large organisation always ensure that he or she has the authority to make the purchasing decision
- if you get a 'yes' answer to your first question this indicates a positive start
- try to keep eye contact and listen carefully to what the customer has to say

Did you know?

The term 'pitch' is used by some service providers, such as marketing firms, when they put a sales proposal to a client. In the Dragons Den, on television, potential small business owners had five minutes to pitch their ideas to a panel to get start-up money.

- it is often better to concentrate on the benefits of the product or service, not the features. Say: 'This coffee machine produces coffee that most people prefer.' rather than 'We only use the best ingredients in our product.'

For more information on personal selling, see Unit 7, page 277.

Did you know?

The Doorstep Selling Regulations have long protected consumers who buy in their own home by giving them a seven day cooling-off period, during which time they can change their mind without any penalty. This now applies to goods bought by telephone, mail order, fax, digital television or on the Internet. See Distance Selling Regulations Unit 7, page 285.

Environmental issues

According to a survey by the Department for Environment, very few small businesses have taken positive steps to limit their impact on the environment. Many, too, did not know about the Environmental Protection Act, which affects most businesses, or about the Duty of Care Regulation, which applies to all businesses producing or disposing of waste.

Most did, however, recognise that there was a link between good practice and increased sales, as well as reduced operating costs. They also knew that bad publicity as a result of being prosecuted for breaking environmental laws was unlikely to endear them to their customers.

Activity

The Business Environmental Training Initiative (BETI) aims to educate small firms and their staff about environmental issues and predicts savings of between 1 per cent and 4 per cent for businesses that implement green policies. Find out more at www.beti.info and about the information and advice available at www.netregs.gov.uk and www.envirowise.gov.uk.

Financial issues

The ultimate test of the success of a business is how much profit it makes. Profit is needed to give the owner sufficient income and for enough money to be reinvested to help the business prosper. If the business makes a loss for some time, it will cease trading. It is therefore important that the financial health of the business is watched closely so that action can be taken at the first sign of trouble.

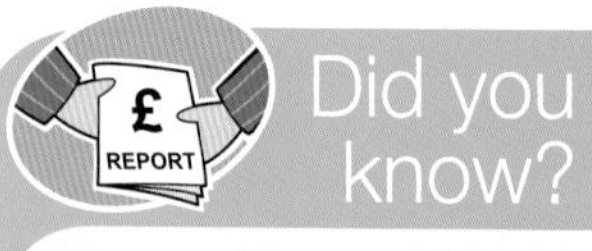

Did you know?

Sole traders and partnerships that fail go bankrupt but companies go into liquidation. This is because they have to be formally wound up as a legal entity.

Sources of finance

All businesses need money to get them started and for running costs for the first few months. The main sources of this are given below.

Own savings Many entrepreneurs have savings from previous income or may have inherited money. A major advantage of this source of money is that interest does not have to be paid. Relatives and friends can sometimes be persuaded to lend money, but they may want interest to be paid and will almost certainly want their money back at some stage.

Entering into a partnership so that there are two sets of savings to use.

Bank overdrafts An overdraft is an agreement with the bank where the customer can 'overdraw' money from the current account. Interest rates are higher than those for a loan but charged on the balance each day. They are far lower for an arranged overdraft than for one that has not been previously agreed with the bank.

Bank loans This is where money is borrowed for a fixed period and repayments (including interest) are paid monthly. Normally, banks ask for some sort of personal security, such as the owner's property which they could claim if the business defaulted on the loan. The government has set up a Small Firms Loan Guarantee system to help businesses which cannot provide security. Often, banks will offer new businesses incentives to open an account and provide an adviser.

Grants and loans There are several types of grants and special loans available from local, national and European governments.

Did you know?

Loans and grants are an example of the government's attempts to encourage more people to start their own small business. Despite this the number of people involved in entrepreneurial activity in the UK in 2005 was only 6 per cent of the population compared with 12 per cent in the USA.

Start-up costs

Businesses need money to get them started. There are two basic costs associated with starting a new business, capital costs and start-up working capital.

Capital items are those which will last for a long time. Start-up capital is needed for items such as:

- purchase of a building or rental deposit
- equipment for production, office equipment, such as a computer and photocopier, any vehicles required
- refitting a building, such as installing shop fitments or a safe.

Start-up working capital is needed to buy stock for production or resale and consumable items such as office stationery and cleaning products.

Activity

Research the section on grants and loans at the Business Link website at www.businesslink.gov.uk to find out what is available. Then visit the Prince's Trust website at www.princes-trust.org.uk and find out about funding for people under 30. If you are Muslim, note that the Prince's Trust support for new businesses complies with Shariah law.

Fact file

Start-up costs are the total amount of capital plus working capital start-up costs. This is the amount the owner needs to borrow or fund from his or her own savings. Even for a small business, there are several types of expenses over a short period of time.

Operating expenses and income

Operating costs are the routine costs incurred to keep the business running. Typical examples include staff wages, materials for production or resale, utility bills (for example gas, water, electricity), telephone and fax bills, rent and business rates, insurance, any interest payable on a loan.

Income is discussed in Unit 3, page 92. It mainly comes from customers paying for goods or services.

Activity

In a group, think of a small business which you may wish to start. Brainstorm as many possible operating costs as you can. If you are feeling adventurous, think how much each item would cost for a month.

Key terms

Cash flow forecasting This is how businesses work out how much money they expect to be in their bank account at intervals in the future.

Start-up capital is needed to pay for items which will not need to be replaced for some time.

Start-up working capital is needed to stock items which are bought repeatedly and which are financed from income once the business is underway.

Organising and controlling expenses and income and cash flow

This topic is covered in Unit 3, page 108. The main points to remember are given below.

- **Cash flow** is the measurement of how much money flows into and out of a business's bank account.
- The critical factor is the **closing balance** which gives the final amount of money in the bank at the end of the period. If it is negative, the business has not got enough money to pay its bills and could be in serious trouble if the situation continues for some time.
- Businesses should monitor creditors, who owe them money, to encourage them to pay their bills promptly. This is called **credit control**.
- **Expenses** should be carefully monitored to keep them to a minimum.
- Businesses should **forecast** cash flow to see if there is likely to be a problem.

Financial records

Recording transactions is covered in full in Unit 3, page 119 and you have already learned about the legal requirements of keeping records on page 378. Businesses also keep financial records so that they can analyse these to check on their performance. This enables them to take timely action when it is needed (see Unit 3, page 134) and check that no unexpected problems are occurring, such as fraud by staff or customers.

External organisations

The main external organisation which has the right to be given detailed information about a business's finances is HM Revenue and Customs (see pages 373–374). This information is needed for tax purposes.

Companies House receives a summary report of the finances of a limited company. Anyone can read these – for a small fee.

Activity

Many specialist organisations help new businesses to form companies and provide other specialist services. Visit Duport services at www.duport.co.uk to find out the type of help that is available.

Measuring financial success

The financial success of a business can be measured in several ways. The following are the most important.

Cash flow The closing bank balance is a measure of a business's ability to pay its debts on time. If it does not do this, suppliers may become wary and refuse to provide goods.

Costs and income Businesses aim to minimise costs and maximise income. You can learn more about this in Unit 3, page 94.

Profit This is the figure arrived at when costs are subtracted from income. Businesses normally only measure profit once or twice a year.

Assets These are also known as capital items. They could include buildings, equipment and furniture. The value of all of these would be taken into account when calculating a selling price if the business was sold.

Financial state of a business The overall performance of a business can be measured by producing a profit and loss account and balance sheet. The first summarises income and expenses to produce an overall profit figure. The second shows how all of the invested money has been spent. Ltd and Plc businesses have to provide this information.

Did you know?

*Profit can be measured as a percentage of the amount of money invested in a business. This is called **R**eturn **O**n **C**apital **E**mployed (ROCE). This figure should be higher than the interest on bank savings accounts or the owner is better off investing any savings and taking it easy.*

Financial priorities

All small businesses aim to make a profit but some entrepreneurs have different priorities to others. These link to the different business aims and objectives you read about in Unit 1.

- One may want to earn as much as possible as quickly as possible, with the aim of retiring whilst still young.
- Another may prefer a quiet life and just want to earn enough to live comfortably.
- One may be prepared to work long hours to earn enough money to expand the business.
- Another may have no wish to be rich or powerful and just invest enough to keep the business running.

Did you know?

Many business owners say that earning money is not their main objective. They enjoy meeting challenges and being in charge of their own destiny.

Did you know?

Under the Enterprise Act 2002, the penalties for responsible business owners who go bankrupt are less harsh than those where the owner has been negligent or reckless. Find out more at www.insolvencyhelpline.co.uk/bankruptcy/what_is_bankruptcy.htm.

Risk

All businesses run some risk. This is why the definition of an entrepreneur is related to being prepared to take a risk. Some of the potential problems encountered in running a business are given below.

Losing money All businesses require an investment of some sort – often from the owner's savings. If the business fails this money and more can be lost, particularly if the owner has unlimited liability, or has secured personal property against a loan.

Security of income Most employed people receive a regular salary each month. People who run small businesses have no such security. Their income depends on the success of the business and will vary from month to month. They are also unlikely to receive any payment if they are ill or when they take a holiday.

Other financial changes Setting up and running a small business often means that personal financial planning becomes more difficult. For example, banks often prefer proof of a guaranteed steady income for someone applying for a mortgage.

Over to you

1 *Research the regulations and licences that apply to different types of businesses. In your group, each person should decide on a different type of business to research.*
   a) *On the Business Link website at www.businesslink.gov.uk choose the section 'regulations' under the 'What applies to me.' heading. Work through the checklist (guess an answer if you aren't sure) and print out the final list of regulations for the type of business you have selected.*
   b) *Still on the Business Link website, go to the licences and find if any apply to that type of business.*

   Compare your list with those obtained by other members of your group who chose other types of businesses. What are the similarities and differences?

2 *Divide into small groups to prepare a marketing campaign for the business of your choice. Do this in three stages.*
   a) *Preparatory stage*
   Prepare a marketing plan which covers:
   - *how you intend to identify and reach your key customers*
   - *the market research you would undertake*
   - *the marketing information you need to obtain*
   - *basic information on your key competitors.*

   b) *Planning stage*
   Add to your plan by stating:

continued ▶

Over to you *continued*

- *how you intend to meet your customers' needs*
- *your proposed customer care package*
- *how you intend to build customer relationships*
- *your proposed selling price(s).*

c) Implementation stage

Complete your plan by deciding:

- *your unique selling point(s)*
- *the methods of promotion you will use*
- *the selling techniques you will use.*

Present your completed plan to the rest of your group in a short presentation. Be prepared to answer questions on any aspect.

3 *Your uncle is quite wealthy and you see him as a useful financial asset, if only you can persuade him to part with some of his money. You have told him you would like to borrow £5,000 to contribute towards your start-up costs and he has said he will lend you the money if you achieve a good score in a quiz he will set you. The quiz is set out below. Ask your tutor if you do not understand any of the terms used.*

For each of the questions decide which answer you think is correct. Then refer to page 404 to see how much your uncle is likely to lend you!

FINANCE QUIZ

1 The Prince's Trust is:
a) a fund set aside by Prince Charles for William and Harry
b) a charitable foundation which supports young business people
c) a new boy band

2 The following costs are start-up costs for a new hairdressing business:
a) deposit on rent, initial stock of shampoo etc., refitting the premises
b) monthly electricity bill, deposit on rent, initial stock of shampoo
c) council tax, monthly electricity bill, refitting premises

3 Bad debtors are:
a) suppliers who have been to prison
b) suppliers who do not pay their bills
c) debtors who pay a week after the deadline

4 The VAT which needs to be added to an invoice amount of £24.00 is:
a) £42
b) 42p
c) £4.20

5 Which of the following is the government body which collects taxes?
a) The Department of Trade and Industry
b) HM Revenue and Customs
c) Companies House

continued ▶

Talking point

View 1: It is better that the penalties for bankruptcy are less stringent now, as this encourages more young people to take risks and start their own business.

View 2: Reducing bankruptcy penalties has been a key factor in the record number of people who were personally insolvent in 2006 – some as young as 19 years of age – because it encourages them to run up huge debts.

With which viewpoint do you agree – and why?

Over to you *continued*

6 The main purpose of monitoring cash flow is:
  a) to make sure that all customers pay
  b) to closely monitor the closing bank balance
  c) to make sure that bills are paid promptly

7 An overdraft is:
  a) money borrowed from a bank which is repaid over a fixed period
  b) interest paid on money in a bank account
  c) approval to go into the red on a current account

8 Which of the following is a financial risk related to starting and running a business?
  a) going bankrupt and losing personal possessions secured against any loans
  b) being fined £100 for sending in a late tax return
  c) being defrauded by your staff

9 What needs to be done in order to maximise profit?
  a) maximise income and expenditure
  b) minimise income and expenditure
  c) maximise income and minimise expenditure

10 Which of the following is not an appropriate reason for a business to keep accurate financial records?
  a) to be able to send accurate information to HMRC
  b) to be able to boast to your friends about how profitable you are
  c) to carefully monitor the financial performance of the business

Case study Assessment practice

Many new entrepreneurs need an overdraft when they start their business. Alex Tew was an exception. His ambition was to become a millionaire before he went to university so that he would not leave with huge debts. To achieve this, he needed to think of something that was easy to understand and set up, would attract lots of publicity and had a good name. The result was the Million Dollar Homepage – a website that contained exactly one million pixels, on sale to (mainly US) advertisers at $1 a pixel. The minimum purchase would be $100 for a 10 x 10 pixel square (the smallest the eye can read) on which would be the advertiser's name or logo. Clicking on that would lead to the advertiser's website.

continued ▶

Case study *continued*

Alex paid £50 for the domain name and a basic web hosting package. The first blocks Alex sold to his brothers and some friends. When he had more than $1,000 he paid for a press release, which was spotted by the BBC. At this point the news also spread across the Internet, as one person after another emailed it to their friends. This generated more interest from advertisers – and the whole thing took off. Later he employed a press officer to help generate publicity and increase sales in the US. He also spent a week there, giving interviews.

Four months later Alex auctioned his last block of pixels on eBay. His total earnings from the enterprise exceeded $1 million (about £545,000).

However, the enterprise encountered a few problems. Hackers launched a DOS (denial of service) attack after Alex refused to give in to blackmail demands which caused problems for a few days.

There are now many copycat sites, but these are far less likely to be as successful as Alex's, simply because his was a 'first'. If you are tempted to set up an Internet business remember that first you need a good idea. You are also likely to need a creative domain name so that you can market your idea and attract funding. You, like Alex, will also have to comply with e-commerce laws and regulations and get up to speed with the technicalities, such as choosing a web host and getting your site designed. Finally, if your idea is unique like Alex's, it is sensible to find out more about intellectual property law and how it can be protected. You can find out more at www.intellectual-property.gov.uk/index.htm and find out more about the aspects involved in setting up an online business at www.platinax.co.uk/.

1(P) Describe how Alex addressed each of the following aspects of preparing for business:
- **a)** regulations and laws
- **b)** marketing and selling products and services
- **c)** financial issues and funding. ***(P2 part)***

2(P) a) How important was good marketing for the success of the site?
Give a reason for your opinion.
- **b)** Access the site at www.milliondollarhomepage.com and assess it from a marketing point of view. What aspects of the site help to 'sell' his idea – and Alex himself?
- **c)** Describe how small businesses prepare to market and sell products and services. ***(P3)***

3(P) From the case study and from reading the site, describe Alex's personal skills and strengths as an entrepreneur. ***(P1 part)***

4(P) Alex wants to sell posters of the completed home page. State why he has the right to do this but other people haven't. ***(P2 part)***

5(M) Explain the benefits you think Alex has gained from running his business. ***(M1 part)***

6(M) a) Analyse the different aspects that a new Internet entrepreneur would need to consider when preparing for business. ***(M2 part)***
- **b)** Describe the financial issues that could affect his or her preparation for business. ***(P4)***

Grading tip

Analysing different aspects means examining each one that applies and explaining its effect.

9.3 Understand how to start and run a business

The main focus of this section is the production of a business plan. A business plan is a comprehensive list of all the factors which need to be considered by anyone planning to start a business. It should include the product or service to be provided, type and number of customers, proposed location and forward plans. Almost all of the factors that must be considered have already been covered in this unit. The business plan brings them all together.

Special note

You will need to decide on a business which you might want to start in the future and produce a business plan. You will be assessed on the quality of the plan you produce. You may find it helpful to discuss your proposed business idea with your tutor before you start this section. Then use the activities on the next few pages to help you to develop this.

Did you know?

At the start of a business plan you should identify your personal goals or objectives (see page 369) and also the proposed legal status of your business (see page 374).

Understanding a business plan

All high street banks provide templates for a business with space to add information under the various headings. If you can obtain one of these you could complete it as part of the assessment for this unit. Alternatively, a template you could use is given on page 402.

The business idea, products or services

Although your business plan is not meant to be put into practice, you should aim to make it as realistic as possible – particularly as you will also have to evaluate it to decide how likely it is that your plan would succeed.

Fact file

New businesses start with someone having a business idea, which they think will attract plenty of customers and make money.

The first step should therefore be to think of a business you would like to set up and run and then think about the feasibility of your idea. Some ideas of how to identify a possible business include:

- identifying a shortage of goods or service – such as something you wanted but could not obtain
- thinking about small businesses you already know, such as a shop where you have worked part-time
- identifying a growing market where more and more products/services are being sold
- having a new or novel idea, like the Million Dollar website
- thinking of opportunities linked to your skills, strengths and preferences, like Alastair Lee.

One basic decision to make is whether to sell goods or provide a service or whether to make a product. Generally, making products requires manufacturing equipment which means the start-up costs are higher.

Possible customers

This subject is discussed on page 381. Basically, part of the new business planning process is to build up a profile of potential key customers and try to find out how many might buy the products or use the services.

Customers' needs

Having identified potential customers it is then necessary to work out the best place and time(s) to deliver the product or service – as you saw in the 'Over to You' activity on page 391. Both will depend upon the nature of the business. Those providing a personal service, such as mobile hairdressers and personal trainers, often have to operate in the evenings and at weekend.

Sales targets

Targets or objectives are discussed on page 369 and in Unit 1, page 22. Basically, targets are standards of performance which the business owner aims to achieve in the future. They are useful because they help the entrepreneur to focus on what needs to be achieved and work out a plan to achieve them.

The need for forward planning

Forward planning means planning for the future. This is needed because action often needs to be taken weeks or months before a planned event can happen and sometimes additional resources are required, such as extra finance. For example, a business that wanted to expand may need to get planning permission before building work can start. It may also need to borrow money to pay for the work and would have to apply to the bank for a loan. All this would take time. Similarly, a business that aims to increase its sales in six months' time will have to plan how to reach and attract new customers.

Did you know?

In 2001 newspapers reported a shortage of plumbers in London and salaries of up to £70,000 a year, so many people left well-paid jobs to go into plumbing. By 2006 the situation was exactly the opposite. There were about 1,500 vacancies for plumbers and 26,000 people on training courses.

Activity

Write a rationale for your proposed business idea and present it to your group. Be prepared to answer questions and to justify your ideas. Then listen to other people and challenge their ideas if you spot any discrepancies.

Key term

Targets are short-term goals which motivate people to try harder.

Fact file

Even the smallest of businesses need to plan ahead so that they can act on opportunities and potential problems. They are also less affected by any unavoidable delays or time lags between planning and taking action.

Starting and running a business

There are several aspects to consider when you are planning to start your business.

The needs of a business

All businesses need resources. These include:

- premises or, at least, space in which the owner can work
- equipment, such as a cash register or computer
- raw materials or stock, if goods will be made or resold
- someone to deal with customers or process enquiries. This may be the owner or additional staff may be needed
- basic consumable items, from carrier bags to printer paper.

The owner needs to list the resources that are required and work out the likely cost of each to calculate the start-up costs and to decide what tasks must be done, and in what order, before the business can start trading.

Did you know?

If passing trade is important then the location of the business can be critical. It is less important if the business will only trade online.

Activity

List the resources that you would need for your proposed business and estimate the cost of each one. Remember that you may be able to save money by buying some basic items of equipment second-hand or leasing instead of buying.

Research techniques

You have already undertaken several research techniques in this unit, for example to find out about laws and regulations that apply to particular types of business. There are basically three methods of carrying out research.

Asking people – called primary research. This was one of the methods discussed under market research on page 381. You can ask people face to face, by issuing questionnaires or by carrying out telephone research. However, it is important to ensure that the people you choose represent your key customers so that their opinions would be representative of the customers you are trying to attract.

Reading publications – called secondary research. This can include local and national newspapers, trade journals and leaflets, brochure or catalogues produced by competitors.

Online – which is the easiest way of obtaining information from the agencies and organisations that offer advice on business start-ups (see page 400). Studying competitors' websites also provides useful information.

Planning ahead and planning techniques

The importance of planning ahead was explained on page 395. Your plans state what you intend to do in the future. It is important that your plans are realistic and link to your financial targets. You cannot plan something that will cost you £5,000 if you only have £500 in the bank.

Planning techniques include:

- thinking about what you want to achieve in 12 months' time and where you want to be, then identifying the steps and resources necessary to achieve this goal
- identifying key times in the year for your business – such as Christmas for all retailers, and then planning activities linked to this
- using a wall planner to enter key events and preparations for these
- recording all commitments and 'to do' lists in a diary or personal organiser so that nothing important is ever forgotten.

Controllable and uncontrollable aspects

Controllable aspects of a plan are those parts over which the owner can take direct action. These would include:

- reducing prices to sell off surplus stock to achieve sales targets
- hiring temporary staff to cover for staff absences due to illness
- rescheduling work to meet an urgent deadline.

Uncontrollable aspects are factors that can affect the plan over which the owner has no control. Examples include:

- changes in interest rates which affect loan repayments
- competitors launching a new product or service
- the local authority introducing new parking restrictions or a one-way system that reduces passing trade
- suppliers increasing their prices.

Although uncontrollable factors usually involve an element of surprise, effective business owners try to be prepared. They do this by asking themselves 'What could really hurt my business?' They then decide if there are any precautions they can take to protect themselves and what action they would have to take if the situation occurred. This is known as a **contingency plan**.

Of course, some uncontrollable factors may change in a way that helps the business. Interest rates could fall or a competitor could go out of business.

Timing

Many markets are seasonal or have quiet times and busy times. Most new businesses like to open in time to benefit from particularly good times, such as retail stores opening in September or October and tourism-related industries in time for the summer season. Adequate time

Activity

Access the websites of two of your competitors, or two businesses that carry out the same activity you plan to do. Note down any ideas you can borrow or adapt for your own business.

Did you know?

Forgetting an arrangement or commitment in your social life or even at college may be overlooked. In business it would cost you money.

Did you know?

A corner shop called El-Jay in Greenwich specialises in African goods and people can travel 30 or more miles to buy items. The business has survived the introduction of a one-way system, a large rent increase, new parking restrictions and two large supermarkets opening opposite! A recent problem was the planned closure of a building society branch next door where customers drew cash to pay for goods.

must be allowed, though, for the business owner and staff to find their feet and for the business to get established and customers to find it. It is not a wise idea to open at the height of the busy season.

Activity

Look back to the case study about Alex Tew on page 392. What uncontrollable factor did he encounter, how did it affect him and what precautions could an Internet entrepreneur take to protect themselves? Now identify the uncontrollable factors that could affect your business and what you could do to prepare for them.

Key terms

Uncontrollable factors are events that can affect a business but over which it has no control..

Contingency plans are business plans to be brought into effect if a predicted possible event occurs.

The work that needs to be done to start and run a business

There are two main stages in planning to start and run a business.

- **The planning stage** involves having the idea, researching it, preparing a business plan and obtaining finance. Until this stage is complete the business is an idea, not a reality. Below you can see the main steps involved in this process.

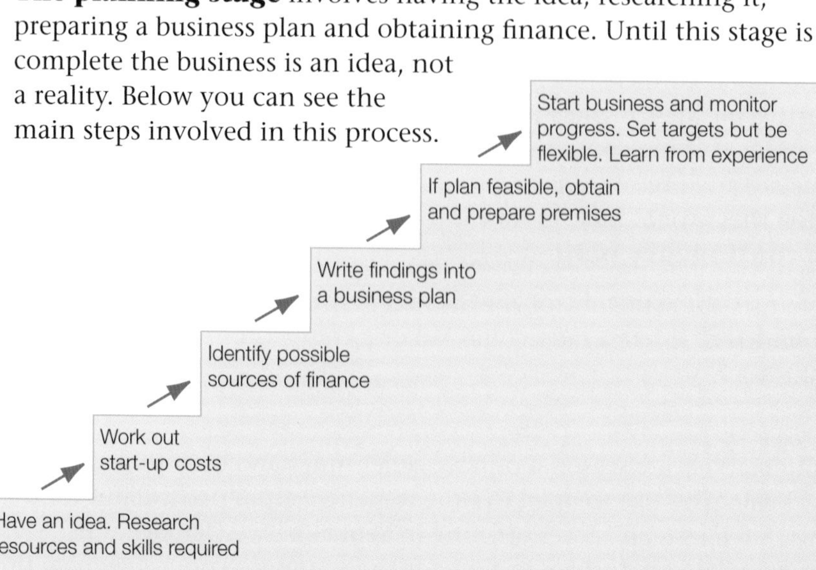

Fact file

People starting a business may want to do so in a quiet period to give them time to get used to running it. They also need a comprehensive and detailed written plan of everything that needs to be done.

- **The preparatory stage** involves putting these plans into action after finance is agreed. Most businesses plan to start trading on a certain day. Before this several tasks must be carried out so that everything will be ready on time. These will depend upon the nature of the business but for a small retailer they may be similar to the list below.

Preparatory tasks for a small shop
Obtain premises
Agree lease/rental terms
Check water, gas, electricity connected
Paint/clean premises
Install shop fittings and fittings
Buy and install equipment, e.g. cash register
Install telephone/fax line/internet connection
Buy stock
Appoint and train staff
Advertise opening

Activity

Prepare your own list of jobs that would need to be done before you could start your chosen business. Then convert these into an action plan by putting them into the most appropriate order for completion and deciding how long you would need for each one.

Next the owner needs to convert the list into an action plan using a wall chart, computer or diary. The plan should also take into account the possibility that things could go wrong, such as stock being delivered late.

When the start date approaches, the owner needs to think about the day-to-day activities which will have to be carried out to keep the business operational such as paying bills, monitoring sales and re-ordering stock or consumables.

Materials and supplies

If a business produces goods then it must regularly purchase raw materials. If goods or services are bought ready to use or sell they are called supplies. In both instances businesses need to find cheap and reliable sources (see Unit 3, page 95). They also need to decide how often to re-order materials and how much to order. This decision would depend on a number of factors, including:

- the storage space available
- the effect on the cash flow of paying for large quantities of goods
- possible discounts for bulk purchases
- the length of time from ordering to delivery. This is called **lead time**.

Whatever is decided, the business will have to decide how much stock is needed to start up and a routine system of re-ordering needs to be established.

Key terms

Order quantity is the quantity of goods ordered at any one time.

Lead time is the time period between placing an order and receiving the goods.

Activity

List the materials and supplies you would need for your business and the quantities you think you would need at the outset. Then research suppliers to estimate the likely cost.

Fact file

Materials are costs to an organisation so purchases should be made very carefully to get the best value for money.

Advice and support

People setting up new businesses need to learn a lot of new skills very quickly. Because of this, they need advice and fortunately there are many sources.

Key term

Networking is developing your business contacts to learn more and increase your business opportunities.

People

People who can give you advice include professional specialists, such as business advisers who work for organisations such as the Prince's Trust, and people who have set up their own business and have learned from experience what to do – and what not to do. Talking to several people will give you a wider range of views than simply talking to one or two, who may have quite fixed views on certain aspects of business.

Did you know?

Shrewd business people build up a network of contacts of people they can turn to for advice and support. You can find out about business networks in your area by entering 'business networks' and your town, city or area into Google.

You will also often hear professional people talk about the benefits of networking. This happens when an individual builds up a number of contacts of people who have knowledge and skills which they are prepared to share. They could be other business people (though not necessarily in the same business) suppliers or customers, for example. Do note that it is unlikely that any direct competitors will want to share their knowledge and skills with you.

Agencies and organisations offering advice and help

There are several agencies and organisations that offer help and/or advice to small businesses. The main ones are listed below.

Business Link This is a government-sponsored organisation which provides a range of support facilities to business. They can also recommend specialist agencies. You have probably already visited the website on www.businesslink.gov.uk. You can find the location of the local branch by entering your postcode. Business Links can also refer enquirers to local Enterprise Agencies.

Banks If someone approaches a bank for a loan to start a business, they would normally be invited to meet a specialist adviser to discuss the business plan. This person would also be available for consultation in the early days of the business.

Your local authority is likely to offer a range of advisory services and may also offer funding for new business start-ups, too.

Solicitors and accountants can give advice in their own specialist areas but they may charge a fee.

Local Chambers of Commerce can also give advice and could also be useful for building up networks of contacts.

Online enterprise sites, such as www.timesonline.co.uk/enterprise, www.bizhelp24.com and www.startups.co.uk.

Technical support

The type of technical support and specialist advice required will depend upon the type of business. An online business will require the expertise of a web host who can advise on security aspects and a website designer who can help to devise an appealing website and advise on how to monitor and market the site. The support you will need is rather different if you are planning to start up in car valeting or window cleaning!

Specialist advice about a particular type of business can often be obtained from a **trade association**. There is usually a membership fee to pay but this is well worth paying because of the specialist support available. This would typically include legal advice, special insurance deals, marketing advice and so on.

Education and training available

Most people starting out in business learn from mistakes and experience, combined with advice from the sources listed above. However, others prefer to enhance their skills by attending a course.

Some courses are useful for almost anyone entering business, such as IT skills and web page design, marketing or accounting. Others are specific to certain trades or industries and concentrate upon technical skills. Often the first step is to undertake a training needs analysis to find out what skills you have and what skills you need to acquire. You can find out more on the Business Links website. Other sources of information include learndirect, your local college, any trade associations or professional bodies for a particular industry and your local Chamber of Commerce.

Activity

The National Federation of Retail Newsagents has nearly 20,000 members. It provides legal advice and represents the trade to Parliament. Find out more at www.nfrn.org.uk.

Activity

Go to www.startups.co.uk and investigate the advice given there about starting up your chosen type of business.

Activity

Access www.businesslink.gov.uk and assess your own potential management skills and find out what skills business owners need. Click on Employing People and then Skills and Training to find the options available.

Did you know?

You can find out if there is a trade association or professional body for your chosen type of business by entering your type of business followed by 'Trade Association' or 'Professional Body' into Google.co.uk. Make sure you are only accessing sites from the UK. Then explore the website to discover what services are available.

Over to you

Work in pairs for the third part of this activity.

1 *Prepare a business plan for your own business idea using either the template below or an outline plan obtained from a bank or other source. Although you do not need to give comprehensive details under each heading, you should cover all the key issues related to starting and running your own business. Use all the information you have collected as you have worked through the activities in this section to help you.*

TEMPLATE FOR A BUSINESS PLAN

1. Names and address(es) of owner(s) and business name
2. Personal objectives
3. Nature of the business and USP
4. Long-term plans for the business
5. Legal status
6. Skill(s) of owner(s)
7. Description of market, types and planned number of customers
8. Analysis of competitors
9. Marketing plan – advertising
10. Financial forecasts – sales revenue, cash flow, profit and loss account
11. Resources needed – start-up capital and working capital
12. Sources of finance
13. Information on suppliers
14. Sources of advice
15. Start-up plans

2 *Evaluate the strengths and weaknesses of your own plan by assessing it against the key issues you have learned in this unit. For each one you identify, give a reason for your choice.*

3 **a)** *Discuss your ideas with a partner and answer any questions about your plan.*

b) *Decide whether either, or both, of the plans are valid by deciding if you would both recommend the businesses should proceed if you were external business advisers. Give evidence to support your views based on information provided in the plan.*

c) *Then both present your findings to the rest of the group.*

Case study Assessment practice

Dom, Zack and Emily met at college. Dom and Zack were learning sound engineering and Emily was on a media course. They soon began talking about starting their own recording studio. Dom spotted cheap premises in a converted church in a regeneration zone and they put down a deposit. Dom and Zack moved their own equipment into the studio and spent the next week doing the wiring themselves to save money. Emily wrote advertising leaflets and sent out flyers to everyone she knew.

After two months they had obtained three commissions but their total income was only £500. They decided they needed a better mixing unit so applied to the Prince's Trust for a grant and a loan. As part of the process they had to complete a business plan and discuss this with an adviser. When they started to draw up the plan they got a few surprises. They had not realised how many competitors were in the area, nor that their first year's projected income would only be about £15,000. They did not need an adviser to tell them that three people could not live on that amount for a year. Doing the research necessary to complete the plan had been a salutary experience and none of them were surprised when the Prince's Trust turned down their application because it didn't think the business was viable unless several changes were made. A month later the friends decided to split up and go their different ways.

Today Dom owns his own restaurant, Zack is a technical director for a software firm and Emily works on a freelance basis for film and TV companies. All used their skills to develop in other directions. They admit that, had their business plan been viable, the future might have been different, but none of them regrets the experience for a moment. They felt that preparing the plan taught them a lot and their only regret was that they didn't do that sooner.

1(P) **a)** Why did Dom, Zac and Emily prepare a business plan?
b) Identify the advantages and disadvantages of doing this after they had already set up their business. ***(P5 part)***

2(P) **a)** Describe the sources of advice and support the group could have used.
b) On what grounds did the Prince's Trust reject their application? ***(P6)***

3(M) Outline the contents of a business plan and explain the key components which Dom, Zac and Emily should have considered before they started the business. ***(M3 part)***

4(D) Had the figures been better, what recommendations could they have made for starting the business and how could they have justified these? ***(D2)***

5(D) Based on all the aspects of business you have covered in this unit, evaluate the issues that need to be considered when starting and running a business. Do this by identifying those that are the most important to the type of business you would like to start one day. ***(D1)***

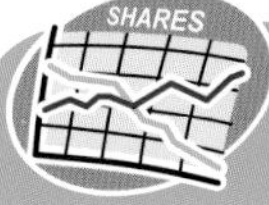

Grading tip

A full explanation involves examining each component and explaining the importance of each one.

Evaluating means deciding the degree to which each item is relevant to a situation and using this decision to support the arguments you make.

Key to self-assessment on page 371

Score	Analysis
8–10	You seem to have most of the qualities needed to run a small business. You may have to address a few areas of weakness.
4–8	You have some of the qualities necessary to run a small business but there are several areas of weakness which you need to consider.
1–3	You do not have many of the qualities needed to run a small business. If you attempted to do so you would have to change considerably and would probably need a lot of help and support.

Key to quiz on page 391

Give yourself one point for each correct answer.

1 b, 2 a, 3 b, 4 c, 5 b, 6 b, 7 c, 8 a, 9 c, 10 b

10 right = £5,000 – congratulations

8 or 9 right = £4,000 – your uncle is strict about finance, as are banks!

6 or 7 right = £3,000 – you may have to cast around for more sponsors.

4 or 5 right = £1,500 – your uncle is really not impressed.

Less than 4 = £0. Brush up on your knowledge before you write your business plan.

Index